The American Theatrical Film

The American Theatrical Film:
Stages in Development

John C. Tibbetts

Bowling Green State University Popular Press
Bowling Green, Ohio 43403

It is a common observation that no art was ever invented and carried to perfection at the same time.... By imitation only, variety, and even originality of invention, is produced.

Sir Joshua Reynolds, *The Sixth Discourse*, 1784

One always begins by imitating.... [Artists] in order to form their talent or to keep it healthy...have had to imitate their predecessors, and imitate them almost unceasingly, whether voluntarily or unwittingly.

Eugene Delacroix, *Journal*, March 1, 1859

...even at an early date in the history of the industry it was commonly recognised that the introduction of general dramatic principles in the production of motion pictures was desirable and necessary.

Edwin S. Porter, 1914

Contents

Introduction

For a long time the medium of the motion picture was regarded as a "new proscenium"—an extension of the popular theater. Plays, players, staging techniques, business practices, and even artificial scenery were brought to the screen. Was it a misguided attempt to transform movies into a semblance of a theatrical event? Or was it merely another legitimate effort to conjoin the arts, an endeavor that can be traced back many centuries? Never mind the official line that too many standard film histories have presented—that contempt by the theatrical establishment toward the fledgling film industry at the century discouraged collaborative efforts. The fact remains that theatrical entrepreneurs, from as early as 1896, actively worked with film personnel on all levels of movie making. Moreover, many theatrical productions on Broadway and in theaters across America subsequently began displaying effects borrowed from motion pictures.

The richest and most productive period of theatrical filmmaking was the 1896-1930 period. In particular, the 1912-1915 and 1926-1930 years produced silent and sound theatrical films, respectively, that best reveal the nature of interaction between film and theater. There are distinct parallels between the two periods that tell us a lot about the ways we have come to define the artistic identity of the motion picture. It is a process that might well shed light on how we define art forms of the future.

We commonly use the term "theatrical film" to designate any film that has a theatrical source, such as a stage play or musical show. But here I use it in a more specific sense to refer to any film that either directly imitates or in some way utilizes the subjects, processes and effects of the stage in a visible and prominent way. Thus, the movie screen quite literally becomes a new proscenium—a playing space that not only supports theatrical forms (such as vaudeville turns, magic acts, melodramas, etc.) but which actually resembles the playing space within a stage proscenium. In other words, the screen space functions like a theater proscenium—enclosing the action, guiding all entrances and exits into lateral directions, fixing the viewer to a stationary vantage point, utilizing artifical scenery, etc.

These practices, we will see, do not necessarily reflect an ignorance on the part of early filmmakers concerning the unique possibilities of their own medium. Rather, as historian Kevin Brownlow has indicated:

Far from being the move of an industry that didn't know what it was doing, the theatrical films were deliberately planned to reproduce the experience of the stage. After all, almost all the cinematic devices existed by the time Bernhardt made *Queen Elizabeth* for Famous Players in 1912. But Edwin S. Porter, Adolph Zukor, and many others kept them out of their early photoplays. They knew that the theatrical "carriage trade" did not appreciate violent changes of

1

scene, moving cameras, or closeups of gargantuan proportions.

And, for various reasons, the same holds true for those theatrical films made early in the 1926-1930 period, the developmental years of the synchronized-sound film.

Unfortunately, due to print deterioration, today's critical indifference and other hazards, many of these theatrical films have disappeared. Films like *The Count of Monte Cristo* (1913) and *Coquette* (1929) seem tediously "stagebound" in comparison with the more sophisticated cinematic achievements of the time. Yet that is precisely their significance for me and this book.

In order to find the surviving titles, I have had to turn to the archives at the University of Southern California at Los Angeles, the Library of Congress Motion Picture Division in Washington, D.C. and to collections belonging to film and theater historians William K. Everson, Miles Kreuger and Kemp R. Niver.

Whenever possible, I have examined primary, rather than secondary, paper materials. In any study of this period, one has to consult the various film and theater journals—*Variety, Moving Picture World, Motion Picture World, Picture-Play Magazine, Billboard, Theatre Magazine, Motography,* and *The New York Dramatic Mirror.* Interviews can also be valuable and I have had the opportunity to talk to filmmakers and players active during these years including Warner Brothers sound engineer Bernard B. Brown, cameraman Glen MacWilliams and actor Lyle Talbot. Many historians and archivists have generously assisted my research, including William K. Everson in New York, David Parker at the Library of Congress in Washington, D. C., Audrey Kupferberg at the American Film Institute in Washington, D.C., Miles Kreuger at the Institute of the American Musical in Los Angeles, Kemp R. Niver at the Locare Research Institute in Los Angeles, Anthony Slide at the Academy of Motion Picture Arts and Sciences in Los Angeles and Kevin Brownlow in London.

One primary resource at my disposal deserves special mention. I was given the opportunity to annotate and edit the transcripts of the Academy of Motion Picture Arts and Sciences Seminar conducted at the University of Southern California in 1929. This occasion—not documented until now—provides invaluable insights into how filmmakers in 1929 regarded the problems of stage and screen interaction. I thank the Academy and the National Film Society for that opportunity.

Finally, in compiling the lists of both theatrical films and their theatrical sources in 1912-1915 and 1926-1930, I have consulted standard references. (These paired lists of films and plays appearing in my study have not, to my knowledge, previously appeared in print.) The reference works for the films are: Howard Lamarr Walls, *Motion Pictures, 1894-1912: Catalogue of*

Copyright Entries (Library of Congress Copyright Office, 1953); Howard Lamarr Walls, *Motion Pictures, 1912-1939: Catalogue of Copyright Entries* (Library of Congress Copyright Office, 1951); Kemp R. Niver, *Motion Pictures from the Library of Congress Paper Print Collection,* 1894-1912 (Berkeley and Los Angeles: University of California Press, 1967); and Kenneth W. Munden, Executive Editor, *The American Film Institute Catalogue of Motion Pictures Produced in the United States,* 1912-1930 (New York and London: R. R. Bowker Company, 1971). The reference works for the plays are: John Chapman and Garrison P. Sherwood, Eds., *The Best Plays of 1894-1899* (New York: Dodd, Mead and Co., 1955); Burns Mantle and Garrison P. Sherwood, Eds., *The Best Plays of 1899-1909* (New York: Dodd, Mead and Co., 1944); Burns Mantle and Garrison P. Sherwood, *The Best Plays of 1909-1919* (New York: Dodd, Mead and Co., 1933); and the annual "Best Plays" series that followed thereafter, from 1919 to 1930, all edited by Burns Mantle and Garrison P. Sherwood. Even here, unfortunately, there are gaps in available information. Only the American Film Institute *Catalogue* provides complete production credits of pertinent films; but a catalogue of films produced in 1911-1920—a period crucial to my study—has not yet been completed and is, at the present time, unavailable. Consequently, I have had to reconstruct from contemporaneous sources the lists of theatrical films produced in 1912-1915, many of which were not copyrighted and, consequently, were not listed in the previously named sources. Thus, the lists I provide in the following pages of my study constitute only a beginning to a comprehensive assessment of theatrical film production.

Finally, my special thanks to Professors Peter Dart, Edward Ruhe, and Robert Findlay of the University of Kansas; and to Dr. Richard Dyer MacCann of the University of Iowa. Their patience and guidance were invaluable in the research and writing of much of this book.

Chapter One
The New Proscenium:
The First Theatrical Films, 1896-1912

Beginning in the early 1890s, the first motion picture promoters tried to profit from the examples of the production and business practices of the popular drama and vaudeville. These promoters came from a variety of backgrounds. Some, like Adolph Zukor and the brothers Warner, were itinerant showmen and theatrical exhibitors. Others, like Thomas Edison and Edwin S. Porter, were inventors, mechanics or engineers fascinated by the new technological apparatus. It was inevitable that they would try to make the film industry into a kind of "new proscenium." After all, the movies had no tradition, no Academy, no system of instruction and training, no centralized industrial plant or business headquarters and no critical record. By contrast, the American stage had inherited theatrical traditions from Europe that extended back to the sixteenth century. Moreover, the theatrical establishment was organized as a business enterprise conducted largely through the central offices of the Syndicate and other booking offices in New York. This centralized authority insured that standards of production and exhibition would be maintained in thousands of theater houses throughout the country—which is to say that it decided what particular kinds of theatrical events would be presented, how they would be mounted and presented to audiences, and how they could reach the widest cross-section of those audiences, both urban and rural. Concepts such as the "star system" were widely exploited in promoting theatrical entertainments. The personalities and peculiar talents of given players could always be expected to appeal to that audience, no matter what the nature of a given play.

The motion picture broke out of the peepshow category around 1895-96 with experiments in projecting movies to mass audiences in France, England and America. By 1903 films lasting from three to ten minutes began telling simple stories. At first they were shown in vaudeville and theater houses (in the latter case, as part of the otherwise "live" bill). But within a year they were finding increased exposure in houses of their own, commonly called "nickelodeons," small stores converted into movie houses of 199 seats. By 1907 the number of these nickelodeons grew to more than four thousand houses, bringing in an estimated two million people a day by 1907.[1] By 1913, when the feature-length film had arrived, audience attendance had grown to an estimated twenty million in ten thousand movie houses. At ten cents admission, that represented two million dollars daily.[2] In 1915, on any given day, one-tenth of the American population (at least ten million) attended the movies. This patronage was six times as large as the daily audiences of all

4

other kinds of entertainment combined.[3]

Around the time that Thomas Edison's projection device (called the Vitascope) was premiered at Koster and Bial's Music Hall in New York City's Herald Square in 1896, some New York-based theater men were forming the Syndicate. The Syndicate was composed of booking agents and theater owners—Sam Nixon, Fred Zimmerman, Charles Frohman, Al Hayman, Marc Klaw and Abraham Erlanger—who sought control of booking for many of the first-class theater houses in the country. Throughout the next twenty years or so the Syndicate—and other emerging interests like the Shuberts— would control the key touring routes, hold the threat of "blackball" over non-cooperative actors and influence the general tenor of the American theater. This centralized control represented advantages and disadvantages to American theatrical development, as has been discussed elsewhere.[4] For our purposes, it is important to emphasize that the Syndicate advocated a standardized kind of theatrical entertainment which was conducted as a business enterprise. These practices would soon be actively imitated by the film promoters.

This state of the theater reflected an international situation. In spite of the Independent Theater movements initiated since 1887 by Andre Antoine in France, J.T. Grein in England, the Moscow Art Theater in Moscow, Otto Brahm in Germany and James A. Herne in America, and the subsequent emergence of tough-minded playwrights like Herne, Henrick Ibsen, August Strindberg, George Bernard Shaw and Maxim Gorki, the contemporary theater was riddled with popular formulas of production, story and distribution. Perhaps Anton Chekhov summed up the situation most cogently in 1896 when he had the character Trepleff in *The Sea Gull* comment on the contemporary theater:

But to my way of thinking, the theatre today is nothing but routine, convention. When the curtain goes up, and by artificial light in a room with three walls, these great geniuses, these priests of holy art, show how people eat, drink, make love, move about and wear their jackets; when they try to fish a moral out of these flat pictures and phrases, some sweet little bit anybody could understand and any fool take home; when in a thousand different dishes they serve me the same thing over and over, and over and over, over and over again....[5]

At this time in America James A. Herne described the Syndicate-dominated theater in similar terms:

And while it is true that we had some excellent plays, they each had a plot, a hero, and a villain, and always ended with virtue triumphant. The hero always got the heroine, and the villain was always foiled before the final curtain fell. The characters in these plays were of a necessity more or less artificial.[6]

A different kind of theatrical entertainment—vaudeville—was also at this time achieving commercial standardizations of its own. Programs of short sketches, or "turns," could be seen in organized chains of theater houses all over America. Their audiences, according to Robert McLaughlin's recent assessment, "never or very rarely attended the legitimate theater." The audience was composed of "working class people with simple tastes, who wanted a cheaper and more approachable kind of entertainment."[7] The kinds of acts and the circuits of theaters were also under a more or less centralized control in New York, including the circuits controlled by Keith, Pantages, Sullivan and Considine, Martin Beck, Gus Sun and the Western Vaudeville Association. The creation of the United Booking Office, the vaudeville equivalent of the Syndicate early in the century, would promote its own kinds of standardized entertainments.[8]

By the time the theatrical Syndicate and vaudeville's United Booking Office were dominating the "living stage" in 1912, film entrepreneurs were actively imitating and exploiting both of them. True, the short one-reel films were commonly regarded as crude and vulgar. Few theater actors were willing to trust their talents to them; few theatrical producers and playwrights saw profitable opportunities on celluloid; only a limited critical establishment was available to consider them in a serious light; and few filmmakers had even a very sophisticated idea of the range of theatrical activity surrounding them.[9] Yet the filmmakers from the early studios—Kleine, Kalem, Edison, Biograph, Essanay and Vitagraph, among others—began a program of imitation of the commercial theater that would anticipate the production of feature-length theatrical films after 1912.

An overview of the commentary that greeted the appearance of the short theatrical films between 1894 and 1911 introduces not only the kinds of theatrical events that were imitated and the presumptions that permitted this imitation, but the nature of the films themselves. There was no organized commentary concerning the motion picture at this time. Excepting early trade magazines that appeared after 1906—*Views and Film Index, Moving Picture World* and *Moving Picture News*—the majority of this commentary came from entertainment and theatrical magazines, like *Billboard, Variety* and the *New York Dramatic Mirror*. A smaller body of commentary came from established journals like the *North American Review, Critic, The Saturday Evening Post* and *Atlantic Monthly*.[10]

From the beginning much of this commentary presumed that the film medium should be a recording device for theatrical events. As early as 1894, a writer in *The Critic* predicted that Edison's kinetoscope would enable an audience to "witness and hear shadowplays in which the only real performer will be the electro-magnetic motor behind the scenes."[11] A year later Edison was quoted as saying that by linking the phonograph and the kinetoscope the movie could preserve and disseminate the theatrical event so that, for example, grand opera could be presented "without any material change from the original, and with artists and musicians long since dead."[12] By 1903, it was acknowledged that the processes of filmmaking were identical with those of theatrical production. Like the stage, observed the *New York Daily Tribune* of June 28 that year, the motion picture had "its stage machinery, its wings, its properties, its lights, its makeups, its exits, and its entrances."[13]

When the proliferation of the nickelodeon theaters began to bring films to all areas of the United States after 1904, more detailed commentary linked the production of motion pictures to that of the stage. In his article, "The Nickelodeons," written for *The Saturday Evening Post* in 1907, Joseph Medill Patterson noted that each film studio owned a property-room, dressing rooms and a completely equipped stage. "The studio manager orders rehearsals continued until his people have their parts 'face-perfect,' then he gives the word, the lens is focused, the cast works rapidly for twenty minutes while the long strip of celluloid whirls through the camera, and performance is preserved in living, dynamic embalment (if the phrase may be permitted) for decades to come."[14]

Many commentators acknowledged at this time that the movies were trying to utilize production techniques that would promote the illusion that the viewer was watching a stage play. For example, in the theater house the viewer sat in a fixed position at an unchanging distance from the action. "On the vaudeville or talking stage," commented a writer, for *The Moving Picture World* in 1909, "figures of human beings do not expand or contract irrationally or eccentrically; they remain the same size." In the movies, therefore, "some sort of attempt should be made by somebody to make things uniform. . . .and [more in] accordance with the need of conveying the correct sensuous impression."[15] Two years later in March 1911, the same magazine reported that the films of Edwin S. Porter, one of the Edison studio's chief producer-directors, were adhering to this correlation with theatrical "uniformity." This is to say that from shot to shot of a film, the size of the figures on the screen did not appreciably change in size. This preserved the illusion that the audience was watching players on a large stage from a fixed vantage point: "Here Mr. Porter works on a large stage, and places his camera at a considerable distance from his actors. The result is that he avoids abnormality of size, and when you see the pictures on the screen, they express the proper sensuous impression of size. . . ."[16]

One consequence of creating the illusion of stage presentation was that many films displayed actors who played to the camera as if they were playing to an imaginary audience. The *New York Dramatic Mirror* on May 14, 1910, noted this tendency. Many players in films "play to the front," the writer said, "thus betraying unconsciously that they know they are being pictured, and giving the impression to the spectators that they are going through their parts before an audience which is not seen in the picture but which appears to be located in front of the scene." The article went on to describe how this illusion was effected:

> The arrangement of the interiors almost invariably accentuates this impression. The chairs almost always face the camera, sometimes reminding one of a minstrel first part. The actor almost always sits at a table sideways, so that he can show his full face front. Sometimes he will seat himself with his back squarely to the table located behind his chair while he faces the camera trying to eat, write, or talk by occasionally twisting his neck and body into unnatural positions. Two people conversing will deliberately walk down front and instead of facing each other as in real life will face the camera, turning only occasionally to look at the person addressed. An entire room full of people may be seen facing front—we see nothing but a sea of white faces with never a back or side view.[17]

Many commentators felt that the story and structure of these short films should follow their stage models with regard to structure and the observance of the "unities." The "well-made" formulations of Scribe and his successors were invoked. As early as 1904, just as the nickelodeons were beginning to be popular and short, story films were appearing, one writer described what he felt should be the proper theatrical orientation of a film's story and structure:

> There should be no lagging in the story which it tells; every foot must be an essential part, whose loss would deprive the story of some merit; there should be sequence, each part leading to the next with increasing interest, reaching its most interesting point at the climax, which should end the film.[18]

This kind of correlation with well-made models was echoed in 1907 by Joseph Medill Patterson in *The Saturday Evening Post*. "Today a consistent plot is demanded," he declared. "There must be, as in the drama, exposition, development, climax and denouement."[19] A year later, writing in the *Moving Picture World*, Rollin Summers elaborated upon some of these parallels, saying that the movies should observe the unity of action—"The presentation of a single consistent story without irrelevant matters." Every moment of a play, he continued, must have the element of doubt and suspense that Scribe advocated. Similarly, the movies should balance character motivation and incident toward those ends. In order to do this, he advocated that more filmmakers study the stage dramas of the past: "The authors and experts employed by the [motion picture] producer should be primarily familiar with the technique of the acted drama."[20]

Yet, how were these stories to be conveyed in a medium that was silent? The use of printed titles was seen as an expedient. For one thing, they could fulfill the role of the printed program during the performance of a play. As Summers reminded his readers, stage plays often employed printed directions to guide the auditor through the action, indicating changes in time and location. The printed title in a movie, he said, was merely a parallel to that program: "It seems equally justifiable to use the device of the printed message...."[21] And for another thing, the written title could be used to convey dialogue. So common was this practice by 1912, that often reviewers of films were moved to protest at the overindulgence of the practice. A reviewer in *The New York Dramatic Mirror* at this point attacked Sarah Bernhardt's film version of her stage success *Camille*. The numerous titles were tedious, he complained, "many things being announced in words that are clearly understandable from the actions themselves."[22]

Much of this early commentary also noted the benefits to filmmakers who emulated the distribution practices of the popular stage. Motion picture distribution was a rapidly developing enterprise during these years, and the biggest profits went to those who best routed movies to the most houses across the country. "The invention of the moving picture machine inaugurated a new era of the amusement business," editorialized *Billboard* in 1906. "The promoters of amusements were not slow in recognizing the merits of the invention, and the manufacture and jobbing of films rapidly grew to the proportions of a business involving the exchange of vast sums of money annually." The article went on to note that film distribution rapidly is a developing business. "There are hundreds of travelling 'shows' that set up in the halls of small opera houses and put on exhibitions of moving pictures...."[23]

Organized routes of distribution had to be developed, and in 1911, Montrose J. Moses in *The American Dramatist* observed that these routes were similar to those of theatrical distribution. It was common for a successful play to appear in many theater houses on simultaneous runs throughout the country. A play that had established a reputation in New York might be sent out on the road; several road companies would perform in prearranged circuits of houses. "I have used the phrase 'exhibited the film'," Moses said, "to indicate that [according to the] way in which the business is managed, the films travel from point to point, just as a stock company would go from theatre to theatre. A film has its 'route'...."[24]

The mass appeal of a play and how successfully it played on the road was often due in large part to the popularity of its leading players. The "star system," so important in the promotion of stage plays, was soon incorporated into the structure of film distribution and production. Robert Grau, reporting on the state of the various branches of entertainment in 1912, wrote that the star system was to play a large part in the future of the film industry. "One must believe that the actor, to a great extent, makes possible the prosperity in the film industry." The appearance in movies of lesser stars of the theatrical road companies as well as the leading lights of the legitimate stage and vaudeville proved that, although "the star phase of the motion picture progress is decidedly in its infancy...it is not to be doubted that the same craze that resulted in advanced vaudeville is now in the process of evolution in the [motion picture] field."[25] The early studios were organizing their own companies of players, moreover. *The Moving Picture World* reported in 1909 that one of these studios, Essanay, "maintained a picked company of permanent players," with "leading ladies and leading men" along with "assisting talent."[26]

The preceeding survey of commentary from 1894 to 1912 suggests some of the kinds of theatrical practices imitated by film entrepreneurs, but it does not indicate the relative proportion of the short theatrical films to the total output of all varieties of movies at the time. The fact is that theatrical films did not constitute merely a tiny percentage of the total output of movies in America during these years. Quite to the contrary, theatrical films may be safely estimated as constituting over one-third of that output. A valuable source in gaining this sense of proportion is Kemp R. Niver's compendium, *Motion Pictures From the Library of Congress Paper Print Collection, 1894-1912.*[27] It is a comprehensive listing of all films made in America that were registered at the Library of Congress. It contains short summaries of all these films and descriptions of their props and scenic effects. Of the thousands of titles listed and described, over one-third contain references that demonstrate that they were either derived from stage plays or that they at least in some way simulated the illusion of a theatrical presentation. The following descriptions of such films are typical: "This was photographed as if from the audience at a theater"; or "all the scenes were photographed from a single camera position and all activity parallels the camera plane"; or "the set is a backdrop painted as an ocean scene"; or "the action consists of the participants being introduced to the 'audience.' " One film, entitled "The Critic" (Biograph, 1906) went to extraordinary lengths to simulate a theatrical event, as witness this description: "The camera, placed as though in the audience, shows several seats with spectators in the immediate foreground and a box to the right. The stage acts are burlesques of regular vaudeville acts."[28]

How closely or loosely film entrepreneurs adhered to these points of contact determined the relative degree of a given theatrical film's "cinematic" nature as opposed to its theatrical dimension. The following is a breakdown of the imitative strategies pursued by filmmakers:

1. The fixed vantage point of the theater house spectator could be approximated in a film by the use of the fixed, unmoving camera providing a medium to medium-long shot of the action.
2. The unit of construction of stage play—the scene—was approximated on film by means of the uncut shot. This uncut shot, filmed from a fixed viewpoint, promoted on the screen a sense of continuous space and real time—i.e., the continuities of time and space were not altered by means of editing or camera movement.
3. Scenes in a play were linked by means of the raising and lowering of a curtain, or by the dimming and intensifying of lights; shots in a film were linked by the simple device of "continuity cutting." (This technique of editing included the use of the "straight cut" and the use of the quick dissolve and the fade-in and fade-out.)
4. The fixed boundaries of the proscenium frame that enclosed the stage's playing space were approximated in the film frame and the movie screen by the fixed borders of both. In effect, the actors could enter and exit laterally (not forward or backward) by means of these external borders, just as they would on the proscenium stage.

5. The scenic artifice of the stage—the painted, forced-perspective backdrops, the two-dimensional props, the shallow-depth playing space, the surrounding proscenium frame, and even the curtains—could be photographed and thus transferred to the playing space of the movie screen.

6. The stage actor's gesture and movement in relation both to his audience and to the artificial world around him could be approximated in film acting, wherein the gesture and movement of the actor were addressed to the camera lens, without regard to the relative proximity of the lens.

Also the following methods of exhibition and distribution were standard to the theater and subsequently pursued by motion picture entrepreneurs:

1. Movies were initially exhibited in theater and vaudeville houses as part of an otherwise "live" bill.

2. Movies were distributed to circuits of movie houses, much in the same way that stage plays toured the "road."

3. Movie entrepreneurs adopted from the stage the concept of the star system as a means of promoting their product.

Production

Many of the film entrepreneurs in these early years did all they could to promote the illusion that the movie viewer was in a theater house watching the action on a proscenium stage. Thus, it is important to understand the physical nature of the proscenium theater house as it had evolved by the end of the nineteenth century. In the late 1500s, the forestage (or apron area), that had constituted the playing space of the theaters of the middle ages (and which was a vital part of Shakespeare's stage) was withdrawn inside a frame called the proscenium. It enclosed the playing area on three sides and, in effect, detached it from the audience, thereby defining a highly specific arena of space and time. The playing area itself became increasingly shallow in depth over the next three hundred years, since the extensive use of painted perspective could supply the necessary illusion of depth.

By the mid-nineteenth century the typical theater house displayed these characteristics. The stage floor was sloped upward from the footlights to the backdrop, a depth of approximately forty to sixty feet. The playing space was equipped with a system of wings, grooves, bridges, traps, and flies devised to control as needed the entrances and exits of the players and the shifting of the scenery. The various appliances were devised to control the two-dimensional side wings or cutouts which, arranged in sequence at either side of the playing space, offered a perspective pictorial illusion. Painted cloth drops could be lowered from the flies and wooden-frame canvas flats called "shutters" were run into the center of the area from the sides. The shutters could be introduced in the foreground of the stage when it was necessary to change the wings and properties behind them. Even the largest of the metropolitan theater houses were no more than elaborations of this basic set up.[29]

This proscenium arrangement presented a pictorial illusion that strikingly anticipated the motion picture screen. This is especially apparent from Perry Fitzgerald's description of the Haymarket Theater in 1881. The frame border, he notes, "is continued all around the proscenium, and carried even below the actors' feet." The actors seem to be "cut off from the domain of prose," Fitzgerald concluded, and, stranger still, "the whole has the air of a picture projected on a surface."[30]

Nicholas Vardac in his *Stage to Screen* has demonstrated that the majority of plays in the nineteenth century reached people by means of the conventional staging devices described here. Vardac explains that the majority of theater audiences were accustomed to these somewhat crude conditions and that such conditions were exactly those that were prevalent at the time of the emergence of the motion picture industry.[31] Most people had seen plays as a result of road companies coming to town to play in the local theater house. It was likely that audiences were accustomed to only the crudest of scenic effects. A travelling company had to "tailor" a play to fit the capacities of these houses. If the company travelled by train or wagon, it had to reduce to the barest minimum the accoutrement it could bring. What scenery it brought had to be measured to the standard dimensions of the doors of American baggage cars—five-feet, nine inches wide, allowing for clearance margins of three inches for the six-feet high doors.[32] Otherwise, the company had to depend upon the available representationally painted backdrops and visual-effects devices common to the theater houses, which had to suffice for all manner of productions. A single backdrop might be used for a variety show, a parlor comedy or a lurid melodrama. Stock scenery was a thriving business by 1870, when commercial scenic studios published catalogues from which stereotypical scenery could be ordered.[33] According to designer Lee Simonson, the situation had become so standardized by 1900 that the American scene-designer was really more of a scene *painter*, "an anonymous craftsman turning out stock-patterns or stereotyped backdrops by the square yard and delivering them to the stage-door without much pre-occupation as to their effect in the theater."[34] Writing in 1904 in *The Old School and the New*, veteran actor William H. Crane noted that all too often these settings and props had no relation either to realism generally or to the specific play at hand:

> When I went on the stage the wooden door was unknown. Everything was pasteboard. Apples and goblets and pies were made of that material, and if perchance one fell upon the floor, it made no sound that could be heard beyond the footlights.[35]

Audiences accustomed to this crudely stereotyped and artificial world certainly had no difficulty accepting its new incarnation in the films that imitated that world. The two-dimensional flats, the artificial props and such constitute the world they had grown up with and were used to. It was the world that, perhaps, they expected to find in the movies as well.

Thus, when the first motion picture production companies erected their own stages, they followed many of these production formulas, although on a somewhat cruder level. At the turn of the century, indoor photography with artificial light was difficult,[36] so it was not yet possible to photograph a theatrical event inside a theater house. The solution was to build stages in accordance with standard theater houses and leave the roofs off (or build the walls of glass) to permit the sunlight through.

The world's first movie studio was constructed for the Edison Laboratory in West Orange, New Jersey, in 1893. This "Kinetographic theater" was dubbed the "Black Maria" and was a constructed stage that revolved 360 degrees on a pivot with its roof open to the sunlight. In order to heighten the clarity of the photographed figures, a backdrop was erected consisting entirely of black draping. Drawings of the time depict the camera anchored at the far end of a narrow room. At the other end was a shallow playing space where many of the stage performers of the day performed.[37]

In 1896-1899 motion picture studios in England and France displayed a far more sophisticated imitation of the traditional theater house, complete with traps, wing and groove arrangements, and flies. One of England's most important early filmmakers, Robert W. Paul, has left us with a description of his first movie studio. It was erected in a corner of a field in 1899. It was, substantially, a miniature stage, approximately twenty-eight feet across and fourteen feet deep, raised above ground level and protected by an iron building with wide sliding doors and a glass roof facing north. At the rear of the stage was a hanging frame to which backdrops painted in monochrome—films at this time were, of course, shot in black-and-white—could be affixed. This frame could be lowered through a slot to facilitate the work of the scene painter. Traps in the stage and a hanging bridge overhead provided means for working "special effects" and scene changes. Behind the studio a scene-painting room was erected. From this stage were produced hundreds of humorous, dramatic and trick films.[38]

The first motion picture studio of Georges Méliès in France bespoke his thorough knowledge of and experience with traditional staging methods. In this way he was more advanced than many other film entrepreneurs, whose exposure to theatrical production methods was limited. In 1896 Méliès abandoned his own Theatre-Robert Houdin and built at Montreuil his first movie studio, the "theatre de prises de vues." It was a shed constructed entirely of glass, containing a stage with a below-stage area and a rigging loft—just like the stage he had formerly operated for "live" productions. The shooting was done with a stationary camera set up in a special recess at the far end of the theater. The actors played facing the camera as though facing an audience. The foot of the camera was connected with the edges of the set with cords or wooden laths, establishing parameters that were the equivalent of proscenium boundaries on a stage. They consisted of painted *tromp-l'oeil* perspective flats that created the impression of relief and suggested depth. There were three different kinds of surfaces for these sets: a large canvas-covered frame was flanked on either side by smaller frames, forming an obtuse angle with the main frame. Sideboards, grandfather clocks, and pictures were all painted on these surfaces. The floor was covered with a canvas painted to simulate either parquet flooring, a carpet, or tiles.[39]

Méliès predilection for painted scenery was, at the turn of the century, far in advance of American practices. Whereas the Edison films coming from the "Black Maria" had only the black backdrop behind the players, Méliès surrounded his performers with spectacularly elaborate scenery. It made no difference to him whether the subject at hand was derived from the *faerie* drama as in "The Palace of a Thousand-and-One Delights" (1905), or from contemporary headlines, as in "The Coronation of King Edward VII" (1903); it always demanded a totally artificial world created in the studio and photographed on film. As Leon Barsacq concluded in his history of the movie designer *Caligaris Cabinet*, Méliès was only conforming to the stereotyped view of stage scenery in his day.[40]

It is hardly surprising that the actors moved within this world as if they were on a proscenium stage. Katherine Singer Kovacs' detailed study of Méliès' staging methods for both film and theater acknowledged that he employed standard theatrical practice in his guidance of his players. It was common in his films, she said, to see the actors entering and exiting from either the side wings or through vampire traps in the floor of the stage. All of their movements, moreover, were executed on one plane along the center of the stage, behind an invisible line of demarcation corresponding to a stage apron.[41]

Méliès' work influenced filmmakers on both sides of the Atlantic. Pathé and Gaumont in France and England, Edison and the Mutoscope Company in America all began to incorporate more elaborate scenic devices into their story films. Whether they produced original stories or whether they appropriated plays, the scenic apparatus was completely artificial and the acting conducted in accordance with the practices of the proscenium stage. Leon Barsacq described how the sets were painted and constructed for Pathé and Gaumont films just at the turn of the century. The direct inspiration for these sets, he said, was the work of the eighteenth century stage designer, Giovanni Servandoni, scenic director of the Paris Opera. His methods were followed by designers from the Opera Comique, the Comedie Française, and other French theaters who came to the screen:

The scenery was painted flat, like stage scenery. The canvas was tacked to the floor, and after applying a coat of glue size and whiting, the designer drew the design in charcoal. For complicated architectural sets a small sketch was made and squared for enlargement. Since the size paint was used hot, a scale of grays running from black to white was prepared in advance in small flameproof buckets. The scene painter worked standing, walking on the canvas (in rope-soled shoes or socks) and using very long-handled brushes; straight lines were drawn with the aid of a long flat ruler, similarly attached to a handle.... The complete canvases were attached either to wooden frames to form the flats, or else, for backdrops, to vertical poles so they could be rolled up.[42]

Many of the Mutoscope films in America between 1896 and 1907 displayed similar scenic aspects. They were shot on the roof of the Mutoscope building at 841 Broadway above the Biograph offices. Films like "An Affair of Honor" (1907) and "Waltzing Walker" (1906) are typical in their usage of artificial scenic backdrops. Douglass Crockwell, an authority on the Mutoscope period, described the appearance and theatrical derivations of these films:

> Ordinary comedy pieces, bedroom farces, kitchen calamities, used crudely painted flats and the action was forced, the comedy broad. Probably many of the acts came directly from the lower vaudeville houses.... Some backdrops were used over and over. A street scene in perspective for one served for six or seven separate themes....[43]

His words could have described the use of stock scenic backdrops used by dozens of the road companies of the day.

Undoubtedly the closest approximation to the theatrical priorities of Méliès as far as American films were concerned were those produced and directed by Edwin S. Porter. In 1902 Porter made for the Edison Company a 250-foot film called "Jack and the Beanstalk," based on a current stage play. It was typical of many such films in that its scenic devices of painted backdrops and shallow-depth playing areas enforced an artificiality upon the entire production. The players froze into tableaux, performed to the camera, and entered and exited through side wings. Entire scenes were played before a fixed camera at a distance allowing the figures to be seen from head to toe. Editing was used only to link scenes together. Porter, like Méliès, did not confine this kind of theatricality to fantasy films. His "factual" films—among which the most famous are "The European Rest Cure," "The Ex-Convict," and "The Kleptomaniac" (1904-05)—displayed startling juxtapositions of location shooting with patently stage-bound scenes. The "real" locales of New York seen occasionally in these films contrast sharply with blatantly artificial shallow-depth sets with painted flats and two-dimensional props. "The Kleptomaniac" even concludes with a written title card with the word "tableau" printed on it, followed by a shot of curtains parting to reveal a posed, draped woman against a black backdrop. Porter's sermon on social injustice is emphasized as the woman holds aloft the scales of justice, one of which is weighted down with a bag of money.

Even when films were shot outside of the studios during this period, the sense that the action was taking place within a proscenium frame was preserved. This is a convincing demonstration of the priorities given to theatrical imitation, even when the circumstances of the filming—in this case, outdoor shooting free of a stage's physical confines—allowed for a different method of staging. Karl Brown, a cameraman who gained his apprentice experience working with D. W. Griffith during this period has given an invaluable description of the ways in which filmmakers set up in outdoor locations. For example, prior to shooting a given scene, it was the cameraman's function to "put down the lines." This process, says Brown, was a standard preliminary to the shooting of every scene. The camera crew would demarcate the boundaries of the playing space with white cord. This cord would be stretched from peg to peg to define not only the height and width of the playing area, but its depth as well. In this way, both the cameraman and the players would know exactly what area would be seen within the four borders of the camera aperture and, hence, within the four borders of the motion picture screen. The camera itself "was not only never to be moved, but...was sometimes even anchored to the floor with strong lash-line secured by a stage screw." The players could not stray from the demarcated area: "Actors would then walk carelessly down toward the camera, secure in the knowledge that as long as they stayed inside that white cord, their feet would not be cut off and audiences would not wonder how people could walk around without feet. They could move from side to side freely so long as they stayed within the lines." Working like this was well suited to players who had experience with stage acting. "It was especially valued by stage-trained actors, who were used to working in a clearly defined area, wings on the side and the apron in front." Without these guidelines, Brown explains, "they were constantly moving outside camera range to deliver their most telling effects. Griffith and his lines removed all that danger."[44]

Thus restricted, players in films had to grapple with the same problems actors on the stage had confronted. Stage players had had to learn to accord their movements and gestures with the fragility of the scenic illusion and the limitations of the physical space. Lee Simonson explains that if an actor moved twelve or fifteen paces up stage he would suddenly have the painted "sky" at his elbow; if he brushed against the scenery it would tremble, and as a result, "the entire structure on which the illusions of scene-painting were based collapsed and the very semblance of reality that mathematically determined perspective had been able to create became an obvious artifice."[45] The Duke of Saxe-Meiningen in 1870 described how the actor's gesture and movement were affected by such conditions. The actor, he wrote, must never lean against painted scenery; if his gesture was free and easy, he might shake the setting; but if he was preoccupied with *not* touching it, his gestures would be forced and obvious. The juxtaposition of painted and plastic objects, moreover, must be subtle, lest their differences be disturbingly apparent. Finally, the actor should avoid getting too far upstage lest his proportions in relation to the scenery's perspective illusion become preposterous. Better he should stay in the center area of the stage, where the prompter's box was.[46]

Thus relatively immobilized, stage actors had developed what Stanislavsky called "full-toned acting," a style of "exaggerated gesture and action." Usually the player's desire, Stanislavsky explained, "was to stand in front of the prompter's box, looking across the footlights at the spectators, exchanging compliments with them, and becoming obsessed by the drunkenness of declamatory speech and theatrical poses."[47] When players appeared in the short theatrical films, they also had the problem of working in a silent medium that reduced a play to eight or ten minutes of pantomime. Save for a few printed title cards, pantomime had to carry all the motivation, plot and action. In 1911, Montrose Moses dubbed this new, shorthand kind of pantomime, "strenuous acting in a mechanical age." He cited the example of what happened when a stock company in New England appeared before movie cameras to perform the first act of David Belasco's production of *Zaza*. "Ordinarily," reported Moses, "this takes from forty-five to fifty minutes for actual performance, but the company ran through all the 'business' in fifteen minutes."[48] Such acting styles in the short theatrical films occasioned some protest from the critics.

For their subject matter, most of the short theatrical films drew at first upon the variety stage.[49] At their crudest, these little films were simply photographed variety turns, their length varying from seconds to eight minutes. Although the history of vaudeville stretches back to the travelling acrobats, jugglers and magicians of antiquity, American's variety players were influenced most by the English variety shows imported early in the nineteenth century. During the 1840s, theaters began to present shows which consolidated many of the acts into regular performances. For example, the Franklin Theater in New York advertised itself as a "variety theater" featuring "Magic Lantern Slides, Comic Lectures, Chemistry, French Plays, Mesmeric Clairvoyance, and Beautiful Arithmetical Diagrams." During the next twenty years, similar theaters and "concert saloons" appeared in the cities, providing a potpourri of acts, often suggestive, aimed at a predominantly male audience. By 1865 Tony Pastor had accommodated vaudeville to draw the same audience sought by every other form of theater, from the well-made play to the melodrama—the mass audience. His Fourteenth Street Theater in New York specialized in "straight, clean variety shows" for the middle-class family trade. Russel Nye maintains that "what Pastor did was to make the variety theater respectable, middle class, mass entertainment, flexible and quickly adaptable to the public taste."[50] So successful was vaudeville at its peak between 1890 and 1913, that it was regularly presented in thirty-seven houses in New York alone, with some 2,000 smaller theaters outside the big cities.

The vaudeville formula basically consisted of a succession of short acts typifying the gamut of popular theater of the day. For example, the first bill at the Palace in 1913 opened with a ballet, a Spanish violinist, a pantomimist, a skit by George Ade, a monologist, a wire act, a cartoonist, and comic star Ed Wynn. It was also not unusual for a leading "legitimate" star like Sarah Bernhardt to appear in an excerpt from one of her famous dramatic successes.

Movies appeared at the time when vaudeville was at its peak. Not only was the length of the short turn—eight to ten minutes—ideal for short films, but the vaudeville house, as we shall see later, was an ideal setting for the first exhibitions of films. Moreover, vaudeville actors were the earliest motion picture players. Paul Spehr, in his study of the early motion pictures in New Jersey, states that most early movie "actors" were professional variety performers recreating their acts on film.[51] They included strong men, jugglers, tumblers, knockabout comedians, trick-shots, exotic dancers, and boxers. Accordingly, many early films were records of Japanese and Indian dances, historical recreations of events—such as the "Execution of Mary, Queen of Scots"—and dances of vaudevillians Annabelle, Dolorita, Carmencita, Lola Yberri, and the Gaiety Girls; and performers from Buffalo Bill's Wild West Show, including Buffalo Bill and Annie Oakley. There were even legitimate performers who had appeared in vaudeville and now appeared on film—such as John Drew and May Irwin.

To say that these recorded vaudeville turns did nothing to advance the artistic nature of cinema is not accurate. It is true that these films recorded the action in unbroken shots from medium-long shot vantage points (approximating the viewer's third row aisle position in a theater house), which did little to exploit the camera's possibilities for movement and the film medium's potential for edition. But it is also true that some aspects of vaudeville did hold out possibilities for the exploitation of the potentiality of the film medium. I refer to the magic shows.

In his study of the magic shows that influenced Georges Méliès, John Frazer in *Artificially Arranged Scenes* demonstrated that a main characteristic of the magic show was the creation of scenic transitions without drawing the curtain. In other words, these transitions had to occur quickly, in full view of the audience. Revolving stages, curtains of light, rolling dioramas, flats raised by elevator, lowered by ropes, or moved horizontally in grooves were used to effect these transitions. Frazer concluded: "The similarity between this presentational style and the vocabulary of transformations created by Méliès for the curtainless cinema suggests the influence that the pantomime spectacle had on early films."[52]

Thus the magical effects staged in some of the famous Paris theaters—the Theatre de l'Ambigu-Comique, le Theatre de la Porte Saint-Martin, and le Theatre Municipal du Chatelet—were imitated in many of Méliès' films. For example, the Ambigu's presentation of *Robert Macaire* in 1903 was imitated in Méliès' "Robert Macaire and Bertrand" (1906); the Theatre de la Porte Saint-Martin's revivals of the fantasy ballet *Biche au Bois* inspired Méliès "The Kingdom of the Fairies" (1903); the theatricalization in 1882 of Jules

Verne's *The Impossible Voyage* was filmed by Méliès in 1904; and the Chatelet's pantomimes of *Cinderella* (1895), *Robinson Crusoe* (1899), and *Little Red Riding Hood* (1901) were filmed before 1902.[53]

The resulting films abounded in trick effects that depended upon the manipulation (editing) of pieces of film or the stopping and starting of the camera. Possibly the most famous trick in the magical repertory of the theater houses became the basis for an important principle in cinema—the creation of effect through editing. The most famous illusion of the conjurer Buatier was "The Vanishing Lady," wherein a woman was made to disappear from under a draped chair. Méliès himself presented this illusion frequently at his Theatre Robert-Houdin; after 1896 he transferred it to film. To make his seated lady disappear, Méliès simply stopped the camera, allowed her to leave the scene, and recommenced filming. This crude editing technique, stated Frazer, "became a landmark in the development of the art of the motion picture, when for the first time Méliès created a magical effect by stopping the camera and rearranging the objects within a scene."[54]

In America, Edwin S. Porter developed cinematic tricks in accordance with Méliès' work. Historian Kevin Brownlow noted that Méliès films directly inspired Porter. Porter had worked as a projectionist for the Eden Musee in New York City in 1896 and had had the opportunity to scrutinize them, frame by frame. Thus, even though relatively ignorant of the magic shows of France, Porter was able to profit from Méliès' imitations of them.[55] He used his newly gained knowledge of trick effects to experiment on his own with ways in which editing could approximate (and even improve upon) theatrical effects. In his first films trick effects were the prime excuse for their existence—"Another Job for the Undertaker" (1901) and "Dreams of a Rarebit Fiend" (1906), for example—and displayed various devices, from pixillation (stop-frame animation of three-dimension objects) to split-screen devices. But eventually Porter incorporated these devices into his story films. Even such simple stories as "Life of an American Fireman" (1902) presented examples of scene transitions effected instantly through editing. Transitions were either done through straight cuts or by the use of dissolves and fade-ins and fade-outs. These latter transitions were gradual transitions that brought to the motion picture the effect of the dimming and brightening of lights on a stage platform.

Vaudeville also held out to filmmakers another concept that was to prove valuable for the development of the motion picture—the excerpted play. The vaudeville turn was just long enough for a special condensed version of a play or for an excerpt from a play.[56] From their beginnings, the movies imitated this practice. One of the earliest examples of the excerpted play on film was an Edison short in 1894 called "Band Drill." It was a photographed scene from Charles Hoyt's *A Milk White Flag* (which had opened at Hoyt's Theatre that same year). It ran for only 593 frames—fifteen seconds at a speed of forty frames per second projection speed. Another Edison film from 1896 was called "The Kiss," and it was one of the first shorts to bring a prominent actress to the screen in an excerpt from a current hit play. "The Kiss" photographed May Irwin in a romantic scene that lasted only a few seconds. It was from her play, *The Widow Jones* (which had opened at the Bijou Theater in New York the year before). And in 1903 Biograph released on four separate reels four scenes from William S. Pratt's popular melodrama, *Ten Nights in a Barroom* (1858). Each "scene" consisted of a tableau recorded in one uncut shot. The titles of each tell the story—"Death of Little May," "Death of Slade," "The Fatal Blow," and "Murder of Willie." This method of excerpting various scenes and releasing them individually on reels was also applied to many operas as well. One example was Edison's release of four individual scenes from *Aida,* each on individual reels, and each utilizing the uncut shot to record the scene.

Short theatrical films also condensed entire plays into one reel of running time. Literally hundreds of popular plays reached audiences at movie houses in this way. In France Méliès reduced many of the melodramas of Guilbert de Pixerecourt—including *Robinson Crusoe* and *The Thousand and One Nights*—to one-reel films under the same names. They were all released around the turn of the century. Méliès also took the complex farce intrigues of Georges Feydeau and translated their spirit and construction (as far as was possible) to film. Feydeau's *La Dame de chez Maxim, On Purge Bebe,* and *La Puce a l'oreille* can be compared, argued John Frazer, to Méliès' style of filmmaking. Both playwright and filmmaker "were attracted to comic reversals, punning names, a vast array of malevolent stage machinery, and the exploitation of pseudo-science for comic purposes."[57]

In America, too, many plays and operas were condensed into short theatrical films. Edwin S. Porter's "Jack and the Beanstalk" has already been mentioned. Another filmed play he produced was "Uncle Tom's Cabin" (1903), which had received its first stage presentation in New York at the National Theater on August 23, 1852 and which had been revived continually thereafter. The film version was only 507 feet in length and it was subdivided into fourteen tableaux-scenes, each of which was recorded in an unbroken shot from a fixed camera. Even D. W. Griffith occasionally made this kind of film. In 1909 he managed to reduce all of the opera, *Rigoletto,* into one reel of film. That same year he made a one-reel version of *The Taming of the Shrew.* And, speaking of Shakespeare, most of his plays had appeared on film by 1912. This may appear unlikely in that movies at this time were silent, but nothing, seemingly, daunted those filmmakers anxious to provide theatrical films for the variety houses and nickelodeons. Robert Hamilton Ball's painstaking study of the silent Shakespearean films has exhaustively demonstrated that.[58] One film company, Vitagraph, was especially active in such endeavors, producing in 1908 alone versions of *King Lear, Macbeth,*

Richard III, and *Antony and Cleopatra.*

One is tempted to ask why film entrepreneurs working in a silent medium sought out the stories of stage plays when it meant having to excerpt or condense them? Why didn't they content themselves with other forms of stories that seemed more appropriate to a medium that could utilize real locations and which had the capacity, through editing, of creating a swiftly paced narrative style? Why weren't the *non-theatrical* films like chases and slapstick comedies preferred more? After all, the chase format, no less than the magic shows of Méliès, held its own potentials for the film medium. But chase films at this time did not exploit story; they exploited *movement*—within the frame and through juxtaposition of pieces of film—and this practice ran counter to that of aligning film with the models of the popular theater. A stage play did tell a *story*; moreover, it was a story that had inherited hundreds of years of traditions in how a story should be constructed. For the melodrama, of course, a story needed only to be simple and clearcut in its moral conflicts. But for the well made play, as shall be discussed at greater length in Chapters Three and Four, the story had to observe certain logical demands in its structure and development. Thus stage plays represented the kinds of stories the public was used to and wanted. It would take some time for the virtues of the chase films to gain rightful recognition in terms of their cinematic potentials.

In addition to the many attractive qualities filmmakers thought they saw in stage plays—their stories, their popularity and audience following, their traditions, and their range of mass appeal—certainly one of the most attractive must have been their accessibility. The copyrights of plays did not protect them from being photographed on celluloid. When Vitagraph made a condensed version of the Broadway hit, *Raffles, the Amateur Cracksman,* the filmmakers got the rights merely by putting the name of the stage producer on the screen. But sometimes filmmakers weren't so open about their thievery. In 1911, Robert Grau reported:

> Recently some of the unprincipled moving picture producers have been pirating copyrighted dramatic compositions, and resorting to changing the titles and scenes to escape detection....[59]

This problem persisted until 1912 when one such theft led to a new copyright law, one that would place the motion picture under the copyright restrictions formerly reserved only to still photographs and printed words.

The case involved was the Kalem Film Company's one-reel version of *Ben Hur* (1908), made without consulting the author's estate or the producers of the stage version—Klaw and Erlanger. A suit was initiated against Kalem that was finally settled in 1912 when the higher courts decided that movie producers could not use copyrighted literary or dramatic material without the consent of the owner. Until then, however, the filmmakers had a relatively free hand in their use of stage material.

These condensed versions of plays, whether lawful or illegal, succeeded in losing whatever dramatic power and complexity they possessed in the first place. Montrose J. Moses summed up the situation in 1911 when he complained about the practice:

> The kinetoscope dramatist, so to speak, takes whatever he can find. He outlines the story of "Treasure Island;" he adapts Boucicault's "The Shaughraun;" he makes a scenario of "Dora;" he modernizes "Oliver Twist;" he receives suggestions for Belasco's "Madame Butterly;" . . . he takes the motive of "Othello" and puts it into a story that is the husk, without the spirit of Shakespeare.[60]

A new audience was being bred, he continued. "The kinetoscopic theatre audience speaks in terms of minutes. . . . When it goes to see 'Othello' it expects to grasp the story in seventeen minutes."[61] Such complaints would become typical as films continued to appropriate stage plays.

Business Methods

Not only were these short theatrical films produced under circumstances imitative of proscenium productional methods, but they were distributed and exhibited in accordance with theatrical precedents. It is difficult to determine exactly when motion pitures began to be shown as part of a vaudeville bill in a vaudeville house, but Robert Grau, writing in 1914, contended that the practice began with the efforts of one Archie Shepard, a theatrical manager with an interest in photography. Grau claimed that Shepard was the first in America to appreciate the entertainment potentials of moving pictures.[62] Beginning in 1895, he took his Armat Magnascope and strips of film to the middle western states, exploiting the films as added attractions on vaudeville bills.

So extensive did this practice immediately become, as George C. Pratt has recently noted in his study of the exhibition practices of early filmmakers, that "motion pictures rode the flying coattails of vaudeville for the first ten years of their existence."[63] A projecting device called the "eidoloscope" screened films for a week's run at the Olympic Theater in Chicago in August 1895. During November of that year, projected films were presented via the "bioscope" at the Wintergarten in Berlin. On December 28, 1895, the Lumière brothers projected moving pictures at the grand Cafe at the Boulevard des Capucines. On April 23, 1896, several Edison films were included in a vaudeville program at Koster and Bial's Music Hall on 34th Street and Broadway in New York City. And in November of 1896, the Mutoscope was unveiled at Hammerstein's Music Hall in New York City.

Sometimes these little films were incorporated into stage routines. An article in the *North American Review* in 1896 speculated that projected films could be used to replace a theater house's artificial backdrops. By projecting the film from behind the screen on the stage, it was argued, scenic backdrops of, for example, a waterfall or a storm at sea could be utilized. "The vitascope would represent these things, taken absolutely from life, with a thousand-fold more effectiveness and pleasure to the audience than anything in the line of the most skillful stage device with which we are now acquainted." Moreover, battle scenes could be achieved, and the author invited us to speculate what a production by Sir Henry Irving would be like if it utilized this technique: "Imagine how much more brilliant and veracious the effect might be with vitascope figures for auxiliaries!"[64]

As if in response to this idea, Georges Méliès that same year began incorporating films into his stage productions. John Frazer has cited many examples of this. For his production in 1905 of *The Devil's Pills* (first produced at the Cirque Olympique in 1839) he filmed the episode of the "celestial carriage" and projected it during the stage performance at the Theatre Municipal du Chatelet. And, to cite just one more example, he filmed a "North Pole" sequence for the ballet called *Near the Stars* at the Olympia Theater a year later. This footage, purportedly, became the basis for one of Méliès' last great films, "The Conquest of the Pole" (1912).[65]

Motion pictures became a regular part of variety bills. Obviously, the more a theatrical short resembled a variety turn, the more it was in keeping with the "live" acts of the bill and the better suited it was to the vaudeville house. On June 28, 1903, a writer for the *New York Daily Tribune* wrote an account of this. He attended a variety bill and patiently waited through the theatrical sketches—including "Is Marriage a Failure?" (with its inevitable "reconciliation" and "kiss-and-make-up conclusion"), the comedy acrobats, a singing duo named Dorothy and Dolly (who "smiled and kicked and danced away into the wings"), a magician with a name from Hindostan ("and a dress suit from Sixth-Ave.") who hatched chickens from the depths of his coattail pockets. Then the house darkened:

And now on the white curtain . . . come scenes of comedy tragedy. Long narrow coils of film are unwound from the bobbins of the kinetoscope, and their thousands of little pictures are flashed on the screen so rapidly that all blend into a single pantomime.[66]

What emerges most strikingly from this long account is that the writer seems to have perceived little difference from the "live" stage routines and ones that existed on film. In this way, according to Benjamin Hampton in his business history of the motion picture, films "became known to theater audiences in all the principal American cities."[67]

Filmmakers sent out their product along organized circuits of variety and legitimate houses. Films began playing their own kind of "road" as early as 1900, when promoter Archie Shepard succeeded in displaying them in the legitimate houses across New England. At that time, theater bookings in that area were controlled by the firm of Cahn and Grant. When Shepard suggested that movies could play a circuit like live plays, they scoffed at first. But, after a successful experiment at Shepard's urging, they collaborated with Shepard's plan. Within months, Robert Grau reported, "Archie L. Shepard's Moving Pictures" became one of the best theatrical attractions in the Eastern states. Several travelling "companies" (composed of advance agents, film equipment, and projectionists) played engagements in the first-class theaters of all the principal cities throughout America and Canada. By 1905, the New York houses had opened to Shepard, also.

Thomas Edison expanded upon his idea when he formed the American Talking Picture Company in 1912. The company represented a partnership between Edison's production company and the largest of the vaudeville circuits, Keith-Albee. This early experiment in synchronized-sound moviemaking recorded on celluloid "turns" and excerpts of plays for distribution in the 1500 theaters across the country. The Keith interests had for a long time shown theatrical shorts as part of their programs; now, with Edison's films, a prosperous future seemed assured. According to Robert Grau, writing in 1914, much of Keith's financial success could be laid at the feet of the motion picture.[68]

The first Edison shorts to appear under this merger included vaudeville turns with titles like "Minstrel Show," "Burlesque Impersonator," and "Wolsey's Soliloquy" (from Henry VIII). By 1913, some of these films expanded to approximately a half hour in length. One of these, "Nursery Favorites," was merely a succession of variety turns while others, like "The Deaf Mute" (after a Civil War drama by Rupert Hughes) were derived from stage dramas. Edison's experiments ended when a fire destroyed most of the American Talking Picture Company's studios in December of 1914. Edison returned to routine silent films and severed the merger with Keith-Albee.[69]

Film entrepreneurs not only took advantage of estabished chains of houses, they also formed their own chains of movie houses along similar lines. How a play toured—that is, where it played, how it was financed, how it could best be staged from theater to theater, etc.—was an important priority of the New York based Syndicate. It had provided the centralized, tough, business-minded control needed to maintain order amid the chaotic conditions of touring plays. Standards of production and exhibition had to be established and maintained, copyrights had to be protected, circuits of theaters to be organized, and an entertainment promoted that best suited a mass audience. Works that did not display good road potential were discouraged. Good potential meant that the play had to display, among other things, a properly conventional moral tone. These producers in the Syndicate, in the words of Oscar Brockett and Robert R. Findlay in *Century of Innovation*, were in a position "to influence (if not dictate) play selection, [refusing] to book any production it thought incapable of attracting a mass audience. Furthermore [they] favored productions featuring stars with large personal followings. Thus, strong pressures were exerted on the theater to remain within the established and popular mold."[70]

It was possible through this kind of organization to present a given drama all over the world in simultaneous productions. For example, when Henry Sienkiewicz' novel *Quo Vadis?* was dramatized in 1899, it was presented in many parts of the country at the same time. A version by Stanislaus Stange was presented in Chicago on December 12, 1899; another by a man named Chase was also playing tank towns. Two productions opened simultaneously in New York on April 9, 1900, one from the Stange adaptation at the New York Theater and the second by Jeannette Gilder at the Herald Square. Wilson Barrett presented it at Edinburgh on May 29, 1900, in London at the Prince of Wales on June 18, and again at the Elephant and Castle on March 4, 1901. In addition, a company appeared at the Castle Square Theatre in Boston on April 16, 1900 and other productions could be seen in San Francisco, Pittsburgh, Denver, and so on.[71]

As impressive as this might sound, it was nothing compared to the distribution potentials of prints of motion picture films. The relative ease and cheapness of print replication, coupled with the increasing numbers of the nickelodeon houses, necessitated centralized control. The theatrical Syndicate was not even ten years old when this urgency was impressed upon the film entrepreneurs. During the earliest years of movie commerce, before 1906, showmen had bought the completed films outright from the manufacturers and exchanged them among themselves. This practice was soon abandoned for a more complex system of film rentals under the control of exchanges scattered about the country. Conditions quickly became chaotic, however, because there were no organized systems, or exchanges, of movie houses under the control of entrepreneurs, no official standards governing the conditions of the houses, and no central influence guiding the nature and the promotion of movies. These were the circumstances that led in 1908 to the formation of the movie industry's version of the Syndicate, the Motion Picture Patents Company.

Although this study is not a business history of the motion picture, it is pertinent at this point to note some of the parallels between the Syndicate and the Patents Company, if only to give a sense of how theatrical business precedents were followed by film people. Like the Syndicate, the Patents Company (whose relative merits continue to be debated[72]) brought phases of movie distribution and exhibition under a centralized control. Just as the Syndicate established and maintained standards of quality for the houses in which touring companies played, so did the Patents Company improve conditions under which movies were shown. Improved film stocks were developed, better projection systems insisted upon, admission prices standardized, and houses themselves kept clean and within the guidelines of local fire laws. Moreover, as the Syndicate was doing, the Patents Company exercised influence upon the kinds of films being made. Stories were encouraged to follow prescribed formulas. They were designed more to fill the houses than to express imaginative and/or challenging concepts. The Patents Company, like the Syndicate, made many enemies of those who sought a more creative and vital kind of entertainment; and many "independent" forces appeared that tried to defy control. Yet the Patents Company was needed if the movie industry was to achieve business stability with houses of its own.

By the time the Patents Company had organized, theaters had to be licensed and films promoted along prearranged routes. As the Syndicate had done, the Patents Company enforced these standardized bookings under the threat of penalties—changes in booking were not allowed, lest the film be paid for without a showing. Soon, it was possible, as *The Moving Picture World* noted in 1909, to distribute films along organized routes of houses, from the largest in the metropolitan areas to the smaller ones of the rural areas. "The first run of the films," the article explained, "are seen in the cities at the best shows, then they go to the next best shows, and on down the line until the expiration of six months finds them delighting the Podunk populace."[73]

Proliferation of films had a disastrous effect on the theatrical road system. Obviously, it was much cheaper to duplicate a print of a film and ship it to a theater than it was to mount a road show company and send it along its circuit. That meant, of course, that audiences had to pay much less to see a film than to see a live stage presentation. Basically, there are two views regarding the movies' role in the decline of the road. The first holds that the movies drew attendance away from the legitimate houses. The second holds that the movies also drew a different audience than that which attended the theater. In other words, the movies created an audience as distinguished from that which regularly attended the theater.

The second view breaks the movie audience into two groups: those who did not attend the theater and those who, when they did attend, constituted the low-paying gallery crowd. The first group was comprised largely of immigrants for whom the silent, pantomime films held obvious attractions. The second group was comprised of those who stopped going to the theater and began attending the movies. This is supported by the fact that the only significant decrease in theater attendance during this period was that of the gallery audience.[74] This decrease may have been unfortunate for the theaters in urban centers, but it was disastrous in the rural areas.

But there is a third view which takes a more comprehensive view of the situation. It holds that the decline of the road shows stems from the movies' growing business structure and, hence, the proliferation of the movie house. Declining stage attendance was only a symptom of a more serious problem— the decline of the legitimate theater itself. People were not going to the theater at this time so much simply because there were not as many theaters to go to! A movie industry growing in strength and organization was beginning to buy up the rival theaters in a given community. It was better to close them up, reasoned the film entrepreneurs, or to convert them into movie houses than it was to let them remain as space for rival theater productions. If the movie entrepreneurs could not buy up the legitimate house they could at least build a movie house next door so as to conspicuously remind the audiences of their own lesser admission prices. And, at the very least, propaganda (some of it admittedly true) could be spread to the effect that patronage of the legitimate house meant that the money would leave town with the road company as opposed to remaining in the hometown coffers of the local movie house.[75]

The result was that touring road companies were finding themselves in financial difficulties. "Every [theatrical] road company has its tale to tell of business ruined by the kinetoscope," noted Montrose Moses in 1911.[76] William Brady, a promoter who depended upon the road show profits of his plays, cited the fate of one of his successful plays, *Way Down East,* as an example of what movie distribution was doing to his business. When filmmakers from one of the Patents companies appropriated his play and sent hundreds of prints of that filmed play around the country for exhibition in the nickelodeons, Brady reported that "one of my companies, composed of thirty-five people—men and women—was forced off the road and sent back to New York. The road company can never play that production again," he continued, "because in nearly every one-night stand in this country, 'Way Down East' is being presented on every street corner...."[77]

The Syndicate-dominated theater held out one model for imitation that filmmakers of the Patents Company-dominated film industry were reluctant to pursue—the star system. The system, which was to become so important to the film industry when the feature-length theatrical film was introduced in 1912, was slow in coming to the movie industry during these early years. In addition to the standardized scenery, plots, and distribution methods, the star system had influenced the nature of the popular theater. It was not uncommon throughout the latter half of the 19th century to find dramas tailored exclusively to the peculiar talents of its star. "The star actor," in the words of Russel Nye, "gave the stereotypes of the formula play a special life," leaving us a record "of an extraordinary number of great performances in an extraordinary number of unimportant plays."[78] As early as the middle of the nineteenth century, W. B. Wood remarked: "The star is the light of everything; the centre about which all must move. He has his own times, his own pieces, his own play of business, and his preferences of every sort."[79] Many American actors became so identified with a certain role that it would follow them throughout their lifetimes—indeed, sometimes throughout the lifetimes of generations of players to come (as in the case of several generations of "Joseph Jeffersons" portraying Rip Van Winkle).[80]

All too often, a play's importance as a self-contained work was subordinated to the actor's participation in it. "We regard the workman first and the work second," said Syndicate producer Charles Frohman. "Our imaginations are fired not nearly so much by great deeds as great doers."[81] Frohman's words capture the essence of the Syndicate attitude, and well he might speak, considering that his own stable of players included Maude Adams, Ethel Barrymore, Otis Skinner, John Drew, and Marie Doro.

As a result, the 19th century American stage presents many examples of star players who influenced the kinds of plays in which they appeared. From Edwin Forrest, early in the century, on through the Booth family—Junius Brutus, Edwin, and John Wilkes—the Jefferson family, and later in the century, James O'Neill and James K. Hackett, players marked roles as their own, even rewriting them to better suit their own talents.[82] (This will be further explored in later chapters in the case of the adaptations of *The Count of Monte Cristo* and *The Prisoner of Zenda* by, respectively, O'Neill and Hackett.) These players were able to appear continually in a single play because of the emergence toward the end of the nineteenth century of the combination company.[83] The star would travel with a supporting group across certain areas of the country, always performing the same play. By 1886 the stock companies had dwindled to a handful while the combination system had grown into the hundreds of companies. The separation of theater management from play production, incidentally, was virtually complete now. The stage manager of the local theater house was now only a janitor, as it were, leasing the house to the travelling company; and, as we have already noted, on the heels of this system came fixed circuits and booking offices.

Although the theatrical entrepreneurs benefited in some ways from this system, they also risked financial hazards. Standardization of plays meant the loss of artistic integrity. But the success of players meant another kind of disaster—demands for increased salaries. This was what George Jean Nathan referred to in 1912 when he attacked the theatrical star system:

> Cast your eye over the records and recall the serious financial injury that has accrued to these producers, and the like injury that has resulted to the portion of the supporting companies and playwrights because of the vanity and momentary whims of 'stars.'[84]

Nathan had pinpointed the problem most feared by the promoters of the Patents Company. All too willing to inherit the systems developed by the Syndicate as far as standardized distribution was concerned, they balked at first at the troublesome economic consequences of copying the star system. Hampton reports that they feared increased expenses in film production attendant upon expenditures for star promotions; and they thought the viewing public would not support films shown at an increase above the nickel to ten cents presently charged at the box offices. As a result, the only celebrities that received any kind of promotion at first were stage stars—and even they were not of the first magnitude, generally.

Before 1909, as Anthony Slide has observed in his *American Film History Prior to 1920*, there were no recognized *film* stars, per se. Those films that in any way played upon the drawing power of players relied upon the services of stage stars of already proven abilities.[85] For the most part, however, these were not stars of the first magnitude, but competent players of proven versatility and experience with companies like those of Charles Frohman. For every Joseph Jefferson (who appeared in several one-reel scenes from his famous stage presentation of *Rip Van Winkle* before 1905) there were dozens more of lesser prestige. They were less likely to make unreasonable salary demands upon their new employers.

The Vitagraph studio was one of the first studios to establish a program of consistent employment of "lesser" stage actors. Two of Vitagraph's most successful players, Florence Turner and John Bunny, were minor stage stars. Turner, Vitagraph's first major star, had been known on the legitimate and vaudeville stages as "Eugenie Florence." She came to Vitagraph in 1905 and filmed some scenes from Shakespeare and from Boker's *Francesca da Rimini* in 1907. Now a film star, she became, according to Slide, the first movie star to make personal appearances—often with another stage actor, her leading man Maurice Costello.[86] Another Vitagraph star, John Bunny, was also stage-trained. From 1898 to 1905 he was stage manager and director for many of William Brady's productions, including *Way Down East* (where he portrayed the character of "Hi Holler"). His remarks about his decision to enter motion pictures reflect a growing consciousness of other stage actors of the time:

> I awoke to the fact that the stage game was not what it had been and that the 'movies' were the coming thing. So I decided I would rather be behind the guns than in front of them. I wanted to be with the 'shooters' rather than with the 'shot' so I cancelled my thirty weeks contract . . . and threw aside all the years of experience and success I had had, and decided to begin all over again.[87]

Stage actors that followed him to Vitagraph included Mr. and Mrs. Sidney Drew. In the early teens, Sidney Drew, with his second wife, Lucille McVey, introduced to the screen the cinematic equivalent of the domestic comedies of the "Roberts-Campbell"-type plays of William Dean Howells.[88] This polite kind of parlor comedy on film was very different from the slapstick variety produced by Mack Sennett. Drew derived his screen style from his experience in presenting excerpts from legitimate drama on the vaudeville stage.

Like it or not, the Patents Company-dominated motion picture industry found itself with a growing roster of stars. Second-rate stage players were becoming some of the brightest lights on the screen. In addition, some of the independent companies that were defying the control of the Patents Company were also trying to promote their own star system. By 1912, according to Robert Grau's estimate, over four hundred stage players were working for the Patent and Independent film companies. The roster of

Vitagraph alone had no less than fourteen actors and actresses formerly from Charles Frohman's company.[89]

The theatrical model of the star system was gradually finding favor in the eyes of the Patents companies and the independents. Benjamin Hampton explained that they had become convinced "that audiences like some actors and actresses more than they did others, and from this observation arose the beginnings of star exploitation on the screen."[90] Moreover, film entrepreneurs were beginning to exploit these names in the promotion of films. The Kalem studio issued posters and stills depicting the players with their names emblazoned beneath, just as the theatrical Syndicate was doing with their productions and stars. The Biograph studios released press information to newspapers and trade periodicals regarding the activities of both screen and stage stars. Some stage players of the day continued to be known on film as "Mr. Sothern," "Miss Adams," "Mrs. Fiske," but movie fans were now talking about stars trained for the screen—"Broncho Billy," "Little Mary," and "Max." Like their theatrical counterparts, these screen stars had their personality traits, their bits of characteristic business, their identifying clothing, etc., by which moviegoers could instantly recognize them. Films were tailored to these characteristics, just as plays were written for their own leading players.

Immediately, some of the problems engendered by the star system on the stage now surfaced in the motion picture industry. Nathan's warnings were justified. *Variety* in November of 1913 explained the problem: Printing the cast of the leading players was causing trouble in the movie industry. "The film directors and executives are now going through the experiences of Broadway impresarios of regular production in attempts to pacify players who want their names mentioned first as well as those who insist that if so-and-so's name is in big type, theirs must be too."[91]

These problems intensified with the proliferation of the feature-length theatrical films after 1912. The movie industry's demands for stars and the stars' demands for greater salaries would prove to the movies, as was the case with the stage, that the star system was both a blessing and a curse. In just a few years the movie industry grew from an awkward toy in penny arcades to a formidable rival of the popular stage. Yet within another decade, something happened to the movies, something so shattering in its impact that the entire industry once again found itself in a formative position. Another period of short theatrical films began—only this time they had synchronized sound. . . .

Notes

[1]Abel Green and Joe Laurie, *Show Biz* (New York: Henry Holt and Co., 1951), p. 5.
[2]Walter Prichard Eaton, "Actor-Snatching and the Movies," *American Magazine*, December 1915, p. 56.

³Thomas H. Dickinson, *The Case of American Drama* (Boston and New York: Houghton Mifflin Co., 1915), p. 101.

⁴See Milo L. Smith, "The Klaw-Erlanger Bogeyman Myth," *Players*, Vol. 44, No. 2 (December-January, 1969), pp. 70-75.

⁵Anton Chekhov, *The Sea Gull*, in John Gassner, Ed., *Twenty Best European Plays* (New York: Crown Publishers, Inc., 1966), p. 350.

⁶James A. Herne, "Art for Truth's Sake in the Drama," *The Arena*, February 1897, p. 364.

⁷Robert McLaughlin, *Broadway and Hollywood: A History of Economic Interaction* (New York: Arno Press, 1974), p. 5.

⁸For a concise explanation of the practices of the United Booking Office, see Robert Grau, *The Stage in the Twentieth Century* (New York: Broadway Publishing Company, 1912), pp. 54-55.

⁹Benjamin Hampton, *A History of the American Film Criticism* (New York: Dover Press, 1970), p. 47.

¹⁰Myron Lounsbury, *The Origins of American Film Criticism* (New York: Arno Press, 1973), p. 3.

¹¹"The Fine Arts: The Kinetoscope," *The Critic*, Vol. 24, No. 638 (May 12, 1894), p. 330.

¹²Antonia and W.K.L. Dickson, *Edison's Invention of the Kineto-Phonograph* (Los Angeles: Pueblo Press, 1939).

¹³Quoted in Marshall Deutelbaum, ed., *"Image" on the Art and Evolution of the Film* (New York: Dover, 1979), p. 32.

¹⁴Joseph Medill Patterson, "The Nickelodeons: The Poor Man's Elementary Course in the Drama," *The Saturday Evening Post*, Vol. 180, No. 21 (November 23, 1907), pp. 10-11.

¹⁵"The Factor of Uniformity," *The Moving Picture World*, Vol. 5, No. 4 (July 24, 1909), pp. 115-116.

¹⁶"Too Near the Camera" *The Moving Picture World*, Vol. 8, No. 12 (March 25, 1911), pp. 633-34.

¹⁷"Spectator's Comments," *The New York Dramatic Mirror*, May 14, 1910, quoted in Stanley Kauffmann, ed., *American Film Criticism* (New York: Liveright, 1972), pp. 39-40.

¹⁹Joseph Medill Patterson, p. 11.

²⁰Rollin Summers, "The Moving Picture Drama and the Acted Drama," *The Moving Picture World*, September 19, 1908, quoted in Stanley Kauffmann, ed., pp. 9-10.

²¹*Ibid.*, p. 11.

²²"Reviews of Feature Subjects," *The New York Dramatic Mirror*, Vol. 67, No. 1738 (April 10, 1912), p. 26.

²³"Editorial" in *Billboard*, Vol. 18, No. 37 (September 15, 1906), p. 16.

²⁴Montrose J. Moses, *The American Dramatist* (Boston: Little, Brown and Company, 1911), p. 207.

²⁵Robert Grau, *The Stage in the Twentieth Century*, pp. 61-62.

²⁶"The Essanay Company Out West," *The Moving Picture World*, Vol. 5, No. 23 (December 4, 1909), p. 801.

²⁷See Kemp R. Niver, Motion Pictures from the Library of Congress Paper Print Collection, 1894-1912 (Berkeley and Los Angeles: University of California Press, 1967). For more of Mr. Niver's research into this period, see also his *The First Twenty Years* (Los Angeles: Locare Research Group, 1968).

²⁸*Ibid.*, p. 26.

²⁹See A. Nicholas Vardac, *Stage to Screen* (Cambridge: Harvard University Press, 1949), pp. 2-8.

³⁰Quoted in John Fell, *Film and the Narrative Tradition* (Norman, Oklahoma: University of Oklahoma Press, 1974), p. 26.

³¹A. Nicholas Vardac, p. 238.

³²Lee Simonson, *The Stage is Set* (New York: Theatre Arts Books, 1970), p. 399.

³³Mordecai Gorelik, *New Theatres for Old* (New York: E. P. Dutton and Company, Inc., 1962), pp. 112-13.

³⁴Lee Simonson, p. 17.

[35]Quoted in Clifford Ashby, "William H. Crane: The Old School of Acting and the New," *Drama Survey*, Vol. 3, No. 3 (Winter, 1964), p. 404.

[36]See Charles W. Handley, "History of Motion-Picture Studio Lighting," in Raymond Fielding, ed., *A Technological History of Motion Pictures and Television* (Berkeley and Los Angeles: University of California Press, 1967), pp. 120-24.

[37]Harold G. Bowen, "Thomas Alva Edison's Early Motion-Picture Experiments," in Raymond Fielding, pp. 90-96.

[38]Robert W. Paul, "Kinematographic Experiences," in Raymond Fielding, pp. 42-48.

[39]Leon Barsacq, *Caligari's Cabinet and Other Grand Illusions: A History of Film Design* (Boston: New York Graphic Society, 1976), pp. 5-6.

[40]Leon Barsacq, p. 7.

[41]Katherine Singer Kovacs, "Georges Méliès and the 'Feerie,' " *Cinema Journal*, Vol. XVI, No. 1 (Fall 1976), pp. 1-13.

[42]Leon Barsacq, p. 9.

[43]Quoted in Andrew H. Eskind, "She Banked in Her Stocking; or, Robbed of Her All: Mutoscopes Old and New," in Marshall Deutelbaum, p. 30.

[44]Karl Brown, *Adventures with D. W. Griffith* (New York: Farrar, Straus, and Giroux, 1973), pp. 15-16.

[45]Lee Simonson, p. 266.

[46]Quoted in Lee Simonson, pp. 270-71.

[47]Constantin Stanislavski, *My Life in Art* (New York: Theatre Art Books, 1952), pp. 306-07.

[48]Montrose J. Moses, p. 201.

[49]For a chatty but invaluable history of the vaudeville stage, see Joe Laurie, Jr., *Vaudeville: From the Honky-Tonks to the Palace* (New York: Henry Holt, 1953). See also Bernard Sobel, *A Pictorial History of Vaudeville* (New York: Citadel Press, 1961).

[50]Russel Nye, *The Unembarrassed Muse* (New York: The Dial Press, 1970), p. 168.

[51]Paul Spehr, *The Movies Begin: Making Movies in New Jersey*, 1887-1920 (Newark, New Jersey: The Newark Museum, 1977), p. 22.

[52]John Frazer, *Artificially Arranged Scenes* (Boston: G. K. Hall and Co., 1979), p. 4.

[53]*Ibid.*, pp. 3-9.

[54]*Ibid.*, p. 26.

[55]Kevin Brownlow, *Hollywood: The Pioneers* (New York: Oxford University Press, 1979), p. 34.

[56]John Fell, p. 15.

[57]John Frazer, p. 8.

[58]Robert Hamilton Ball, *Shakespeare on the Silent Screen* (New York: Theatre Arts, 1973).

[59]Robert Grau, *The Stage in the Twentieth Century*, p. 273.

[60]Montrose J. Moses, p. 212.

[61]*Ibid.*, p. 201.

[62]Robert Grau, *The Theatre of Science* (New York: Benjamin Blom, 1969), p. 28.

[63]George C. Pratt, "No Magic, No Mystery, No Sleight of Hand," in Marshall Deutelbaum, p. 39.

[64]George Parsons Lathrop, "Stage Scenery and the Vitascope," North *American Review*, Vol. 163 (September 1896), p. 379.

[65]John Frazer, p. 8.

[66]Quoted in Marshall Deutelbaum, p. 32.

[67]Benjamin Hampton, p. 12.

[68]Robert Grau, *The Theatre of Science*, p. 21.

[69]The best history of this enterprise is contained in Rosalind Rogoff, "Edison's Dream: A Brief History of the Kinetophone," *Cinema Journal*, Vol. XV, No. 2 (Spring 1976), pp. 58-68.

[70]Oscar Brockett and Robert R. Findlay, *Century of Innovation* (Englewood Cliffs, N.J.: Prentice-Hall, 1973), p. 50.

[71]These statistics are derived from A. Nicholas Vardac, pp. 76-77.

[72]The best history and assessment of the Motion Picture Patents Company can be found in Gertrude Jobes, *Motion Picture Empire* (Hamden, Connecticut: Archon Books, 1966), pp. 44-110.

[73]"The Essanay Company Out West," p. 802.

[74]See Jack Puggi, *Theatre in America: Impact of Economic Forces,* 1870-1967 (Ithaca, New York: Cornell University Press, 1968), p. 41.

[75]See Alfred L. Bernheim, *The Business of the Theatre* (New York: Benjamin Blom, Inc., 1932), p. 89.

[76]Montrose J. Moses, p. 214.

[77]Quotes in Moses, p. 208.

[78]Russel Nye, p. 78.

[79]Quoted in John Perry, *James A. Herne: The American Ibsen* (Chicago: Nelson Hall, 1978), p. 12.

[80]For a fine account of the Jefferson family's portrayal of Rip Van Winkle, see Ima Honaker Herron, *The Small Town in American Drama* (Dallas: Southern Methodist University Press, 1969), pp. 94-106.

[81]Quoted in Arthur Hobson Quinn, *History of the American Drama: From the Civil War to the Present Day,* p. 388.

[82]For a general discussion of the actor-families, see Montrose J. Moses, *Famous Actor-Families in America* (New York: Benjamin Blom, 1968); see also Dale Shaw, *Titans of the American Stage* (Philadelphia: The Westminster Press, 1971).

[83]For a valuable discussion of the growth of the "combination company" system, see Alfred L. Bernheim, pp. 28-30.

[84]George Jean Nathan, "Falling Star System," *Theatre Magazine,* January 1912, p. 14.

[85]Anthony Slide, *American Film History Prior to 1920* (Metuchen, N.J.: The Scarecrow Press, 1978), p. 1.

[86]Anthony Slide, *The Big V* (Metuchen, N.J.: The Scarecrow Press, 1976), p. 35.

[87]Quoted in Slide, *The Big V,* pp. 42-43.

[88]*Ibid.,* pp. 42-43.

[89]Robert Grau, *The Stage in the Twentieth Century,* p. 61.

[90]Benjamin Hampton, p. 87.

[91]Anthony Slide, *Aspects of Film Prior to 1920,* p. 4

After 1915 the Lasky and Famous Players Companies merged with Paramount under Adolph Zukor.

Chapter Two
"Now Hear This":
The First Talking
Theatrical Films, 1926-1930

On Friday, August 6, 1926, Warner Bros. studio premiered the Vitaphone sound-on-disc process at Warners Theater on Broadway and 52nd Street. A number of short, synchronized-sound theatrical films were shown that starred currently popular opera and stage celebrities. Only a few months later, on January 21, 1927, William Fox premiered his Movietone sound-on-film program of theatrical shorts, also featuring popular performers. Within the next two years all of the major film studios were producing short theatrical films of similar types. Numbering in the thousands, these films offered opportunities for the development of sound engineering techniques that soon made feasible the production of feature-length sound films. Although this two-year period is much briefer than the eighteen-year span already outlined, striking parallels between them can be traced. Like the short, silent theatrical films, these films recorded vaudeville turns and short plays (or excerpts of plays). And, again, they were distributed and exhibited in accordance with current theatrical business practices.

They derived from a popular theater in America little changed since 1912. It was a theatrical system controlled by powerful booking agencies like the Syndicate and the United Booking Office. The Syndicate had been successfully defied by the Shubert interests since 1912, but the Shuberts had gone on to establish their own Trust and eventually to control one-fourth of the plays American audiences saw.[1] The Shuberts' tactics in maintaining this control were no less ruthless than those of their competitors.

Some contemporary critics attacked this formula-ridden theater for the same reasons that James Herne had attacked the American stage in 1896. Writing in 1929, Erwin Piscator could have been echoing Herne's words when he said, "So little have the old forms changed in a new world." Drama had not kept up with the changing life styles and technological advances, Piscator continued. Into the unchanging box stage "our dramatists must set a time of storm and change, fall of dynasties, revolutions! Everything has been changed by new techniques; the waging of wars, our behavior, even our thinking. Everything but the stage!"[2] Joseph Wood Krutch summed up the state of the contemporary stage in similar terms. He realized that many of the same formulas, subjects, and playwrights active before 1912 were still operating late in the 1920s. With few exceptions, Krutch wrote:

...the American playwright...tended to think of himself, not as an artist, but as an artisan practicing an absurdly specialized trade. His favorite maxim and the favorite maxim of his admirers was the oftquoted dictum, "plays are not written but rewritten," by which it was meant to imply simply that the best play was the one which most painstakingly exploited the tricks of the trade.[3]

Vaudeville reached its peak in 1913 with the opening of the Keith Palace Theater in New York; but, suffering from the competition of the movies, it had been declining ever since. The motion picture, after beginning as simply another "turn" on a vaudeville bill was, by the late 1920s, threatening to destroy it. It was becoming more common to see a "live" act as part of a motion picture bill than the other way around. Movies, along with radio, were offering the public a cheap brand of entertainment that vaudeville could not hope to rival. It is ironic to note that, by 1933, the Palace had reverted to an all-motion picture policy.[4]

A new kind of variety entertainment, the revue, appeared in the 1920s that also siphoned off many of the vaudeville entertainers. Unlike vaudeville, the revue catered to the carriage trade audiences of Broadway, featuring sumptuously elaborate and expensive settings—such as the work of Joseph Urban for the Ziegfeld Follies. The revue always emphasized American ideals of femininity, producing a blend of the archetypal *Black Crook* "leg" show (extant since 1866) and the more respectable fashion show. In addition to the Ziegfeld Follies, which had begun in 1907 and had achieved mature form by 1919,[5] there were many other revues throughout the twenties, including twenty-two editions of the Ziegfeld series, eight Greenwich Follies, four Irving Berlin Music Box Revues, thirteen George White's Scandals, nine Earl Carroll Vanities, and innumerable Winter Garden extravaganzas (the site of a series of revues by Al Jolson, Raymond Hitchcock, and Ed Wynn). Many of the performers and routines of the revue were utilized in the short theatrical sound films, and they also appeared in the full-length theatrical films after 1928.

If the popular stage had changed little in America since 1912—and, for now, I am not considering the growth of the Little Theatre movement and of producing organizations like the Theatre Guild—the motion picture presented a strikingly different history. The emergence of the feature-length theatrical film after 1912 helped spur numerous changes in both the industry and the ways in which people regarded movies. Motion picture studios such as Fox, Warner Brothers, Famous Players-Paramount, Metro-Goldwyn-Mayer appeared after 1912 and developed into enormous combines with production, distribution, and exhibition arms. In effect, these studios secured in the film industry the kinds of controls that had been exercised by the Syndicate and the Shuberts. Moreover, the idea that the film medium was merely an extension of the stage, a recording mechanism for theatrical events, was modified. Since 1915, cinematic theory had appeared from Hugo Muensterberg, Vachel Lindsay, Sergei Eisenstein, and many others. People were now speaking of the "art" of the screenwriter, cameramen, director, and actor, as distinct from their stage counterparts. Where formerly the cinema had borrowed liberally from the actors, stories, and productional methods of the stage, such appropriations had noticeably diminished by 1926. Many actors currently popular—Tom Mix, Gloria Swanson, and Mary Astor (to name but a few)—had little, if any, stage experience. Story departments were now a regular feature of the studios. Scenario writing was regarded as an endeavor separate from the work of the playwright, stories had to be written that took into account the potentials of the medium. Many of the most profitable feature films of the twenties—*Robin Hood* (1923), *Foolish Wives* (1922), *Nanook of the North* (1920), and *The Crowd* (1928)—owed nothing to theatrical sources. A survey taken by *Variety* in 1928 noted that of the 157 directors under contract to the eight major studios, only 70 had had previous stage experience; and of the 186 players, only 146 had "trained" voices.[6]

Thus, the success, as well as the artistic standing of a film was no longer dependent upon its theatrical source materials. Methods of editing montage, camera movement and special effects—although they may have originally grown out of theatrical precedents—had so developed that they now had become unique achievements altogether. Indeed, it was now the stage play that was borrowing techniques and effects from the motion picture. This had occurred as early as 1914 when Elmer Rice's *On Trial* displayed a non-linear time sequence in its arrangement of scenes; and later in the episodic structure and swift narrative pace evident in many German Expressionist dramas such as Hasenclever's *Der Sohn* and Toller's *Man and the Masses*. (For a more detailed examination of this, see Chapter Six.)

When the Vitaphone process premiered in 1926, the film industry's independence from the stage changed virtually overnight. For the next three years the producers of theatrical films turned their backs on these advances and again reverted to the stories, players, and effects of the popular stage. The initial products of this imitation, as had happened before 1912, were theatrical short films that prepared the way for the feature-length films to follow.

Much of the commentary that greeted the synchronized-sound shorts indicated that movies were returning to their role as a recording medium for theatrical events. Artists, critics, and entrepreneurs like George Bernard Shaw, Luigi Pirandello, Sam Warner, Howard Barnes, and Rudolf Arnheim all promoted this idea. Shaw, long a photography enthusiast and outspoken commentator on the motion picture, hailed the synchronized-sound film as the ideal vehicle for plays—especially his own. Cinema was, for Shaw, striving toward the perfection of the theater, a perfection that had been lacking in the voiceless silent films. With sound that was all changed. Movies were no longer a medium essentially different from the theater in the use of dramatic dialogue, action, and effects: "I tell you flatly and violently that there is no difference whatever. The dramatic technique is precisely the same."[7] Incidentally, when Shaw had the opportunity in 1930 to produce a sound film of one of his plays, he followed through on this idea.

Other reactions were similar. When Luigi Pirandello discussed talking pictures in the *New York Times* in 1929, he said that the cinema was now begging to be turned into theater—although, at best, a poor imitation of it. "The greatest victory which the cinema can ever hope to achieve," he said, "...will be that of becoming a more or less bad photographic and mechanical copy of the theater...."[8] Sam Warner, who since 1925 had been predicting that the movies "could take a Broadway drama, word and action, exactly as it is presented on the stage and reproduce it without change,"[9] was now saying that the Vitaphone "will bring to audiences in every corner of the world the music of the greatest symphony orchestras and the vocal entertainment of the most popular stars of the operatic, vaudeville, and theatrical fields."[10] Commentator Francis Taylor Patterson agreed that the new theatrical films

...are content to be to the art of the drama what the phonograph is to the art of music: a reproducing medium.... The essentials of the cinema, fluidity and rhythm, mass composition, scenic progression, and the use of light, have no part in the new movies.[11]

And Broadway critic Howard Barnes also compared the cinema to a recording medium:

From being a distinctive expression with its own peculiar problems and capacities for fine achievement, the films suddenly were placed in the not particularly enviable position of camera and phonograph for stage plays and musical shows.[12]

Once again the movies were imitating productional and business methods of the stage. Howard Barnes noted that the motion picture was primarily concerned "with the goings-on of the theater proper," offering "nothing but a hodge-podge of familiar stage...techniques."[13] When Paramount began filming stage routines in 1928 in their Astoria Studios on Long Island, it was announced in *Variety* that the acts would be "brought intact to the studio, scenery and all;" and the routine to be filmed "as it is done on the Paramount stage in New York."[14] When British-born director Edmund Goulding came to America to study filmmaking, he described the new sound techniques in similar terms. After preliminary rehearsals to a pre-conceived script, he said, the producer would "witness a rehearsal in a specially designed small theater. He will hear the dialogue, watch the action in much the same way as a stage producer now watches the final rehearsals." Sound stages would then be utilized in exactly the same way producing a filmed record of that theatrical event.[15]

Accordingly, acting and writing, it was thought, had the same functions in both stage play and on film. Movie acting was no different from that of a play, commented Alexander Bakshy; what was in question was solely the quality of its reproduction.[16] As for the film script, it could—and should—be consigned to the hands of experienced playwrights. Through the Vitaphone, a *Variety* reviewer remarked, the player could now speak the titles. Thus, remarked Major Albert Warner, "It will be necessary to acquire writers with a knowledge of the theatre for the construction of effective speaking lines."[17]

Some theorists and commentators agreed that the new film medium must abandon the techniques of moving camera and montage. Rudolf Arnheim in *Film As Art* argued that the addition of sound made film's illusion of reality stronger and more complete than it had been. The more complete the illusion the less necessary was editing. Thus, his description of the new film technique indicates a return to the idea that an uncut length of film could approximate a scene:

> Scenes will have to be taken in their entire length and with a stationary camera, and they will have to be shown exactly as they are. The artistic potentialities of this form of film will be exactly those of the stage. Film will no longer be able in any sense to be considered as a separate art.[18]

Fitzhugh Green agreed, although his own argument was based upon more practical considerations. Admitting that editing and the moving camera had helped realize the artistic potential of the motion picture, he noted at the same time that because of the huge, soundproofed booths that contained the cameras, and because of the difficulty of editing the sound on phonograph discs, scenes were best recorded with uncut shots. The camera had to remain motionless, at one height, and the action had to be brought in front of it.[19]

As the synchronized-sound shorts appeared, they began to be reviewed regularly in the pages of *Variety*, and critics immediately singled out for comment the return to the frontal acting styles and fixed viewer vantage points that had been so prevalent in the pre-1912 shorts. Two shorts from Fox in 1928, for example, were adversely criticized for these effects. "The Bath Between" featured vaudevillains Clark and McCullough in a sketch they had perfomed in a Music Box Revue. A reviewer complained about the lack of closeups—"medium shots were employed...which long distanced facial expressions...."[20] Another short, "Napoleon's Barber," was reviewed in terms that seem to sum up most of these films: "it screens and talks like a straight dramatic sketch."[21]

It should not be surprising, considering how closely these short films imitated productional methods of the theater, that they were distributed in accordance with theatrical business practices. "Indications are," reported *Variety* in March, 1928, "that talking pictures may eventually usurp the place of the legitimate road show, which has become practically extinct."[22] And in July of that year, it was reported that RCA Photophone (later to be known as RKO) had the outlets of the Keith and Orpheum houses available for its films—which featured, by no means incidentally, many of the stars of Keith and Orpheum. Again, these chains of houses were beckoning to have the new series of theatrical shorts exhibited. And again, both film and theater entrepreneurs sought mergers by which films of popular plays with stage players could be sent on the "road," just as, once, "live" theatrical productions had been.[23]

Production

Like the early studios of Edison, Méliès, and Paul, the first sound stages of Warner Brothers, Fox, and Paramount (to name but a few studios) were closely modelled after proscenium stages. The first Warners shorts were made in the spring of 1926 in the old Vitagraph studios in Flatbush, Brooklyn. The building, "close to the vaudeville and operatic centers,"[24] was converted into a standard proscenium stage with a frame, a shallow playing area, and standard wing and border arrangement. When it was found in the autumn of that year that the acoustics of the Manhattan Opera House nearby were better, operations moved there. This house, the source of some of America's greatest musical artists, was located on 34th Street. It had been built by Oscar Hammerstein in the days when he was rivalling the Metropolitan Opera House in operatic prestige. Since Hammerstein's day, it had housed a variety of theatrical entertainments—Sothern and Marlowe's Shakespeare, minor opera companies, and ballets. The Warner Brothers operation decked over the seats and extended the stage over the auditorium. The boxes became equipment rooms and sound mixing was done on the sixth floor in a room overlooking the stage. Production of sound shorts proceeded there at the rate of four shorts a week, and it was here that the shorts featuring Marion Tally, Mischa Elman, and Giovanni Martinelli were produced for the Vitaphone premiere.

Production continued there and at the Vitagraph studios all through this two-year period so that the filmmakers could remain close to the New York variety and legitimate players. Yet, even when the Warner Brothers studio built its new sound stage in Los Angeles in 1927, it was with an eye toward readily available talent. It would be just as advantageous to build a studio on the west coast and send stage stars overland as it would be to utilize only a studio in New York. In addition, Los Angeles was an important center on the Orpheum vaudeville circuit, which booked the same artists as did its eastern affiliate, Keith. In short, there was plenty of vaudeville talent in the west that could be utilized.[25]

The west coast studio of Warner Brothers was dubbed "Stage Three" and, like its eastern affiliate, was constructed along the lines of a proscenium stage. Because all sound shooting was done indoors, it was a self-contained theater house with a staging area and facilities for the building of sets and props. There was a bridge for the suspending of lighting equipment and microphones; also overhead were numerous catwalks corresponding to the files of a theater for the handling and suspending of scenery. The stationary, anchored camera booths faced the stage to record the action from only one angle and direction.

Other studios followed the example of Warner Brothers and built their own stages along the lines of theater houses. Paramount built a miniature theater house at its Astoria, Long Island studios in 1928. It was built to accommodate the sets and props of Broadway stage productions. Metro-Goldwyn-Mayer took over the old Hearst Cosmopolitan studios in New York and refurbished them into proscenium-style sound stages midway through 1928. Film Booking Offices (FBO) moved their operations into an old theater in the Bronx where they, too, could remain close to Broadway talent.

The Fox studio went its competitors one better when, in July 1928, it negotiated with several broadway legitimate houses to produce and film variety acts on their stages. This practice had been impossible for the production of theatrical films before 1912; but now, it was thought that interior lighting had developed sufficiently that such filming could now proceed. "The only extra effort the use of ordinary stages involves," reported *Variety* in October, 1928, "is the organization of a group of property boys into traffic cops outside the studios to keep vehicles on the lot from passing the stage while scenes are being shot."[26] Yet this kind of arrangement caused problems, as Alexander Walker has noted in his recent study, *The Shattered Silents*. "An attempt to shoot one production ran into deep trouble. The stage sets photographed flat; the actors were too white against the backdrops; the theater lights could not muster the candlepower that talkies required."[27]

Yet the use of artificial settings and props were necessary, due to the sensitive microphones and closed environments of the early sound stages. Shooting had to be restricted within muffled walls lest outside sound intrude upon the sound recording. The player was surrounded by a totally artificial world of two-dimensional scenery and artificial props.[28] Noted Francis Taylor Patterson in 1930: "Now that the subject matter of the talkies is identical with the subject matter of the stage," said Patterson, "the settings require no vaster space than that which is bridged by the proscenium arch of any theater.... To a microphone-ridden industry great open spaces mean nothing. Nothing at all."[29] Thus, the early operatic shorts of Vitaphone had been made with the regular opera scenery leased from the warehouses that supplied the Metropolitan. Fitzhugh Green has left a charming contemporary description of the artificial contrivances that filmmakers had to resort to in the making of an early Vitaphone theatrical short called "The Volga Boatmen." A set was constructed, Green reported, of a river bank with the opposite shore painted on the background flat. A boat was constructed— actually just part of one—of canvas which was then pushed about by a willing stagehand during the singing of the songs.[30] In an effort to improve upon such patently artificial sets, filmmakers began working with rear-screen projection to provide naturalistic effects while remaining within the sound stage's confines. This bore out the prophecy of 1896, that rear-screen projection of films could provide scenic effects for a stage. *Variety* noted in October of 1928, actors "could perform before a blank background on a studio stage."[31]

The use of rear projection indicates an important feature of these early sound stages—they presented a shallow playing space. Players had to be kept close to the background screens to avoid focussing problems—both background projection and the "live" players had to be kept in focus. This shallowness was a logical consequence of the development of multiple-camera shooting. Because the Warner Brothers sound-on-disc process did not easily permit editing of sound, the camera had to record an entire scene in an uninterrupted take. In effect, this marked a return to the idea that a single camera should record a given scene and preserve the continuities of space and time. The only way to record image and sound uninterrupted and yet allow for some shifting of camera vantage point was to record a scene with several cameras shooting simultaneously from different angles to the action. Splicing together these different angles produced a composite film which was still exactly synchronous with the uninterrupted sound recording. Obviously, the cameras had to stay out of each other's view during the shooting, so they had to remain on the same side of the 180-degree line fronting the set. This kind of setup did not permit any reverse angles—indeed, it necessitated a set that was shallow in depth and whose space remained essentially unexplored and inviolated. The sense of "editing" that was created kept the viewer in front of the action and at restricted distances and angles. In effect, one had the sense of moving from one seat to another in a theater house, the action always remaining fixed in a planar space to the front.

These artificial surroundings and sensitive microphones influenced the frontality, stiffness, and posed quality of the acting styles. Figures were seen from head to toe because the mutliple camera setup necessitated their being kept at a sufficient distance so that all the cameras could record the action without being in each other's view. Thus, all the cameras were fixed at medium to medium-long shot from the action. The frontality of the acting styles came about because of the unpredictable nature and fixed placement of the crude microphones. Because microphones were unidirectional, players had to remain in fixed positions lest their voices stray from their range. Even the angle of the head had to remain constant because any variation would distort the sound quality. Stage actress Louise Closser Hale and director Paul Sloane have left contemporary accounts of this problem. The actor, said Hale, had to have one eye on the chalk marks that kept him or her within range of the microphone and the other eye on that microphone hidden inside the flowerpot, the telephone, the lamp, etc. Lest her speech be distorted, she was instructed not to talk while sitting down or getting up, not to sigh, not to pitch her voice too high, not to let it range too much, and not to project her tones as she had learned to do on stage. All of these things could spoil the recording.[32] Sloane's account, written in 1928, is more detailed:

> Unfortunately, engineers have not yet developed the microphone to the point where it can be unobtrusively placed about the set ready to receive at all times the voices and sound which emanate from the scene. The microphone must be placed just so. The actors must to a great extent completely disregard the logical and dramatic positions and groupings which the scene demands, and must instead be ready always to stand at just so many inches from the microphone; their heads at just such an angle; their voices at just such a level, varying the position of their heads as to the quality of their voice changes....[33]

Players found themselves scattered about the shallow sets in tight clusters, frozen into immobility, in patterns oddly reminiscent of the stage tableau described by the Duke of Saxe-Meiningen and Stanislavsky. It was a cramped, artificial world whose illusion was shattered if the players moved too much. If one problem for actors in the silent theatrical films had been to *avoid* contacting the artificial scenery, in the new sound shorts, it was to *break* contact with the immobile microphones.

Because most of the players were stage performers, they acted on film as if they were performing to a live audience rather than to the camera. As Fitzhugh Green noted in 1929 about these performances, the actors "had gone through their stuff so many times that they could do it in the face of hell or high water. They would get up in front of the microphone and 'play' to it as though it were an audience of 5000; and in so doing, would play to and please its audience of many millions."[34] An early Phonofilms which presented Eddie Cantor's celluloid debut was made in 1924 and was shot in a theater with the proscenium in full view. Cantor entered the stage and stood in the center for a full shot. He told a few jokes, spoke to an imaginary audience and to his band leader off screen, George Olsen. After the jokes, he walked off stage and then returned to sing a comedy song—the whole procedure recorded in an uninterrupted take with only a slight tilt of the camera to keep Cantor's feet in the frame after the first entrance. Another Phonofilm, this one of Weber and Fields' famous vaudeville sketch, "The Pool Room Scene," actually begins with a curtain opening onto a stage and the players bowing to an imaginary audience. One Vitaphone short in 1927 featured opera singer Benjamino Gigli who sang a solo from Mascagni's *Cavalleria Rusticana*. After the song, he walked upstage to join an ensemble, where he paused, as if listening to applause; then he turned around and took a bow while his supporting singers stood stiffly in a row behind him.

Thus far, this discussion has been linked to the synchronized-sound filmed variety turns; but there were many other kinds of theatrical shorts in this period, the most significant of which were the short plays. At Warner Brothers, ex-vaudevillian Bryan Foy had, by 1928, grown restless with filming variety turns. None of the studios had as yet produced a feature-length talking picture—*The Jazz Singer* does not really qualify, since it had only a few talking sequences—but Foy wanted to test complete dramas on film. The problem with the filmed vaudeville turn had been the limitations of using only one set and one camera setup for the simple story lines. At first, Foy's own stage experience had been invaluable for these little films. For example, he filmed his own family ("The Seven Little Foys") in several Vitaphone shorts, including "Foy Family" and "The Swell Head" (both released in August of 1928). All of the brothers and sisters recreated their stage routines. The latter film contained a recreation of the late Eddie Foy Srs.'s last vaudeville act. But, according to contemporary accounts, aside from an occasional camera movement, they were simple films confined to one set and to one camera setup.[35]

While at Stage Three in Los Angeles, Foy began experimenting with more complex dramatic structures that involved some scene shifting. Two short films appeared by August, 1928 that contained action in three separate locations. To affect these transitions, Foy had to resort to a crude device borrowed from 19th century stagecraft. He constructed triple sets with synchronized cameras focused on each of them. Action would start on the left hand set and, when finished, the lights would black out and the actors duck around behind the second set so that when the lights came up again the action could continue there; then that set would black out and filming began on the third set. All of this would proceed in an unbroken sequence so that the wax disc could record sound uninterruptedly. Thus, Foy's "French Leave" could take the action from a setting of front line trenches of World War I to an inn setting, to, finally, a jail set; similarly, "The Bookworm" (derived from a playlet by Willard Mack) could shift from a bookstore to a woman's home to, finally, a train interior. Films that utilized this technique included "The Lash" (a film version of Hall Crane's popular one-act drama), "Solomon's Children," and a revue-like sketch called "The Pullman Porters." A *Variety* reviewer noted that in this last film, the scene shifted from the rear train car, where the porters were singing, to the passengers in the forward car. All this time, the reviewer said with obvious astonishment, the singing of the unseen porters continued to be heard.[36] Such an effect is commonplace in filmmaking today, but in 1928 the joining of sound and image from two different set locations was a novelty worth mentioning. Crude as it was, it was an early example of the asynchronous union of sound and images.

Foy's triple-set technique had advantages and disadvantages. On the plus side, it enabled him to experiment with story films and gave him the experience he needed to make for Warner Brothers the first full-length, all-talking picture, *The Lights of New York* (August, 1928). At the same time, he was able to liberate the cumbersome sound-on-disc system from its single set confines. On the negative side, the technique forced him to stay with shallow-depth stages and artificial props and scenery. He was only doing what had been commonplace in many 19th century plays. The action progressed from scene to scene not by bringing down the curtain but by spotlighting different areas of the stage. The lights would black out on one portion of the stage and come up on another, thereby conveying the necessary sense of a shift from one place and time to another place and time. The best Foy could hope for was the kind of review that greeted his playlet, "Across the Border" (August, 1928). *Variety* noted that the film "was good enough to be presented on a stage just as it stands."[37]

By late 1928 other film companies like Film Booking Offices (FBO) and Paramount were doing their own experiments with filmed plays. FBO's Bronx sound stage was utilized for a number of these playlets, including "Taxi 13," "Joy Ride," "The Scoop." The proximity to Broadway talent was advantageous for FBO, which, in turn, provided good try-out spots for minor theatrical talent.[38] Paramount's playlets (in addition to their filmed variety turns) began production late in 1928 in the Astoria Studios on Long Island, guided by production chiefs Walter Wanger and Monta Bell. One of the many theater people called in to help was George Abbott. Abbott, already very successful as an actor (Lawson's *Processional*), producer (*Broadway*), and writer/director (*Coquette, Gentlemen of the Press*), was fascinated by the movies. Like Foy, he too thought the synchronized-sound medium could make longer and more sophisticated stories than permitted in the one-reel vaudeville turns. "I for one believe that it is as unwarranted to estimate the talking pictures' future by the present state of its mechanical advance as it would have been to judge the potentialities of the phonograph from the cater-waulings it emitted in its first phase."[39] He put his theories to the test in the production of at least two short filmed plays while at Astoria. They were called "The Bishop's Candlesticks" and "The Carnival Man" and both starred stage actor Walter Huston in his screen debut. They will be discussed later in this study in terms of their contributions to the development of asynchronous sound techniques. Abbott's own play, *Gentlemen of the Press,* incidentally, would be filmed early in 1929 in feature-length form, also starring Walter Huston.

Business Practices

At the time of the Vitaphone premiere in 1926, most of the major studios had their own chains of houses—both movie and theater—in which their silent films were exhibited. Paramount operated five hundred houses worth four hundred million dollars; First National, in association with the Stanley Theater chain had three hundred-fifty houses worth three hundred-fifty million. MGM, through its owner, Loew's, Inc., had about three houses worth three hundred million dollars. The remaining studios had smaller chains—Fox, Universal, Pathé, and United Artists accounted for some four hundred theaters valued at four-hundred-fifty million dollars.[40]

The arrival of the Vitaphone and Movietone sound processes enabled Warner Brothers and Fox to overtake and surpass the other majors in terms of circuits of movie houses. Fox greatly expanded his modest chain of houses while Warner Brothers, which before this had possessed only a handful of houses, moved quickly to a commanding position. Indeed, one studio newly formed in 1928—RKO—started from nothing and within a year was able to boast of a vast chain of houses that came from a merger between RCA and the Keith and Orpheum vaudeville chains. While the rest of the industry lagged behind, these three companies used their theatrical shorts to propel them toward the ownership of the entire vaudeville circuits. The policy of distribution and exhibition that had begun before 1912 was now, with the talking picture, active again. It was a period that was best summed up by *Fortune* magazine as constituting "beyond comparison the fastest and most complete revolution in the whole history of industrial revolutions."[40]

William Fox formed the Fox Theatre Corporation for the purpose of expanding his chain of movie houses. It eventually made him the most powerful man in the industry.[42] By 1927 he had built up a chain of 800 houses with New York's 6,000-seat Roxy as his flagship theater. Within two years he had within his grasp, albeit temporarily, the chain of legitimate and vaudeville houses controlled by Loew's, Inc., and the Keith-Albee circuit.

Harry Warner started from scratch with his empire building. By the autumn of 1926 he had three theater houses on Broadway wired for sound with eight more scattered about in as many large cities across the country. Within three years he acquired some 800 theater houses, a consequence of obtaining the houses formerly owned by the Stanley Company of America and those owned by the First National chain. Despite the awesome expenditures necessary to equip them all with sound systems, this move brought Warner Brothers to a position of leadership in the industry by 1930. Small wonder that Gertrude Jobes, in her study of the movies' industrial growth during this period, called Warner Brothers' acquisitions "the most sensational single event in the history of motion pictures."[43]

Warner Brothers' distribution practices reveal how closely the distribution of sound shorts was based upon the distribution practices of "live" vaudeville. Because the Vitaphone shorts presented a complete range of vaudeville—from legitimate and variety stars in turns and short plays—they appealed to different sections of audiences (just as the bill of the Palace would appeal to a different group than that of the local, smaller houses). Accordingly, as Fitzhugh Green reported in 1929, these shorts "had to be booked more like vaudeville than like pictures (which had a more universal appeal). Some cities liked opera numbers; others would not stand for them.

Western and southern states in particular objected to highbrow stuff."[44] Thus, much as promoters on the Keith-Albee or Pantages circuits had had to determine the best routes for given acts, Warner Brothers had to determine where particular kinds of the short films could best play.

The popularity of talking movies caused more and more theater owners to convert their houses to films. Some booked special films for limited engagements and went on to convert to films permanently, dropping their "live" productions entirely. McLaughlin reports that by 1929 in New York alone as many as eleven legitimate theatres were showing films. Nearly half of the nation's 20,500 movie houses (which now included most of the large theaters in urban areas) were showing sound films; and by 1931 fully 20 percent of all legitimate theaters in New York were used for film exhibitions.[45] The movie industry's encroachment on theater houses, begun before 1912, was now virtually completed.

Sound theatrical shorts brought a new impetus to the film entrepreneurs' exploitation of the theatrical star system. The movie industry had developed its own star system since 1915 but, since the arrival of the talkies, it was again felt that only players trained in the theater could adequately meet the new challenge. Not since the arrival of the feature-length silent film in 1912 had there been such an emigration of stage actors to the movies. By late 1928 it was estimated that over 250 legitimate actors had gone over to the movies in hopes of supplanting the silent film actors now in trouble. Of the 750 movie stars, at least a third of them were in peril, and "one investigator says that the only film actor he has met not worrying about his voice and the talkies is Rin-Tin-Tin."[46] Movie stars went into a panic, hiring voice coaches and studying diction. Those whose voices were beyond help even found themselves talking on "voice doubles"—stage trained people whose voices were dubbed over their own.[47]

Stage actors were enthusiastic about the situation. Emil Jannings, who had achieved considerable fame in both stage and screen roles in Germany and America, noted that, regardless of the fate of the stage at the hands of the talkies, there was at least a new opportunity for the actor: "We no longer have to act pantomimes and attempt to work on our public with overdone mimicry to make up for our silence."[48] His words echoed Montrose Moses' outcry who complained of the undue stress placed upon actors working in a silent medium. Lupino Lane was also enthusiastic: "Actors once prominent on the Broadway stage, who haven't been able to get a break in the movies, are jubilant beyond words. A new gate is being opened in the hitherto impregnable fortress of the motion picture. . . ."[49]

But it was the drawing power and prestige of their names that made stage players epecially important to the film entrepreneurs. As *Variety* reported late in 1928, "Legitimate actors as a class, and the names particularly, are on the crest of a wave with all of the New York sound studios contemplating dramatic people exclusively in their film dialogue productions."[50] From the very beginnings of the synchronized-sound film—stretching back to 1900 when Sarah Bernhardt, Coquelin, and the English comedian Little Tich headlined talking pictures at the Paris Exposition Internationelle—it was the players' names that figured most prominently in advertising and promotions. A survey of some of the films produced in the 1920s and the famous players that appeared in them will demonstrate how closely filmmakers clung to the star system as a means of promotion. Lee De Forest's Phonofilms, while never as popular as Warner's shorts, pioneered Hollywood's promotion of stage stars as early as 1923. By the time Warners' Vitaphone premiered in 1926, De Forest had already made more than a thousand short theatrical films of players working in New York theaters—including opera singers in scenes from *Lakme, Rigoletto,* and *Lucia de Lammermoor;* ballet sequences with Pavlova and Fokine; bandleaders Roger Wolfe Kahn, Ben Bernie, and Paul Specht; monologues by Bernard Shaw, De Wolf Hopper, and Elsa Lanchester; dialogues by Weber and Fields; minstrel acts, both Negro and blackface; and headliners like Eddie Cantor, George Jessel, Sir Harry Lauder, and Chic Sale.

When the Vitaphone system premiered on August 6, 1926 in New York, the names of Giovanni Martinelli, Marion Tally, and Mischa Elman "sprang like spotlights out of the advertising page and caught the eye of critics, public, and the film industry."[51] The short films that played that night were, in order: an opening speech by Will H. Hays, President of the Motion Picture Producers and Distributors; Henry Hadley conducting the New York Philharmonic Orchestra in the "overture" from *Tannhäuser;* Marion Tally of the Metropolitan Opera singing the "Caro Nome" from Verdi's *Rigoletto;* comedian Roy Smeck in "His Pasttimes;" Anna Case singing "La Fiesta;" violinist Mischa Elman performing Dvorak's "Humoresque;" and tenor Giovanni Martinelli singing "Vesti la Giubba" from Leoncavallo's *I Pagliacci.* The second Vitaphone program, which premiered in October of 1926, included Al Jolson singing "The Red, Red Robin" "April Showers," and "Rock-a-Bye-Baby with a Dixie Melody;" and performances by Elsie Janis, George Jessel, and Roy Smeck. Warners' program of vaudeville shorts was fully launched with the work of Bryan Foy who, as earlier noted, took advantage of his vaudeville contacts to make over 500 shorts before the end of 1928. Their variety of starring players was as diverse as most vaudeville bills— Joseph Rosenblatt in recital; opera routines by Benjamino Gigli, Giovanni Martinelli, and John Charles Thomas; comedy routines by Leo Carillo ("At the Ball Game"), George Jessel ("A Theatrical Booking Office"), Bert Lahr ("Hold Everything"), Fred Allen ("The Little Show"), and Harry Conley ("Broadway Nights"); musicians like Horace Heidt; and legitimate leading ladies like Irene Franklin (Arthur Hammerstein's "Sweet Adeline").

Fox and Paramount also exploited the drawing power of theater players to launch their sound films. Fox's Movietone process, an elaboration upon De Forest's Phonofilm system, premiered on January 21, 1927, with a program of songs sung by the Spanish entertainer Raquel Meller. On May 25, 1927, a second Movietone Program appeared, with Meller reciting "Corpus Christi," Gertrude Lawrence singing a hit from one of her revues; and a comic sketch by Chic Sale entitled, "They're Coming to Get Me." As was the case with Vitaphone, these shorts were to number in the hundreds before the decade was through. Paramount, also, began producing a program of headliners in the closing months of 1928. Some of the first entries were films featuring Ruth Etting. Others were entries from popular revues, such as "If Men Played Cards as Women Do," based on George Kaufmann's blackout sketch in a Music Box Revue. Kaufmann himself appeared in the sketch on film.

From the reviews regularly appearing in *Variety*, it is clear that the vast majority of all the short, synchronized-sound films from this time had theatrical origins and featured famous stage players. Yet a smaller group of films were also reviewed that will prove to be of great significance later in this study. We already know that some of the pre-1912 shorts were newsreels, or, as Raymond Fielding has called them, "Actualities."[52] Similarly, in the 1926-28 period a number of synchronized-sound actualities appeared, newsreels that forsook the cramped, artificial worlds of the sound stages for locales and events of the real world. Now, films brought to audiences the sound of Lindbergh's voice, the roar of the motor of his "Spirit of St. Louis," the marching feet of Westpoint Cadets, the blaring horns of New York street traffic. Silent newsreels captured the natural world; now the sound newsreels not only recorded the natural world, but it sounds as well. Most of these came from the Fox Studios.

The era of the synchronized-sound short theatrical films peaked in 1928. Thereafter, more and more studios in Los Angeles and New York committed budgets and personnel to the production of feature-length films, both theatrical and non-theatrical. By 1930, although short films continued to be made as "programmer" material, the feature film again assumed a preeminence that it had not enjoyed since the introduction of sound. (I am not considering here the *silent* feature films that continued to appear even as late as 1930.) An important part of that development, as it had been with the appearance of feature films beginning around 1912, was the theatrical film....

Notes

[1] Jerry Stagg, *The Brothers Shubert* (New York: Random House, 1968), p. 3.

[2] Erwin Piscator, "The Theatre Can Belong to Our Century," in Eric Bentley, ed., *The Story of the Modern Stage* (New York: Penguin Books, 1976), p. 471.

³Joseph Wood Krutch, *The American Drama Since 1918* (New York: Random House, 1939), p. 13.

⁴Robert Sobel, *A Pictorial History of Vaudeville* (New York: Citadel Press, 1961), p. 109.

⁵Robert Baral, *Revue: The Great Broadway Period* (New York: Fleet Press Corporation, 1962), pp. 44-102.

⁶"Film People Who Can Talk," *Variety*, July 25, 1928, p. 5.

⁷Quoted in Donald Costello, *The Serpent's Eye* (Notre Dame: University of Notre Dame Press, 1965), p. 14.

⁸"Pirandello Views the 'Talkies,' " *The New York Times Magazine, July 28, 1929, p. 1.*

⁹Quoted in Charles Higham, *Warner Brothers* (New York: Charles Scribner's Sons, 1975), p. 55.

¹⁰*Ibid.*, p. 51.

¹¹Frances Taylor Patterson, "Will Hollywood Move to Broadway?" *New Republic*, February 5, 1930, p. 42.

¹²Howard Barnes, "Talkie-Town," *Theatre Magazine*, Vol. LII (July 1930), p. 36.

¹³*Ibid.*, p. 36.

¹⁴"Tests Start at Paramount's New Studios," *Variety*, July 25, 1928, p. 7.

¹⁵"Talkers in Closeup," *Variety*, June 13, 1928, p. 7.

¹⁶Alexander Bakshy, "The Talkies," *The Nation*, Vol. 128, No. 3320 (February 20, 1929), p. 236.

¹⁷"Vitaphones Play Talking Films as Road Show Substitutes," *Variety*, March 28, 1928, p. 5.

¹⁸Rudolf Arnheim, *Film As Art* (Los Angeles: University of California Press, 1960), p. 157.

¹⁹Fitzhugh Green, *The Film Finds Its Tongue* (New York: G. P. Putnam's Sons, 1929), p. 166.

²⁰Review of "The Bath Between," *Variety*, November 28, 1928, p. 15.

²¹*Ibid.*, p. 15.

²²"Vitaphones Play Talking Films," p. 5.

²³"The Great World Theatre," *Theatre Arts Monthly*, October 1928, p. 693.

²⁴Fitzhugh Green, p. 183.

²⁵*Ibid.*, p. 183.

²⁶"Talkies on Ordinary Stages," *Variety*, October 3, 1928, p. 4.

²⁷Alexander Walker, *The Shattered Silents* (New York: Oxford Press, 1979), p. 91.

²⁸For detailed accounts of some of these difficulties, see the following: "Interview with Cameraman Hal Mohr," in Leonard Maltin, ed., *Behind the Camera* (New York: Signet Film Series, 1971), pp. 91-138; "Interview with Sound Engineer Bernard Brown," by John Tibbetts, *American Classic Screen Magazine*, Vol. 3, No. 1 (September-October, 1978), pp. 33-38, 40, 42, 46; and "Trials of the Talkies," *Photoplay Magazine*, Vol. 36, No. 2 (July 1929), pp. 52-53, 113-16.

²⁹Frances Taylor Patterson, "Will Hollywood Move to Broadway?", p. 297.

³⁰Fitzhugh Green, pp. 58-59.

³¹"Transparent Backgrounds," *Variety*, October 10, 1928, p. 4.

³²Louise Closser Hale, "The New Stage Fright: Talking Pictures," *Harper's Monthly Magazine*, September 1930, pp. 420-21.

³³Paul Sloane, "Hysteria Talkerfilmus: New Movie Maladay," *Theatre Magazine*, October 1928, p. 70.

³⁴Fitzhugh Green, p. 213.

³⁵Review of "The Swell Head," *Variety*, July 18, 1928, p.

³⁶Review of "The Pullman Porters," *Variety*, June 27, 1928, p. 14.

³⁷Review of "Across the Border," *Variety*, August 29, 1928, p. 15.

³⁸Alexander Walker, p. 92.

³⁹George Abbott, "The Big Noise," *Vanity Fair*, April 1929, p. 79.

⁴⁰Alexander Walker, p. 46.

⁴¹"Color and Sound on Film," *Fortune*, Vol. 2 (October 1930), p. 33.

⁴²Norman Zierold, *The Moguls* (New York: Coward-McCann, Inc., 1969), p. 226.

⁴³Gertrude Jobes, *Motion Picture Empire* (Hamden, Connecticut: Archon Books, 1966), p. 275.

⁴⁴Fitzhugh Green, p. 83.

45Robert McLaughlin, *Broadway and Hollywood* (New York: Arno Press, 1974), p. 97.

46Frances Taylor Patterson, p. 42.

47The use of stage actors' voices to "double" for silent stars in talkies occasioned much comment. This practice often had to be done in a post-synchronization process, one of the first uses of this technique. Post-dubbing was one step in the liberating of the hitherto fixed microphone. It meant that sound and image could be recorded separately. See Mark Larkin, "The Truth About Voice Doubling," *Photoplay*, July 1929, pp. 32-33, 108-110.

48Emil Jannings, "Why I Left the Films," *Living Age*, July 1, 1930, p. 558.

49Lupino Lane, "To Talk or Not to Talk—In Pictures," *Theatre Magazine*, August 1928, p. 28.

50"Heyday for Legitimate Talent," *Variety*, December 5, 1928, p. 43.

51Fitzhugh Green, p. 8.

52See Raymond Fielding, *The American Newsreel: 1911-1967* (Norman, Oklahoma: University of Oklahoma Press, 1972).

Sarah Bernhardt's *Queen Elizabeth* (1912) was imported to America by Adolph Zukor as Famous Players' first release (directed   by Louis Mercanton; adapted from the play by Emile Moreau).

Chapter Three

Feature Attractions:
Theater/Film Collaborations, 1912-1915

The premiere of *Queen Elizabeth*, starring Sarah Bernhardt, in New York on July 12, 1912, marked a significant step in the development and acceptance of the feature-length film in America. The "new proscenium" was no longer confined to short plays, vaudeville turns, and dramatic excerpts; soon, it would be the standard mode for the full-length theatrical event. *Queen Elizabeth* appeared at a time when, according to statistics cited by the *New York Dramatic Mirror* that year, there were already more than 12,000 picture theaters in America showing films to a weekly attendance of 36,000,000.[1] Although it was filmed in France, *Queen Elizabeth* was one of the first feature-length films to have a commercial distribution in America. It was based upon a play by Emile Moreau in which Bernhardt had appeared in Europe and America. Its subsequent four-reel length on film more than doubled the average length of a motion picture of the day. Bernhardt's presence and the film's initial exhibition at Daniel Frohman's famous Lyceum Theater on Broadway lent the film a prestige beyond that of any motion picture that had been made up to that time. Its release through the newly-formed Famous Players company, controlled by film entrepreneur Adolph Zukor and theatrical entrepreneur Daniel Frohman, represented a new spirit of cooperation between the theatrical Syndicate and the Motion Picture Patents Company. The Famous Players endeavor would inspire more such cooperative ventures between these formerly competitive organizations during the feature-film making years immediately ahead.

The concept of the feature-length theatrical film came to America from Europe. The organization of the Film d'Art Company in France in 1908 was the first alliance between filmmakers and theatrical personnel expressly for the purpose of making feature-length films from popular and prestigious stage plays. Representatives of Film d'Art, which grew out of a meeting of a congress of film and theatrical entrepreneurs in France on February 2, 1908, stated that its aim was to "raise the prestige of the cinema and erase the memory of its lowly past."[2] That "lowly past" referred to the crude short films of the shooting galleries, boardwalk nickelodeons, and vaudeville houses with their largely blue collar and immigrant audiences. By contrast, legitimate dramas could be filmed and controlled by cooperatives of film and theater personnel. Great stars of the legitimate stage could appear before the camera. Methods of film distribution and replication would insure that these filmed plays would be shown to middle class audiences in legitimate houses all over the world.

The Laffite brothers founded the Film d'Art Company. They recruited actors from the Comedie Francaise and gained the services of prominent stage designers like Emile Bertin from the Theatre Français. The first production from Film d'Art was *The Assassination of the Duc de Guise*—a popular subject throughout the 19th century for painters and playwrights alike. The film premiered on November 17, 1908. It was scripted by Henrie Lavedan, designed by Bertin, and played by actors from Comedie Française. The players performed before impeccably detailed and beautifully designed painted backdrops. They faced an imaginary audience and confined their movements within the compass of a shallow-depth plane parallel to the camera plane. Scenes of the play were recorded on uncut lengths of film by means of a camera fixed at a medium distance from the action (keeping the heads and feet of the figures visible). The film created a sensation. Its academic credentials, opulent production values and its exhibition in legitimate houses insured it an audience hitherto disdainful of movies.[3]

Film d'Art's initial success immediately spurred competitors Pathé, Gaumont, and Eclair to make their own feature-length filmed plays. They drew from the popular well made plays and melodramas of the time—the works of Sardou, Brieux, and Lavedan. Thus, by 1909, films appeared of Sardou's *La Tosca* (1887) and *Madame Sans-Gene*, Brieux's *The Red Robe* (1900), and melodramas such as *Oliver Twist* (1874). Likewise, those actors best known to the theater-going public in France appeared—A. Albert Lambert, Henri Krauss, Silvain, Severin, Max Dearly, Mounet-Sully, Max Linder, and Mesdames Tessandier, Barat, Robinne, Taillade, Cecil Sorel, Bartel, Megard, Geniat, Mau, Catherine Fontenay, and Trouhanowa. Eleonora Duse appeared for the Italian firm of Ambrosio-Caesar-Film, and Sarah Bernhardt and Rejane appeared for Film d'Art.

These productions placed control in the hands of the theatrical personnel. M. Jourjon of the Eclair Company believed that theatrical personnel should be able to make the decisions regarding camera placement, for example. Historian Robert Grau commented on this practice in 1914 when he noted theatrical films had been made solely from the perspective of the original stage play with little regard for the special problems and potentials of the film medium. Members of the Comedie Francaise, who in all likelihood had never been inside a movie house, were controlling the productions. Lou Tellegen, a player in Film d'Art's *Queen Elizabeth*, confirmed this when he recalled in his autobiography that he and his company "hadn't the remotest idea of camera angles, make-up for the camera, or anything."[4]

One of the first features to reach America was Pathé's *Incriminating Evidence*, which premiered in New York in February of 1909. It consisted of a pantomime by M. Severin. The *New York Dramatic Mirror* applauded it as "a revelation in the production of motion picture drama" and recognized its fidelity to its stage original (currently playing in New York): "The...scenes are almost exactly like those of the pantomime."[5] A few weeks later *The Assassination of the Duc de Guise* premiered in New York and was promptly cited by the same journal as "one of the few masterpieces of motion picture production."[6]

The positive critical and popular reception given these foreign films was not lost upon American film entrepreneurs. Writing in 1911, Robert Grau noted that American entrepreneurs were competing with foreign productions with multi-reel films of their own. Vitagraph, Kalem, Biograph, and Edison, he said, "must emulate the methods of the highest grade of producers of the stage...."[7] "Almost overnight," wrote Epes W. Sargent in February of 1912, "the two, three, and five-reel subject has come into its own." And two months later Sargent declared: "The cry for feature films is more insistent than ever."[8]

In 1912 there appeared more theatrical features, most of them foreign-made, some of them American products. The great majority of them derived either from melodramas or well made plays. For example, in March and April of 1912, both Sarah Bernhardt and Rejane appeared in, respectively, *Camille* and *Madame Sans-Gene*. Both films played at the Majestic Theater, a famous legitimate house in Brooklyn. *Camille*, according to a trade advertisement, "raised [movies] to the level of the Comedie Française"[9] and featured players from the Theatre Sarah Bernhardt. In May, actress Jane Fearnley appeared in a film version of *Lady Audley's Secret* (produced by the Independent Motion Picture Company) and Nat C. Goodwin appeared in General Film's four-reel *Oliver Twist*. In June Max Reinhardt supervised the filming in Vienna of his *The Miracle*, featuring his original cast. It duplicated the play "in every detail."[10] July was a productive month with at least three important theatrical features, in addition to the exhibition of *Queen Elizabeth* at the Lyceum (and later at Daly's Theater). Frederick Warde appeared in a three-reel version of *Richard III*, Vitagraph released a three-reel *As You Like It* (with Rose Coghlan as Rosalind and Maurice Costello as Orlando). And late in December Scribe's *Adrienne Lecouvrer* appeared in a three-reel version with Sarah Bernhardt.

Like the short theatrical films that had preceeded them, these features closely imitated theatrical presentations. "Spectator," the columnist in the *New York Dramatic Mirror*, described in March of 1912 correlations: "Characters will enter a scene in the background and walk deliberately down to the front to carry on a conversation that would naturally have occurred where they first met," the writer reported. When the characters converse, "they will in many cases keep their faces turned fully or partly to the front instead of looking at each other as people do when they hold conversations in real life." Exaggerated acting, sometimes necessary on the stage, was evident on the screen, signalling to the spectator that "it is all acting...."[11]

Specifically, the actress Rejane was cited for her "stage method" of acting, "the sin of playing direct to the front and for a supposed audience."[12] Attempts to convey a play's dialogue by means of written titles could lead to problems, this writer reported in June that same year. The number of titles threatened to impede the flow of images: "It is in the picture adaptation from a play...that this error is most prevalent in larger films...since the producer in his desire to adhere to the original finds himself unable to ignore those features of the plot which are totally unsuitable for presentation in consistent motion picture action."[13] When the restrictions of the proscenium stage playing space were carried over into film, the results were questioned. For example, *Queen Elizabeth* was described as "a mere photographed stage production," where "the characters sit and talk at each other without explicit action, which carries forward the movement of the story."[14] And *Martin Chuzzlewit* exemplified yet another characteristic of so many of the filmed plays—the use of artificial scenery. Few outdoor scenes were employed, noted one writer—"most of the exteriors as well as interiors being studio made."[15]

If these features did little to advance cinematic technique, they did provide prestige value to the motion picture that, in the opinion of some, was badly needed. The *New York Dramatic Mirror* closely followed the rise of the feature-length theatrical film in America during the crucial period of 1911-1913. The *Mirror* was unique among the trade publications in that it had, since 1909, featured a regular column of commentary on the motion picture written by Frank Woods under the pseudonym of "The Spectator."[16] This column was founded on the conviction that "photoplays were to be handled with the same respect, seriousness and freedom that have always characterized this publication's treatment of the stage productions." No other publication, the *Mirror* boasted in 1913, had followed such a course.[17] At any rate, a survey of its pages reveals a consistently held attitude toward feature-length films that carried on the ambitions of the Film d'Art Company, i.e., feature films, especially those derived from stage plays, could elevate the prestige of the motion picture and thereby expand its audience base to include the middle class theater-goer.

First, feature-length film gave filmmakers the chance to present sophisticated drama that was more complex than had been possible in shorter-length formats of the past. "The people who want nothing but boisterous burlesque will like it just as well if it has some meaning to it," Spectator said early in 1912; "and, on the other hand, the presence of a little genuine humor will make the mess palatable to the more fastidious...." Melodrama, "a perfectly legitimate type of drama," could thus appeal both to the "lowbrows" and, at the same time, could be done "so that it will have a universal appeal."[18] Vitagraph's three-reel version of *Uncle Tom's Cabin* proved the point, Spectator noted late in January of 1912: "House managers...had found [it] a money maker for them [and] became eager for other subjects of feature length."[19]

Second, theatrical features could appropriately be exhibited in both legitimate houses and movie houses. In February of 1913, Spectator reported that devotees of the legitimate stage, who had shunned the "vulgar" movies heretofore, "now accepted these films because they so closely resembled the legitimate drama they were used to seeing."[20] Spectator said in July of 1913, "that patrons not addicted to motion pictures will flock to a 'legitimate' theater to see a film production of consequence." Moreoever, "such audiences are in the main composed of theater-goers and, of course, it is their support that the new producing firms rely upon.... Screen drama will be handled by theater men with a view to reaching patrons of the stage."[21] The presence in these dramas of respected stage players like Mrs. Fiske could only aid in that ambition: "It is hardly likely that her admirers would regard a house in which the films were shown as unworthy of their support." Similarly, movie house exhibitors could use these films to attract patrons accustomed to attending only legitimate houses: "He may gain recruits from among those who would not think of entering the average picture house."[22]

Third, theatrical features could be shown on the "road" just as their "live" counterparts could. As early as February of 1912, Spectator observed that the European-imported features were "—the more exclusive types of motion picture productions that are coming more and more to be sent on tour like any theatrical attraction.... Could anything be more indicative of the higher plane which the motion picture art is attaining than the mere mention of this subject?"[23] American theatrical features can follow this example, Spectator said in April of that year. "They are pictures that an exhibitor can book as he would an actor or a play, billing them ahead and thereby attracting extra business to his house. They can be taken on tour as any other travelling attraction and for these reasons they may have long and profitable lives."[24]

Fourth, in addition to new patrons and attractive touring routes, the new features garnered a lot of attention from the press. "As movies get longer," said Spectator in February of 1912, "in which a single subject will furnish a night's entertainment with extended runs and road tours, we may expect to see film criticism also develop to meet the new conditions. The daily press may then take up motion picture reviews seriously and the great critics may even condescend to discuss their individual merits."[25] Sure enough, within the next two months, Spectator reported that the Hearst papers were running regular space on film information and that, generally, "other papers in various parts of the country are giving news space to motion picture affairs in a way that indicates an awakening in the newspaper fraternity to the news value of motion picture productions."[26]

Finally, as the movies gained in prestige through increased attention, more and more legitimate stars were willing to try the film medium. The years of the short theatrical films were ones that largely saw second rate and stock company players coming to the movies. With some exceptions, legitimate stars had remained aloof. Now, according to Spectator in October of 1912, the situation had changed. The idea that legitimate players would accept the film medium was "comparatively new and like most ideas it must battle against prejudices. In this case the notion to be overcome is that to appear in motion pictures detracts from stage prestige—that it means a loss of dramatic dignity. Such a viewpoint is biased and it is encountered much less frequently than a year ago, say."[27] Certainly, it was assumed, the stage player's presence could only enhance the film's prestige value. "The famous player by entering the picture field," said Spectator in September of 1913, "is advancing and elevating the film drama. A great star is an asset to a picture before it is shown. The name draws.... People want to be educated to the best—they want to see the better class of films. They are tired of rubbish."[28]

Between 1912 and 1915 several motion picture production companies were formed by combinations of theatrical and film personnel for the purpose of bringing famous plays and players to legitimate and movie houses across the country. The first such company was Famous Players, which released *Queen Elizabeth* in July of 1912. One of Famous Players' founders, Broadway entrepreneur Daniel Frohman, was, at that time, one of the few men in the American theater willing to see his name publicly linked with theatrical films. The *New York Dramatic Mirror* reported at the time that "prominent theatrical managers, including no less a person than Daniel Frohman and others, who have vigorously opposed pictures in the past, have come together for the purpose of presenting a series of motion picture productions, which will feature well-known stars and successes of the dramatic stage." Mr. Frohman, the article emphasized, "is the only manager who is willing that his name should be presented to the public...." The writer went on to emphasize the company's ambition (which was shortly to become that of the many other enterprises soon to enter the field):

The men back of this movement have become fully convinced that the time for the amalgamation of the legitimate stage and the motion picture has come.... It is felt that the last barrier has been removed between the picture and the stage.... The films will comprise for the most part past and present successes of the European and American stage.[29]

Before examining in detail the formation of Famous Players and the other companies that followed it during the 1912-1915 period, it is important to note that those "past and present successes of the European and American stage" were comprised of famous melodramas and well made plays. Each of these forms of drama had its own peculiar attractions to American entrepreneurs, just as they had appealed to foreign entrepreneurs. The melodrama, because of its enduring popularity in the big cities and on the road with American audiences throughout the 19th century, was especially attractive. Melodrama first came to America through adaptations of foreign plays by native playwrights. William Dunlap's adaptation of L. C. Caigniez' *Le Jugement de Salomon* (1873) was, according to Quinn, "the first example in this country of an adaptation of the French melodrama."[30] By mid-century, native melodramas like *Uncle Tom's Cabin* (1852) and *Ten Nights in a Barroom* (1859) were beginning runs that would continue throughout the rest of the century. Dozens of road companies brought these plays to rural and urban audiences alike. William A. Brady's perennially popular *Way Down East* (1898) proved to be as popular with audiences on the road company routes as it was with audiences attending the lavishly appointed legitimate houses in New York City.

Significantly, melodrama appealed to the kinds of audience that also attended nickelodeons. "Melodrama reflected the topical excitements of a growing working class," explains John Fell in his survey of late 19th century popular entertainment. "Speech, behavior, and settings were coded to instant recognition," which "presented a world of problems and characters made fraudulently comprehensible, then costumed with palatable thrills, climaxed in reassuring resolutions."[31] Plots about crime, military adventure, wilderness explorations, and working girls dominated the stage in plays that all would be made into motion pictures in 1912-1915—respectively, William Gillette's *Sherlock Holmes* (1899), David Belasco's *The Heart of Maryland* (1897), and Augustin Daly's *Under the Gaslight* (1867). So-called "problem" subjects were exploited in sensational fashion in *Uncle Tom's Cabin* (1852), *The Octoroon* (1859), and *The Clansman* (1906)—which involved racial issues like miscegenation and slavery; *The Lure* (1913) and *Bought and Paid For* (1911)—which involved prostitution; *The Boss* (1911) and *The City* (1909)—which involved labor unrest and political corruption.[32]

Unlike the well made play, melodrama did not emphasize the logic and rigor of plot construction. Rather, as one of the first practitioners of the form, Guilbert de Pixercourt of the Theatre Français explained, the melodrama was relatively free of the observance of the strict dramatic law of cause and effect.[33] The structure was episodic and events hinged upon improbable coincidences and violent conflicts. Situation was more important than plot complexity, and there was always a "danger" scene, a "rescue" scene, and a "recognition or reunion" scene.[34] An entire play was built around this formula as Montrose Moses has explained. "The bill-board posters are drawn a long while before pen is even put to paper," he said in 1911. After situations are decided upon, there is little subsequent shaping of plot elements. The trapdoors, the bridges about to be blown up, the walls to be scaled, the instruments of torture for the persecution of hapless heroines, the onrushing trains—"all these melodramatic accessories are determined upon before the manuscript takes shape."[35]

Not surprisingly, characters in these melodramas were as stereotyped as were the situations surrounding them. While the characters in the well-made play were often complex and ambivalent in their moral posture and motivation, characters in melodrama were like two-dimensional cutouts, ciphers of right and wrong. In recent essays, Robert Heilman and John Fell agree that this was a consequence of the working class audiences.[36] Characters had to be "fraudulently comprehensible" to be easily identified. Owen Davis, one of the most successful playwrights specializing in melodrama, noted this necessity for instant viewer identification. The hero, for example, "must be labeled at his first entrance. Nothing must be left to inference." Because many in the audience were immigrants and semi-literate workers, these characters had to be presented more in terms of actions than dialogue. "I therefore wrote for the eye rather than the ear," Davis explained. This description could also be applied to the silent film.[37]

The ways in which many melodramas were staged also helps explain why filmmakers drew upon them. In two recent studies, *Stage to Screen* and *Film and the Narrative Tradition*, Nicholas Vardac and John Fell conclude that narrative speed and quick transitions in space and time were common to 19th century melodramas, making them suitable later for adaptation to film.[38] Unlike the well made play, the melodrama displayed frequent shifts in time and space, and while the play commonly confined its action to one or two set changes and a restricted span of time, the melodrama employed an average of ten to twenty different scenes, each marking a change in time and space. This characteristic, it was noted at the time the first theatrical features were being exhibited in America, was well suited to the motion picture medium. When Boucicault's *The Octoroon* was filmed by the Kalem Company in 1913, for example, one writer reported that the play "is peculiarly adapted for the motion pictures with its many thrilling situations, which depend largely upon pantomime."[39]

Rapid transitions among scenes imparted speed and mounting tension to the play. Thus, two or more playing areas would often be employed during a given act so that the action could shift from one to the other or be carried on in both simultaneously without pausing for a curtain. For example, in W.J. Thompson's *A Race for Life*, the house set was opened to the audience, permitting the action to progress simultaneously on both stories of the façade. Many of the plays of Dion Boucicault, especially *Forbidden Fruit* (1876), utilized this device. The play presented two connecting offices on stage, the action going from one to the other and back again without a curtain delay. Such devices, contend Fell and Vardac, reveal that "the nineteenth century theater explored transitional devices which clearly anticipate the techniques of the motion picture."[40] By splicing pieces of film, filmmakers could achieve instantaneous scene transitions. And by cutting back and forth from one storyline to another, he could maintain a simultaneity of parallel actions.

The typical melodrama also anticipated cinematic technique in that its emphasis was upon pictorial elements rather than upon dialogue. *A Race for Life*, for example, is cited by both Vardac and Fell for its long scenes of virtually wordless pantomimic action.[41] Similarly, Boucicault's *Arrah-na-Pogue* (1865) had a third set wherein the hero, Shaun, escaped his prison in a long, wordless sequence of special stage effects, including a number of "dissolves" where scenes quickly changed while the lights faded in and out. And in *Under the Gaslight* and *The Heart of Maryland* (1897) there were lengthy rescue scenes where plucky heroines hacked through doorways to rescue men tied to railroad tracks and climbed bell towers to silence the pealing of a bell. That this pictorial emphasis was suited to the film medium was noted in the *New York Dramatic Mirror* in May of 1913 when the Belasco-produced play, *The Good Little Devil*, was described as a play suitable for the movies: "It is peculiarly adapted to motion pictures, offering unequalled opportunities for illusions, visions, and other camera effects."[42]

Another form of drama—the well made play—was very attractive to film entrepreneurs during 1912-1915 for very different reasons than were melodramas. The value of the well made play to the movies has been virtually ignored in available scholarship. While studies like those already cited—especially those by Fell and Vardac—have emphasized the importance and appropriateness of melodramas and the movies, they have altogether dismissed the great body of good plays that were so important to the early feature-length theatrical films. True, the good play relied more upon dialogue than action; plot complexity than a loosely episodic narrative structure; and restrictions in shifts in space and time than the more widely ranging actions and locales of melodrama. All these factors seemingly rendered excellent plays, inappropriate for the cinema. Yet, these plays, unlike the melodramas, appealed to a more affluent audience; they represented prestige and respectability to those entrepreneurs engaged in that "seduction of the affluent" described by Russell Merritt.

I use the term "well made play" in its broadest sense, to include both the *pièce bien fait* of Eugene Scribe during the first third of the nineteenth century and the "satisfactory" dramas of Bronson Howard and Clyde Fitch in America late in the nineteenth and early in the twentieth centuries. According to Eric Bentley in *The Life of the Drama*, the well made play linked the popular stage of the nineteenth century with the neo-classical drama promoted by the French Academy in the seventeenth century. It was a modern form of classical tragedy, Bentley notes—"that can be called degenerate or ultimate, according to the point of view."[43] It represented both entertainment and respectabilty for the growing middle-class audiences.

To one degree or another the well made play has traditionally observed the so-called "unities" of time, place and action. (This is an important point, as it was on this basis that the form would ultimately prove, as we shall see in later chapters, to be inappropriate for the film medium.) Taken to its furthest extreme, this theory held that a play's action should be confined to twenty-four hours (or, as some theorists like Chapelaine held, to the two or three hours in which the play could be staged[44]), to a single location (or, at least, to locations immediately contiguous to one another),[45] and to a causal unfolding of events (avoiding incidental and extraneous material and subplots[46]). Such theoretical grounding, notes Bentley, "laid down the rules for the rest of the world. Never perhaps in the whole history of theatre has a given way of writing plays been so insisted upon and other ways so scorned."[47]

The most widely imitated model of well made play came, of course, from the hundreds of plays written by Scribe between 1811 and 1860. This form has been analyzed by many commentators—Stephen Stanton, Patti Gillespie, John Russell Taylor and Maurice Valency[48]—and they all agree that it was interspersed with upsets and reversals, the whole highly dependent upon expository dialogue and action which occurs offstage and usually before the beginning of the first act. Stanton notes that a typical well made play presents only the *crisis* of the whole story. This means that the first act is usually expository, devoted entirely to describing events that have occurred before the rise of the curtain.[49] The rest of the play, Stanton continues, leads toward a *scene a faire*—the confrontation toward which every action has been moving—and *denouement*—the unravelling of the plot. Moreover, as can be seen from a survey of Scribe's work, there are, at most, only two or three different settings in each play; and the duration of time is usually limited to only a few days. One of Scribe's most popular plays, *The Glass of Water*, restricts the action to only one room and a span of time of only forty-eight hours.

Into these "respectable" formulae, Scribe infused a lightly satiric spirit that gave his plays substance, as well as entertainment value. This in itself increased the legitimate standing of his work. *Reves d'amour* (1859) and *Les Doights de fee* (1858) are two examples that presented satiric views of both class pretensions and the oppressions of women. Thus they anticipated the social dramas of Augier and Dumas *fils*, and later, the tougher plays of Henrik Ibsen, August Strindberg and Henri Becque. If a typical play of Scribe's was not so uncompromising as any of these later plays, note Helen Koon and Richard Switzer in their study of Scribe, at least "the play still provides a delightful evening in the theater; if a thoughtful residue leads to insight, a deeper value is added to the amusement."[50]

By mid-century, Scribe's influence had extended to England, as can be seen in the work of Tom Robertson and, later, Henry Arthur Pinero. Pertinent plays here include Robertson's *Society* (1864), *Caste* (1866) and *M.P.* (1870); Jones' *Wealth* (1889); and Pinero's *The Second Mrs. Tanquery* (1893) and *Trelawney of the Wells* (1898). These plays, and many others like them, all adopted Scribean devices, says John Russel Taylor in *The Rise of the Well Made Play*—soliloquies, asides, slightly-based misunderstandings and strong curtain tableaux.[51] In addition, they balanced light social commentary with popular entertainment. The action, moreover, was confined to small parlors, anterooms and bed chambers, while the passage of time rarely spanned more than a few days—or, at the most, weeks.

By the time Bronson Howard established the American equivalent of the well made play—the "satisfactory" drama—in 1878, the form had been somewhat diluted. Not so "pure" in construction or in its allegiance to the unities, the American dramas of Howard and his successors resembled their European counterparts in that they were relatively confined in their use of time and space and wholly dependent upon dialogue instead of physical action. Moreover, as Howard explained, regarding his *The Banker's Daughter* (1878), it was a form of drama that, like Scribe's and Pinero's, combined the respectability of classical dramatic form with the entertainment values so necessary for mass audience popularity:

A dramatist should deal, so far as possible, with subjects of universal interest, instead of with such as appeal strongly to a part of the public only . . . . Furthermore—and here comes in another law of dramatic construction—a play must be, in one way or another, 'satisfactory' to the audience . . . [and] whatever audience you are writing for, your work must be 'satisfactory' to it.[52]

So important did this model become for American playwrights by the first decade of the 20th century, that Montrose J. Moses in *The American Dramatist* noted that American writers were frankly dependent upon it. "We are learning technique from the European writers of social plays," he said; "we need not be ashamed of the well made dramas by Augustus Thomas and William Gillette."[53]

Such plays constituted a large portion of the "legitimate" theater in America at the turn of the century. When producer Daniel Frohman organized his Lyceum stock company in New York in the late 1880s, he followed the "satisfactory" model in encouraging the social satires of Henry C. De Mille and David Belasco. *The Charity Ball, Lord Chumley* and *Men and Women* (1887-1889) were a consistent blend of light parlor comedy with mild social satire.[54] Similarly, Syndicate producer Charles Frohman promoted the work of Clyde Fitch—in the opinion of many, the American master of the well-made form.[55] Fitch's *The Girl With the Green Eyes* (1902) and *The Truth* (1907) are two of his popular, lightly satiric comedies. After writing two of the most popular melodramas of the century—*Under the Gaslight* and *Horizon* (1871)—another producer, Augustin Daly, turned to the social drama when he instituted his own theatrical company in New York at Broadway and 30th street. His work was described by William Dean Howells as "the nearest approach to a national school of acting we have had in America. His work in elevating the American stage can scarcely be overestimated."[56] And when David Belasco became an independent producer, he too promoted many important social satires of the day, including Charles Klein's *The Music Master* (1904) and Eugene Walter's *The Easiest Way* (1909).

The most important film production companies in the 1912-1915 period were the Famous Players Company, the Protective Amusement Company, the Jesse L. Lasky Company, World Film Corporation, and the Triangle Film Corporation. They were all amalgamations of film and theater entrepreneurs that utilized chains of theater and movie houses for exhibition.

"Famous Players in Famous Plays"

The formation of Famous Players in 1912 by Adolph Zukor and Daniel Frohman created the model from which sucessive production and companies were patterned. By 1910 Zukor had become established as a theater exhibitor interested in promoting motion pictures in New York's theater district. This Hungarian immigrant had gone from a penniless lad sweeping out a fur store to the manager of his own fur business, to managing penny arcades, and, finally, to managing nickelodeons and movie houses. From Zukor's office on 14th Street it was but a long look "uptown" to New York's legitimate theater district, and this ambitious young man longed to establish motion pictures there as a successful enterprise. He felt that the feature-length film—especially the theatrical film—would be crucial to the success of this endeavor, but the restrictions of the Motion Picture Patents Company had kept films to one to two reels in length. This was an insufficient length in which to tell a story—especially a story derived from a stage play. With the success of the European film companies like Film d'Art in mind, he reasoned that feature-length filmed plays could help overthrow this restriction. If M. Jourjon of Eclair could ally himself with the Comedie Française, then Zukor could ally himself with its only American equivalent, the legitimate Broadway theater.

When Sarah Bernhardt made a film version of her play *Queen Elizabeth* for Film d'Art early in 1912, Zukor decided it would be a suitable test case to determine the feasibility of feature films for the American market. He bought the American rights for $35,000 from Joseph Engel of the Rex Company. He next sought out a partner from the New York theatrical establishment who would insure a guaranteed exhibition of the film on Broadway. He first approached William A. Brady. Although he had once worked with Brady in managing some nickelodeons, Brady had by now become somewhat embittered toward the motion picture industry. As we have already seen, filmmakers had frequently appropriated some of his theatrical properties, like *Way Down East*, and successfully competed against his road companies. Zukor turned next to the Frohman brothers.

The Frohmans stood with David Belasco at the top of New York's theatrical establishment. Through Daniel's Lyceum Theater in New York, American audiences had first seen plays by Henry C. De Mille and David Belasco. Famous productions by these and other playwrights included *The Wife* (1887), *An American Duchess* (1898) by Clyde Fitch, *The Prisoner of Zenda* (1895) by Anthony Hope, *Trelawney of the Wells* (1898) by Arthur Pinero, and *The Dancing Girl* (1891) by Henry Jones. Charles Frohman was also a producer whose first success, Bronson Howard's *Shenandoah* (1888), established him as one of the most prominent theatrical men in the country. He organized several important stock companies, at the Twenty-third Street Theatre in 1890 and at the Empire Theatre in 1893. As a result, many important playwrights and players were encouraged, including James M. Barrie, Clyde Fitch, Maude Adams, John Drew, Margaret Anglin and Ethel Barrymore. Some of Charles' most successful productions included William Gillette's *Too Much Johnson* (1894) and *Secret Service* (1895), Clyde Fitch's *Captain Jinks of the Horse Marines* (1902) and James Barrie's *The Little Minister* (1897).

But, according to Daniel in his autobiography, brother Charles was derisive and left it to Daniel to consider a partnership with Zukor.[57] (Charles' attitude would soon change, as we will see later in these pages). "Prominent theatrical managers derided me somewhat for going into the 'movies'," Daniel recalled in 1914: "but I did not mind it."[58] Thus, Daniel Frohman became the Director of Production for Zukor's newly formed Famous Players Company.

Frohman's importance to Famous Players has usually been ignored in the standard film histories. He is not mentioned in Lewis Jacob's *The Rise of the American Film* (1939) and in John Fell's *A History of Films* (1979), for example; and in one of the best general histories, A.R. Fulton's *Motion Pictures* (1960), Frohman is only credited with bringing his prestige to the Famous Players enterprise.[59] Yet, at the time he joined Famous Players, commentators of the day recognized the precedent he established. To Daniel Frohman, wrote Spectator in the *New York Dramatic Mirror* in July of 1912, "belongs the credit of leading the way among the prominent managers. He sees in the pictures true dramas, as *The Mirror* almost alone for four years has been pointing out ...." There can be no question, Spectator continued, "that he will eventually prove his eminence in it as he has in stage production."[60] In fact, there might not have been a Famous Players Company had it not been for Daniel Frohman. Not only did his venture encourage other entrepreneurs to follow his lead in the next few years, but he was able to supply Zukor with many successful plays and players. And, reportedly, it was largely he that finally gained a license for *Queen Elizabeth* from the General Film Company, enabling the film to be shown and distributed.[61] Without a successful exhibition of it, Famous Players could never have continued. In their recent history of Paramount (the distribution company that absorbed

Famous Players after 1915), I.G. Edmonds and Reiko Mimura even claim that on several crucial occasions during 1912 and 1913, Frohman's own money kept Famous Players alive.[62]

Queen Elizabeth was promoted and exhibited as if it were a stage play. Emile Moreau's story of the legendary affair between Elizabeth I of England and Robert Devereaux, Earl of Essex, was laid out along accepted "well made" guidelines. It gives a fictionalized treatment of historical incidents; its action is confined to a few rooms; its dialogue bears the weight of exposition; and its tragic outcome hinges entirely upon a seemingly insignificant object—in this case a ring that Elizabeth had given to the Earl. For most Americans, *Queen Elizabeth* was the first opportunity to glimpse Sarah Bernhardt (even though she had made her first American stage tour with co-star Lou Tellegen two years earlier). Although the film was successful and, because of its showings in legitimate theaters like the Lyceum it attracted the notice of prominent critics and play-goers, *Queen Elizabeth* demonstrated many of the faults that would be singled out in subsequent filmed plays. The reliance upon written titles to carry the verbal dimension of the play, the uncut and static camera views, the artificiality of the scenic devices constituted a few of the problems.[63] These will be examined in detail later in this study, but for now it is enough to indicate that at least one critic balked at the intention of Famous Players to imitate so faithfully the illusion of a stage production. Trouble lay ahead for these theatrical features, noted Robert Grau in February of 1913, six months after the premiere at the Lyceum of *Queen Elizabeth*:

> If a canvass of the Bernhardt audiences were possible, it would be found that a majority of those who had seen these pictures on the screen would emphatically state that they did not wish to renew the experience, and that a still greater majority would express a preference for a similar production along the lines of ordinary releases. In fact, the fame of the 'divine Sarah' ... while it was potent enough to attract huge crowds, and to insure a successful financial outcome for the films, was not great enough to warrant the 'repeats' that mean so much in the box-office records of the theatre .... [Why] did she allow [*Queen Elizabeth*] to be presented at all? Madame could not resist the temptation to add to her annual income; that is the only explanation.[64]

Recently, Henry Knepler in *The Gilded Stage* claims that *Queen Elizabeth* may have used the play's original sets; he also confirms Grau's suspicion of Bernhardt's mercenary motives, saying, "Sarah did not believe in films and used this particular one as an attempt to recoup some of the 200,000 francs she had lost in the production of the play itself."[65]

However, the initial success of *Queen Elizabeth* convinced Zukor and Frohman to make more feature-length theatrical films that would promote the illusion of a proscenium stage presentation. Joining the artistic staff at the New York studios located in the top two stories of an old armory on West 26th Street were veteran filmmaker Edwin S. Porter and veteran stage personnel Hugh Ford (leading stage producer of the popular *Potash and*

Perlmutter), Frederick Stanhope (English producer of *The Garden of Allah*), and Edward Morange (one of the best known authorities on scenic art and effects in America), and J. Searle Dawley. Dawley soon became one of the most important directors for Famous Players, responsible for many filmed plays, including *Tess of the D'Urbervilles* and *The Good Little Devil* (both in 1913). He brought a thorough grounding in the stage to the filmmaking process. Prior to this time he had written and produced fifteen plays, three of which had at this time been on the road for long runs. One of his biggest successes, *Marie Antoinette*, was described in June of 1913 as being a "decided hit [which] is still popular in many sections of the country."[66] In the most complete account of Dawley's work extant in recent scholarship, Jack Spear's essay "Edwin S. Porter," it is indicated that it was Dawley's stage experience that made him especially useful in rehearsing the actors, blocking the action and handling the dramatic details.[67]

Zukor and Frohman decided to follow *Queen Elizabeth* with their first American-produced filmed play, *The Count of Monte Cristo*. Because of Frohman's urging, the popular stage star James O'Neill agreed to appear in what had become his most popular starring vehicle.[67] O'Neill had long been associated with *The Count of Monte Cristo* and, because he had seldom played in New York (appearing mostly on the road before more rural audiences), he had escaped some of the negative prejudices many other actors harbored toward the movies. He was eager to play the role of Dantes before the cameras and the film was shot in two weeks and released in a four-reel length. At the same time, Frohman persuaded James K. Hackett and the majority of his stage company to repeat before the cameras their popular success, *The Prisoner of Zenda*. Like O'Neill, Hackett had become "typed" in the dual role, which he had played regularly since 1895.[68] This film, costing $7,000, became the first release of Famous Players. The release of *The Count of Monte Cristo* was delayed because of the release at that time from the Selig studio of another version of the story.

The Prisoner of Zenda premiered at Frohman's Lyceum Theatre on February 18, 1913, six months after the premiere of *Queen Elizabeth*. A writer in the *New York Dramatic Mirror* reported that Frohman made a curtain speech in which he emphasized that the motion picture could be a recording device for many of the popular plays and players of the day. This same writer concluded that "to see Mr. Hackett in this film is to get considerable knowledge of his original playing of the role."[69]

Frohman's contract with Famous Players insured that for the next five years every theatrical release would bear the title "Daniel Frohman Presents." He was able to sign up many of the important players of the day. In 1913 Minnie Maddern Fiske signed to do the screen version of her stage success, *Tess of the D'Urbervilles*. David Belasco not only agreed to let Famous Players film his success that year, *The Good Little Devil*, but he also appeared in the prologue. Other players and celebrities to appear included John Barrymore, Hazel Dawn, Pauline Frederick, Arnold Daly and Marguerite Clark. With Zukor, Frohman was willing to let his players assume some of the control of the filming, just as M. Jourjon had at Eclair in France. For example, when Dawley directed Mrs. Fiske in Tess, he assured her that "if the production did not meet her approval, the film would be destroyed."[70]

In addition to the players and plays over which he had personal interests, Frohman was also able to gain the rights to plays written by his associates. For example, by February of 1914, he acquired the plays of Henry W. Savage. Savage, like Mrs. Fiske and Daniel Frohman, waged a continual war with Syndicate interests when his own independence was threatened but his friendship with Frohman led him to entrust him with his plays, including *The Million, Top o' the Morning, The Great Name, The Merry Widow* and *Excuse Me.*

The film output of Famous Players was organized into three classes: the Class A films were the theatrical features, the Class B films presented trained film actors with a reputation and the Class C films were those with obscure players, usually in original scenarios. By 1915, the studio had established an immense manufacturing and distributing business all over the world with four studios: the 23rd Street Studio in New York, on Long Island, one in Los Angeles and one in London.

The experience of filmmaking was, in some instances at least, a favorable one for the stage actors. James K. Hackett was convinced that his experience with Famous Players had profited him considerably at the box-offices of the legitimate theaters. Contrary to the fear held by many players that their appearances in films might injure their reputations, Hackett saw only benefits. In 1914 he looked back upon a year of increased profits for himself for his touring road shows. This can be charged, he said, "to nothing but the advertising and interest in me created by the Famous Players for my performance in *The Prisoner of Zenda*, I am absolutely convinced."[71]

At the same time, people like Hackett still had not learned that the motion picture and the stage were distinctly different media. Rather he still regarded the motion picture as a mere extension of the stage, subject to its methods. He even proposed a plan by which the motion picture process could aid stage producers in their own productions. It is worth quoting in its entirety since it gives a detailed look at a typical presumption that united the methods of stage and screen:

The idea is this—I am going to rehearse my company in the usual way until they have reached the stage of perfection at which a dress rehearsal is called. Then at a dress rehearsal I am going to have a moving picture made of the play, and I am confident that when I have this before me and can repeat it time after time without the slightest change that I shall be able to discover many helpful ideas and improvements which cannot be seen in the regular rehearsal or performance. Even more valuable than to the manager or stage director will this film be to the player. Watching themselves on a screen with every detail reproduced in exact and pitiless sharpness, would enable actors to correct faults, and make improvements in their work far more intelligently than by the directions of any director.[72]

This practice continued into the late twenties when filmmakers prepared for their own versions of stage plays by photographing the play in its entirety for study before actual filming began.[73]

Between 1912 and late 1915 the following filmed stage plays were released by Famous Players. Records are incomplete, since not all of Famous Players' releases (such as *The Prisoner of Zenda*) were copyrighted at the Library of Congress; therefore, my compilation here is admittedly incomplete. It provides, whenever possible, the title of the film, its release date, director and star, and information on its theatrical source material:

Queen Elizabeth, July 1912. Starring Sarah Bernhardt and Lou Telegen and directed by Louis Mercanton. Filmed in France by Film d'Art and released in America by the Engadine Amusement Company (changed to Famous Players).

The Count of Monte Cristo, December 1912. Starring James O'Neill (duplicating his stage characterization) and directed by Edwin S. Porter. Dumas' novel was first dramatized in 1850. O'Neill first played in it on February 12, 1883 at Booth's Theater in New York.

The Prisoner of Zenda, December 1912. Starring James K. Hackett (duplicating his stage role) and directed by Edwin S. Porter. Anthony Hope's novel first dramatized by Edward E. Rice and first staged by Daniel Frohman at the Lyceum Theater on September 4, 1895 for 112 performances. James K. Hackett took over the role from E.H. Sothern in 1896 and continued to play it throughout the rest of his life.

Tess of the D'Urbervilles, September 1913. Starring Minnie Madern Fiske (duplicating her stage role) and directed by J. Searle Dawley. Thomas Hardy's novel was dramatized by Lorimer Stoddard in 1897 and staged at the Fifth Avenue Theatre in New York on March 2, 1897 for 88 performances with Mrs. Fiske in the title role.

An American Citizen, January 1914. Starring John Barrymore in his screen debut and directed by J. Searle Dawley. Madeleine Lucette Ryley's play premiered at the Knickerbocker Theatre on October 11, 1897 for 96 performances with Nat Goodwin in the title role.

A Good Little Devil, March 1914. Starring Mary Pickford and the entire original cast. Based on David Belasco's 1913 production. The film features Belasco in a prologue.

A Lady of Quality, August 1914. Starring Cecilia Loftus in her screen debut. Based on the play by Francis Hodgson Burnett and Stephen Townsend which premiered at Wallack's Theatre on November 1, 1897 for 48 performances.

In the Bishop's Carriage, September 1914. Starring Mary Pickford. Based on the play by Channing Pollock which premiered at the Grand Opry House on February 25, 1907 for eight performances.

The Dictator, 1914. Starring John Barrymore and directed by Oscar Eagle. Based on the play by Richard Harding Davis which premiered at the Criterion Theatre on April 4, 1904 for 64 performances with John Barrymore and William Collier.

Are You a Mason? 1914. Starring John Barrymore. Based upon the German farce of Lauf and Kratz as adapted by Leo Ditrichstein and produced by Charles Frohman at Wallack's Theatre on April 1, 1901, for 22 performances.

Port of Missing Men, 1914. Starring Arnold Daly. No performance statistics given.

Clothes, 1914. Starring Charlotte Ives and House Peters. Based on the play by Avery Hopwood and Channing Pollock which premiered at the Manhattan Theatre on September 11, 1906 with Grace George for 113 performances.

Lost Paradise, 1914. Starring H. B. Warner. Based on the play by Henry C. De Mille which premiered at Proctor's Twenty-Third St. Theater on November 16, 1891.

Monsieur Beaucaire, 1914 (?). Starring James K. Hackett. Based upon E. G. Sutherland's dramatization in 1901 of Booth Tarkington's novel which premiered at the Herald Square Theater on December 2, 1901 with Richard Mansfield.

The Brute, 1914 (?). Based on the play by Frederic Arnold Krummer which premiered at the 39th St. Theater on October 8, 1912 for 22 performances.

The Masqueraders, 1915 (?). Starring Hazel Dawn. Based on the play by Henry Arthur Jones which premiered in New York at the Empire Theatre on December 3, 1894 with Henry Miller and William Faversham for 120 performances.

Bella Donna, November 1915. Starring Pauline Frederick. Based upon James Bernard Fagan's dramatization of Robert Hickens' novel as premiered at the Empire Theater on November 11, 1912 with Alla Nazimova for 72 performances.

The Red Widow, November 1915. Starring Pauline Frederick. Based on the musical play, book and lyrics by Channing Pollock and Rennold Wolf and Charles J. Gebest as presented by Cohan and Harris at the Astor Theater on November 6, 1911 for 128 performances.

The Mummy and the Hummingbird. November 1915. Starring Charles Cherry in his screen debut. Based on the play by Isaac Henderson as produced by Charles Frohman at the Empire Theatre on September 4, 1902 with John Drew for 85 performances.

The Old Homestead, December 1915. Based on the play by Denman Thompson (1878) (No performance statistics available).

Under Cover, July 1916. Starring Hazel Dawn. Based on the play by Roi Cooper Megrue as produced by Selwyn and Company at the Cort Theatre on August 26, 1914 for 349 performances.

The Moment Before, April 1916. Starring Pauline Frederick. Based on the play by Israel Zangwill (no performance statistics available).

Diplomacy. February 1916. Starring Marie Doro. Based on the play "Dora" by Victorien Sardou which was first performed in New York at Wallack's Theater on April 1, 1878.

Snow White, December 1916. Starring Marguerite Clark (duplicating her stage role). Based upon the dramatization in 1912 of Grimm's story by Jessie Graham White as produced by Winthrop Ames at the Little Theatre on November 7, 1912 for 72 performances with Marguerite Clark.

Wildflower, 1916. Starring Marguerite Clark. No performance statistics available.

The Protective Amusement Company: "Famous Plays in Pictures"

Before Syndicate producers Marc Klaw and Abraham L. Erlanger joined forces with the Biograph Company to produce filmed plays in 1913, they had mixed feelings toward the film industry. They had run one of the leading theatrical booking offices in America since 1887. As two of the original founders of the Syndicate, Klaw and Erlanger controlled some two hundred theaters across the country. The history of these two men is long and full of controversy.[73] Their vision of popular theater was one of centralized control. This control was occasionally ruthless and threatened the livelihood of those independent producers who refused to subscribe to their methods and aims. Yet, their first involvement in film resulted in them being on the receiving end of some of their own methods.

Klaw and Erlanger decided in 1897 to produce a film version of the *Passion Play* as staged in Hoeritz, Bohemia. The film constitutes perhaps the very first feature-length film version of a theatrical event in America, and it probably was the very first major collaboration anywhere between filmmakers and theater producers.

The Passion Play was made less than three years after the first motion picture was copyrighted and just eighteen months after the Koster and Bial Music Hall program of projected Edison films. It was photographed directly from a production in Bohemia and, after cutting, was about fifty minutes long. Some documentary footage of the two and some tableaux that identify each of the principal actors were added to the events of the play.

Klaw and Erlanger bought the rights to film the play from W. B. Hurd, the American representative of the French Cinematographe movie camera at a cost of $10,000. Another $10,000 was expended in the production to dispatch a cameraman, one "Doc" Freeman, to Europe to handle the photography.

The film was promoted as if it were a play. It opened on Monday,

November 22, 1897, in Philadelphia, then as now one of the principal cities in which to try out a new production. An admission price comparable to a play, 50 cents to a dollar a performance, was charged. The premiere took place at Philadelphia's Academy of Music, a setting reserved ordinarily for operas.

Critics judged the film as if it were a play. The Philadelphia *Public Ledger* referred to it as "a really remarkable series of moving tableaux" and as "lifelike reproductions made by this wonderful machine." The Philadelphia *Inquirer* spoke of "the dramatic movement of the personages, and the eye seemed to be looking upon real flesh and blood men and women who were taking part in the working out of a tragedy."[74]

The film was sufficiently successful to inspire imitations. One Richard G. Hollaman decided to make his own version on a New York City rooftop with painted flats to simulate the Bohemian countryside. It premiered at the Eden Musee in New York only two months after the Klaw and Erlanger production.

But Klaw and Erlanger were working in defiance of the Edison patent interests. The Edison Company alleged that the filmmakers were using patent-infringing motion picture equipment. Klaw and Erlanger, themselves leaders of the theatrical Syndicate, now, ironically, were caught in the machinery of the movie industry's own version of a monopoly. The Edison organization would grow in power until by 1908, when it would spearhead the Motion Picture Patents Organization.

Klaw and Erlanger had no further dealings with the film industry until 1907. That year the Kalem Company made a one-reel film version of *Ben Hur* without obtaining copyright permission from Klaw and Erlanger. They brought suit against Kalem, obtaining an injunction against the exhibition of the picture. Because copyright laws had not anticipated the advent of motion pictures, filmmakers had been relatively free to appropriate for their own use the stage plays of the day. In 1911 Kalem finally settled for $25,000. The higher courts decided that movie producers could not use copyrighted literary or dramatic material without consent of the owner.[75]

Within the next two years, Klaw and Erlanger decided to return to film production. Films were needed for the increased number of movie houses. By 1912 movies were making an appreciable dent in theatrical revenues. Weekly, more and more legitimate houses teetered on the brink of bankruptcy and changed over to motion picture exhibition. By September of 1913, 480 movie theaters in New York alone needed film programs. Paid admissions had reached a figure of better than 300 million dollars a year. And that money was divided among only a handful of individuals who controlled the film distribution and exhibition business.

These figures were not lost upon the business-minded Klaw and Erlanger. With the precedent of Zukor and Frohman's Famous Players Company in mind, they set out to form a company of their own that would film famous plays and, hopefully, reap great profits. With a vast chain of theater houses under their control, moreover, they could be assured of exhibition houses for their product. On March 22, 1913, *The Moving Picture News* printed an announcement declaring, "The Protective Amusement Company, formed by Klaw and Erlanger...has been formed for the purpose of exploiting by the means of motion pictures the biggest dramatic successes of the Age!"[76] A total of 104 "film-plays" were announced each year, two productions a week, with the first delivery to be on Monday, September 2, 1913. These filmed plays, according to the *New York Dramatic Mirror* of March 19, 1913, were to be the "answer to the question of what is to be done with the many high class theaters throughout the length and breadth of the land."[77] Joining Klaw and Erlanger in the project was the Biograph Company, one of the most important film studios of the day. The method of exhibiting through the Klaw-Erlanger-controlled theater houses and other exclusively franchised theater houses soon became a standard procedure in theatrical film exhibition, copied by subsequent companies which will be examined in this chapter. Of course, the stage properties to be filmed were already controlled by Klaw and Erlanger. They hoped initially to contract D. W. Griffith to direct the productions, but because of Griffith's dispute with Biograph over his *Judith of Bethulia* project, he had left the studio and gone to another company.[78] The preliminary selection of Klaw and Erlanger plays to be filmed included *Seven Days, Thelma, The Three Guardsmen, The Round Up, A Japanese Nightingale, The Liberty Belles, The Pink Lady, Broadway After Dark, Divorcons, Dr. Jekyll and Mr. Hyde, Mam-Zelle, The Devil, Strongheart, Peer Gynt, St. Elmo, The Land of the Midnight Sun,* and *Rebecca of Sunnybrook Farm.* The plays of Henry C. De Mille and David Belasco were also under consideration.

Economic advantages to Klaw and Erlanger's plan were: actors for a film would be on salary only for the time of the actual shooting; the story itself had already been paid for; the costumes and sets had already been paid for; and, once the film was completed, there would be no other production costs. Rentals from theaters would be $50 a day—quite an increase over the average motion picture rental of $150 a week.

These grandiose plans, however, produced a less than glorious reality. Unfortunately, information is scant on the Protective Amusement Company and only one scholar, Kemp R. Niver, has devoted any attention to researching its short history. His book, *Klaw and Erlanger: Famous Plays in Pictures*, remains the only source on the subject, and it is hardly definitive. We do know, however, that the Protective Amusement Company established facilities in Los Angeles at Georgia and Girard Streets and that there were two units—one headed by David Miles for the three and four reel theatrical features, and one headed by Del Henderson for the production of comedy shorts. We also know that of the 104 announced theatrical films, only twenty-six were actually made. The first premiered at the prestigious Palace Theater in New York on Monday, January 19, 1914. It was called *The Fatal Wedding*, based on a play by Theodor Kramer. Other filmed plays included popular melodramas, such as those adapted from Augustin Daly's *Under the Gaslight* and Wall Spence's *The Woman in Black;* Puritanian romances such as *Beverly of Graustark;* and well made plays by Henry C. De Mille and David Belasco—*The Charity Ball, The Wife, Lord Chumley,* and *Men and Women.*

The Protective Amusement Company failed within three years. Terry Ramsaye contends that it folded because its film rentals were too high. At this time the better movie theaters were just beginning to charge an admission price of ten cents—hardly enough to support the fifty dollar a day rentals imposed by Klaw and Erlanger.[79] (It would not be the first time that film producers would charge high ticket prices in excess of the standard nickel or dime of those times, and it would not be the first time that the plan would fail.) Kemp Niver adds that the films were put on sprocketed film stock usable only on Klaw/Erlanger equipment, limiting the ubiquity of the films. Moreover, the plays themselves generally were too dated, too tied to Victorian manners and mores. The acting styles of the Klaw/Erlanger players were generally more natural than those in the films from Famous Players—due to the fact that many of the players in the Klaw/Erlanger films, like Lionel Barrymore and the Gish sisters, had made films before—the filming technique was limited to static camera setups, awkward juxtapositions of artificial scenery with real locales, and too few expository and dialogue titles. "It is doubtful if more than a fraction of the money invested in these 'pretentious' productions...ever was recouped," Niver concludes; "largely because neither Klaw nor Erlanger could seem to realize that the legitimate theater and motion pictures were worlds apart."[80]

In other words, the complaint voiced by Robert Grau concerning the theatricality of *Queen Elizabeth* may also be applied to the Klaw/Erlanger series of filmed plays. Niver says that these films "made the mistake of transferring plays to the screen exactly as they had appeared on the stage, using a motion picture camera as if it were a spectator in the audience rather than to move it about as filmmakers had begun to do...."[81]

My own research, moreover, has shown that only a handful of these films received any kind of critical attention. This could be due to their limited exhibition. Without a means of exhibition and distribution more extensive than that envisioned by Klaw and Erlanger, the films simply could not generate enough interest. Those that were reviewed, however, confirm Niver's conclusion. For example, *The Billionaire* (based on *Brewster's Millions,* by George Barr McCutcheon) was released in April of 1914. The conclusion of one critic was succinct: It was "as nearly like that of the stage as camera and screen permit."[82]

The following list of the filmed plays of the Protective Amusement

Company between 1913 and 1915 is based on available—and incomplete—resource materials. Whenever possible, the film titles are followed by their approximate release dates, casts, and the performance statistics of their source plays:

The Fatal Wedding, 1914. Starring Walter Miller, Charles Hill Mailes, Irene Howley, and Millicent Evans. Based on the play by Theodore Kramer as produced by Sullivan and Harris at the Grand Opera House on October 28, 1901 with Edwin Mordant for eight performances.

Classmates, 1914. Starring Henry B. Walthall, Blanche Sweet, Lionel Barrymore, and Thomas Jefferson. Based on the play by William C. De Mille and Margaret Turnbull as produced by Henry B. Harris at the Hudson Theater on August 29, 1907 for 102 performances with Frank McIntyre and Sydney Ainsworth.

The Billionaire, 1914. Starring Vivian Prescott, Dave Morris, and Charles Hill Mailes. Based on a dramatization of George Barr McCutcheon's book, *Brewster's Millions.* No performance statistics available.

Strongheart, 1914. Starring Henry Walthall, Lionel Barrymore, Blanche Sweet, and Antonio Moreno. Based on the play by William C. De Mille as produced by Henry B. Harris at the Hudson Theater on January 30, 1905 for 66 performances with Robert Edeson.

Lord Chumley, 1914. Starring H. B. Walthall, Charles Hill Mailes, Lillian Gish, and Mary Alden. Based on the play by Henry C. De Mille and David Belasco as produced by Davis Belasco at the Lyceum Theatre on August 20, 1888 with E. H. Sothern in the title role.

Seven Days, 1914. Starring Dave Morris, Charles Hill Mailes, Louise Orth, and Florence Lee. Based on the play by Avery Hopwood and Mary Roberts Rinehart as staged at the Astor Theatre on November 10, 1909 for 397 performances with Herbert Corthell.

Men and Women, 1914. Starring Lionel Barrymore, Blanche Sweet, Gertrude Robinson, and Marshall Neilan. Based on the play by Henry C. De Mille and David Belasco as produced at Proctor's Twenty-Third St. Theatre on October 20, 1980 for over 200 performances with Maude Adams in her debut as "Dora."

Liberty Belles, 1914. Starring Dorothy Gish, Gertrude Bambrick, Spottiswoode Aitken, and Viola Smith. Based upon the play by Harry B. Smith as produced by Klaw and Erlanger at the Madison Square Theatre on September 30, 1901 for 104 performances with Elsie Ferguson.

A Fair Rebel, May 1914. Starring Charles West, Charles Perley, and Clara T. Bracy. Based upon Harry Mawson's play as staged in March of 1898 (no performance statistics available).

The Power of the Press, May 1914. Starring Lionel Barrymore, Betty Gray, and "Spike" Robinson. Based on the play by August Pitou and George H. Jessop as staged at the Star Theatre on March 16, 1891.

The Squaw Man's clash of cultures and ideologies was brought to the screen as the first Lasky Company release in 1913 (directed by C. B. De Mille; adapted from the play by Milton Royle).

The Wife, May 1914. Based on the play by Henry C. De Mille and David Belasco as presented at the Lyceum Theatre on November 1, 1887 for 239 performances with Georgia Cayvan and Herbert Kelcey.

The Charity Ball, June 1914. Starring Franklin Ritchie and Viola Smith. Based on the play by Henry C. De Mille and David Belasco. First produced at the Lyceum on November 19, 1889 with Herbert Kelcey and Effie Shannon for 200 performances.

The Road to Yesterday, June 1914. Starring Walter Miller and Kenneth Davenport. Based on the play by Beulah Marie Dix and Evelyn Greenleaf Sutherland as presented at the Herald Square Theatre on December 31, 1906 for 216 performances with White Whittlessey and Minnie Dupree.

The Rejuvenation of Aunt Mary, July 1914. Starring Kate Toncray and Audrey Kirby. Based on the play by Anne Warner (no performance statistics available).

The Woman in Black, August 1914. Starring Lionel Barrymore, Charles Mailes, and Mrs. Lawrence Marston. Based on the play by Wall Spence (no performance statistics available).

Beverly of Graustark, August 1914. Starring Gertrude Robinson. Based on a dramatization of George Bar McCutcheon's novel (no performance statistics available).

The Indian, September 1914. Starring Alfred Paget and Bert Williams. Based on the play by Lorimer Johnstone as produced at the People's Theatre on September 6, 1896 for eight performances.

Under the Gaslight, November 1914. Starring Lionel Barrymore. Based on the play by Augustin Daly as produced in New York Theatre on August 12, 1867.

The Jesse L. Lasky Feature Play Company: "The World Is Our Studio"

Like the Famous Players Company and the Protective Amusement Company, the Jesse L. Lasky Feature Play Company was founded on the premise that it was both prestigious and profitable to make feature-length theatrical films with stage stars duplicating their famous roles. In addition to bringing many prominent stage actors to the screen, the Lasky Company acquired the active services of playwrights Edwin Milton Royle, William C. De Mille, and David Belasco. From 1913 to 1916 it presented many features derived from stage plays. After 1916 it ceased to be an independent production company and merged with Zukor and Paramount.

The Lasky theatrical films of 1913-16 were very successful, unlike those made by the Protective Amusement Company. Moreover, Lasky's films had a flavor that caught and held the public—they were, in the main, films derived from the western melodramas and regional adventures filmed in natural western locales. They were chosen because of their regional color, strongly contrasting main characters, and abundance of physical action. No films could have been more different from the parlor dramas of the Protective Amusement Company. These films revealed a relatively successful integration of theatrical and cinematic elements; thus, they pointed the way out of the stranglehold of close imitation of theatrical events seen in the early Famous Players and Klaw-Erlanger plays.

The Lasky Feature Play Company was formed in the summer of 1913 by Samuel Goldwyn (or, as he was then known, Samuel Goldfish), Jesse Lasky, and Cecil B. De Mille (son of playwright Henry C. De Mille). Lasky was the president. Primarily a theatrical promoter, he became enthusiastic about the financial possibilities of the motion picture after seeing the feature-length *Queen Elizabeth*. Another enthusiast, Cecil B. De Mille, was appointed director-general of the company, although he had never before handled a camera. He was assisted by Oscar Apfel who had had training both in the theater and more recently as a cameraman. Samuel Goldfish's job was to sell the finished films to exhibitors.

"I realized at once," Lasky commented in 1914, looking back upon the formation of the Lasky Feature Play Company in 1913, "what an opportunity there was for a producer of the experience, particularly one accustomed to catering to types of vaudeville audiences and the great public. Further study convinced me that the future of the business will be absolutely in the production of large features."[84] For him, as for others, filming stage plays seemed the likeliest course in pursuing that ambition. Unlike Zukor, however, Lasky did not feel that feature-length filmed plays could appeal primarily to the "carriage trade" audiences. Rather, he thought these films could still retain the audience base that viewed short films in vaudeville houses: "...we can do novel and unusual things on the screen that are impossible on the stage, and anything that is original has an appeal for a vaudeville audience." At the same time, he foresaw that the movies could improve upon certain aspects of the stage. For example, the use of artificial scenery in films should be abandoned:

We have adopted the motto, 'The World is Our Studio.' As an earnest of that, we are sending the present company to Southern California and Wyoming for the atmosphere of the story. We will not hesitate to go wherever the best interests of any production require. If necessary, we will send companies abroad. We intend to erect outdoor stages in different parts of the country.[85]

Thus, he selected for filming only those stage plays that implied outdoor locations and which presented action that ranged over those locales. These factors he identified as "screen value."[86]

He put his theories into practice with the company's first release, *The Squaw Man*. Stage actor Dustin Farnum was contracted to duplicate his success in Edwin Milton Royle's regional melodrama, *The Squaw Man*. Farnum had taken over the role of the title character from William

Faversham, who had premiered it in 1905. While Goldwyn and Lasky remained in New York to sell the film, De Mille and his co-director, Oscar Apfel, journeyed westward to California to shoot the picture.[87] *The Squaw Man*, while certainly not the first American feature film, as some historians have claimed, was at least one of the first feature films entirely shot in areas near Hollywood. Other filmed plays followed that took advantage of these natural locales—including Owen Wister's and Kirk La Shelle's *The Virginian* (1904), and two films derived from David Belasco productions, *Rose of the Rancho* (1906) and *The Girl of the Golden West* (1905).

It was not accidental that some of the Lasky feature-length theatrical films were based on plays by David Belasco. Belasco had worked in the theater as actor, stage manager, playwright, and producer since his days in San Francisco in the 1860s. He not only emphasized the importance of *scene* in his many plays, but he came to recognize in the motion picture the logical extension of that priority. By 1914, he was actively participating in the Lasky endeavor. He had collaborated with James A. Herne (on *Hearts of Oak*, 1879) and with Henry C. De Mille in the 1880s (*The Charity Ball, Lord Chumley, The Wife,* and *Men and Women*) where he worked at Daniel Frohmans Lyceum Theatre in New York as playwright, director, and teacher in the theater's acting school. With the production in 1895 of his melodrama, *The Heart of Maryland,* starring his protege, Mrs. Leslie Carter, he emerged as an independent producer. In 1902 he acquired his own theater and in 1907 acquired yet another, the Stuyvesant. By the time he decided to go into the movies, his most famous plays were behind him, including the regional melodrama, *The Girl of the Golden West,* and his production of Eugene Walter's *The Easiest Way* (1909), a strong portrait of a woman drawn into the world of prostitution.

These two examples of his writing and stagecraft reveal what seems in hindsight to be a distinct affinity for the medium of film.[88] Whether Belasco's work embraced the social satire of the parlor drama in *The Easiest Way* or the adventure and open air romance in *The Girl of the Golden West,* his plays were at all times characterized by an exact and detailed concern with realism. In her recent study of Belasco, Lise-Lone Marker calls particular attention to this realistic emphasis:

> Every feature in his productions not only resembled but *was* that which it seemed to be, down to the smallest detail. In his mature period he never allowed the use of a set which consisted simply of conventional canvas flats stretched out on wooden frames. Everything had to be real.... Both countless photographs and enthusiastic reviews of his productions testify to the fact that his settings appeared like marvels of solid walls and authentic accessories.[89]

This predilection for what Vardac has called "photographic realism" produced in *The Easiest Way* a literal transfer of a Manhattan tenement apartment onto the stage. Vardac contends that Belasco was not only extolling the brand of naturalism deriving from the Theatre Libre productions of Antoine but was directly vying with the motion picture in the firm delineation of specific interiors.[90]

It is quite likely that Belasco came to see in the motion picture realization of his own predilection for realism. He was involved in the New York productions of *The Good Little Devil* and *The Governor's Lady* when he consented to allow Famous Players to film the former. It is also quite likely that he saw in the film medium a way to preserve his productions for future generations. As W. Stephen Bush commented in the *Moving Picture World* in June of 1914: "Had he not recognized the quality and power of art in the motion picture the great Belasco plays would have remained lost to the film for probably another generation."[91]

Initially he refrained from active participation in film production. He explained, "A few years ago I never thought that I would ever be associated directly or indirectly with any enterprise in motion pictures. I had a poor opinion of the motion picture then."[92] He refused initial overtures from film production companies because "it seemed to me that under the methods of productions as I had seen...my plays might have suffered the fate of travesty."[93] But then a viewing of the Italian-imported feature film, the spectacular *Quo Vadis*, coupled with subsequent viewing of the first Lasky films (probably *The Squaw Man* and *The Virginian*) made him realize that the movies had, as he described it, put on seven-league boots: "...I felt I should hesitate no longer. I gave the rights to Mr. Lasky and his company on their merits. They were indeed generous in the financial inducements offered but I am free to say that if the mere gain of money had been my object, I might have made other arrangements."[94]

Indeed, the Lasky productions must have seemed a breath of fresh air to Belasco after *The Count of Monte Cristo* and *The Good Little Devil*, with their artificial scenery and shallow-depth playing space. It was possibly this kind of motion picture that Belasco rejected—"the cheap, little pictures of the Dick Turpin variety, the crude and tawdry attempts at portraying life...."[95] The Lasky films, by contrast, excited Belasco:

On the stage we must give you a bit of painted canvas for Niagara Falls or the Nile; you show us the real thing. The world is your stage. These considerations and my abiding faith in the Lasky people have induced me to give my plays to the screen and to help when necessary in doing them justice in the films.[96]

Belasco had the right to cancel with Lasky any productions he deemed unsuitable but there is no indication that he ever exercised that perogative. Instead, his support seems to have been unequivocal. On June 6, 1914, his contract with Lasky and Goldwyn was cited in a notice in *The Moving Picture World*. His letter to them was reproduced:

My Dear Mr. Lasky: I am forwarding you, under separate cover, contracts giving you the motion picture rights to all my productions, both past and future, and even while writing this acknowledgement, I am congratulating myself upon the fact my productions are to see the light of the day in the motion picture field under your auspices. For the past six months, in fact ever since dramatic successes became popular upon the screen, I have made a careful study of the situation. Personally, I have seen numerous feature motion pictures, and concluded after seeing the three productions already made by you that no other firm is as open to conviction as to the value of untried methods, no other firm as willing to innovate and no other firm allows their directors the freedom to create new methods of production to take the place of those which we have outgrown.[97]

It was also announced that, whenever possible, the original Belasco stars would be secured for the filmed plays. This, however, proved to be seldom the case. While featuring many prominent Broadway stars like Theodore Roberts and Frank Keenan, the Lasky filmed plays more often than not presented different cast members in the films than had been in the plays. The Lasky-Belasco association resulted in the filming of at least five Belasco productions. They were, in order, *The Girl of the Golden West* (near the end of 1914), *The Case of Becky* (August, 1915), *The Woman* (April, 1915), *The Warrens of Virginia* (February, 1915), and *Sweet Kitty Bellairs* (May, 1916).

In addition to the Belasco plays, many other plays were brought to the screen in Lasky productions—some of which duplicated members of the original casts. For example, the film of *Brewster's Millions* (1906) brought Edward Abeles to the screen in 1914 duplicating his role of "Brewster," a part he had played over 1800 times. The film versions of *The Virginian* and *The Squaw Man* in 1913 and 1914 gave Dustin Farnum the chance to repeat his roles as the title characters in each. And Edgar Selwyn and Charlotte Walker repeated their stage portrayals in, respectively, *The Arab* (1911) and *The Trail of the Lonesome Pine* (1912). Both films appeared late in 1915.

The history of the Jesse L. Lasky Feature Play Company as an independent production and releasing company ends by 1915. At that time Lasky joined with other production companies, Famous Players, Morosco and Pallas Inc., in releasing his films under the banner of Paramount. Yet this brief span of three years was a significant one in the history of the feature-length theatrical film. Unaccountably the Lasky Company has had little attention from film scholars. *The Squaw Man* is usually cited as an important entry in the development of the American feature film, but its significance as a *theatrical* film, as well as that of the theatrical features that followed it, such as *The Virginian* and *The Girl of the Golden West*, has been ignored. The fact is, these films did more to bring a *cinematic* element into adaptations of stage plays than the early features of the Zukor and Klaw-Erlanger companies. In this respect, they were productions that looked forward to the full development of the motion picture as a medium relatively distinct from the stage. This was due in large part to the insistence of Lasky and Belasco upon the utilization of natural locales in the filming. When Cecil B. De Mille began filming *The Squaw Man* in the Uintah country in eastern Utah and in Ah Say, Wyoming, he described how the use of such locations helped him to

William de Mille's play, *The Warrens of Virginia* (1907), was brought to the screen in 1915 for the Lasky Company brother, Cecil B.

throw aside the stage techniques he had learned during his association with Belasco in New York. Writing in January of 1914, he noted:

> Imagine, the horizon is your stage limit, and the sky your gridiron. No height limit, no close-fitting exits, no conserving of stage space, just the whole world open to you as a stage and a thousand people in a scene does not crowd your accommodations. . . . I felt lost at first. I could not get the stage idea out of my head at first, I looked skyward for sets of lines, borders and drops. . . . [98]

Practical conditions necessitated a different response, he continued: "I learned all over again the art of directing. This time a universe as a working basis . . . . Instead of a set mountain, with the paint yet wet, I had a real, honest-to-goodness mountain . . . ."[99]

Critics were quick to single out the natural locales as among the chief attractions of *The Squaw Man*. *The Moving Picture World* applauded it for its "compelling beauty and nobility of actual scenery as compared to stage affectations."[100] And Robert Grau praised the film's location shooting as well: "The realities of life not only prove the most compelling attractions with the public, but will enable one to point to the influence of the motion picture in the natural life."[101]

The following is a chronology of filmed stage plays from the Lasky Feature Play Company from 1913 to 1916. Whenever possible, the film's release date, cast and the performance statistics of the stage plays are given:

The Squaw Man, February 1914. Starring Dustin Farnum and directed by Cecil B. De Mille and Oscar Apfel. Based upon Edwin Milton Royle's play as presented by Royle and William Faversham at Wallack's Theatre on October 23, 1905, for 222 performances. Dustin Farnum appeared in the play's revival at the Broadway Theatre on January 9, 1911 for eight performances.

Brewster's Millions, April 1914. Starring Edward Abeles (duplicating his stage success). Based on the play by Winchell Smith and Byron Ongley as dramatized from George Bar McCutcheon's novel. First produced by Thompson and Dundy at the New Amsterdam Theatre on December 31, 1906, for 163 performances with Edward Abeles.

The Master Mind, May 1914. Based on the play by Daniel D. Carter as staged at the Harris Theatre on February 17, 1913, for 128 performances with Edmund Breese and Elliott Dexter.

The Virginian, August 1914. Starring Dustin Farnum and directed by Cecil B. De Mille and Oscar Apfel. Based on the dramatization by Owen Wister and Kirke La Shelle of Wister's novel. First produced by La Shelle at the Manhattan Theatre on January 5, 1904, for 138 performances with Dustin Farnum and Guy Bates Post.

Cameo Kirby, December 1914. Starring Dustin Farnum. Based on the collaboration in 1907 between Booth Tarkington and Harry Leon Wilson which was first presented in New York on December 20, 1909.

The Warrens of Virginia, February 1915. Directed by Cecil B. De Mille. Based on the play by C. De Mille as produced by David Belasco at the Belasco Theatre on December 3, 1907, for 190 performances with Frank Keenan and Mary Pickford (in her New York debut).

The Country Boy, February 1915. Starring Marshall Neilan and produced by C.B. De Mille and Edgar Selwyn. Based on the comedy by Edgar Selwyn as produced by Henry B. Harris at the Liberty Theatre on August 30, 1910, for 143 performances with G.C. Staley.

The Governor's Lady, March 1915. Directed by Cecil B. De Mille. Based on the play by Alice Bradley as produced by David Belasco and William Elliott at the Republic Theatre on September 19, 1912, for 125 performances with Milton Sills.

The Woman, April 1915. Based on the play by William C. De Mille as produced at the New National Theatre in Washington, D.C. on April 17, 1911, with Helen Ware and William Courtleigh.

The Arab, June 1915. Starring Edgar Selwyn (duplicating his stage role) and directed by Cecil B. De Mille. Based on the play by Edgar Selwyn as produced by Henry B. Harris at the Lyceum Theatre on September 20, 1911, for 53 performances.

The Case of Becky, August 1915. Based on the play by Edward Locke as produced by David Belasco at the Belasco Theatre on October 1, 1912, for 95 performances with Frances Starr.

Rose of the Rancho, October 1915. Based on the play by David Belasco and Richard Walton Tully as produced by Belasco at the Belasco Theatre on November 27, 1906, for 240 performances with Frances Starr and Jane Cowl.

Trail of the Lonesome Pine, February 1916. Starring Theodore Roberts and Charlotte Walker (duplicating her original stage role) and directed by Cecil B. De Mille. Based on the play by Eugene Walters from the novel by John Fox, Jr. and first produced by Klaw and Erlanger at the New Amsterdam Theatre on January 29, 1912, for 32 performances.

Sweet Kitty Bellairs, May 1916. Based on the play by Davis Belasco as based on the book "The Bath Comedy" by Agnes and Egerton Castle and produced by Belasco by arrangement with Maurice Campbell at the Belasco Theatre on December 9, 1903, for 206 performances with Jane Cowl.

The World Film Corporation: "Well-known Plays by Well-known Players"

Unfortunately, the history of the World Film Corporation and the theatrical features it produced, have been generally ignored by film historians. The "standard" histories by Terry Ramsaye and Benjamin Hampton discuss World only in terms of some of its business practices, while books on William A. Brady and the Shubert brothers (all partners in the enterprise) either ignore it entirely or mention it only in passing.[102]

Nonetheless, the World Film Corporation was a fascinating amalgamation of film and theater entrepreneurs; and, although short-lived (1914-1917), it put on film some of the finest American plays that were written between the turn of the century and the appearance of Eugene O'Neill in 1915.

In the winter of 1914 World Film Corporation was organized by Arthur Spiegel, mail-order Chicago merchant, in conjunction with film entrepreneur Lewis J. Selznick. World Film engaged as its director of production William A. Brady. Brady, of course, was one of the most powerful of the New York-based theatrical producers. His wide experience in the theater ranged from his management of James. J. Corbett, the pugilist, to business associations with the early nickelodeons, to producing stage productions for some of the most successful and respected of American playwrights, including Clyde Fitch.

On February 7, 1914, notice of Brady's association with World appeared in the *Moving Picture World*. The plan as announced would make available for filming all of the plays presently under Brady's control. This enterprise would proceed under three fronts: a program of films based on the plays of George Broadhurst (including *Bought and Paid For*, 1911); a program of films made by the stage actor Robert Mantell and his own repertory company; and films that would be personally controlled by Brady.[103] This last venture would be presented under the separate title of "William A. Brady Picture Plays." Brady's properties numbered over sixty-five stage productions.

A few months later the Shuberts entered into this combination. In June an announcement appeared stating that the three million dollar corporation was "to add in photoplay form, throughout the civilized world, the big dramatic and spectacular successes controlled by the Shubert Company to the regular output of the World Corporation."[104] The Shuberts would control their productions under the aegis of their own Shubert Feature Film Corporation while the world interests would handle the distribution and sales. In his study of stage and screen economic interactions, *Broadway and Hollywood*, Robert McLaughlin notes that the Shuberts intended to utilize their own theaters for exhibition of the films, just as the Klaw-Erlanger interests had intended to do.[105] Again, the failing road system was a prime factor in such ambitions. Combined with Brady's properties, the Shuberts raised the total number of available plays for the screen to over two hundred.

The guiding motto of the World Film Corporation was similar to that of Famous Players: "Features Made From Well-Known Plays by Well-Known Players." However, the theatrical films that were made derived from a very different kind of play than those used by Famous Players, the Protective Amusement Company, and the Lasky Company. I refer to a body of plays that represented the work of new and courageous playwrights in America. They included George Scarborough's *The Lure* (1913), Edward Sheldon's *The Boss* (1911) and *Salvation Nell* (1908), George Broadhurst's *The Dollar Mark*

(1909) and *Bought and Paid For* (1911), Clyde Fitch's *The City* (1909), and Channing Pollock's dramatization of Frank Norris' *The Pit* (1904). Such plays had been praised in an article in *The New York Dramatic Mirror* in 1912 as indicating new and tougher directions for the American playwright. "Even though none of them goes resoundingly through the ages as the final and loftiest expression of the spirit of the 20th Century," noted the writer, "one can feel only gratification that our own playwrights are struggling along the right path. Their efforts may make the advent of some later genius an easier matter."[106] This is not to say that these plays entirely broke away from the styles of melodramas and well made plays that preceeded them; the conflicts and violence of the former as well as the social satire of the latter were still very much in evidence. But they dealt with "problem" issues in a tougher and more uncompromising manner than their predecessors. *The Boss* and *The City* were both plays about political and moral corruption. They contained harsh language and violent situations such as murders and labor strikes. More than other American plays of the time, they approached the naturalistic dramas of Brieux, Hauptmann, Shaw, and Ibsen.

Unfortunately, due to nitrate deterioration and popular neglect the film versions of these plays have been lost. I have had to rely upon contemporary reviews to gain a sense of what they were like. Maurice Tourneur's version of Channing Pollock's *The Pit* for example, was praised by George Blaisdell in *Moving Picture World* in January of 1915 for the "spectacular value" of the interiors of the Chicago Opera House and the pit of the Chicago Wheat Exchange. Norris' naturalistic tendency to avoid melodramatic villainy was captured, evidently, in Milton Sills' ability to portray a villain "without being villainous," and the emphasis in the film upon its "story of a business battle" without "the usual tempestuous love scenes." Indeed, the play's climactic scenes about the battle among the stock brokers appears to have been fully realized in the film: "The views of the speculators fighting in the pit are the best this writer has seen.... There are hundreds of men employed in them."[107] The realism of the sets was praised by Peter Milne in *Motion Picture News*, and his words echo Belasco's pronouncements that the motion picture should abandon the artificiality of the stage's scene accoutrement: "In an exchange scene we have been accustomed to seeing shaky walls, men taking the parts of brokers who apparently have spent most of their lives as truckmen or the like, and the whole spectacle has been grossly exaggerated. Here it is not; it is realistic; the men look as if they might have come from State Street offices."[108] The film of Thomas Buchanon's play, *The Cub* (1910), was likewise praised by Mr. Milne for its realism—in this case, location shooting: "Wild mountain land is the background for all the exteriors, while the settings, comprising mainly the interiors of the feudists' cabins, are excellent."[109] That the opportunities for action were fulfilled in the film is indicated by the note that "the final fight, in which an entire house is completely wrecked, is truly thrilling."[110]

However, Edward Sheldon's play *Salvation Nell* (1908) appears to have fared rather differently at the hands of the filmmakers. This "street scene" play had an intricately staged first act that presented dozens of carefully delineated anecdotes and snatches of dialogue conveying a sense of the rough life on the Bowery. The diction and tone of the dialogue was relatively crude and vulgar. Nell herself was first seen as a Bowery slave who was rough, unkempt and brutal in her language. But Margaret MacDonald's review in *Moving Picture World* in August 1915 indicated that while some time was spent in the first reel depicting Sheldon's carefully drawn Bowery milieu, the main plot elements of Nell's illegitimate child, her relationship with the drunkard Jim Platt, and her own personality were "diluted" considerably for the movie. Possibly fearing negative audience response, the filmmakers omitted references to the illegitimate child and portrayed Nell herself as "a type that is sweet and dignified, living in the midst of vice yet preserving within herself an atmosphere of righteousness . . . ."[111] And the pictures that survive from the production reveal Beatriz Michelena's portrayal of Nell as a kind of Bowery Joan of Arc.[112] Sheldon's play was, for its time, brave and relatively uncompromising in its stripping away of the genteel women's image from the character of Nell. Therein lay its greatness. But the film bowed to pressures, which left it looking like just another melodrama. This problem in adapting stage plays to the screen—especially controversial stage plays like *Salvation Nell*—would trouble filmmakers in the future, as we shall see later with George Abbott's play, *Coquette* (1927).

With so many different producers releasing film versions of their plays through the World releasing organization, it is small wonder that the combine did not last long. After Arthur Spiegel died in 1917, Lewis J. Selznick left the project, William A. Brady returned to the stage, and its most promising director, Maurice Tourneur, went to work for another production company, Artcraft. The constant infighting between the Shuberts and Brady did not contribute to the working relationship when it came to guaranteeing the availability of theaters for the exhibition of the films. Finally, it is also possible that the very nature of the filmed plays—in many cases derived from "problem" plays and other contemporary dramas—limited their audiences to smaller numbers than those that attended the action melodramas of the Lasky Company.

Yet a significant record was left of some of the greatest stage stars of the day. Holbrook Blinn duplicated his stage role in Edward Sheldon's *The Boss*, as did Wilton Lackaye in Pollock's dramatization of *The Pit*, Thurlow Bergen in Fitch's *The City*, and Emma Dunn in *Mother*. And among the other stars brought to the screen, there were C. Aubrey Smith, Alice Brady (William Brady's daughter) and Barbara Tennant.

The following is a chronological listing of the World films made from stage plays:

The Dollar Mark, September 1914. Based on the 1909 play by George Broadhurst as staged by William A. Brady at the Wallack Theatre on August 23, 1909 for 48 performances with Pauline Frederick.

The Gentlemen from Mississippi, September 1919. Based on the 1908 play by Thomas Wise and Harrison Rhodes as produced by William A. Brady at the Bijou Theater on September 29, 1908 for 407 performances with Douglas Fairbanks.

Mother, September 1919. Starring Emma Dunn in her original stage role and directed by Maurice Tourneur. Based on the play by Jules Eckert Goodman as produced by William A. Brady at the Hackett Theater on September 7, 1910 for 133 performances.

Across the Pacific, October 1914. Based on the play by Charles E. Blaney (no performance statistics available).

The Lure, 1914. Based on the 1913 play by George Scarborough as produced at Maxine Elliott's Theatre, on August 14, 1913 for 132 performances.

The Wishing Ring, October 1914. Directed by Maurice Tourneur. Based on the play by Owen Davis (no performance statistics available).

After Dark, September 1915. Based on the play by Dion Boucicault as produced in New York at Niblo's Garden Theatre on November 16, 1868.

Salvation Nell, October 1915. Starring Beatrix Michelena and directed by Alexander E. Beyfuss. Based on the play by Edward Sheldon as produced at the Hackett Theatre on November 17, 1908 for 71 performances with Minnie Maddern Fiske.

The Boss, 1915. Starring Holbrook Blinn in a duplication of his stage role. Based on the play by Edward Sheldon as produced at the Astor Theatre on January 30, 1911, for 88 performances.

M'Liss, March 1915. Starring Barbara Tennant and directed by O.A.C. Lund. Based on the dramatization of a story by Bret Harte (no performance data available).

The Builder of Bridges, May 1915. Starring C. Aubrey Smith. Based on the play by Alfred Sutro as produced by Charles Frohman at the Hudson Theatre on October 26, 1909 for 47 performances with Kyrle Bellew.

The Family Cupboard, November 1915. Starring Alice Brady (duplicating her stage role). Based on the play by Owen Davis as produced by William A. Brady at the Playhouse on August 21, 1913 for 140 performances.

The Pit, December 1915. Starring Wilton Lackaye (duplicating his original stage role) and directed by Maurice Tourneur. Based on the dramatization of Frank Norris' novel by Channing Pollock as produced by William A. Brady at the Lyric Theatre on February 10, 1904 for 77 performances.

The Model, May 1915. Based on the play "Woman and Wine" by Arthur

Shirley and Benjamin Landeck as produced at the Manhattan Theatre on April 11, 1900 for 69 performances with Howard Kyle and Minnie Dupree.

Trilby, 1917. Directed by Maurice Tourneur. Based on the dramatization by Paul Potter of du Maurier's novel that was staged at the Garden Theatre on April 15, 1895.

The Cub, February 1917. Starring John Hines. Based on the play by Thomas Buchanon as produced by William A. Brady at the Comedy Theatre on November 1, 1910 for 32 performances with Douglas Fairbanks.

Bought and Paid For, November 1916. Starring Alice Brady and directed by Harvey Knoles. Based on the play by George Broadhurst as produced by William A. Brady at the Playhouse Theatre on September 26, 1911 for 431 performances.

The City, January 1918. Starring Thurlow Bergen (duplicating his stage role). Based on the play by Clyde Fitch as produced by the Shuberts at the Lyric Theatre on December 21, 1909 for 190 performances.

Kalem, All-Star Feature Company, Morosco, Lubin

Thus far this chapter has emphasized those film production companies that were newly formed for the purpose of making theatrical features in the 1912-1915 period. This is not to say, however, that the other, established, production companies did not produce theatrical features at this time. A case in point is the Kalem Company, which was founded in 1907 by the group partnership of George Kleine, Samuel Long and Frank Marion (K-L-M). I have already mentioned Kalem in connection with its one-reel adaptation of *Ben-Hur* in 1908. The only other aspect of the Kalem enterprise that is at all remembered today was its production in 1912 of a feature-length film shot on location in Egypt called *From the Manger to the Cross* in five reels.

The company had no indoor studios and therefore shot most of its product outdoors on locations throughout the United States and extending as far as Italy, Palestine and Ireland. Even before Lasky began filming plays in outdoor locales, the Kalem company, as early as 1911, was making three and four-reel films of famous stage plays. Virtually forgotten today, these filmed plays represented an important attempt to bring melodrama to the screen. I will consider here the feature-length versions of a number of plays by Dion Boucicault.

The Boucicault-inspired features between 1911 and 1913 were shot in locations in Ireland and Florida. A. Nicholas Vardac suggests that these helped break the two-reel limitation imposed upon the movie industry at this time. These "experiments with the longer film ... served as the basis for further progress."[113] This "progress" lay in Kalem's realizing of the scenic potentials present in Boucicault's plays. "It is not at all surprising that the Boucicault melodrama should have been taken into the films," declared Vardac. "For these plays, by virtue of their independence upon external effects, as well as by virtue of the values inherent in their dramatic style, were prime cinematic material."[114] The Boucicault films were, in order of release:

The Colleen Bawn, October 16, 1911. Based on Boucicault's drama of the same name, which was first produced in America at Laura Keene's Varieties on March 29, 1860.

Arrah-na-Pogue, November 21, 1911. Based on Boucicault's drama of the same name, which was first produced in America at Niblo's Gardens, July 12, 1865.

The Shaughraun, December 25, 1912. Based on the Boucicault drama of the same name, which was first produced in America at Niblo's Garden Theatre, September 24, 1894.

The Octoroon, December 1, 1913. Based on Boucicault's drama of the same name, which was first produced in America at the Howard Athenaeum in Boston, 1863.

It will be recalled that *Arrah-na-Pogue* presented on stage a famous escape scene typical of the penchant in melodrama for long, wordless sequences. During an escape scene a prisoner leaves his chamber and clambers up the outside of a tower. It was done with an inset frame (itself like a movie screen's border) which enclosed a vertically moving series of flats, each one representing a portion of the tower wall that was higher than the last. When they moved in sequence, the prisoner seemed to be climbing upward. Scenery likewise was important in *The Colleen Bawn*. This drama of rocks, seacoast and caves depended heavily upon the use of cut-outs, sections of landscape painted upon drops that could be quickly "flown" to reveal other drops behind it. There was also some extensive "cross-cutting" from one scene to another:

> Throughout the play ... the effort is made to picture upon the stage every scene necessary for the development of the story, and one scene is dissolved into another, or, under cover of lights, the changes are faded out and in. Four scenes are needed in the first act, five in the second, and five (including the multiple scene of the moving wall) are used for the last act.

This type of staging characteristic of 19th century melodrama was, according to Vardac, anticipatory of cinematic syntax.[115]

This is all by way of indicating what kinds of material were utilized by Kalem for its Boucicault series. The films were directed by Sidney Olcott, who, with the rest of the Kalem crew, left for Beaufort, Ireland in August of 1910, and returned there later in 1911 for more work on the series. Olcott also starred in the films, George Hollister serving as the cameraman and Gene Gauntier filling in as a supporting actor.

Since these films are all lost, it is again necessary to turn to contemporary reviews to gain a sense of what they were like. As happened later with the Lasky features, critics praised the use of natural locales as opposed to the artificial scenery of the stage. *The Colleen Bawn* was lauded by the *Moving Picture World* as "the chef d'oeuvre of American motion picture production ... not alone typical of the company immediately concerned, but of American picture-making as an enterprise, alert, resourceful, and progressive."[116] *Arrah-na-Pogue* was described in the same periodical: "There is not a dull moment in the entire three reels of this subject and there are many situations that are intensely gripping. For sustained action it is the best three-reel subject we have seen up-to-date."[117] And *The Shaughraun* was described by the magazine at length, which is worth quoting in full:

When this company began filming Irish plays on Irish soil it entered a new field of cinematographic endeavor. It demonstrated beyond all cavil that the motion picture is vastly more than a mere vehicle of cheap dramatic composition. Because of its efforts we can challenge the novelist, the historian, and the dramatist to a combat of portrayal and description with no fear of the result for the prestige and superiority of the motion picture .... In *The Shaughraun*, it seems to me, they have well nigh touched perfection in the use they made of outdoor scenery. Nothing in art or literature can approach the ability of the gifted and painstaking producer in creating atmosphere. After we have seen the weird and rugged beauty of the stern and cliff-bound Irish coast, much of the temperament and much in the history of the Celtic race becomes as clear as crystal. We enjoy the sensation. We thrill with delight at this new way of learning things by the roots .... Imposing, however, as all these scenes are, they form but a part of the true story and the true atmosphere, and we feel constantly that they have been selected for that purpose only .... I have seen splendid outdoor scenery in motion picture plays, but my enjoyment was greatly lessened by the fact that the producer evidently counted on the scenery to 'pull through' a time-worn plot or a lot of amateurish actors and actresses. *The Shaughraun* gives us its scenic splendors as merely one item in its program of uniform excellence.[118]

Just as the locales were natural, so too did the characters inhabiting them also transcend the wooden stereotypes of so much stage melodrama:

The attention to details, without which a play like this would lose much on its way from the stage to the celluloid, does infinite credit to the director. When the action of the play calls for the interior of a country lawyer's office to which the camera pays a careful visit. A real 'Dan' works in a real blacksmith shop and even the 'Dinny Doyle,' who peers over the fence and hears the villains plotting and rejoicing, is the kind that you would expect to meet on an Irish country road on a workday's afternoon.[119]

Thus the circumstances that necessitated the shooting of Kalem pictures outside a studio led, inevitably, to their emphasis upon local color, action and detail. What could only be suggested on stage could be fully realized on the screen. Admittedly, it is difficult to assess these pictures since they have disappeared, but if we can trust contemporary reviewers, they made substantial contributions to a species of filmed play that broke the bonds of proscenium space and time and, to paraphrase Jesse Lasky and David Belasco, make of the world a stage.

Of all the production studios that at this time specialized in filming feature-length versions of famous plays, the All-Star Feature Company is probably the least known. One looks in vain for references to it in the standard histories. Instead, what little can be gleaned about it comes from the trade journals and writers of the day. Although Robert Grau states that it was formed in August of 1913, the first reference I can find in the trades predates that, in late July of that year. An advertisement appearing in the *New York Dramatic Mirror* states that the company will, in words sounding very much like the pronouncements of other film companies, present "the world's greatest plays enacted by distinguished stage celebrities, under the personal direction of Augustus Thomas."[120]

Augustus Thomas was one of the most popular and respected playwrights of the day. After working for Charles Frohman as his Art Director in the 1880s, Thomas established himself as a playwright with a series of popular dramas, many of them regional melodramas, beginning in 1891 with the production of *Alabama*. *In Mizzoura* (1893), *Arizona* (1899), *The Witching Hour* (1907) and *The Copperhead* (1918) were other popular plays that followed. Applauded by Montrose J. Moses for his masterly "well made" craftmanship, by Ima Honaker Herron for his touches of regional color, and by Arthur Hobson Quinn for his practical approach to native drama, Augustus Thomas was, seemingly, well suited for the challenge of the motion picture.[121] Indeed, his position at All-Star as the "Director-General" (a position De Mille occupied with Lasky at this same time) was unique. It may be the only instance during this period where a famous playwright actually went into the field, as it were, to personally produce films of his and other playwright's works. More is the pity that virtually all of his filmed plays are lost to us today.

Joining Thomas in the All-Star venture were theatrical producers Archibald Selwyn and Philip Klein. They announced late in July that the forthcoming feature-length filmed plays would include several films based on Augustus Thomas' successes—*Arizona, In Mizzoura, Colorado, Alabama* and *The Witching Hour*—as well as other distinguished plays—Eugene Walter's *Paid in Full* (1908), James A. Herne's *Shore Acres* (1892) and Edgar Selwyn's *The Arab* (1911), *The Country Boy* (1910) and *Pierre of the Plains* (1908). All these films appeared in the 1913-1915 period. Some, like the Selwyn pictures—were eventually released through the Lasky Company. Many of them presented on film some of the original cast members of the Broadway productions. For example, *Arizona*, All-Star's first release in September of 1913, brought Cyril Scott from the Broadway company to the screen along with "a mighty cast of original 'Arizona' players."[122] And the Selwyn filmed plays featured Selwyn himself duplicating his stage roles. Augustus Thomas directed at least some of the productions attested to, in part, by an article in the *New York Dramatic Mirror* in August of 1913 that described his journeys to various locations in Fox Hill and Staten Island for the shooting of *Arizona*. In another article the next month, his film of *Arizona* was praised by the *Mirror* for Thomas' ability to realize in cinematic terms his own play:

> ... in this instance the author of a drama is also the author of the photoplay adaptation. Where an alien hand might observe the letter and lose the spirit, the creator of the original knows just what he was driving at ... and rebuilds accordingly .... Mr. Thomas has retained the spirit that made *Arizona* famous; he has reconstructed his characters for the screen, remodeled his big scenes and revived his climaxes in an effective fashion.[124]

Curiously, information on Thomas' films in the trade magazines becomes increasingly hard to find by late 1914; and it is impossible, based on information available, to determine the fate of the All-star company. August Thomas' own autobiography, *The Print of My Remembrance*, was, unfortunately, written in 1911, two years before the venture began. We do know that by April of 1914 Thomas had apparently ceased to direct the All-Star productions, for the name of "Lawrence McGill" appears on the credit listings for *Pierre of the Plains* and *In Mizzoura*. At this time, the story of one of Broadway's most eminent playwright's involvement with cinema remains incomplete.

Another subject for further study is the feature-length theatrical film output of the Morosco Company. Morosco is known today primarily for its release by former stage actor Hobart Bosworth of several films based on Jack London novels. Otherwise, information is scant. However, a cache of Morosco films, some of them stage-to-screen adaptations, has come to light and is presently being catalogued at the Library of Congress.[124] According to a notice in the *New York Dramatic Mirror* in June of 1913, Morosco, like the Klaw-Erlanger venture, planned to release its theatrical films via a chain of theater houses—in this case a circuit of houses called the "Northwestern Theatrical Circuit." Morosco did not survive long as an independent production company. By 1915 it was absorbed by Paramount and, shortly thereafter, apparently sank without a trace.

Some of the theatrical features released before Morosco's demise included *The Yankee Girl* (released in September of 1915), which presented Blanche Ring duplicating her stage success in the play by George V. Hobart (1910); *Madame La Presidente* (released in January of 1916) with Anna Held in her screen debut in the farce by Maurice Hennequin and Pierre Veber (as translated for Charles Frohman's version in 1913 by Jose G. Levy); and *The Tongues of Men* (released in December 1915) with Constance Collier in the film version of Edward Childs Carpenter's play of 1913.

The Lubin Company was, like Kalem, formerly one of the members of Edison's Trust during the 1909-1914 period. From 1912-1916 Lubin presented many theatrical features which, like those of Kalem, All-Star and World, are lost to us today. This is especially unfortunate because many of them were derived from some of the most important plays of the day by established English and American playwrights. They included:

The Lion and the Mouse, January 1914. Starring Ethel Clayton and directed by Edgar Lewis. Based on the play by Charles Klein as produced by Henry B. Harris at the Lyceum Theatre on November 20, 1904 for 686 performances.

The Daughters of Men, March 1914. Directed by George W. Terwilliger. Based on the play by Charles Klein as produced by Henry B. Harris at the Astor Theater on November 19, 1906 for 59 performances.

The Wolf, June 1914. Directed by Barry O'Neil. Based on the play by Eugene Walters as produced by the Shuberts at the Bijou Theatre on April 18, 1908 for 81 performances.

The District Attorney, July 1915. Directed by Barry O'Neil. Based on the play by Charles Klein and Harrison Grey Fiske as produced at the American Theatre on January 21, 1895 for 40 performances.

The Great Divide, December 1915. Starring Ethel Clayton and House Peters and directed by Edgar Lewis. Based on the play by William Vaughn Moody as produced by Henry Miller at the Princess Theatre on October 3, 1906 for 238 performances.

The Evangelist, January 1916. Starring Gladys Hanson and directed by Barry O'Neil. Based on the play by Henry Arthur Jones as produced by Klaw and Erlanger at the Knickerbocker Theatre on September 30, 1907 for 19 performances.

This incomplete list indicates the high calibre of plays used as source material for films. They were all by playwrights of considerable reputation and prestige who had made their names in a kind of naturalistic drama that America had inherited from Europe. Klein's *The Lion and the Mouse* was one of the first plays produced in America that combined the zeal for reform with well-made intrigues. His *The Daughters of Men* and *The District Attorney* used the stage to launch satiric attacks on, respectively, socialism and political corruption. *The Great Divide* and *The Evangelist* took on issues that were uncommon on the stage in America—rape, prostitution and fraudulent religious practices. All the plays attempted the realistic depiction of life as opposed to the more artificial formulas of the parlor comedies and the stereotypes of the melodramas.

Contemporary reviews indicated that these filmed plays, in common with those of Lasky and World, revealed a penchant for outdoor shooting in real locales. Thus, *The Lion and the Mouse* shot its exteriors in Washington, D.C. *The Great Divide* was shot in the Grand Canyon, where the events in the first act took place. It evoked from reviewer W. Stephen Bush in *Moving Picture World* on December 18, 1915, this remark: "All the art of the conventional stage cannot produce the effect which these sublime settings of Nature produce instantaneously .... No picture was ever made which reproduces atmosphere as 'The Great Divide' does."[125]

Although these films were able to realize the scenic implications of the plays, they were not able to confront their thematic dimension. Adapting a play like Moody's *The Great Divide*, which was a relatively harsh dissection of love and violence (including a near gang-rape in the first act), proved to be too much for the filmmakers. One of the key speeches in the play had occurred when Steve Ghent returned to take his estranged wife Ruth back with him to Arizona. What followed was an important discussion about duty and morality as opposed to the contrary impulse of sensual love. But in the movie, according to the review, all this was lost. Ruth returns to Steve *only* when she learns he has been supporting her mother during the period of their estrangement!

The Triangle Film Corporation: An Exodus of Stage Stars

Late in 1914 feature-length theatrical films were receiving mixed critical and popular reception. Those films that most closely imitated a proscenium event occasioned negative comments, while those that utilized uniquely cinematic characteristics—such as location shooting—were praised. At the same time, James O'Neill, Sarah Bernhardt, Minnie Maddern Fiske and many other stage stars had made a film or two and then quickly retired from the movies. Questions were being raised—namely, were their acting techniques unsuited to the film medium? Yet, in the face of all that, the Triangle Film Corporation announced early in 1915 that it was forming three production companies for the purpose of presenting famous stage players in film versions of their most famous plays.[126] Entrepreneurs Harry Aitken, D.W. Griffith, Thomas Ince and Mack Sennett proposed to make, with Wall Street's backing, theatrical films that would compete with the principal theatres of the country. These productions, they predicted, would "elevate" the screen and establish new standards of film entertainment. Moreover, they proposed to imitate the top Broadway admission price of the two-dollar seat for the theatrical houses they were remodelling for film production.[127]

The three Triangle production companies—Fine Arts, Ince and Sennett—were designed to take advantage of the widest possible range of popular theater. For example, the Fine Arts Company, controlled by Griffith, was aimed at the prestige drama of the day (social satire, Shakespearean drama, etc.); Ince specialized in outdoor dramas, corresponding to the regional melodramas of Augustus Thomas and David Belasco; and Sennett was already known for slapstick farces, the screen equivalent to vaudeville burlesque.

As the three production companies began making films in the summer of 1915 in or near the Los Angeles area, the trades began reflecting some of the excitement generated by the enterprise. The two-dollar seat policy for film exhibition was highly controversial, although Griffith's *The Birth of a Nation* had already commanded such a price earlier that year. But for Triangle, such prices were to be part of a general policy:

Triangle is the first company to offer a program of feature photoplays at the $2 scale of prices customary in theaters of better class. Neither *The Birth of a Nation* nor *Cabiria* may be cited as precedents, for both are extraordinary productions that provide a full evening's entertainment . . . .[128]

The high prices offered to stage celebrities by Triangle also aroused comment. As we have seen, it had been feared all along that the presence of stage stars might contribute to a growing inflation of salaries. Triangle now fulfilled that prophecy. Harry Aitken hired Arthur Klein, a theatrical agent, to help entice notable stage talent to the movies at salaries ranging from $1000 to $2500 per week. Throughout the summer Edwin Fitzgerald ("Eddie Foy") was contracted at $1200 a week, Douglas Fairbanks at $2000 a week, Weber and Fields at $3500 a week, and still the salary levels kept climbing. Even though many stage players were accustomed to receiving only $250 to $500 a week for thirty or forty weeks out of the year (and much less if their plays were unsuccessful), the players were nonetheless fearful that screen appearances would jeopardize future theatrical bookings. Thus, Aiken and Klein had to double, treble and even quadruple player salaries for a guaranteed period of at least a year.[129]

Two of the most extravagant contracts Triangle offered to stage celebrities indicate the commitment to obtaining these players. For example, $40,000 for five weeks work was offered to Frohman star Billie Burke, then married to Florenz Ziegfeld. In addition, Burke was offered a special railway car to bring her from New York, the use of an automobile while in Los Angeles, and $50,000 down payment to close an option on her services twenty-four weeks out of the next three years. $100,000 would come if she fulfilled the contract. While Triangle insured itself for $50,000 against rain, Burke severed her connections with the Frohman office (which had a policy that did not permit its stars to appear in movies).[130] De Wolf Hopper, a popular star of the musical comedy stage (especially renowned for his Gilbert and Sullivan repertoire), overcame his initial hesitation and signed with Triangle when $83,000 was promised for a year's service. Probably the most extravagant of these players' contracts was that offered to England's renowned Sir Herbert Beerbohm Tree, $100,000 to spend thirty weeks in Los Angeles filming an adaptation of his previous film presentation of *Macbeth*.

Mixed reactions greeted this exodus of stage stars to the movies. William A. Brady, himself involved with motion pictures through his own connections with World Pictures, admitted that "the actor will die out because the movies offer inducements and the drama doesn't. Through active connection with the theater I find where ten years ago there were twenty young men ambitious for a stage career, today there is not one. In another year there will be no actor."[131] In a reply to Brady the New York *Evening Post* noted that the American legitimate theater had many things wrong with it— big business, syndicates, booking privileges—that could be corrected by the film industry. By satisfying the public appetite for "action," the writer said, the movies might yet, in effect, drive "pistol-waving from the theater and leave the stage clear for a real spoken drama. People will go to the movies for one thing and to the theater for another."[132] Such perception hints at a fundamental difference between stage and screen that was later echoed in Professor Brander Matthews' assertion that the movies can do certain kinds of melodrama better than the "regular" theater, whereas comedy and tragedy are beyond the movies' reach.[133] This vision of the film as a magnet for the "undesirable" aspects of the popular stage was also noted by critic Alan Dale:

I discovered that the screens were the veritable scavengers of the amusement world, that they could be relied upon to remove from the theater all that the theater couldn't possibly want—things that it had ignobly fattened upon in less felicitous days—and that like certain beetles, they gorged themselves upon the very material that the 'legitimate' had never before been able to rid itself of.[134]

While the movie industry held out fat salary checks to stage stars, Dale continued, the theater, as a result, was free to go in other, more artistic directions. He did not elaborate on those directions.[135]

Yet, ironically, most of the stage celebrities who came to Triangle proved to be ill-suited to the film medium. Very few theatrical films were produced, and very few players achieved any kind of popular or critical success in the movies. As one of those failures, De Wolf Hopper recalled:

Before anyone else can say it first, let me admit that I was no earth-shaking success in the movies. If the truth must be known, I died on the silver screen; I sank majestically beneath the oily waves of the cinema sea and never was heard of again. Not so much as a life belt or a spar was picked up. The fact that a gallant company of stage celebrities perished with me made my demise less poignant personally, but not the less indisputable.[136]

Long before Triangle ceased to be an important production enterprise in 1918, its policy of presenting famous stage players in their most noteworthy successes changed to one promoting the production of films that had little to do with the opportunity to see how stage players confronted the new medium of film and why so many of them failed in that endeavor. Fortunately, Triangle's history has been relatively well documented in several recent works, including Kalton Lahue's general history, *Dreams for Sale* (1971), Anthony Slide's history of Griffith's Fine Arts Unit, *The Kindergarten of the Movies*, (1980), and my own Master's thesis (unpublished).[137]

Before selecting three of Triangle's stage stars for discussion it is pertinent to indicate something of the number and range of stage stars who came to Triangle in the 1915-1916 period. Collated from the works just cited, here is as comprehensive a list as is presently possible. It is tentative, since many stage players who came to Triangle never made a film at all. For Griffith's Fine Arts studio: Fay Tincher, De Wolfe Hopper, Marie Doro, Douglas Fairbanks, Frank Campeau, John Emerson, Tully Marshall, Orrin Johnson and Herbert Beerbohm Tree; for the Sennett studio: Raymond

Hitchcock, Weber and Fields, Joe Jackson, Eddie Foy, Sam Bernard and William Collier; and for the Ince studio: Bessie Barriscale, Billie Burke, William Desmond, William S. Hart, Frank Keenan and Mary Boland. Other stage stars known to have worked at Triangle include Hale Hamilton, House Peters, Julia Dean, Forrest Winant, Louise Dresser, Harry Woodruff, Willard Mack and Jane Grey.

The list is impressive because it ranges from players in vaudeville to light opera, comedy and legitimate theater. Some of them had very brief film careers. Eddie Foy signed on at Sennett and, under the direction of Del Henderson and Ed Frazee, made only one comedy, *A Favorite Fool* in 1915. Personality clashes with the film crew and with Sennett led to his suspension. Foy filed a court suit for back pay, lost and headed back to New York. Weber and Fields already had some film experience with the World Film Corporation of Brady for a much lower salary. Their stay at Triangle lasted less than a year. Their comedy styles were dependent upon dialogue and dialect—which, of course, was completely lost on the silent screen. One of their only known films was called *The Worst of Friends*, made early in 1916. No further information can be found at this time concerning their short-lived film career.

The experiences at Triangle of De Wolf Hopper, Herbert Beerbohm Tree and Douglas Fairbanks shed some light on the problems they and other stage stars encountered during the process of filmmaking. For Hopper and Tree the movies brought challenges not only to their acting techniques but to their life styles as well. It was at best a dubious experience for them, one from which they were only too glad to withdraw before the end of 1916. For Fairbanks, however, the movies brought new opportunities for a kind of acting that Montrose J. Moses earlier in this discussion dubbed "strenuous acting." It was an athletic style incompatible with the spatial restrictions of the proscenium stage.

De Wolfe Hopper's career had spanned light opera by Gilbert and Sullivan, John Phillip Sousa operettas and the plays of Shakespeare. In the late 1880s he had popularized the ballad "Casey at the Bat" and had made a name for himself in the portrayals of colorful American rustic types like "Old Bill" in *The Better 'Ole*. By the time Hopper came to Triangle in 1915 his name had become synonymous with robust, good-humored character roles. In the late spring of that year he was playing Gilbert and Sullivan repertoire at the 48th Street Theater in New York when Aiken of Triangle offered him a picture contract for one year at $83,000. "I had not taken the movies very seriously," recounted Hopper, "but I took the eighty-three thousand and an early train for Hollywood."[138]

A combination of money and restlessness lured Douglas Fairbanks to Los Angeles.[139] By contrast to the venerable Hopper, the thirty-one year old Broadway star was a leading new juvenile who had come a long way from bit parts in the Frederick Warde company to the leads in two successful light Broadway social comedies of 1914 and 1915, *He Comes Up Smiling* and James Forbes' theatrical satire, *The Show Shop*. His style displayed a kind of physical exuberance that threatened to burst the bounds of the proscenium. This penchant often led him to leap off balconies, run about the stage and climb stairways on his hands. It is entirely likely that in addition to the two thousand dollars a week Aitken offered, Fairbanks saw other, non-monetary possibilities. Given his athletic tendencies and restless temperament, the motion picture must have seemed a welcome kind of breathing space. He recalled:

Oftimes the question of why I deserted the speaking stage for the films has been hurled at me. Because of the possibilities and the outdoor life. Three years ago when I played with W.H. Crane in The New Henrietta we often spent our time between shows seeking vivid melodramatic pictures, especially Western subjects. We were amused by the primitive emotions and active life in the West ....[140]

Similarly, for Sir Herbert Beerbohm Tree the movies must have fed not only his pocketbook but his quixotic temperament as well. Although he was an established star of the English stage, Tree had long been accused by some critics of being only a virtuoso with make-up, a quick-change artist otherwise lacking in professional polish. If for the public he had inherited the mantle of Henry Irving, for others, mostly critics, he was more of a showman than an artist. But everyone agreed that as a producer he was formidable. The scenic accoutrements of his productions—the richness of costuming, the sense of spectacle—were opulent, even if (it was whispered) his own performances sometimes fell short of that level of accomplishment.[141]

Tree toured America for the first time in 1895. The thirty-four year old actor-manager brought his London Haymarket Company as well as his half-brother Max, who served as secretary for the tour. The tour began at Abbey's Theatre in New York on January 28, and went on to Chicago, Philadelphia and Boston before returning to New York in early April. A year later, Tree came back for a second tour (now with the rights to Paul Potter's stage adaptation of du Maurier's *Trilby* in hand). He presented other plays such as Ibsen's *An Enemy of the People, Hamlet* and *The Merry Wives of Windsor*, which sparked a moderate public response in addition to mixed critical reviews. Tree's final visit to America was in 1915 when he accepted Triangle's offer to make a film of *Macbeth*. He was now a knight (the honor having been bestowed upon him in 1909) and at the zenith of his popularity in England and America. Following his Hollywood assignment, Tree planned to participate in the American observance of the Shakespeare Tercentenary Celebration at the New Amsterdam Theatre.

Hopper, Fairbanks and Tree all arrived at Triangle from different points of the theatrical compass. The initial reception accorded to these three was enthusiastic. Fairbanks and Tree were received with a great deal of fanfare and publicity. Fairbanks arrived to a uniformed band and drum majors (supplied by the Sennett studio) while Tree was greeted by the Los Angeles mayor and a banquet given by the Los Angeles *Examiner*. Tree, recalling his first visit to the Fine Arts Studio was astonished at the number of motor-cars, the size of the movie sets (Griffith was filming *Intolerance* at the time) and the sheer energy of the place:

At the Studio, as our car stops, we are surrounded by a motley crowd, all painted and costumed, among whom are Red Indians, cavaliers, moderns, gorgeous Babylonians, and cowboys. Suddenly there is a terrific explosion as a dozen cowboys fire their pistols into the air. This is a welcome! Recovering from the shock, and finding myself, happily, unwounded, I raise my hat to the cheering crowd. My instinct tells me that I am in the midst of a democratic society.[142]

But after this initial warmth, all accounts point to growing dissension between stage stars and screen players. Unlike the Famous Players and Protective Amusement Studios, which had been located near theatrical centers in New York and Brooklyn, the Triangle studios were in Los Angeles. Anthony Slide in his study of the Fine Arts Studio reports that a sturdy pride existed among the members of the film colony that came to resent the invasion of the legitimate actors. Broadway actors, particularly, represented effete manners and excessive temperament. Their salaries, so much higher than for those already working at the studios, also occasioned much envy and antagonism. Slide points out that by this time many of those actors trained only for the screen were gaining a lot of publicity. Their performances, when measured against those of stage actors in films like *Tess of the d'Urbervilles* and *The Squaw Man*, seemed more natural, less forced.[143] Some of these actors, like Francis X. Bushman and Lottie Briscoe, even took their own talents so seriously as to refuse to take lower billings than stage stars on the credits of films where they jointly appeared. Briscoe had cancelled her contract with Lubin because she felt it was ill-fitting to submit to such an indignity.[144] Nevertheless, the salaries were disproportionate for these two groups of actors. De Wolf Hopper commented on the disparity:

The men and women of the California film colony who had been laboring at twenty-five to one hundred and fifty dollars a week viewed this descent in force of the one-thousand dollars-a-week high hats of Broadway with a jaundiced eye. They had toiled and sweated long in the vineyards and now that the grapes were ripe we fair-haired boys and girls of the legitimate were to eat the fruit; eat it patronizingly with slightly curled lips.[145]

Interestingly, the film colony's adjustment to Tree was not so difficult as one might imagine from the foregoing paragraph. While D.W. Griffith and Harry Aitkin worried about such things as how to address properly an English knight, the film crew merely followed his good-natured advice to call him "Herb" and soon found him to be personally unaffected and funloving.[146] By contrast, there were frictions between Fairbanks and the film crew. The young star exuded a brash cocky energy that appalled Griffith and, reportedly, irritated the crew. Alistair Cook in his monograph on Fairbanks relates that the animosity that developed between Fairbanks and the crew led to acts of sabotage. It would have been easy enough for the wrong kind of makeup to be given the actor. A "pancake" makeup for the footlights was one thing, but the unknowing actor did not realize that it was entirely inappropriate to the orthochromatic film used by filmmakers:

> The crew that worked with Griffith was a busy unit, jealous of its habits and, as small contented staffs are apt to be, unwilling to change its routine. They took a dislike to Fairbanks not as a person but as a symbol. There had been much speculation over the move to recruit theater stars, and by the time Fairbanks arrived the crew had come to the conclusion that they were against it . . . . According to G.W. Bitzer . . . they saw to it that Fairbanks was given a wrong and rather ghastly make-up . . . . The combined effect of acrobatic levity in comedy scenes with strenuous hamming was enough to convince Griffith that there was little hope for Fairbanks in Triangle's ambitious program.[147]

A screening of Fairbank's first Fine Arts films, *The Lamb* and *Double Trouble*, does indeed reveal in the closeups a makeup that seems ashen and clay-like. How was he to know at first that proper makeup for appearing before the cameras consisted of lemon-colored substance applied to the face?

Beyond these kinds of problems, of more immediate interest were the challenges the film medium brought to actors trained to project voice and gesture on stage. Describing her experiences before the camera in 1915, an unidentified actress noted that she had to unlearn a great many things she had learned on the stage. For example, she had to learn greater restraint of gesture and facial expression. "In the test picture I had frowned so realistically that I or my counterfeit looked horrible," she said. "My arms when I waved them about looked like the wings of a windmill in a tempest. It was a lesson to me in restraint."[148] At the same time, the stage player was likely bewildered by his first exposure to a typical movie set in 1915. On either side of a given set were other sets where other films were cranked out, where other directors shouted out cues and directions, where other musicians provided different moods of music, where other carpenters threw up or tore down set constructions to the din of constant hammering, crashing and banging. And all kinds of people wandered about, some of them actors in various costumes, some of them technicians hurrying from set to set, some of them hair-dressers, relatives of the assistant directors, and curiosity-seekers. The actor might be called into a barn-like cavern of a building for a particular scene where the artificial lights were raw and intense and could temporarily blind a person because of the ultra-light emissions; or they might be called to an outdoor set erected under the glaring sun where the reflected light bounced onto the set from the great aluminum-covered boards that ringed the set. Then they would have to stand around while the cameraman checked his focus and the light and while other scenes were being filmed; and then, after hours of standing first on one foot and then the other, they would be called before the camera once again and register love, hate, fear, envy while the sound of the grinding crank clattered on and on. Such conditions must have been difficult for an actor at the best of times, but the stage actors accustomed to the dark, emotionally-charged space of the theater, to the audience out front, and to acting in sequence and building up a characterization, must have been bewildered and a little frightened.

This was the world that now surrounded Hopper, Tree and Fairbanks. Hopper's first Triangle film was *Don Quixote*, Tree's was *Macbeth* and Fairbanks' was *The Lamb*. They were released, respectively, in December of 1915, June of 1916 and September of 1915. All three projects were designed to exploit the unique talents of each actor. Fairbanks' film was ostensibly based on Bronson Howard's popular social comedy, *The New Henrietta*. Tree's vehicle drew upon his reputation as a Shakespearean actor, and Hopper's film drew upon his abilities to portray eccentric characters.

De Wolf Hopper's reaction to the world of filmmaking was decidedly unenthusiastic. He had to be up and on the lot in makeup by nine o'clock in the morning—a scandalous hour for the ordinarily nocturnal stage actor. His whole "working day" had to be rearranged because photography in those days was largely dependent upon available sunlight.[149] Like most stage actors Hopper was accustomed to building up a role in narrative continuity and the method of filming in bits and pieces, out of narrative sequence, was bewildering. He felt that he was no longer in control of his work. In words that foreshadow remarks made by Pirandello in 1929, Hopper noted that "the actor in the films is the creature of the director." He continued:

> The director is an important factor in the speaking stage, more so than the spectator often realizes, but in the pictures he dwarfs the players. They are puppets dancing at the ends of strings to his piping, seldom knowing anything of the sequence of the story they are enacting and little of its sense .... No more initiative is expected or desired of them than of a squad of soldiers being drilled by a top sergeant in the manual of arms.[150]

The absence of an audience was also disconcerting. A sense of a live audience had been a part of his training:

> The appeal of acting to those who practice it lies in the enkindling of the emotions of an audience and the reward of applause, laughter and tears then and there. This is the actor's daily bread, and the movies offer him a stone. One cheer in the hand, as far as I am concerned is worth ten thousand in the bush. I would not swap the audible applause of the couple in the last row upstairs for all the fan mail in the post-office.[151]

He was also soon to learn that filmmakers rarely respected a given story line. Cervantes had had Don Quixote die of brain fever, but Hollywood chose a more melodramatic and certainly more exciting visual death:

> ... it was down in the scenario that I was to be shot. So I fell mortally wounded, why or by whom I had not then the remotest idea, and contorted my face and limbs this way and that way as the megaphone told me to do."[152]

Don Quixote took twelve weeks to film and ran for seven reels (approximately eighty minutes). After its first run, the film dropped from sight without turning in a profit. There were critical complaints of Hopper's theatrical acting style, as might be expected. The New York *Times* reported that "He looked a bit too well-fed for the part and grimaced and used certain gestures with so great a frequency that they became monotonous."[153] Aside from the stagy acting style, however, the film demonstrated other, decidedly more cinematic characteristics. Double-exposures were used in the scene where the Don mistakes distant windmills for belligerent giants. Ghostly figures fade in and out in front of the mills as the audience shares the subjective viewpoint. Action scenes quicken the pace during the episode at the country inn where the Don mistakes the serving maid for his beloved Dulcinea. There is a knockout brawl that takes the Don and the landlord up and down the stairs and over the furniture in a series of swiftly edited shots. Similarly, the tilt with the windmill affords another action sequence. The Don's lance is caught in the sail and he is picked up and whirled about (or, to be accurate, the double for Hopper is picked up and whirled about). Subtle satire it may not be, the *Times* complained, and a successful job of acting for Hopper it may not be, but as a cinematic achievement it achieves a level of success far surpassing *Queen Elizabeth*.

Available informaton indicates that Hopper made only two more films for Triangle before returning to the stage. The first was called *Sunshine Dad*, about which no information can be found; the second was drawn from his popular stage monologue, "Casey at the Bat." The poem's slim story was expanded into a film that included a portrait of a small country town and a gallery of eccentric characters, including Casey (Hopper), whose famous strikeout was, apparently, intentionally engineered so the opposing team's pitcher could save face and keep the girl!

The experiences of Sir Herbert Beerbohm Tree were, if anything, even more disastrous than Hopper's. Like Hopper, Tree detested the working hours. But unlike Hopper, he remained firm to his habits and flatly refused to appear on the lot until after noon. This necessitated his working far into the night occasionally and thus caused the filmmakers to employ more artificial lighting than was usual for 1915. "Let no one imagine that the moving picture actor's fate is one of mere fun," Tree recalled later in 1916. "It is work, work of the hardest kind. Some days we labored for eighteen hours at a stretch, taking and retaking scenes until one was fairly ready to drop."[154]

Initially, Tree regarded motion pictures favorably. "I am a socialist in Art," he declared, "and I believe equally in the films and in the legitimate drama. The true artist uses the material that his epoch puts ready to his hands."[155] Moreover, the "photodrama" can perpetuate for posterity a sense of history and give it a new sense of pictoral narrative, "swift, sure, direct, and intensely dramatic."[156] But after facing the challenges of making *Macbeth* Tree had occasion to rue those words. For example, he found the scenarist to be a young woman still in her teens, Anita Loos, who had chosen to eliminate the drunken porter scene and had instead introduced into the script a mysterious "Lady Agnes." The film's director, John Emerson, refused to shoot artificial scenery and drops representing the Scottish heath; he preferred to find his authentic Scottish scenery around Los Angeles. Lack of privacy became a real nuisance for Tree. But worst of all, Tree, according to Anita Loos' memoirs, insisted upon speaking every word of Macbeth's long speeches. Filmmakers by now had learned to abridge such speeches into a couple of sentences for a subtitle. But Emerson was unable to dissuade Tree from saying every word before the camera; so he finally resorted to saving film by unplugging the camera's crank during the declamations and discreetly plugging it back in toward the end of the speech—all unbeknownst to Tree, of course.[157] And finally, Tree was used to moving in the circumscribed space of a proscenium theater's shallow stage. Before the camera, he continually moved out of the frame, grandly exaggerating his pantomime as if to make up for the lack of audible speech. So cavalier was he to the camera that he even turned his back upon it on a number of occasions.[158]

Working pace on the film slowed to a virtual halt and Monte Blue, who had doubled earlier for Hopper, was called to double for Tree. Blue allegedly doubled for Tree in every scene except those in which Tree's face would be recognizable. In other words, for $30 a week Blue appeared in the majority of the picture's scenes, doubling for an actor receiving $100,000.[159] No doubt the subsequent critical reviews lauding Tree's "athletic ability" pertained to Monte Blue rather than to Tree.[160]

After shooting was completed, Tree displayed an altered attitude toward the motion picture medium. This "strange new art," he was quoted as saying, "offered something very beautiful and wonderful—not precisely a play in the Shakespearean sense, perhaps, but a dramatic narrative of great power."[161] The film should not be considered an extension of the theater, he added: "I believe the art of the moving picture has not yet found its feet. It is likely that a natural cleavage between the spoken and pictorial drama will take place."[162]

One of *Macbeth*'s severest critics was none other than De Wolf Hopper. Hopper flatly stated that the film was not a success: "Tree was like a drowning man clutching at a straw and no straw there. Reduced to pantomime, interspersed with occasional emasculated quotations as captions ... *Macbeth* became a stick tea party salad set before a hungry harvest hand."[163] He cited the scenes following the death of Duncan as especially awkward, because too many titles had to be used to maintain the narrative clarity.

On the other hand, *Macbeth* did display on film a number of events that occur offstage in the play. Thus, the coronation and the killing of Macbeth are visualized in great detail. Double-exposure is used in some effective ghost and phantom scenes. And set-pieces like the witches' lair yield by striking images of the craggy ground and rocks under an overcast sky. The battle scenes at the end are swiftly edited as pots of boiling oil, catapults, rocks, lances and the moving Birnum Wood take over as far more effective actors than the human cast. Shakespeare's original play was filled with the drama of action, said Tree about the original play. "It is, perhaps, the least dependent upon words of any of the plays."[164] When the film itself was least dependent upon words, it was at its best; but when it depended too much upon Tree, it faltered.

Macbeth was not Tree's last American film appearance. After finishing his duties with the Shakespearean Tercentenary in New York, he returned to Triangle. Aitkin, apparently dissatisfied with the venerable star, sought to force Tree out of his contract by casting him in a "potboiler" called *The Old Folks at Home.* Tree described the project:

I am doing a perfectly awful picture here, but I suppose it has to be. I play the part of a virtuous American senator-farmer who would wear elastic side-spring boots and a toupee, has the old testament in one hand and the ace of diamonds up his sleeve. It is called "The Old Folks at Home" and is not entirely in my line.[165]

Actually, Tree did not even appear until near the end of the picture, although his name was liberally used in the advertising. Subsequently, he requested release from his Triangle contract and returned to England.

By contrast with Hopper and Tree, the career of Douglas Fairbanks blossomed at Triangle.[166] So successful a film actor did he become that the American public virtually forgot his earlier association with the stage. Fairbanks found in his first film, *The Lamb*, a whole world in which to stretch out and move. There are few resemblances between Fairbanks' Broadway success, *The Lamb*, and the film version. The play was about Wall Street finance and a ne'er-do-well young man who, in a moment of crisis, risks his entire fortune to save his father from bankruptcy. But beyond the fact that in the film a wealthy young idler achieves maturity in a moment of crisis, the similarities end. The scenario was credited to one "Granville Warwick" (a pseudonym of D.W. Griffith). It substitutes the wilds of Yaqui Indian-infested Arizona for Wall Street. The second half of the film is all action as Fairbanks leaps, tumbles and climbs his way through many adventures. Its use of masses of people in long shot, parallel editing during the rescue scene, outdoor locales and accelerated editing pace at key moments made it a cinematic experience that was both critically and financially successful. Taken in its entirety, *The Lamb* juxtaposes scenes in the first half that are dependent upon parlor comedy with scenes in the second half that are far removed from such a restricted form. Fairbanks himself moves from a stilted performance in the early scenes to a lithe and energetic superman in the later scenes. Thus, it is both interesting and instructive to see two styles of filmmaking and acting—one dependent upon an imitation of the proscenium stage and the other entirely independent of it—brought together.

In this latter aspect, it is typical of the more cinematic achievement that would dominate movies for the next ten years.

Notes

[1]"The Spectator," *The New York Dramatic Mirror*, February 21, 1912, p. 24.

[2]Joseph H. North, *The Early Development of the Motion Picture 1887-1909* (New York: Arno Press, 1973), p. 272.

[3]*Ibid.*, p. 272.

[4]Quoted in Joseph North, p. 277.

[5]"Many Notable Films," *The New York Dramatic Mirror*, February 13, 1909, p. 12.

[6]"The Assassination of the Duc de Guise," *The New York Dramatic Mirror*, February 26, 1909, p. 13.

[7]Robert Grau, *The Stage in the Twentieth Century* (New York: Broadway Publishing Co., 1912), p. 138.

[8]Quoted in John Allen, *Vaudeville and Film* (New York: Arno Press, 1980), p. 138.

[9]"The Spectator," *The New York Dramatic Mirror*, February 21, 1912, p. 29.

[10]"Reinhardt's Mystery Play in Pictures," *The New York Dramatic Mirror*, June 26, 1912, p. 22.

[11]"Spectator," *The New York Dramatic Mirror*, March 27, 1912, p. 24.

[12]"Spectator," *The New York Dramatic Mirror*, April 10, 1912, p. 26.

[13]"Spectator," *The New York Dramatic Mirror*, June 12, 1912, p. 24.

[14]"Bernardt As Queen Elizabeth," *The New York Dramatic Mirror*, July 16, 1912, p. 31.

[15]"Spectator," *The New York Dramatic Mirror*, July 3, 1912, p. 31.

[16]For a discussion of the development of film criticism and film-related journals, see Myron Lounsbury, *The Origins of American Film Criticism* (New York: Arno Press, 1973), p. 3.

[17]"Suggestions and Comments," *The New York Dramatic Mirror*, June 11, 1913, p. 23.

[18]"Spectator," *The New York Dramatic Mirror*, January 10, 1912, p. 28.

[19]"Spectator," *The New York Dramatic Mirror*, January 31, 1913, p. 51.

[20]"Spectator," *The New York Dramatic Mirror*, February 19, 1913, p. 25.

[21]"Comments and Suggestions," *The New York Dramatic Mirror*, July 2, 1913, p. 24.

[22]"The Spectator," *The New York Dramatic Mirror*, February 7, 1912, p. 28.

[23]"The Spectator," *The New York Dramatic Mirror*, February 7, 1912, p. 28.

[24]"The Spectator," *The New York Dramatic Mirror*, April 3, 1912, p. 24.

[25]"The Spectator," *The New York Dramatic Mirror*, March 13, 1913, p. 24.

[26]"The Spectator," *The New York Dramatic Mirror*, March 13, 1912, p. 24.

[27]"The Spectator," *The New York Dramatic Mirror*, October 23, 1912, p. 25.

[28]"Comments and Suggestions," *The New York Dramatic Mirror*, September 3, 1913, p. 25.

[29]"Theatrical Stars in Pictures," *The New York Dramatic Mirror*, July 10, 1912, p. 34.

[30]Arthur Hobson Quinn, *A History of the American Drama: From the Beginning to the Civil War* (New York: F.S. Crofts & Co., 1946), p. 103.

[31]John Fell, *Film and the Narrative Tradition* (University of Oklahoma Press, 1974), p. 14.

[32]The proliferation of "problem" plays on the American stage after 1900 is examined in Maxwell Bloomfield, "Muckraking and the American Stage: The Emergence of Realism, 1905-1917," *The South Atlantic Quarterly* (Spring 1967), pp. 165-178; "Is the American Theater Deteriorating?" *Current Opinion* (December 1913), pp. 413-4; "Is the Realism of the Stage Running to Seed?" *Current Literature* (January 1912), pp. 88-89; "The Rising Tide of Realism in the American Drama," *Current Opinion* (October 1913), pp. 250-51.

[33]Quoted in Arthur Hobson Quinn, p. 103.

[34]See Russel Nye, *The Unembarrassed Muse* (New York: Dial Press, 1970), pp. 157-8.

[35]2Montrose, J. Moses. *The American Dramatist* (Boston: Little, Brown, 1911), pp. 196-7.

[36]See John Fell, pp. 12-13; and Robert Heilman, "Tragedy and Melodrama: Speculations on Generic Form," in James L. Calderwood and Harold E. Toliver, eds., *Perspectives on Drama* (New York: Oxford Univ. Press, 1968), pp. 148-62.

[37]Quoted in Frank Rahill, *The World of Melodrama* (University Park, Pennsylvania: Pennsylvania State University Press, 1967), p. 278.

[38]See John Fell, pp. 18-24; and Nicholas Vardac, *Stage to Screen* (Cambridge: Harvard University Press, 1949), pp. 20-67.

[39]"*The Octoroon* on Film," *The New York Dramatic Mirror*, May 7, 1913, p. 26.

[40]John Fell, p. 18.

[41]See John Fell, p. 22; and Nicholas Vardac, pp. 23-24.

[42]"A Good Little Devil," *The New York Dramatic Mirror*, May 14, 1913, p. 26.

[43]Eric Bentley, *The Life of the Drama* (New York: Atheneum, 1967), p. 22.

[44]For a discussion of Chapelaine's formulations, see Julian M. Kaufman, *Appreciating the Theater* (New York: David McKay Company, 1971), p. 177; for a more general discussion of the "unity of time," see Pierre Corneille's "Discourse on the Three Unities (1660)," reprinted in James L. Calderwood and Harold E. Toliver, eds., *Perspectives on Drama*, pp. 210-13.

[45]For a critical rebuttal to the rule of the unity of place, see John Dryden, "An Essay on Dramatic Poesy," (1668) in James L. Calderwood and Harold E. Toliver, eds., pp. 214-29.

[46]For a discussion of how this and other academic tenets of the unities relate to Aristotle, see Francis Fergusson, *The Idea of a Theatre* (Princeton, New Jersey: Princeton University Press, 1949), pp. 229-34.

[47]Eric Bentley, p. 21.

[48]See Patti Gillespie, "Plays: Well-Constructed and Well-Made," *Quarterly Journal of Speech* (October 1972), pp. 313-21; Patti Gillespie, Stephen Stanton, ed., *Camille and Other Plays* (New York: Hill and Wang, 1957), pp. vii-xxxix; John Russel Taylor, *The Rise of the Well Made Play* (London: Methuen and Co., Ltd., 1967); and Maurice Valency, *The Flower and the Castle: An Introduction to Modern Drama* (New York: Macmillan, 1963), pp. 40, 62-68.

[49]Stephen Stanton, p. xiv.

[50]Helene Koon and Richard Switzer, *Eugene Scribe* (Boston: Twayne Publishers, 1980), p. 67.

[51]John Russel Taylor, pp. 27-29.

[52]Quoted in Arthur Hobson Quinn, *A History of the American Drama: From the Civil War to the Present Day* (New York: S.F. Crofts & Co., 1943), p. 44.

[53]Montrose J. Moses, p. 9.

[54]See Robert Hamilton Ball, ed., *The Plays of Henry C. De Mille, Written in Collaboration with David Belasco* (Princeton: Princeton University Press, 1941), pp. x-xxiii.

[55]For an appreciation of Clyde Fitch's plays and a comparison of them to the work of European playwrights (especially Henry Becque), see William Lyon Phelps, *Essays on Modern Dramatists* (New York: Macmillan, 1921), pp. 142-78.

[56]Quoted in Marvin Felheim, *The Theater of Augustin Daly* (Cambridge: Harvard University Press, 1956), p. 18.

[57]Daniel Frohman, *Daniel Frohman Presents* (New York: Claude Kendall and Willoughby Sharp, 1935), p. 275.

[58]"Daniel Frohman Talks Pictures," *Moving Picture World*, April 11, 1914, p. 194.

[59]A.R. Fulton, *Motion Pictures* (Norman: University of Oklahoma Press, 1960), p. 73.

[60]"Spectator," *The New York Dramatic Mirror*, July 17, 1912, p. 24.

[61]The story of Daniel Frohman's visit to Thomas Edison to obtain licensing from General Film to exhibit *Queen Elizabeth* and *The Prisoner of Zenda* has appeared in many volumes, including Frohman's autobiography. For a recent assessment of this episode, see I.G. Edmonds and Reiko Mimura, *Paramount Pictures* (San Diego and New York: A.S. Barnes and Co., 1980), p. 30.

[62]*Ibid.*, pp. 34-35.

[63]A detailed examination of *Queen Elizabeth* can be found in A.R. Fulton, *Motion Pictures*, pp. 62-72.

[64]Robert Grau, "A Word About Celebrated Stars in Photoplay," *Motion Picture Story Magazine*, February 1913, p. 127.

[65]Henry Knepler, *The Gilded Stage* (New York: William Morrow and Co., 1968), p. 287.

[66]"Engage J. Searle Dawley," *New York Dramatic Mirror*, June 11, 1913, p. 25.

[67]Jack Spears, "Edwin S. Porter," in *The Civil War on the Screen and Other Essays* (Cranbury, N.J.: A.S. Barnes, 1977), p. 173.

[68]For an account of O'Neill's long association with *The Count of Monte Cristo* see Dale Shaw, *Titans of the American Stage* (Philadelphia: Westminster Press, 1971), pp. 94-115.

[69]Anthony Hope's novel was dramatized by Edward R. Rice and staged by DanielFrohman at the Lyceum Theatre on September 4, 1895 for 112 performances. E.H. Sothern originally appeared in the dual role. James H. Hackett took over the roles in the 1896 revival at the Lyceum for 88 performances.

[70]Anthony Slide, *American Film History Prior to 1920* (Mettuchen, N.J.: Scarecrow Press, 1978), p. 43.

[71]James K. Hackett, "Hackett's Strong Arguments for Pictures," *Moving Picture World*, July 1914, p. 1701.

[72]*Ibid.*, p. 1701.

[73]Author's interview with Miles Kreuger in Los Angeles, May 24, 1979.

[74]Quoted in Kemp R. Niver, *Klaw and Erlanger: Famous Plays in Pictures* (Los Angeles: Locare Research Group, 1976), pp. 9-11. For information on another "Passion Play" that emulated the K&E film, see Joseph H. North, *The Early Development of the Motion Picture* (1887-1907) (New York: Arno Press, 1973), pp. 142-44.

[75]Benjamin Hampton, *History of the American Film Industry* (New York: Dover Press, 1970), p. 35.

[76]Quoted in Kemp R. Niver, p. 35.

[77]"Klaw and Erlanger New World Project," *The New York Dramatic Mirror*, March 19, 1913, p. 13.

[78]See Robert M. Henderson, *D.W. Griffith: The Years at Biograph* (New York: Farrar, Straus and Giroux, 1970), pp. 151-57. The Biograph studio chiefs objected to Griffith's insistence that *Judith* be longer than one or two reels in length. By the time Biograph began producing feature-length films with Klaw and Erlinger, Griffith had departed for Mutual. *Judith* was not released by Biograph until March of 1914.

[79]Terry Ramsaye, *A Million and One Nights* (New York: Simon and Schuster, 1964), p. 610.

[80]Kemp R. Niver, pp. 174-75.

[81]*Ibid.*, p. 175.

[82]"Review of The Billionaire," *The New York Dramatic Mirror*, April 8, 1914.

[83]Edmonds and Mimura, p. 38.

[84]"Lasky Gets Belasco Plays," *Moving Picture World*, June 6, 1914, p. 1412.

[85]"Jesse L. Lasky in Pictures," *Moving Picture World*, January 3, 1914, p. 35.

[86]*Ibid.*, p. 35.

[87]First-hand accounts of the filming of *The Squaw Man* can be found in William C. De Mille's *Hollywood Saga* (New York: Dutton, 1939); and Cecil B. De Mille's *Autobiography* (Englewood Cliffs, N.J.: Prentice-Hall, 1959), pp. 81-94. For an overview, see Edmonds and Mimura, pp. 38-47.

[88]For accounts of the original staging of these two plays, see Lise-Lone Marker, *David Belasco: Naturalism in the American Theatre* (Princeton: Princeton Univ. Press, 1975).

[89]*Ibid.*, p. 60.

[90]A. Nicholas Vardac, *Stage to Screen* (Cambridge: Harvard University Press, 1949), p. 131.

[91]W. Stephen Bush, "Belasco on Motion Pictures," *Moving Picture World*, June 13, 1914, p. 1513.

[92]*Ibid.*, p. 1513.   [93]*Ibid.*, p. 1513.   [84]*Ibid.*, p. 1514.   [95]*Ibid.*, p. 1514.   [96]*Ibid.*, p. 1514.

[97]"Jesse L. Lasky in Pictures," p. 35.

[98]"Making a Picture Director," *The New York Dramatic Mirror*, January 14, 1914, p. 62.

[99]*Ibid.*, p. 62.

[100]Louis Reeves Harrison, "Review of *The Squaw Man*," *Moving Picture World*, February 29, 1914, pp. 1068-69.

[101]Robert Grau, *The Theatre of Science*, p. 104.

[102]See Jerry Stagg, *The Brothers Shubert* (New York: Random House, 1968), p. 132.

103Advertisement in *Moving Picture World*, February 7, 1914, pp. 696-97.

104"Shuberts and World Film in Big Deal," *Moving Picture World*, June 20, 1914, p. 1700.

105Robert McLaughlin, p. 50.

106"Spectator," *New York Dramatic Mirror*, February 28, 1912, p. 32.

107"Review of *The Pit*", *Moving Picture World*, January 2, 1915 (no page number), for a collection of clippings at the Library of Congress.

108"Review of *The Pit*," *Motion Picture News*, January 2, 1915 (no page number), from a collection of clippings at the Library of Congress.

109"Review of *The Cub*," *Motion Picture News*, July 24, 1915 (no page number), from a collection of clippings at the Library of Congress.

110*Ibid*.

111"Review of *Salvation Nell*," *Moving Picture World*, August 28, 1915 (no page number), from a collection of clippings at the Library of Congress.

112See the photographs reprinted in Geoffrey Bell, "The Rise and Fall of the California Motion Picture Company," *American Classic Screen*, March/April 1981, pp. 15-23.

113A Nicholas Vardac, p. 187.

114*Ibid*., p. 187.   115*Ibid*., p. 27.

116Quoted in Anthony Slide, *American Film History Prior to 1920*, p. 91.

117*Ibid*., p. 91.   118*Ibid*., p. 94.   119*Ibid*., p. 93.

120Advertisement in *The New York Dramatic Mirror*, July 30, 1913, p. 26.

121See Montrose J. Moses, pp. 166-75; Ima Honaker Herrron, pp. 140-49; and Arthur Hobson Quinn, p. 174.

122Advertisement in *The New York Dramatic Mirror*, July 30, 1913, p. 26.

123"Review of *Arizona*," *The New York Dramatic Mirror*, September 24, 1913, p. 32.

124Letter to author from Paul Spehr of the Film Archives, Library of Congress, January 24, 1980.

125W. Stephen Bush, "Review of *The Great Divide*," *Moving Picture World*, December 18, 1915 (no page number), from a collection of clippings, Library of Congress.

126"Announcement of New Film Corporation," *Variety*, June 25, 1915, p. 19.

127Benjamin Hampton, pp. 141-42.

128"The Triangle Premiere," *The Theatre*, November 1915, p. 238.

129Benjamin Hampton, p. 144.

130Walter Prichard Eaton, "Actor-Snatching and the Movies," *American Magazine*, December 1915, p. 33.

131"Camera Drama Versus Spoken," *Current Opinion*, December 1915, p. 405.

132*Ibid*., p. 405.

133"Are Movies a Menace to Drama?" *Current Opinion*, May 1917, p. 331.

134Alan Dale, "Dramatic Critics and Photoplays," *Theatre Magazine*, June 1916, p. 334.

135*Ibid*., pp. 334, 346, 364.

136De Wolf Hopper, *Once a Clown, Always a Clown* (Boston: Little, Brown, 1927), p. 135.

137See Kalton Lahue, *Dreams for Sale* (Cranbury, N.J.: A.S. Barnes, 1971); Anthony Slide, *The Kindergarten of the Movies: A History of the Fine Arts Company* (Metuchen, N.J.: Scarecrow Press, 1981); and John Tibbetts, *The Triangle Film Corporation*, unpublished Master's Thesis, University of Kansas, 1975.

138De Wolf Hopper, p. 141. Hopper's salary is cited at a different amount $125,000 in "What They Really Get—Now!" *Photoplay*, March 1916, pp. 28-29.

139See John Tibbetts and James Welsh, *His Majesty the American: The Films of Douglas Fairbanks, Sr.* (Cranbury, New Jersey: A. S. Barnes, 1977), p. 21.

140Unidentified press clipping from a collection of clippings, New York Public Library, Lincoln Center, New York City.

141Leonard H. Knight, "Beerbohm Tree in America," *Theatre Survey*, May 1967, p. 39.

142Max Beerbohm, ed., *Herbert Beerbohm Tree* (London: Hutchinson and Company [1920?], p. 281.

143Anthony Slide, *American Film History Prior to 1920*, pp. 3-6.

144Anthony Slide, "Evolution of the Film Star," *Films in Review*, December 1974, p. 593.

[145]De Wolf Hopper, p. 142.

[146]Anita Loos, *A Girl Like I* (New York: Viking Press, 1966), p. 110.

[147]Alistaire Cooke, *The Making of a Screen Character* (New York: Museum of Modern Art, 1940), p. 14.

[148]Richard Savage, "Trying Out for the Movies,' *Theatre Magazine*, February 1916, p. 75.

[149]De Wolf Hopper, p. 157.

[150]*Ibid.*, p. 149.

[151]*Ibid.*, p. 170.

[152]*Ibid.*, p. 151.

[153]"Review of *Don Quixote*,"   The New York Times, December 20, 1915, p. 11.

[154]Edward Coward, "Sir Herbert Tree, England's Actor Knight," *Theatre Magazine*, May 1916, p. 291.

[155]Quoted in Leonard Knight, p. 43.

[156]Beerbohm Tree, "The Worthy Cinema," *The New York Times*, January 30, 1916, p. 8.

[157]Anita Loos, p. 110.

[158]Kalton Lahue, p. 134.

[159]*Ibid.*, p. 135.

[160]"Review of *Macbeth*," *The New York Times*, June 17, 1916, p. 28.

[161]Leonard Knight, p. 43.

[162]Max Beerbohm, ed., p. 282.

[163]De Wolf Hopper, p. 161.

[164]Beerbohm Tree, "The Worthy Cinema," p. 8.

[165]Kalton Lahue, p. 135.

[166]See John Tibbetts and James Welsh, *His Majesty the American*, pp. 19-36.

The beautiful "Pirate Ship" set from RKO's film version of the Ziegfeld smash, *Rio Rita* (1929). (courtesy Academy of Motion   Picture Arts and Sciences)

Chapter Four
More Feature Attractions:
Theater/Film Collaborations, 1926-1930

The premiere in New York on November 16, 1928, of Paramount's first all-talking feature-length film, *Interference,* was strikingly similar in significance to the premiere of *Queen Elizabeth* sixteen years earlier. Both films ushered in a new cycle of feature-length theatrical films for the silent and sound periods, respectively. Both were derived from prestigious, "well made" dramas; both were made under the aegis of Adolph Zukor and Daniel Frohman (whose Famous Players company had by now merged with Jesse L. Lasky and other companies under the banner of Paramount); and both were introduced to "first night" audiences on broadway by theatrical impresario Daniel Frohman. The only substantial difference between the two films, besides the element of sound, was that *Queen Elizabeth* had been a foreign-made feature film exported to an America still hesitant about the commercial and artistic possibilities of the feature-length format. *Interference,* on the other hand, was American-made, and it resumed the feature film format that had been temporarily interrupted by the period of the synchronized-sound short films, 1926-1928.

In his filmed, spoken prologue to *Interference,* Daniel Frohman described the significance of the new feature-length talking theatrical pictures. He renewed the same philosophy he had espoused with Famous Players in 1912: the feature-length film could help elevate the prestige of motion pictures; and the movie medium could serve as a vehicle for disseminating theatrical events all over the world. Frohman's speech, spoken from the screen, should be quoted at length:

It was only last winter that this play [*Interference*] we are about to see tonight was enacted on the boards of the Lyceum Theatre. It was presented by the company which was founded by my brother, the late Charles Frohman. Tonight, carrying on the Frohman tradition, I once more welcome you on behalf of the greatest era in entertainment—an era made possible through this miraculous invention, the talking picture. No more will our best plays be confined to the few big cities. These plays, with their stirring drama enhanced by the richness of the human voice, will go to the whole world.[1]

Usually, any discussion of the development of the feature-length talking picture—especially the theatrical feature—begins with Warner Brothers' *The Jazz Singer,* which preceeded *Interference* by a full year. *Interference,* if it is now remembered at all, is dismissed as tedious and static and of no consequence to the development of synchronized sound.[2] Yet, I do not consider *The Jazz Singer* as a *talking* picture at all. Harry M. Geduld's *The*

Birth of the Talkies, which contains the most thorough analysis of *The Jazz Singer* extant, emphasizes that synchronized speech occurs in only two brief sequences. In the first, a nightclub scene, we hear only Jolson's voice; in the second, where Jolson converses with his mother (Eugene Besserer), there are no more than about 300 words spoken. The rest of the film, aside from the singing sequences, employs standard silent film inter-titles and the techniques of fluid camera movement and crisp editing typical of the sophisticated techniques of silent film making.[3] *The Jazz Singer* and the many other part-talkies that subsequently followed from Warner Brothers and other studios during the next ten months came to be known as "goat gland" pictures.[4] Their talking sequences were literally "injected" into otherwise silent pictures to give them new box office life during the sound revolution. These hybrids included, from Warner Brothers, *Glorious Betsy* (April, 1928), based on the play by Rida Johnson Young (1908); *The Lion and the Mouse* (June, 1928), based on the play by Charles Klein (1905); and from Metro-Goldwyn-Mayer, *Alias Jimmy Valentine* (November, 1929), based on the play by Paul Armstrong (1910). Edmund Goulding, a film director for MGM, summed up the situation in 1929 when he described them as "silent motion pictures accompanied by synchronized, but wholly mechanical and artificial sounding voices or instrumental music.... They are scarcely even examples of that which is to come."[5]

Interference, on the other hand, provided the stage play for the first time with a feature-length, all-talking format. It was a *talking* picture from beginning to end. The techniques and methods of silent filmmaking, as they had developed by 1927, had little or nothing to do with how *Interference* was made and how it looked to audiences. It was, in short, a film completely representative of a new technology and of how that technology translated theatrical events into celluloid.

Other all-talking theatrical features soon followed. Late in November, Universal released *The Last Warning*, based on a play by Thomas F. Fallon; nearly at the same time MGM released *The Bellamy Trial*, based on a play by Frances Noyes Hart (1927). In February, 1929, the Fox Film Corporation released *The Ghost Talks* based on Max Marcin and Edward Hammond's *Badges* (1924). In April, United Artists presented Mary Pickford in *Coquette*, based on the play by George Abbott and Ann Preston Bridgers (1927). That same month Paramount followed its own *Interference* with another theatrical feature, *The Letter*, based on the play by Somerset Maugham, which had first been staged in America at the Morosco Theatre in New York in September 1927. Between April and the end of 1929 several filmed versions of Broadway musical shows and revues also appeared. These included Warner Brothers' *The Desert Song*, based on the popular operetta that had been playing in New York since November, 1926; Radio-Keith-Orpheum

RKO's *Rio Rita* based on the Ziegfeld production that had been playing since February 1927.

It is amazing how quickly the motion picture industry changed and grew as the feature-length sound films were gaining in number and popularity during 1928-30. *Variety* reported that the movie industry had taken fifteen years to create a production structure valued at $65,000,000; but in only eight months since mid-1928, it had expended another $20,000,000 for the talking picture.[6] By the end of 1928, over 1,000 theaters had converted to sound, many of them formerly reserved only for legitimate theater. For example, in New York's Times Square, *Variety* reported in April, 1929, eleven legitimate houses were showing feature-length talking pictures at the standard top price of $2 a seat. There was not a single "live" legitimate attraction between forty-second and fifty-third streets.[7] The major studios, after experimenting with theatrical short films in 1926-28, were, by March, 1929, predicting that approximately two-thirds of their future features would have synchronized sound.[8] Many of these would have theatrical origins. And, in fact, the film industry bought the rights to eighteen new Broadway plays and musicals in 1927-28; the next year the industry bought nearly forty plays and musicals.[9] Warner Brothers led the way with a predicted output for 1929-30 of thirty features, all of which would have synchronized-sound; RKO predicted an output of thirty features, all of them talking; Paramount and MGM announced that three-fourths of their next sixty features would be talking; and United Artists, Fox, Universal, and Columbia all announced schedules indicating that at least half of their output would be talking.[10] Meanwhile, the statistics for average weekly motion picture attendance reflected a growing trend. Attendance went from fifty-seven million per week in 1927, to sixty-five million in 1928, to eighty milion in 1929, and, finally, to ninety million in 1930.[11] It was obvious that the synchronized-sound feature was responsible for a booming box office.

Studios developed a system for "scouting" new Broadway shows. Studio representatives would attend out-of-town tryouts and opening nights on Broadway—judging the productions solely on their worth as a potential motion picture. Robert McLaughlin, in his study of the economic interactions of stage and screen, has noted that story editors of the studios judged plays by the following rules: First, they would write synopses of the action and a detailed report of the play, including its merits and faults as possible film material, and rush the reports to Hollywood. If the top story editors were interested, the studio obtained a copy of the playscript. And last, a final decision was made on the value of the play as a film property. If a purchase was decided upon, the property could sell for as little as $35,000 or for as much as $255,000.[12]

By May 1, 1929, *Variety* estimated that over 205 stage people were working in the major studios in Hollywood and New York. This number was broken down into groups of fifty-one playwrights, seventeen stage and dance directors, sixty-four actors, thirty-one actresses, and forty-two song writers, musical directors, and composers.[13]

Between the premiere of *Interference* and the end of the 1920s, many of the synchronized-sound theatrical features displayed the same formal correlations with proscenium staging that I have already noted in the silent short films and features; i.e., the spatial field of the motion picture screen was treated as if it were the playing space within the proscenium frame of a stage platform. Robert Herring, an English critic writing about these American theatrical sound films, summed this up when he noted that they "successfully put the movies inside a proscenium."[14]

What is most immediately apparent about these filmed plays is their relative fidelity to their theatrical origins. The film medium again served primarily as a recording medium for theatrical events. Commentary of the day demonstrates this. While preparing his film version of James M. Barrie's playlet, *Half an Hour,* William de Mille announced that he would faithfully preserve the action and dialogue of the stage play; that he would *not* "add situations, sequences, or elaborations" to further the story.[15] When Paramount released Somerset Maugham's *The Letter* in 1929 with stage star Jeanne Eagels in her screen debut, *Variety* praised it for its fidelity to the original production: "Any summary of the picture must record that the merits of the screen production belong to the original play, written for and played on the stage." The reviewer continued, the film itself contributed only "atmosphere," which is to say that the production was "entirely a transcription of a stage work and the cinema version does little to make the subject matter its own."[16] Again and again, theatrical features of this early talkie period were cited for this faithfulness. Released by the William Fox studios, *Thru Different Eyes,* a courtroom drama by Milton E. Gropper and Edna Sherry, released in April, 1929, "follows the play in every detail...."[17] MGM's *The Trial of Mary Dugan* (March, 1929), based on the popular drama by Bayard Veiller, was described by Mordaunt Hall in the New York *Times:* "...with the exception of a few scenes, this is virtually a reproduction of the play."[18] RKO's *Rio Rita,* based on the Ziegfeld production of 1927, was "virtually an audible animated photographic conception of the successful Ziegfeld show."[19] And *Disraeli,* a starring vehicle for George Arliss, from Warner Brothers, was described in The New York *Morning Telegraph* as "no more than an audible photograph of the stage piece."[20] The prevailing attitude on the part of the critics toward these films was grudging tolerance. If a play like *Bulldog Drummond* (1925) was preserved intact on the screen in the version released by United Artists, noted *Variety* in May, 1929, it "seems the best, in an all-dialog."[21]

While the use of written intertitles in early theatrical silent films had all too often overwhelmed the visual dimension of the filmed play, now the use of recorded speech all but replaced physical action. Thus, these early theatrical sound features displayed a resumption of long shots, tableaux-groupings of immobile actors, shallow-depth playing areas, and the exaggerated acting styles characteristic of the filmed plays of 1912. In other words, now that the movies could talk, filmmakers seemed determined to allow the players to remain fixed in an unchanging medium shot and talk their heads off. In *The Doctor's Secret*, wrote Herbert Cruikshank in *Motion Picture* in 1929, there was nothing but "long photographic discussions between characters."[22] When George M. Cohan's *The Home Towners* (1926) reached the screen in a Warner Brothers production late in 1928, the dialogue exchanges occurred during stiff tableaux where the characters "just grouped in front of the microphone and wished they were on the stage...."[23] Referring to the Fox production in 1929 of Henry Arthur Jones' playlet, "The Knife," *Variety* noted that "people stand still and talk" with "never a raised voice or a spirited gesture."[23]   And George Abbott's play *Coquette*, when filmed by United Artists early in 1929, was similarly greeted by the pronouncement that it had "a repeated tendency to become too talkie and motionless."[24] Now that dialogue was possible on the screen, *Variety* summed up in March, 1929, "progress comes out of the spoken word instead of from essential action, which is strictly an attribute of the stage."[25]

Commentators greeted the presence of Broadway stars in these films with mixed feelings. On the one hand, as a New York *Times* writer said about *The Letter,* their presence was a distinct benefit: "It is the first offering of its kind in which there are true passages of life-like drama, a fact that is chiefly due to the abilities of the players who are all well known to the stage."[26] Even when the acting style seemed a bit too broad for the intimacy of the camera, noted the New York *Morning Telegraph* with reference to George Arliss in *Disraeli,* the style was "robust and forthright, the acting of the new-old masters who earned universal recognition for the American stage in the days when the rest of the world considered us barbarians."[27] On the other hand, there were dissenting voices. When Robert McWade brought his stage role in *The Home Towners* to the screen the New York *Times* noted: "Mr. McWade was given to shouting on the stage, and his voice is even more stentorian in this shadow translation."[28]

We already know that theatrical films often employed artificial sets and props. This was no less true in the early talking features, since they were filmed entirely inside cramped sound stages. When Paramount constructed sound stages at its production plant in Astoria, New York, special care was taken so that the sets could be easily transported by overhead trolleys from one part of the studio to another. They had to be light, portable, easily dismantled and quickly reconstructed, and interchangeable for use in many different films.[29] This practice was reminiscent of the standardized sets for the travelling shows of the 19th century. Artificial scenery, then, was a conspicuous part of most of the theatrical features of 1928-30, from musical films like *The Desert Song* and *Rio Rita* to dramas like *Disraeli* and *Coquette*. Referring to this situation, Robert Herring said that the presence of synchronized sound now only *reinforced* this detectable artifice, showing up what he called the "studioness of the sets." This was a fatal mistake, he warned, somewhat ungrammatically: "The real noises among cardboard walls and canvas deserts won't do. The better the sounds, the more false are the sets going to be shown up...."[30]

It is apparent from the plays referred to that, excepting for the moment the musical productions and reviews, filmmakers were once again drawing upon well-made plays and melodramas. In 1930 *Close Up* magazine reported that "the microphone gives us talk, and it rules out action and much change of scene," so that current films merely "talked and talked in one room."[31] Such conditions, coupled with the prestige always attached to well made plays, made them ideal for translation into feature-length films with sound. Their relative adherence to the unities of time, space and action was also advantageous to a medium confined at this point to indoor sound stages. Historian Ron Haver notes that the play *Interference*, for example, was ideal for the early talkies—"it was suspenseful, had a small cast, and only three main sets, which could be easily confined within the confines of the crude sound stage."[32] Likewise, Barrie's "Half an Hour" (which became Paramount's *The Doctor's Secret*) was confined to one set—"the Garson mansion near Park Lane"—and to a span of just one-half hour in time. Louis Parker's *Disraeli* (1911), which Warner Brothers brought to the screen in October 1929, was a kind of latter-day *Men and Women* in its preoccupations with the intrigues of money and power that motivated its characters. It had no physical action whatever save that which was conveyed by the dialogue. Elmer Rice's *Street Scene*, the Pulitzer Prize winning play of 1929, which King Vidor brought to the screen for United Artists late in 1930, had but one set, the exterior of a walk up apartment house in a "mean quarter" of New York, and action which spanned less than twenty-four hours. Another drama, Philip Barry's *Holiday*, which Pathé filmed in June 1930, confined the action to two floors of the Edward Seton house; the time span was but one month. And George Abbott's *Coquette* was also confined to a single set, the living room of Norma Besant.

Melodramas were also popular with filmmakers. In May 1929, *Variety* reported "that at present the talking screen is flooded with the trial picture for the drama ...."[33] While melodramas of regional color and open-air adventure had been very popular with filmmakers in 1912-15, this new kind of melodrama was much more confined. In his extensive examination of melodrama on Broadway during the 1920's, Edmond M. Gagey in *Revolution in American Drama* concluded that the melodrama changed in the late twenties from outdoor locales to claustrophobic dramas of trials, spies, police actions and racketeers set in courtrooms, night clubs and police stations. Gagey cited as examples Bayard Veiller's *The Trial of Mary Dugan* (1927), Philip Dunning and George Abbott's *Broadway* (1927), Bartlett Cormack's *The Racket* (1927), Louis Weitzenkorn's *Five Star Final* (1930) and John Wray's *Nightstick* (1927)—all of which were made into films by 1931.[34] Thus, like the well made plays, these melodramas were suited to the small sound stages. In their recent examination of MGM's *The Trial of Mary Dugan*, Al Manski and Dan Navarro note that "in those experimental days of sound, many plots had to focus on indoor scenes and what more suitable setting than a courtroom?"[35] Accordingly, for most of its 113-minute length, *The Trial of Mary Dugan* is a one-set film production, just as most of the film version of *Nightstick* (*Alibi*) is restricted to interrogation rooms and nightclubs.

Another benefit to filmmakers with all these plays was the presumption that they would add prestige to the movie industry. This had been a prime factor in the selection of plays as a basis for the silent theatrical films; now, in the sound era after the motion picture had long been established as a powerful entertainment medium, this ambition, while not so pronounced, was still very much in evidence. *Interference*, for example, was praised by Daniel Frohman as an example of America's "best plays," while the New York *Times* praised it as a "melodrama of the more sophisticated type, without any shouting or screaming."[36] George Arliss, the eminent stage actor who appeared in several films of his plays for Warner Brothers late in 1929 and 1930, recalled in his autobiography that attracting "respectable" audiences was a primary reason behind Warner Brothers' securing his services:

> I believe that the plays I was doing in the theatre might be looked upon as "high-brow," and I was regarded as an actor devoted to that exalted plane of the drama. This was the time when everybody didn't go to the movies—the prehistoric days .... There is no doubt that a considerable percentage of the people that came to see me in the theater never went to the movie-tones at all [sic] .... The Warner Brothers realized that these lost sheep must be collected and brought into the fold .... And that was why they came to think of me, Harry Warner told me afterwards.[37]

Such films, Arliss wrote in 1930, could "set the standard of good English, good diction, perfect delivery of speech." At the same time, viewers who rarely went to the legitimate drama, "will learn through audible pictures to know stars they never had a chance of seeing before, and this will mean many more patrons for the legitimate theater ...."[38] For some viewers, these films did indeed raise cinema to a higher plane. The New York *Evening Post*, for example, observed about *Disraeli*: "The picture, of course, is one of the few works of art produced in the cinema world."[39]

Many prominent and respected stage stars followed Arliss to the movie studios. Hal Skelly's characterization of "Skid" in Watters and Hopkins'

Burlesque (1927) was repeated for the Paramount cameras in *The Dance of Life* (1929); Dennis King duplicated his appearance in *The Vagabond King* (1925) for Paramount in 1930; James Gleason and Lucille Webster recreated their roles in *The Shannons of Broadway* (1927) for United Artists in 1929; Eddie Cantor followed Florenz Ziegfeld to Hollywood in 1929 to duplicate his role in *Whoopee*; Hershell Mayall and Minna Gombell converted their success in *The Great Power* (1928) into a film for MGM in 1929; Mary Lawler repeated her success in *Good News* (1927) for MGM in 1930; Leslie Howard and Beryl Mercer brought their *Outward Bound* (1924) to Warner Brothers in 1930. And, on a less "elevated" plane, the Marx Brothers filmed their stage production of *The Cocoanuts* for Paramount in 1929.

The major studios in 1928-30 produced 511 films during the 1927-30 period, 141 of which were based on stage plays and musical shows. The information and statistics in succeeding pages come from a number of sources—including *The American Film Institute Film Catalog, 1921-30*, the *Library of Congress Copyright Entries, 1912-39* and the series of "Best Plays" volumes compiled by Burns Mantle. My conclusion is that at least twenty-eight percent of all the feature-length talkies during this period was based on theatrical events. This is a high percentage, especially when it is remembered that all of the studios included within their total output a body of "programmer" films like westerns and serials. (In 1930 alone Universal produced, out of its total output of thirty-five talkies, eleven westerns.) If the programmer material is deducted from the total of all the studios, it can be seen that the theatrical film represents a high percentage of total output indeed.

Warner Bros.: From Jolson to Arliss

From the premiere of its part-talkie *The Jazz Singer*, on October 6, 1927 to the premiere of the all-talking *Outward Bound* on November 19, 1939, Warner Bros. studio released ninety-seven feature-length talkies and part-talkies. Of that number, thirty-two were either based on stage dramas and musical shows or were original revues patterned after Broadway models. Thirty-three percent of the total output, therefore, was theatrical in nature. In 1927 *The Jazz Singer* was the studio's only synchronized-sound theatrical feature; in 1928 sixteen talkies were released, four of which were theatrical features; in 1929, thirty-nine talkies appeared, sixteen of which were theatrical features; and in 1930 forty-one talkies appeared, twelve of which were theatrical features. Warner's first *all-talking* theatrical feature was *The Home Towners*, which was released on November 3, 1928. It was based on a play by George M. Cohan that had been produced at the Hudson Theater on August 23, 1926 for sixty-four performances. Warner's first film version of a musical show was *The Desert Song*, which premiered on April 8, 1929. It was based on the operetta by Otto Harbach, Oscar Hammerstein II, Frank Mandel and Sigmund Romberg which had been staged at the Casino Theatre on November 30, 1926 for 465 performances.

Encouraged by the success of three part-talking theatrical features—*The Jazz Singer* (based on Samson Raphaelson's production of 1925), *Glorious Betsy* (based on Rida Johnson Young's production of 1908) and *The Lion and the Mouse* (based on Charles Klein's production of 1905)—Warner's pushed ahead to increase its production of filmed plays and its complement of theater personnel. In March, 1928, *Variety* reported that "Warner Bros. are negotiating for the Vitaphoning of successful Broadway stage productions. By next season, it is understood, two or three legit hits, with the original New York casts, will be released throughout the country as talking pictures."[40] The first stage play to be filmed, it was reported, was to be *The Trial of Mary Dugan*. When the deal fell through, Elmer Rice's stage drama *On Trial* (1914) was substituted and premiered late in December 1928. Moreover, in an effort to attract Broadway stars to the screen, Warner's "submitted proposals to some of the best known legit stars on Broadway to appear in talkers." The studio let it be known that "the demand for legitimate players in talking pictures will be considerable." Included also were to be writers "with a knowledge of the theatre for the construction of effective speaking lines."[41] As of July 1928, there were eight directors and actors with prior stage experience under contract. These people included directors Lloyd Bacon, Archie Mayo and Bryan Foy; and actors Helen and Dolores Costello, Conrad Nagel, Myrna Loy and Louise Fazenda. Within the next twelve months that number had increased to twenty-three, now including playwright Arthur Caesar; stage director Bryan Foy; actors Al Jolson, George Arliss, Frank Fay, Ted Lewis, Joe E. Brown; actresses Charlotte Greenwood, Bette Davis; and songwriters Al Dubin, Harry Akst, Herman Ruby, Oscar Hammerstein II and Sigmund Romberg.[42]

One of the most important producers of theatrical features was Bryan Foy. I have already mentioned his role in the development of Warner's theatrical short films. Foy's vaudeville experience was most useful in this endeavor. At the rate of four shorts a week, Foy had produced approximately 600 by the end of 1930, many of which were photographic records of the famous vaudeville performers of the day. A direct outgrowth of his experience with the sketches, Foy's *The Lights of New York*, the first all-talking motion picture, premiered on July 8, 1928. For the first time in movies, the spoken dialogue, rather than written titles, carried the story. While not directly based on a stage play, its underworld story was characteristic of the spate of crime thrillers currently on Broadway. Moreover, Foy insisted that the film's writers and actors were vaudeville trained. *The Lights of New York* was written by Hugh Herbert and Murray Roth, two sketch writers from vaudeville. Starring were Eugene Pallette and Cullen Landis, who had had stage experience. The supporting cast, as *Variety* phrased it, "was as vaudeville as stealing bows."[43]

These players included Jere Delaney, Walter Percival, Tom McGuire, Tom Dugan, Harry Downey and Gladys Brockwell.

Before 1930, Foy directed two more features that were based on stage plays. *The Home Towners* was released on November 3, 1928 and was based on a recent play by George M. Cohan. And, late in 1929, he directed *The Royal Box*, based on Charles Coughlan's dramatization of *Kean*, by Alexander Dumas. These films were archetypes in the development of theatrical films at Warner Bros. although they all suffered from stage-bound qualities. It is unfortunate that so little information is available today concerning Foy's career. Inquiries at the Academy of Motion Picture Arts and Sciences and at the Warner Bros. archive at the Wisconsin Center for Film and Theater Research have yielded little beyond what I have already reported. After these features Foy abandoned a directing career and became a producer for Warner's during the 1930s of the "B," or program picture, unit. He went on to produce an estimated twenty-six features with low budgets. But of his value to Warner Bros. there can be no doubt. His contacts with entertainers, his knowledge of stagecraft, and his ambitions to bring dramatic dialogue to the sychronized-sound film, gave the studio an advantage over its competitors early in the talkie period.

Of all the actors who came to Warner's during this time, certainly none was more prestigious than George Arliss. As Arthur L. Marble noted in his protrait of Arliss, "he has done more than any other actor to win assent for the union of stage and screen."[44] Arliss' career pivoted around three starring vehicles on the stage: the title role in Louis Parker's *Disraeli* (1911), the evil Rajah in William Archer's *The Green Goddess* (1921) and the elderly gentleman in John Galsworthy's *Old English* (1924). Warner Bros. had signed Arliss to make talking pictures of these plays in an attempt to elevate the motion picture drama of the time. Accordingly, he appeared in *Disraeli*, released on October 2, 1929 (his wife, Florence, with whom he had played in the original production in 1911, duplicated her role in the film as Disraeli's wife). On February 13, 1930 Warners released, *The Green Goddess*. And on August 21, 1930 the studio released *Old English*. These three films, especially *The Green Goddess*, blended touches of melodrama with the refined surface and form of the well made play. There were only a handful of exterior shots in the whole series. The dialogue, for the most part, was retained from the original plays. And the staging kept the players in a frontal posture to the camera, arranged in a plane parallel to the lens. In the next chapter I will examine in more detail the film and stage versions of *The Green Goddess*.

Warners produced many musical films. Its biggest musical star was, of course, Al Jolson. After Jolson's success in *The Jazz Singer*, he appeared in an even more successful vehicle, *The Singing Fool* (September 19, 1928). Although not based on a particular play or show, *The Singing Fool* was tailored to Jolson's reputation as a singer and it gave him the chance to sing three smash hits, "Sonny Boy," "There's a Rainbow Round My Shoulder" and "I'm Sitting on Top of the World." The film represented the peak of Jolson's film career, which would extend through the middle thirties. Jolson did two other musical films for Warners during 1928-30 that were based on Broadway shows—*Mammy*, released on March 20, 1930, which was based on Irving Berlin and James Gleason's *Mr. Bones* (1928); and *Big Boy*, released on September 6, 1930, based on Harold Atteridge's musical (1925).

Other musical productions included the first all-color (two-color Technicolor) musical revue, *On With the Show* (May, 1929). Later in November of that year another revue, *Show of Shows*, appeared, featuring seventy-seven players. The first was a "backstage" story that cleverly juggled two narrative lines—one backstage and the other involving the production going on onstage. This device became the model for dozens of subsequent musicals, most notably *42nd Street* in 1932. The second film brought to the talking picture the form of the revue, complete with master of ceremonies, curtain divisions for each act and a variety of musical and dramatic numbers. As for adaptations of Broadway musicals, Warners' first entry was *The Desert Song*, 1929, based on the operetta by Harbach, Hammerstein, Mandel and Romberg (1926). It was followed by *The Golddiggers of Broadway* in August 1929, based on Avery Hopwood's comedy (1919). Then came *So Long Letty* in October 1929, with Charlotte Greenwood repeating her original role in the 1916 production; *Song of the West* on February 26, 1930, based upon Laurence Stallings' and Oscar Hammerstein's *Rainbow* (1928); *Hold Everything* on March 20, 1930, based on the musical by Buddy De Sylva, John McGowan, Ray Henderson and Lew Brown (1928); *Golden Dawn* on June 14, 1930, based on the musical by Hammerstein, Harbach, Kalman and Herbert Stothart (1927); *Oh! Sailor, Behave!* on August 16, 1930, based on Elmer Rice's *See Naples and Die* (1930).

Because many of these films had songs like the popular "Sonny Boy," Warners initiated a policy that made songwriting a vital part of the filmmaking process. The song writer of Tin Pan Alley usually had a difficult time promoting a song and keeping it before the public. There was a big difference in writing for motion pictures, however, as *Photoplay Magazine* reported in September 1929: "To a song-writer there is no greater comfort than the knowledge that once a number is set in a movie—it *stays* in.... Within a month of a film's release, the average motion picture song with commercial possibilities will sell from 100,000 to 500,000 copies, plus an equal number of records." Before the advent of talking and singing pictures, the writer continued, the song "would be fortunate to sell 30,000 copies in three months."[45] Reportedly, the first song written especially for the motion picture to be sung as part of its action was Louis Silvers' "Mother I Still Love You." The team of De Sylva-Brown-Henderson demonstrated to Warners that this concept could not only contribute to musical films but could also yield great profits to everyone involved. After the success of "Sonny Boy" in *The Singing Fool*, therefore, Warner Bros. "decided not to overlook any future possibilities" and purchased one of the oldest music publishing firms in America, Witmarks, Inc. All future songs written for Warner Bros. films by De Sylva-Brown-Henderson, for example, would be controlled by Warners and Witmarks, the royalties to be split between them.[46] Within months, as other studios more prominently featured original songs in their musical films, other alliances between studios and music publishers resulted.

In the desire to acquire stage properties, Warner's displayed such zeal that the studio tried to secure the screen rights to certain Broadway plays and musicals *before* they were put into production. *Variety* reported on September 19, 1928 that Warner's wanted to finance productions of the Shuberts in order to acquire advance rights to them. In addition, the Shubert houses "could be alternately employed for special dialog full-length films or legit stage attractions."[37] This promised a double benefit for the studio—a ready-made supply of theatrical properties to put on film and a chain of legitimate houses in which to exhibit them. "An offer nowadays by a picture firm to bankroll a stage producer is very common," *Variety* had noted a month earlier. The idea was to promote stage plays that "would be easily adaptable to the dialog screen." The writer continued that the "dialog picture maker calculates it could produce a stage play, erect prestige for it by a Broadway run, and [photograph] the play, sending it on the road, but in the picture houses ...."[48] It was a gamble, to be sure, but at the high prices commanded by many of the legitimate producers in selling properties to the movies, it was likely to save money.

However, Warner's plan proved to be in direct violation of the provision concerning screen rights to dramatic properties written into the Minimum Basic Agreement by the Dramatists Guild in 1925. In his detailed examination of the creation of the Minimum Basic Agreement, Robert McLaughlin in *Broadway and Hollywood* notes that one of the most important aspects of this agreement had been that Hollywood "could not under any circumstances secure film rights to [plays] before the Broadway opening." Only after a stage production had opened and had had a run for three weeks could film companies bid for screen rights. In other words, just because a film company backed a show, it could not have an advantage in the bidding for screen rights. McLaughlin concludes that this agreement "guaranteed an open market for film rights and also allowed for either the author or producer to submit or secure bids, or bid on their own behalf."[49]

The proposed Warner's/Shubert agreement violated the Minimum Basic Agreement, and the Dramatists Guild issued a warning to all studios that these deals should be terminated. Action was taken in 1930 when playwrights Herbert Fields and Cole Porter were found guilty of signing a pre-production contract with the producer of their play, *Fifty Million Frenchmen*, in an arrangement allowing the backer, Warner Bros., to secure the rights for a price considerably less than would have been possible on an open market. As a result of this action, explains McLaughlin, it was thought "that the suspensions and fines would stop future violations of the MBA. It was also thought that this action would slow the rising tide of film financing of Broadway shows, because by discouraging producers and playwrights from entering into these pre-production deals, film companies would no longer have reason to back plays."[50]

The Fox Film Corporation: "A Stage Stock Company for the Screen"

Since 1927, the Fox Film Corporation had been making newsreels and theatrical shorts with its sound-on-film process, Movietone. The regular inclusion of these short films in movie programs of the time did as much as Warner Bros.' Vitaphone to establish synchronized-sound films as a familiar part of the moviegoing experience by 1929. As a producer of sound features during 1928, the Fox Film Corporation was second only to Warner Bros.— although these films were either only part-talkies or silent films with synchronized music score and sound effects added. In 1929, forty-six sound features were released, eight of which were based on stage plays. Of the ninety-two talkies and part-talkies made between 1928 and 1930, twenty were theatrical films, comprising almost twenty-two percent of the total. The first all-talking theatrical feature was *The Ghost Talks* (February 24, 1929), based on Max Marcin and Edward Hammond's *Badges* (1924); near the end of 1930 came *Scotland Yard* (October 19, 1930), based on Denison Clift's play (1929).

Fox led all other studios in employing theatrical personnel. Because of the Movietone shorts, Fox had established an efficient method of screen-testing Broadway talent. In fact Fox, through its general manager, W.R. Sheehan, had been one of the earliest Broadway raiders, signing up Fanny Brice, Gertrude Lawrence and Beatrice Lillie in 1928. Whatever stars like these thought of the new medium of sound, they apparently could not resist the money, as another Fox star, George Jessel, admitted: "It's simply a business proposition with me. I want the money. It's not ideals or anything else. I can't honestly tell you that I have entered motion pictures to express a suppressed desire, or to make people happy."[51] At Fox, Jessel went on to make *Love, Live, and Laugh* (November 3, 1929), based on Leroy Clemens and John B. Hymer's *The Hurdy-Gurdy Man* (1922).

In July, 1928, Sheehan announced some of the policies the Fox Studio would pursue in the future. "We are after the best people of the legitimate stage available today," he said. He explained that the studio was forming a speaking stage stock company for their 10th Avenue studios in New York. Daily tests of legitimate actors were being conducted to gather together at least twenty "legit" people for the company. Significantly it was decided that two directors, from both stage and screen, would be assigned to each feature film in the future.[52] Some of the theatrical personnel that began working for Fox at this time included playwrights George Middleton, Zoe Adkins, Cyril Hume, Clare Kummer, R.H. Booth and Gilbert Emery; stage and dance directors Edward Royce, Donald Gallaher and A.H. Van Buren; actors Paul Muni, Will Rogers, William Collier and George Jessel; actresses Helen Twelvetrees, Marguerite Churchill, Helen Chandler and Helen Garden.[53]

The majority of Fox's theatrical features during 1928-30 were drawn from crime melodramas and musical shows of the time. *The Ghost Talks* was based on the police thriller *Badges* (1924); *The Valiant* (with Paul Muni) was based on a one-act psychological drama by Holworthy Hall and Robert M. Middlemass (1924); and *Scotland Yard* (with Edmund Lowe) was based on Denison Clift's play (1929). There was even a regional melodrama, *Cameo Kirby* (1909) that received fresh life in a film released in January, 1930. Fox also produced several musical revues and shows in addition to Jessel's *Love, Live, and Laugh*. Heading the list in popularity was *Sunny Side Up* (October 3, 1929), which, although not based on a currently running Broadway musical, was very much in the Broadway style. For this film the songwriting team of De Sylva-Brown-Henderson came over from Warner Bros. and wrote two smash hits, "Sunny Side Up" and "Turn on the Heat." Two editions of the *William Fox Movietone Follies* appeared in 1929 and 1930. They were both full-length revues that followed in the mold established by Warner Bros.' *On With the Show* and *Show of Shows*.

William Fox, like the Warner Bros., was also interested in investing in Broadway productions with an eye toward securing their future screen rights. Fox had experimented with this policy even before his competitors. In the summer of 1925, he arranged with at least seven stage producers—including Al Woods, Sam Harris, John Golden, Robert Milton and Archie Selwyn—to finance their plays in return for a fifty per cent share of the profits and the opportunity to secure the film rights in advance. "It was also alleged," observed Robert McLaughlin, "that the deal allowed for a salary to be paid the stage producer up to $500 a week plus $150 expenses. If true, this removed all risk from producing and put the producers entirely in the employ of Fox."[54] By the middle of the fall season, Fox had bought a twenty-five per cent interest in three Al Woods' productions for over $100,000, and he contracted to finance all of Robert Milton's productions for the season. Thus, in the 1925-26 season, *The Pelican*, *The Monkey Talks* and *The Grand Duchess and the Waiter* were all produced under Fox's plan. Broadway was, in effect, becoming a testing ground for film material—an artistic and economic threat, especially to the playwrights. The Fox plan could have destroyed the principle of competitive bidding by film companies for screen rights to plays. It was also feared that Fox would cut short a play's Broadway run in order to save expenses and get the play into screen production. This could also cut short the royalties of the playwrights.

William Fox's activities were the initial spur to the Dramatists Guild to write the Minimum Basic Agreement in 1925. Yet it was difficult to pinpoint illegalities in the Fox arrangements with Broadway producers. Almost all activity of this kind, notes McLaughlin, "transpired under a veil of secrecy in order to avoid unpleasant notoriety." Therefore it is impossible to know how much financing Fox provided for Broadway productions. However it would be difficult, notes McLaughlin, to underrate the business ambition, "however unscrupulous," of producers in both the movie industry and the theatre.[55] What was to be feared most at the time, as a New York *Times* editorial stated early in 1926, was that there was too much temptation on Broadway to produce plays "not with regard to their dramatic, to say nothing of their literary, qualities, but solely with regard to their scenario value."[56]

If Fox's attempts to underwrite the production of stage plays was clouded in controversy, at least there was nothing problematic about trying to negotiate for plays that had already run on Broadway. He sought out Al Lewis, who worked in association with Sam Harris, to obtain the rights to ten plays under his control. These included *The War Song* (with George Jessel), *Mister Bones*, by Fulton Oursler and Bide Budley, *Black Belt*, by William Jourdan Rapp and Wallace Thurman, and *Street Scene*, by Elmer Rice. "It is understood the original New York casts will appear in the talkers to a large extent," reported *Variety* in July, 1928. Further, Lewis reportedly had signed a three-year contract with the Fox Film Corporation to handle the transference of the screen rights to these plays. "His main duties are to pass upon stage plays and story material for Fox's talking subjects in addition to promoting the development of the new type of player necessary for sound pictures."[57]

One can only speculate what might have happened as a result of these plans. William Fox shortly found himself in such financial straits that such plans had to be discontinued. On the verge of becoming the film industry's most powerful magnate as a result of attempts to buy up the other major studios, Fox became involved in a government antitrust action, the stock market collapse and a personal injury in an automobile crash. It was an incredibly complicated story and has been fully documented by Upton Sinclair;[35]; but the final result was that Fox was forced to sell his share in the Fox Film Corporation to a group of bankers; thereafter, he was involved in a succession of court litigation actions. In 1936 he declared bankruptcy. The history of the theatrical film—at least at the Fox Film Corporation—had come to an abrupt end.

Paramount: Marching to Astoria

Paramount's first theatrical film with talking sequences was *Abie's Irish Rose*. It was released just before the end of 1928 and was based on the play by Anne Nichols which had been running on Broadway since 1924. With the premiere of *Interference*, an all-talking theatrical feature, just weeks later, Paramount had at last launched its production schedule of talkies. Although it lagged behind Warner Brothers and the Fox Film Corporation in talking picture production, it quickly caught up before the end of 1930. By that time Paramount had released approximately 120 films, about twenty-four of which were based on stage plays. The theatrical films comprised about twenty per cent of the total output. In 1929 fifty films were released, fourteen of which were based on stage plays. In 1930 seventy films appeared, ten of which were based on stage plays.

Paramount had a long tradition of theatrical film production. It will be recalled that two of the companies that now comprised the Paramount production group had first organized in 1912 and subsequently made some of America's first theatrical feature films—Zukor's Famous Players and the Jessie L. Lasky Company. In 1916 Zukor and Lasky had merged their companies to form the Famous Players—Lasky Corporation with Zukor as president and Lasky as vice president in charge of production. Within another year other production companies—some of which, like Morosco, had been involved in theatrical film production—had joined in the merger. Then, with the acquisition of a distribution company called Paramount a little later, the huge conglomerate now known simply as "Paramount" had been formed.

During the transition to sound in 1927-28, Paramount built a series of sound stages on Long Island, New York. These studios, which I will refer to hereafter to as the "Astoria studios," would prove to be extremely important to Paramount's plans to produce theatrical sound films. Yet the story of the Astoria studios and their significance in the development of the talking theatrical film has been ignored in recent scholarship. There is no reference at all to Astoria, for example, in I.G. Edmonds and Reiko Mimura's recent history of Paramount Pictures (1980) and there are only a few passing references to it in Alexander Walker's important book on the early talkie period, *The Shattered Silents* (1979). As far as this study is concerned, however, the Astoria studios are especially significant. Astoria represented a return to the collaborative spirit in theatrical filmmaking that marked the 1912-15 period.[59]

The Astoria plant was established just as Paramount's general production manager, Walter Wanger, and his assistant, Monta Bell, arranged with Broadway talent to make screen tests in the New York area. Paramount's campaign to contract theatrical talent was in full swing by December, 1928; and by May, 1929 there were a reported twenty-nine theater people under Paramount contract—most of them gaining their apprenticeship in movies at the Astoria studios nearby—including playwrights Melville Baker, Bartlett Cormack and George Abbott; stage directors John Cromwell, Robert Milton, Irving Rapper and George Cukor; actors Maurice Chevalier, Hal Skelly,

Edward G. Robinson; actress Ruth Chatterton; dance director Maria Gambarelli; and song writers Leo Whiting and Frank Harling.[60]

Monta Bell supervised the Astoria operations and made sure that "the producers who readied the plays for the stage will be on hand to direct them ... with a regular cinema director who will simply advise of the camera and sound possibilities, as well as of tempo and timing of work."[61] This collaborative spirit was extended to the writers as well. Many Broadway playwrights, reported *Variety*, "may be pressed into service for the preparation of the talkie scripts, with a silent script man on hand to point out possibilities and handicaps."[62]

It is not surprising that Broadway people looked favorably at a film studio right on their doorstep. Writing in the *Saturday Evening Post*, Frank Condon noted that the "New York actors generally loathe the thought of hustling out to Hollywood in a lower berth." Their homes and their plays were in New York, "and when they go traipsing off to the Coast, they lose touch, abandon their own business, and the managers of plays think of them as dead." Fortunately for the Broadway people, however, the Astoria studios confined the search for theater people to New York City, "which is at its doors." The method by which actors and directors were put under contract at Astoria has been described by Condon in an account that should be quoted at length:

Discovery of new material comes about as follows: A film executive or department head thinks of a director on Broadway who is doing well with stage material ... or he happens one evening to wander into a Broadway playhouse and beholds an actor doing his bit with more than usual zest. The executive sends a letter, or his secretary telephones saying that Mr. Jones, of the studio, would like to talk things over with Actor Smith and that five cents spent on subway fare might produce results. If he is a fair actor, drawing $750 a week, the studio offers him another $750 a week to make a motion picture, which makes two jobs where one grew before, daytimes at the studio and nights in the theater .... But this desirable contract depends entirely on the success made by the gentleman in his first shot. If he goes over with a roar heard round the cinema universe, he certainly continues to draw his $750, but if his first essay is a gentle flop, or if his work marks him a mediocre man before a camera, he is rushed off the pay roll like lightning....

Following this system, the company sidesteps contracts with untried actors and actresses and a fine bill of expenses which would automatically occur if Hollywood tried to employ New York talent direct.[63]

Many stage stars got their start in motion pictures in the Astoria studios. Jeanne Eagels, who had created a sensation on Broadway in the role of Sadie Thompson in Somerset Maugham's *Rain*, made her talking debut in *The Letter*; Ruth Chatterton made her debut in William C. de Mille's talking version of Barrie's "Half an Hour" called *The Doctor's Secret* (January 26, 1929); Frederick March and John Cromwell first appeared in *The Dummy* (March 9, 1929), based on the play by Harvey J. O'Higgins and Harriet Ford (1914); Claudette Colbert and Edward G. Robinson made their talking debuts in *The Hole in the Wall* (April 27, 1929), based on the play by Fred Jackson

(1920); the Marx Brothers brought their stage productions of *The Cocoanuts* (1925) and *Animal Crackers* (1928) to Astoria and made film versions in 1929-30; Hal Skelly brought his role of "Skid" in *Burlesque* (1927) to Astoria and made a film version called *The Dance of Life* (September 7, 1929); Dennis King and Jeanette MacDonald first appeared in *The Vagabond King* (April 19, 1930), based on the musical production by Rudolph Friml in which King had starred (1925).

Several notable stage directors joined the ranks of the Astoria unit and went on to become successful film directors. George Abbott has already been mentioned in connection with his work on the Paramount talking theatrical shorts. Rouben Mamoulian had first trained for the stage at the Moscow Art Theater under Vakhtangov. In 1918 he organized his own drama studio in Tiflis, Russia and two years later toured England with the Russian Repertory Theater. He came to the United States in 1923 and for three years directed operas and operettas at the George Eastman Theater in Rochester, New York. Then he produced three plays at New York's Theatre Guild and the following year directed on Broadway the Guild's highly successful production of Dubose Heyward's *Porgy*. It was at this time that Mamoulian received an offer from Walter Wanger and Jesse Lasky of Paramount to come to Astoria. According to Mamoulian's biographer, Tom Milne, he spent five weeks at Astoria watching Jean de Limur directing Jeanne Eagels in her follow-up to *The Letter, Jealousy* (September 13, 1929).[64] Then Mamoulian began work on his first film, *Applause*. This was not a film based on any particular film production, but a film *about* the theater—particularly, the sleazy environments of the burlesque houses. Its fluid camera and its imaginative use of sound—not to mention the talking picture debut of Helen Morgan—made it a landmark in the development of the talking picture. *Applause* was filmed at the Astoria studios. Thereafter, Mamoulian would work in Hollywood. Because he was famous as a stage director when he came to Hollywood, it was assumed that he would work only on dialogue at Astoria. But he preferred to explore the expressive resources of camera movement and multiple-channel sound mixing. Thus, it is ironic that although he came from the stage, Mamoulian was eventually to help liberate the theatrical film from the proscenium confines. Mamoulian now looks upon his apprenticeship at Astoria with affection. "It might have taken me years to leave Broadway," he has recently recalled, "but Paramount was still making movies in its Astoria studio in 1929, so I broke into the movies without leaving New York, something you couldn't do later on."[65]

John Cromwell was another Broadway director who came to Astoria. He had received his first stage assignment in 1913 as a director of *The Painted Woman*. From 1915 to 1919 he worked as an actor and stage director for the New York Repertory Company and appeared in the American premieres of Shaw's *Major Barbara* (Playhouse, December 9, 1915) and *Captain*

Brassbound's Conversion (Playhouse, March 29, 1916). He had also appeared with Edward G. Robinson in Bartlett Cormack's play *The Racket* in 1928.

Before leaving for RKO in 1932, Cromwell worked both as an actor and director at Astoria. At Astoria, Cromwell had recalled, "there was a great aura about the men from the New York stage and their experience with dialogue. The attitude of almost everybody in the studio at the time reflected an absolute fear ... a panic at what was going to happen to their careers with sound coming in, so they really laid down the red carpet for me."[66] As an actor, he appeared in *The Dummy* (directed by stage director Robert Milton), *The Dance of Life*, *The Mighty* and *Street of Chance* (all in 1929). *The Dance of Life* was based on George Manker Watters and Arthur Hopkins' *Burlesque* (1927). He co-directed it with veteran film director Edward Sutherland. Cromwell also co-directed *Seven Days Later* (January 25, 1930), based on James M. Barrie's one-act play, "The Old Lady Shows Her Medals" (1918). Accustomed to rehearsal time for stage productions, Cromwell had to fight to extend the practice to film-making at Astoria. After being told by B.P. Shulberg of Paramount that rehearsal time had to be cut, Cromwell insisted and eventually prevailed.[67]

George Cukor also served as a dialogue director for Paramount in 1929-30, although he spent only part of that time at Astoria. He entered the theater professionally in 1919 as stage manager for a Chicago company and a year later became the resident director of a stock company in Rochester, New York. By 1926 he was directing such stars as Ethel Barrymore, Jeanne Eagles and Laurette Taylor on Broadway. His first experience in filmmaking came when Paramount sent him to their West Coast studio to work on *River of Romance* (June 29, 1929), based on Booth Tarkington's drama *Magnolia* (1923). After a brief period at Universal where he worked with Lewis Milestone as a dialogue director (uncredited) for *All Quiet on the Western Front* (1929), he returned to Los Angeles and Paramount where he worked as a co-director with Cyril Gardner, a veteran filmmaker. The picture was *Grumpy* (August 1, 1930), based on the play by Horace Hodges and Thomas Wigney Percyval (1921). Gardner and Cukor both then went to Astoria where they co-directed a film version of one of Broadway's biggest successes, *The Royal Family of Broadway*, by George S. Kaufman and Edna Ferber.

Like Mamoulian, Cukor, although a stage-trained director, chafed at the restrictions of the sound stages and the still prevalent use of the unmoving camera. Strangely, this early period of Cukor's career has been virtually ignored by historians. What we do know, according to the Rev. Gene Phillips' interviews with Cukor, is that Cukor's ideas about liberating the camera and avoiding the "stagy" dialogue characteristic of early talkies were, like Mamoulian's, ahead of the time. "When I got to Hollywood," Cukor has recalled, "the studios were all petrified about the coming of sound to motion pictures. Directors lost their heads and began to abandon everything that they had learned about camera movement in the silent days .... But gradually the techniques of making sound films were perfected and everyone got used to them. After all, as Lionel Barrymore quipped at the time, 'human speech had been a success for thousands of years; there is no reason why talking pictures should not work out'."[68]

True to the pattern established by Warner Brothers and the Fox Film Corporation, Paramount produced several musical shows and revues during 1928-30. In order of release, the first was *The Cocoanuts* (August 3, 1929), a filmed version made at Astoria of the Marx Brothers' success in 1925. *The Cocoanuts* has been regarded as "the best record we have of [the Marx Brothers'] vaudeville style," showing them "at the height of their stage art rather than a record of their film beginnings."[69]

Another musical film documented a Ziegfeld revue, *Glorifying the American Girl*, was shot at Astoria with Ziegfeld himself on hand as co-producer. By the fall of 1928 Florenz Ziegfeld was riding a crest of success. No less than four shows had scored spectacular successes within the last year and a half—*Rio Rita, Rosalie, Show Boat, The Three Musketeers* and *Whoopee*. The Astoria location was convenient for Ziegfeld and his stars, so Ziegfeld committed himself and members of his current productions for the filming of *Glorifying the American Girl*. The film is indeed an evocation of the Ziegfeld style. Helen Morgan, Eddie Cantor, Rudy Vallee and Mary Eaton all appeared. Moreover, the Ziegfeld name is featured prominently throughout, and there is even some newsreel footage of an opening night at the Ziegfeld Theatre (with shots of Fanny Brice, Texas Guinan and Mayor James J. Walker, among others). The last third of *Glorifying the American Girl* is a mini-revue featuring several full-scale tableaux mounted by the Ziegfeld Girls. This would not be Ziegfeld's last venture into filmmaking, incidentally, as we shall see in discussing the theatrical films made by United Artists.

Two filmed operettas should be mentioned. Ernest Lubitsch chose Leon Zanrof and Jules Chancel's *The Prince Consort* (1919) and Hans Mueller's *The Blue Coast* (publication undetermined) as the basis for, respectively, *The Love Parade* (November 19, 1929) and *Monte Carlo* (August 27, 1930). While they helped establish the vogue for operettas on film—Sigmund Romberg would write *Viennese Nights* for Warner Bros. late in 1930—they also displayed wit and imagination in a more cinematic sense.

Paramount also produced a spectacular original revue, as did all the other studios. All the skits in *Paramount on Parade* (April 19, 1930) take place on a stage—a *real* stage. Three "masters of ceremony"—Jack Oakie, Skeets Gallagher and Leon Erroll—face the camera and, in sustained, uncut shots, do patter-numbers and songs. They even lean knowingly toward an imaginary audience (the camera) and indulge in asides and private jokes. The device of opening and closing curtains introduces and ends each routine.

No survey of Paramount's theatrical films between 1928-30 can be complete without mention of *The Virginian* (November 9, 1929), starring stage star Walter Huston. It will be recalled that the first filmed version of Owen Wister's dramatization in 1904 of his novel was made by the Lasky Company in 1914. The play's implications for open-air adventure had stimulated filmmakers Cecil B. De Mille and Oscar Apfel to utilize natural locales and the deep frame to create a uniquely cinematic experience. The talking version of *The Virginian* displays a similar penchant for location shooting. To shoot outdoors forced director Victor Fleming to utilize the newly-developed blimped cameras. Once again, the open-air romance of a melodrama had stimulated filmmakers to liberate the camera from the confines of a proscenium stage.

Several of the theatrical films referred to here—*The Cocoanuts, Glorifying the American Girl, The Virginian* and *Paramount on Parade*—will be discussed in more detail in the next chapter.

Metro-Goldwyn-Mayer: Courtrooms and Musical Revues

MGM's first talking theatrical films were both released in January 1929. They were *The Bellamy Trial*, a courtroom drama based on the play by Frances Noyes Hart (1927), and *Alias Jimmy Valentine*, a part-talkie based on the play by Paul Armstrong (1910). Sandwiched between them and *Paid* (December 30, 1930), based on Bayard Veiller's *Within the Law* (912), were seventy-four features displaying synchronized-sound appeared, twenty-three of which were stage-based. Out of the total film output, therefore, thirty-one per cent were theatrical in origins.

There are a number of significant theatrical films in this output. Several were crime melodramas and courtroom dramas characteristic of the period. In addition to *The Bellamy Trial* and *Paid*, MGM produced *The Trial of Mary Dugan* (June 8, 1929), based on Bayard Veiller's 1927 play; *The Thirteenth Chair* (October 19, 1929), based on Bayard Veiller's 1922 play; and *The Woman Racket* (January 24, 1929), based on Philip Dunning's *Night Hostess* (1928). Others were well made plays, including *The Last of Mrs. Cheyney* (July 6, 1929), based on Frederick Lonsdale's 1925 play; *Madame X* (August 17, 1929), based on the 1927 play by Alexandre Bisson; *A Lady to Love* (February 28, 1939), adapted by Sidney Howard from his Pulitzer-Prize-winning play, *They Knew What They Wanted* (1925); *Strictly Unconventional* (May 3, 1930), based on W.S. Maugham's *The Circle* (1921); and *Romance* (August 26, 1930), based on the 1913 play by Ned Sheldon.

MGM was an amalgamation of the Metro Picture Corporation (formed in 1915) and the Goldwyn Picture Corporation (formed in 1918). It was put under the corporate control of Loew's Inc. in 1923. Louis B. Mayer was the first vice president and head of the studio; his associate was Irving Thalberg. MGM prospered rapidly after 1923 until by 1929 it was considered the

One of many courtroom dramas to be adapted from the stage in 1929-1930 was MGM's *The Trial of Mary Dugan*. Playwright Bayard Veiller directed the film version of his 1927 play.

"prestige" studio in Hollywood. By May 1928, only Fox had more theatrical personnel under contract. *Variety* estimated that thirty-two stage-trained people were at MGM during the first flush of the talkie revolution. These included playwrights Willard Mack, Bayard Veiller, Edgar Selwyn, Gus Edwards and John Howard Lawson; dance director Sammy Lee; actors Cliff Edwards, Raymond Hackett, Charles King, Joel McCrea, Basil Rathbone, Robert Montgomery; and song-writers Nacio Herb Brown, Arthur Freed and Billie Rose.[70]

Before coming to MGM playwright Bayard Veiller had been, in Barret H. Clark's opinion, an author of "acceptable and occasionally superior plays," including *Within the Law* and *The Thirteenth Chair*.[71] When he was contracted by MGM to direct his own adaptation of *The Trial of Mary Dugan* in 1929, the play had already run for a spectacular 437 performances. Its sole set was a New York courtroom. The film version, except for a prologue visualizing action only referred to in some of the play's original dialogue, is itself confined to one courtroom set. Thus, Veiller was able to stage it very much in the manner of the original play. In his autobiography, *The Fun I've Had*, virtually the only reference source for this subject, Veiller recalls that the artifice of the sound stages was troublesome; that the stages necessitated the lack of realism:

[The scenery] wasn't painted on canvas—sound reflected from canvas—so the sets were painted on the thinnest kind of cheesecloth. The floor had to be covered with heavy pieces of felt—the floor reflected sound. Table tops were made of felt. We couldn't have any fans to let out the super-heated air—they made a noise—so the temperature on the stage in those ran to about 120 or 130 degrees, and that's what we worked in.[72]

Another playwright who came to MGM in the 1929-30 period was John Howard Lawson. Whereas Veiller's plays had been confined to space within the proscenium, Lawson had always worked with more radically experimental techniques that "broke" the proscenium frame. Brockett and Findlay in their *Century of Innovation* have noted that during the 1920s "Lawson made the most extensive use of nonrealistic techniques of any American playwright."[73] His first Broadway play was *Roger Bloomer* in 1923, where he used the techniques of European expressionism to portray the frustrations of American life. His next play, *Processional*, a year later, was produced by the Theatre Guild. It was a savage story of a strike in the coal mines of West Virginia that utilized jazz music and burlesque characterizations in its mixture of violence and slapstick humor. Early in 1927 he joined Michael Gold, John Dos Passos, Francis Edwards Faragoh, and Em Jo Basshe in founding the New Playwrights Theatre, which pursued the kinds of experimentation advocated by Piscator in Germany and by Meyerhold in the Soviet Union. Lawson's *Loudspeaker* (1927) was the first production of the New Playwrights, enacted on a constructivist setting designed by Mordecai Gorelik. During the last production of the group, Upton Sinclair's *Singing Jailbirds* (1928), Lawson received an offer from MGM and left for the West Coast to get involved in talking pictures. Fortunately, he has left a brief account of his stay during 1928-30.

"The jump from *Singing Jailbirds* to Hollywood seems abrupt," Lawson recalled in his *Film: The Creative Process*, "but I regarded it as a means of gaining cinematic knowledge which would be invaluable for future work either in drama or film." He saw in the talking cinema far more than the proscenium-bound productions of the time. "I cherished the hope that films would offer possibilities of continuing the experimental work begun by the New Playwrights." Admittedly, Lawson's dreams were far removed from the realities of American film production at MGM. Yet, at the same time, the experience gave him an "insight into filmmaking which challenged my craftsmanship as a writer and deepened my approach to creative problems."[74] In Irving Thalberg, Lawson saw the guiding energy behind a studio that represented the "safe" but lively entertainment expected of MGM. Thalberg's first meeting with Lawson resulted in the assignment for Lawson to write a sound sequence for the otherwise silent film, *Flesh and the Devil* (1927). "Since the stars could not speak," Lawson remembers, "I prepared a fantastic dream sequence for *Flesh and the Devil*, with sounds and voices coming from a void."[75] Although Thalberg liked it, the scene was never used. It was not until Lawson wrote dialogue for Cecil B. De Mille's first all-talkie, *Dynamite* (1929), that he actively worked with the filmmaking process. Nonetheless, all that Hollywood actively taught Lawson, it seems, was that "Hollywood had not so much mastered dialogue as it had been mastered by it." This dependence on speech "was magnified by the employment of personnel trained in the theatre. Directors, writers, and performers did not change their methods of work when they crossed the continent from New York to Hollywood. They were hired because of their stage experience and they had no incentive to abandon it or to risk experimentation."[76] Lawson went on to co-found the Screen Writers Guild and become its first president in 1933. Today, he is chiefly remembered from the notoriety he received as one of the "Hollywood Ten" during the House Un-American Activities Committee investigation in the late 1940s.

MGM made several significant contributions to filmed revues and musical shows. Its *Broadway Melody of 1929* (February 1, 1929) was, according to historian Alexander Walker, "the first Hollywood musical in the modern sense of the term."[77] It helped set the shape of a new genre that has not substantially changed since then. The score by Arthur Freed and Nacio Herb Brown had to be recorded on the set as it was being sung (with the orchestra just out of camera-range). Although, like Fox's *Sunny Side Up*, it was not based on a particular Broadway musical show, it *looked* like a stage production with dialogue written by veteran Broadway writer James

Gleason. The songs, "Broadway Melody" and "You Were Meant for Me," were so successful that all Hollywood frantically rushed to Tin-Pan Alley for more musical material. MGM's original revue that year was *The Hollywood Revue of 1929*, released just two months after *Broadway Melody*. Again, composers Freed and Brown produced a popular score, including "Singin' in the Rain" and "Pagan Love Song." Typically, the sketches were filmed head on on a proscenium setting, featuring some twenty numbers introduced by two masters of ceremonies, Jack Benny and Conrad Nagel. There were also two filmed versions of musical shows—*The Rogue Song* (1930), based on the 1912 operetta by Franz Lehar, and *Good News* (August 23, 1930), with Mary Lawler repeating her stage role as Constance in the 1927 show by Laurence Schwab, B.G. De Sylva and Lew Brown. *The Rogue Song*, incidentally, was the first musical feature film to bring to the screen a Metropolitan opera star—Lawrence Tibbett.

MGM's most prestigious talking theatrical film was *Anna Christie* (February 21, 1930), based on the Eugene O'Neill play produced by Arthur Hopkins in 1921. It survives today as one of the most proscenium-bound theatrical films of the period. With the exception of the barroom, each interior was shot from only one side. There was a preponderance of medium shots. The actors tended to remain stationary when speaking. They tended also to move around a focal point in a scene, such as a table in the ship's cabin, a filmic equivalent of unimaginative proscenium staging. Dialogue was more important than action. Anna's past could have been revealed cinematically, through the use of flashbacks or a visualized prologue; rather, the soliloquies were retained and spoken, as they had been on the stage, in sustained shots from an unchanging camera angle. The only moments where the film acquired a more cinematic quality came during the added scenes of the barge at dock and in a storm and during the added scene of the amusement park sequence (which utilized four separate sets). Here the use of natural locales and a quickened sense of pace through editing stood out in contrast with the artificial sets and deliberate pacing of the rest of the film.

United Artists: Shakespeare to Ziegfeld

The first all-talking film from United Artists was a theatrical feature—*Coquette* (April 12, 1929), based on the 1927 play by George Abbott and Ann Preston Bridgers. It was followed by a number of theatrical talkies characteristic of the period—crime thrillers, courtroom melodramas and musical shows. The crime thrillers included *Alibi* (April 20, 1929), based on the play, *Badges* (1927), by John Wray; *Bulldog Drummond* (August 3, 1929), Sidney Howard's adaptation of the British drama; *Raffles* (July 26, 1930), based on the 1903 play by Eugene Presbrey and W.W. Hornung. And there was even an old-fashioned melodrama, *The Bat Whispers* (November 29, 1930), based on Mary Roberts Rinehart's long-running *The Bat* (1926). Out of a total of twenty-nine talkies for the 1929-30 period, ten were based on stage productions.

United Artists had been formed in 1919 to give its four producers—Douglas Fairbanks, Mary Pickford, Charles Chaplin and D.W. Griffith—independent status as filmmakers. Each had his own studio and sold and distributed his pictures free of the usual block booking procedures of the day. In 1927 producer Sam Goldwyn joined the partnership, retaining autonomous status like the others. Aside from two theatrical talkies released by Mary Pickford and Douglas Fairbanks in 1928 and 1929, it was Goldwyn who supplied the bulk of United Artists' theatrical sound features during the 1928-30 period.

For the first all-talking film from United Artists, Mary Pickford chose *Coquette*, by George Abbott and Ann Preston Bridgers, a major hit of the 1927 Broadway season. The play was jazzy and contemporary, yet, ultimately, tragic in its consequences. Pickford followed a customary practice by taking a "screen test" of the play—i.e., she filmed parts of the play with its original cast to determine its suitability for the screen.[78] According to Alexander Walker, she had the test run and promptly pronounced the cast unsatisfactory, excepting for Miss Hayes, whose part she was determined to play.[79] She began shooting late in 1928 and released the film in April 1929. It won her an Academy Award. The play was ideally suited for early sound production, since it was confined to a single set and conveyed its actions entirely through dialogue. For the most part, the film version retained this simplicity, although it catered to a trend of the time and included a long courtroom scene at the end that is only suggested in the play.

Pickford and Fairbanks both appeared in *The Taming of the Shrew* (October 26, 1929) based on the play by William Shakespeare.[80] Unlike many theatrical films of the period, it treated the material very freely and, to a great extent, relied upon visual gags written by its director, Sam Taylor (who had been a gag writer for Harold Lloyd) to convey the characterizations. This quality of the film makes it seem today rather modern and refreshingly free of the endless dialogue exchanges typical of other talkies of the period.

United Artists's most famous musical film of the period reveals a determination to treat theatrical material in a manner far different from what had been done in *The Taming of the Shrew*. *Whoopee* (September 1, 1930) was based on the Ziegfeld production in 1928. It was produced by Samuel Goldwyn working in collaboration with Florenz Ziegfeld. When sound arrived Goldwyn was determined to work with the best talents Broadway had to offer.[81] He had already brought playwright Sidney Howard to Hollywood to work on an adaptation of the British play *Bulldog Drummond*, with Ronald Colman, one of the more witty and imaginative theatrical talkies of the period. Now he went after Ziegfeld and the writer of *Whoopee*, William Anthony McGuire. In addition, he was determined to have Eddie Cantor recreate on film the role of the hypochrondriacal Easterner out in the Wild West. For the dance sequences he also signed Busby Berkeley who, as a dance director on Broadway, had been successful recently with Rodgers and Hart's *A Connecticut Yankee*, Emmerich Kalman's operetta *The Golden Dawn*, Rudolf Friml's *The White Eagle* (based on Edwin Milton Royle's *The Squaw Man* 1905) and the *Earl Carroll Vanities of 1928*.

Ziegfeld and Goldwyn were both content with transferring *Whoopee* to the screen as faithfully as possible. Miles Kreuger has said that it is "as close as you'll ever see to seeing a Broadway show of that period."[82] Filmed in two-color Technicolor, which preserves the sense of color of a typical Ziegfeld production, it was shot entirely on a stage, save for a few silent shots of horsemen galloping across the desert.

I have selected three of the theatrical films referred to here—*Coquette, Taming of the Shrew* and *Whoopee*—for detailed discussion in the next chapter.

Universal Studios

In the first full year of sound, 1928, Universal produced three talkies and part-talkies, none of which were based on stage plays. But within the next year twenty-five talkies were produced, eight of which were from stage productions. In 1930 thirty-five talkies were produced, seven of which were based on stage productions. Out of a total of sixty-three films in the 1928-30 period, a total of fifteen were stage-based, comprising almost twenty-four percent. The first talking theatrical feature was *The Last Warning* (January 6, 1929), a part-talkie based on the play by Thomas F. Fallon (date unknown). Late in 1930 *The Cat Creeps* was released (November 10, 1930), based on the play by John Willard (date unknown).

The transition to sound was marked at Universal by a transfer of power from Carl Laemmle to his son, Carl Jr. It was a time of uncertainty for the studio and there was no consistent policy regarding the production of theatrical talking pictures. However, by May 1929, Universal had eleven theatrical people under contract—most of whom were actors, like Eddie Leonard and Benny Rubin.

Probably the most important director to come to Universal from the stage at this time was James Whale. His dramatic career had begun in a World War I prison camp in Holzminden, Germany, where the young Englishman acted in plays presented by his fellow prisoners. Back in England after the Armistice his work in the theater ranged from working as a stage manager to that of a scenic designer and director. In January 1929 he brought R.C. Sherriff's *Journey's End*, a tale of the spiritual ravages of war, to London's West End. After taking it to Broadway and Chicago, Whale went to Hollywood with an eye toward making movies. Like so many other stage directors, he began his new career as a dialogue director at Paramount, where

An innovative early talkie was Roland West's *Alibi*, based upon John Wray's 1927 play, *Badges*. The bizarre nightclub set was   on film's set pieces.

he worked on *The Love Doctor* (1929). He also worked for Howard Hughes on *Hell's Angels* (1930). For his first assignment as a director he went to Tiffany Studios, one of the smaller studios in Hollywood, where he made the film version of *Journey's End.*

Whale's reputation rested so firmly upon his stage success with *Journey's End* that no one else was seriously competing to take on the film version. Although he did not end up utilizing members of his New York stage cast, as he wished, he was able to retain the services of his lead, Colin Clive. After the film was released to general acclamation, both in America and abroad, Whale continued to direct yet another stage company in New York—a rare instance of one director simultaneously directing stage and screen versions of the same property.

Whale's association with playwright R.C. Sherriff was continuing with his direction of another play, *Badger Green,* when Universal studios beckoned in 1931. Young Carl Laemmle, Jr., had been so impressed with the film of *Journey's End* that he went on to film *All Quiet on the Western Front,* another wartime story directed by Lewis Milestone. He offered Whale a contract at a top salary of $2,500 weekly. Back in Hollywood, Whale made for Universal such films as *Waterloo Bridge,* adapted from the two-act play by Robert Sherwood, *Frankenstein* (1931), *The Old Dark House* (1932) and *One More River* (1934).

Whale never lost his sense of the theater while at Tiffany and Universal. Although his camera fluidity and witty cutting imparted a cinematic quality to all his films, they remained nonetheless very much a product of his stage training. For example, he uses "cut-away" sets in most of his films, especially in *Journey's End*; German expressionist set distortion in *Frankenstein*; and the models of well made play construction in *One More River.* His *Show Boat,* released in 1937, is still one of Hollywood's most witty and loving tributes to the vanished days of the melodrama, containing as it does a full-scale recreation of something called *The Parson's Bride.* Even *Frankenstein* was based upon a play—John Balderston's adaptation of Peggy Webling's drama (premiered at London's Preston Theatre in 1927). The play had been revived in 1930 and thus originally come to Laemmle's attention.

Three of Universal's theatrical films deserve special mention. They were all musical films, and each in its own way drew upon elements of the American musical theater. *Broadway* (May 27, 1929) was not based on a musical but a drama by Jed Harris, Philip Dunning and George Abbott. It conveyed a convincing sense of a musical show, however, by means of its nightclub settings and incidental show sequences. Its use of a seemingly unfettered camera (placed atop a giant camera boom by director Paul Fejos) seemed to explode the bounds of the proscenium. The camera swooped down from heights and angles above and across the art deco sets of the Paradise Night Club. *Show Boat* (July 28, 1929), partly a silent film, based on the musical comedy by Oscar Hammerstein II and Jerome Kern (1927), contained a most interesting prologue. The prologue portrayed film producer Carl Laemmle, Sr. and impresario Florenz Ziegfeld jointly introducing members of the Broadway cast performing in the production in January 1929. Collaborations of stage and film personnel had frequently displayed these kinds of introductions, and it will be recalled that Belasco had "introduced" the Famous Players version of his *The Good Little Devil* in 1913 and that Daniel Frohman had done it for Paramount's first all-talkie, *Interference*, in 1928. After the introductions here, the next eighteen minutes featured three principals from the stage presentation—Tess "Aunt Jemima" Gardella and the Jubilee Singers singing "C'mon, Folks" and "Hey, Feller!", Helen Morgan singing "Bill' and "Can't Help Lovin' Dat Man"; and Jules Bledsoe and chorus singing "Ol' Man River."

Today only the Aunt Jemima numbers survive, but they are enough to indicate the film's close imitation of proscenium staging. The viewer's angle approximates a balcony viewpont overlooking a stage (the Fox Movietone studios on West 54th Street in New York). The curtains part revealing Gardella and the chorus singing and dancing in place, facing an imaginary audience. Midway through the uncut scene, the curtains fall into place and then are again drawn back so the second song can continue. Historian Miles Kreuger, whose *Show Boat: The Story of a Musical* is a definitive history of the show, has told me that he thinks that the Ziegfeld pit orchestra is used in the film as well as the original costumes. "But everything about it is sleazy and cheap," he said; "done at a moment's notice to capitalize on the stars' names."[83] In an interesting twist of irony, Universal promoted this film prior to its premiere by sponsoring on Broadway an actual show boat company of actors under the direction of Norman F. Thom. The company presented "The Parson's Bride"—the same melodrama that is depicted in the musical.

Perhaps the most innovative of the Universal theatrical films was *King of Jazz* (May 7, 1930), an original musical film directed by John Murray Anderson, a famous director of Broadway revues who brought to the film medium a fresh ambition to annihilate the sense of a proscenium frame. The significance of this film will be discussed in the next chapter.

Radio-Keith-Orpheum

RKO was formed in 1928, "the first studio to be formed directly as a result of the sound revolution . . . ."[84] RKO resulted from a merger between RCA, headed by David Sarnoff, the theatre chains of the Keith-Orpheum circuits, and a small production unit in Los Angeles called the Film Booking Office (FBO). David Sarnoff was chairman of the board. As early as October 1928, Sarnoff had advocated the sound film as a new field of dramatic expression and RKO would make only talking pictures, he announced. "A really new art was created when [movies and sound] finally met on the silver screen . . . .

Neither sound nor motion can go forward without the other's cooperation. Sound has opened an infinitely wider field of dramatic expression for the motion picture."[85]

In 1929-30 RKO released thirty-six sound features, seventeen of which were based on stage productions. Rounding out the period, *Seven Keys to Baldpate* was released on December 25, 1929; it was based on the play by George M. Cohan (1913). *Variety* estimated that in May 1929, nine threatrical personnel were under contract, including Ben Hecht and Charles MacArthur, writers; dance director Pearl Eaton; actors Wheeler and Woolsey; and songwriters Dorothy Fields and James McHugh.[86] William Le Baron was vice-president in charge of production. Le Baron had also had some experience with the New York theater world.[87]

Several of the theatrical features were based upon the well made plays of the time. These included *Second Wife* (February 9, 1930), based on Charles Fulton Oursler's *All the King's Men* (date unknown); *He Knew Women* (April 18, 1930), based on S.N. Behrman's *The Second Man* (1927) with Lunt and Fontanne; *The Fall Guy* (June 15, 1930), based on the 1924 comedy by George Abbott and James Gleason; and *Inside the Lines* (July 5, 1930), based on the 1915 play by Earl Derr Biggers.

Perhaps the most noteworthy of the theatrical releases during this period, however, were the adaptations of musical shows. These were *Rio Rita* (October 6, 1929), based on the 1927 play by Guy Bolton and Fred Thompson, which retained Bert Wheeler and Robert Woolsey from the original cast; *Hit the Deck* (January 14, 1930), based on the 1927 production by Herbert Fields and Vincent Youmans; *The Cuckoos* (May 4, 1930), based on the 1926 production by Bert Kalmar and Harry Ruby; *Dixiana* (August 1, 1930), based on the production by Harry Tierney and Anne Caldwell (date unknown); and *Leathernecking* (September 12, 1930), based on the 1928 production by Herbert Fields, Richard Rodgers and Lorenz Hart, *Present Arms*.

The films were under the general control of William Le Baron, with music direction by Victor Baravalle. Joining the RKO staff late in 1929 was another musican who had had extensive experience in the musical theater, Max Steiner. Steiner's fifteen years of musical show experience was to prove of great advantage to RKO. While orchestrating and conducting *Sons o' Guns* (1929) on Broadway, he was approached by the studio. Accounts differ about the circumstances of his signing with RKO. In his autobiography (unpublished) Steiner indicates that his friend Harry Tierney—whose show *Rio Rita*, Max had arranged and conducted—invited him out to the studio.[88] But in an interview in 1967, Steiner mentioned William LeBaron as his first contact. He reiterated this in an interview reprinted in *The Real Tinsel*.[89] In his recent book on film composing, *Music for the Movies*, Tony Thomas says it was Tierney's invitation that resulted in a contract.[90] Whatever, it is doubtful that Steiner arrived in time to work on the film version of *Rio Rita*, as he claimed in the 1967 interview. It is also doubtful that he had the opportunity to work on *Hit the Deck*, which was released just two months after his arrival in Hollywood. Probably the first musical film Steiner worked on was *Dixiana*, by his friend Henry Tierney.

The presence of people like Tierney, Steiner and Le Baron at RKO did much to insure that the music and stage stylings of Broadway were accurately transferred to the motion picture screen. When the musical film fell out of favor late in 1930, and after Le Baron left RKO, Steiner remained to work on original scores to films. As a pit conductor, Steiner was accustomed to playing incidental music throughout a show, sometimes underlying passages of dialogue with it, sometimes creating moods during wordless sequences. After 1930 he would begin employing these techniques in motion picture composing. Prior to his work, the use of incidental music in motion pictures was limited, for the most part, to scenes where the source of that music could be seen.[91] Steiner's experience on the musical stage on Broadway would soon aid him in changing this situation.

In an editorial in February 1931, *Cinema* magazine looked back on three years of talking pictures. "The mechanical improvements have gone so far that it is now possible to listen to voices from the screen without minding them, sometimes even forgetting that they are mechanically reproduced," noted the editorial. Moreover, "a way of combining sound with action has been gradually arrived at that restores most of the fluency that the motion picture lost in its first struggles with the microphone."[95] In the next chapter I examine some of the filmed plays that represent both the close imitation of the stage and the shift away from that close imitation. In that shift can be seen the beginnings of an enriched sense of the unique effects and possibilities of film—properties that, while indirectly related to the stage, could be applied to promote the motion picture as a medium of artistic expression.

Notes

[1]Quoted in Mordaunt Hall, "Interference" (review), New York *Times*, November 17, 1928, p. 23.

[2]In at least two "standard" film history texts, A.R. Fulton, *Motion Pictures* (Norman: University of Oklahoma Press, 1960), and John L. Fell, *A History of Films* (New York: Holt, Rinehart and Winston, 1979), *Interference* is not mentioned at all. In his *The Detective in Film* (Secaucus, N.J.: The Citadel Press, 1972), William K. Everson dismisses *Interference* as "one of the talkiest and most static of all early sound films." (53)

[3]See Harry M. Geduld, *The Birth of the Talkies: From Edison to Jolson* (Bloomington: Indiana University Press, 1975), pp. 166-94.

[4]For a discussion of several of these hybrid motion pictures, see Alexander Walker, *The Shattered Silents* (New York: William Morrow, 1978), pp. 56-62.

[5]Edmund Goulding, "The Talker in Close-Up," *Variety*, June 13, 1928, p. 7.

[6]"What Sound Has Done," *Variety*, March 13, 1929, pp. 1, 60.

[7]"11 Legit Sites Playing Films," *Variety*, April 10, 1929, p. 49.

[8]"About One-Third Silent for 1929-30," *Variety*, March 20, 1929, p. 7.

[9]Robert McLaughlin, *Broadway and Hollywood: A History of Economic Interaction* (New York: Arno, 1974), p. 115.

[10]"About One-Third Silent for 1929-30," p. 7.

[11]See the figures in Table Seven in Robert McLaughlin, p. 287.

[12]Robert McLaughlin, pp. 115-6.

[13]"205 Stage People West," *Variety*, May 1, 1929, p. 57.

[14]Robert Herring, "Twenty-Three Talkies," *Close Up*, February 1930, p. 114.

[15]William C. de Mille, "No Stage Director or Writer Required for Talkers," *Variety*, October 17, 1928, p. 4.

[16]"The Letter" (review), *Variety*, March 13, 1929, p. 14.

[17]"Thru Different Eyes," (review), *Variety*, April 17, 1929, p. 22.

[18]"The Trial of Mary Dugan," (review), The New York *Times*, March 29, 1929, p. 21.

[19]"Rio Rita" (review), The New York *Times*,

[20]Quoted in "Disraeli Speaks," *Literary Digest*, April 12, 1930, p. 19.

[21]"Bulldog Drummond" (review), *Variety*, May 8, 1929, p. 20.

[22]Quoted in Alexander Walker, p. 127.

[23]Robert Herring, p. 119.

[23ffi]"The Knife" (review), *Variety*, May 29, 1929, p. 26.

[24]"Coquette" (review), *Variety*, April 10, 1929, p. 25.

[25]"The Letter," p. 14.

[26]"The Letter" (review), The New York *Times*, March 8, 1929, p. 30.

[27]"Disraeli Speaks," p. 19.

[28]"The Hometowners" (review), The New York *Times*, October 24, 1928, p. 26.

[29]"Overhead Trolleys for Sets," *Variety*, April 24, 1929, p. 7.

[30]Robert Herring, p. 123.

[31]*Ibid.*, p. 119.

[32]Ron Have *David O. Selznick's Hollywood* (New York: Knopf, 1980), p. 49.

[33]"Madame X ' (review), *Variety*, May 1, 1929, p. 17.

[34]For a discussion of the stage melodramas of the 1920s see Edmond M. Gagey, *Revolution in American Drama* (New York: Columbia University Press, 1947), pp. 234-42.

[35]Al Manski and Dan Navarro, "Hollywood Goes to Court: *The Trial of Mary Dugan*," *American Classic Screen*, Vol. 5, No. 2, p. 30.

[36]Mordaunt Hall, "Interference" (review), The New York *Times*, November 17, 1928, p. 23.

[37]George Arliss, *My Ten Years in the Studios* (Boston: Little, Brown, 1940), p. 12.

[38]Arthur L. Noble, "George Arliss and the Merger of Stage and Screen," *Photo-Era*, September 1930, p. 178.

[39]Quoted in "Disraeli Speaks," p. 19.

[40]"Vita's Play Talking Films as Road Show Substitutes?" *Variety*, March 28, 1929, p. 5.

[41]*Ibid.*, p. 5.

[42]"205 Stage People West," p. 57.

[43]"Vaudevillians Mostly in First 100% Talking Film, 'Lights of New York'," *Variety*, July 11, 1928, p. 27.

[44]Arthur L. Marble, p. 178.

[45]Jerry Hoffman, "Westward the Course of Tin-Pan Alley," *Photoplay Magazine*, September 1929, p. 39.

[46]"Musical Firms' 'Tie-Ups'," *Variety*, April 17, 1929, p. 71.

[47]"Plays Mostly: No Theatre Deal," *Variety*, September 19, 1928, p. 5.

[48]"Dialogue Menace," *Variety*, August 15, 1928, p. 44.

[49]Robert McLaughlin, pp. 76-77.

[50]*Ibid.*, p. 118.

[51]George Jessel, "Why I Alternate on Stage and Screen," *Theatre Magazine*, February 1928, p. 22.

[52]"Fox Assembling List for Talkers," *Variety*, July 4, 1928, p. 5.

[53]"205 Stage People West," p. 57.

[54]Robert McLaughlin, p. 67.

[55]*Ibid.*, p. 65.

[56]Quoted in Robert McLaughlin, pp. 68-69.

[57]"B'way Legit Producers Tying Up With Talker Makers on New Plays," *Variety*, July 25, 1928, p. 49.

[58]See Upton Sinclair, *Upton Sinclair Presents William Fox* (Los Angeles: Published by the author, 1933).

[59]For an account of present activities at the refurbished Astoria studios, see Joe Masefield, "Feature Filmmaking Returns to Astoria," *Making Films in New York*, December/January 1975-76, pp. 22-24.

[60]"Heyday for Legit Talent," *Variety*, December 5, 1928, p. 43.

[61]"Tests Start at Paramount's New L.I. Sound Studios—1st Full Length in November," *Variety*, July 25, 1928, p. 7.

[62]*Ibid.*, p. 7.

[63]Frank Condon, "Over the Bridge to the Movies," *The Saturday Evening Post*, January 16, 1932, pp. 31, 48.

[64]Tom Milne, *Mamoulian* (Bloomington: Indiana University Press, 1969), p. 17.

[65]Andrew Sarris, ed., *Interviews With Film Directors* (New York: Avon Books, 1969), p. 345.

[66]Kingsley Canham, *John Cromwell* (New York: Barnes, 1976), p. 64.

[67]*Ibid.*, p. 64.

[68]Rev. Gene Phillips, S.J., *George Cukor* (Boston: Hall, 1982), pp. 15-16.

[69]Paul D. Zimmerman and Burt Goldblatt, *The Marx Brothers at the Movies* (New York: Putnam's, 1968), pp. 19-20.

[70]"205 Stage People West," p. 57.

[71]Barrett H. Clark and George Freedley, eds., *A History of Modern Drama* (New York: Appleton-Century-Crofts, 1947), p. 714.

[72]Al Manski and Dan Navarro, p. 30.

[73]Oscar G. Brockett and Robert R. Findlay, *Century of Innovation* (Englewood Cliffs, N.J.: Prentice-Hall, 1973, p. 527.

[74]John Howard Lawson, *Film: The Creative Process* (New York: Hill & Wang, 1967), pp. 101-02.

[75]*Ibid.*, p. 104.

[76]*Ibid.*, pp. 104-06.

[77]Alexander Walker, p. 135.

[78]Author's interview with Miles Kreuger in Los Angeles, May 24, 1979.

[79]Alexander Walker, p. 92.

[80]See John C. Tibbetts and James M. Welsh, *His Majesty the American: The Cinema of Douglas Fairbanks, Sr.* (Cranbury, N.J.: Barnes, 1977), pp. 175-84.

[81]Arthur Marx, *Goldwyn* (New York: Norton, 1976), p. 166.

[82]Author's interview with Miles Kreuger in Los Angeles, May 3, 1980.

[83]Author's interview with Miles Kreuger in Los Angeles, May 3, 1980.

[84]Ron Haver, p. 66.

[85]"Sarnoff's Talker Views," *Variety*, October 24, 1928, p. 3.

[86]"205 Stage People West," p. 57.

[87]See Ron Haver, p. 67.

[88]Max Steiner, *Notes to You* (unpublished autobiography in the possession of Mrs. Leonette Steiner).

[89]Bernard Rosenberg and Harry Silverstein, eds., *The Real Tinsel* (New York: Macmillan, 1970), p. 389.

[90]Tony Thomas, *Music for the Movies* (Cranbury, N.J.: Barnes, 1977), p. 112.

[91]Steiner comments on this in Nancy Naumburg, ed., *We Make the Movies* (New York: Norton, 1937), p. 219.

[92]Quoted in John Kobal, *Gotta Sing Gotta Dance* (New York: Hamlyn Publishing Group, 1970), pp. 49-50.

Chapter Five
Plays and Photoplays:
Analyses of Selected Theatrical Films

Several criteria governed my selection of theatrical films for examination in this chapter. First, they came from the two periods of time under discussion, 1912-1915 and 1926-1930. Second they are feature length, encompassing an entire theatrical event and not just a condensation or an excerpt. Third, they are among those relatively few theatrical films of that time that survive today (in spite of loss by print deterioration and other hazards). Fourth, they demonstrate the widest possible range of theatrical imitation—i.e., some being indiscriminately imitative of their theatrical source materials; others more *selectively* imitative of their sources. Fifth, they represent the most popular theatrical formulas of the day—melodramas, well made plays, musical shows, etc. And finally, they were made by those American production and/or distribution companies discussed earlier.

Thus, from the 1912-1915 period: in chronological order, *The Count of Monte Cristo* (Famous Players, 1912), *The Squaw Man* (Lasky Feature Play Company, 1913), *Men and Women* (The Protective Amusement Company, 1914), *The Virginian* (Lasky Feature Play Company, 1914), *The Girl of the Golden West* (Lasky Feature Play Company, 1915), and *The Birth of A Nation* (Triangle/Epoch, 1915); and from 1928-30—*Coquette* (United Artists, 1929), *The Green Goddess* (Warner Brothers, 1929), *The Taming of the Shrew* (United Artists, 1929), *The Virginian* (Paramount, 1929), and examples of the filmed musical shows—*The Cocoanuts* (Paramount, 1929), *Whoopee* (United Artists, 1930) and *King of Jazz* (Universal, 1930). Finally the source plays of these films represented a cross-section of American drama from the middle of the 19th century to the late 1920s. *The Count of Monte Cristo, The Green Goddess* and *The Cocoanuts* represent starring vehicles for popular stage players (who, subsequently, appeared in the film versions); *Men and Women* and *Coquette* represent the American style of well made plays that limited physical action to an indoor locale, emphasized dialogue and restricted the compass of time and space; *The Squaw Man, The Virginian* and *The Girl of the Golden West*, by contrast, represent the western melodramas that exploited a sense of action set against outdoor locales; finally, the musical revues represent a form of theatrical entertainment peculiar to the 1920s.

Closely Imitative Theatrical Films
The Count of Monte Cristo (Famous Players, 1912-13)

The Count of Monte Cristo was the first American-made release by

Famous Players. Filmed in October and November 1912, it was directed by Edwin S. Porter and featured members of the original New York stage cast, including James O'Neill in the role of Edmund Dantes. Alexandre Dumas had published the novel *The Count of Monte Cristo* in 1845 and dramatized it three years later. It was an extravagant melodrama, with twenty acts, thirty-seven tableaux, 221 scenes and fifty-nine characters. It was first performed in London in 1848 and premiered in New York later that year. A subsequent version, known as the "Webster" version, failed on the boards in London in 1868. The author, Benjamin Webster, after condensing the play in 1870, presented it at the Globe Theatre in Boston and at the Grand Opera House in New York three years later. Then John Stetson of the Globe Theatre took over the play and opened it at Booth's Theatre in New York on February 12, 1883. For the first time, James O'Neill appeared as Edmond Dantes. Although the play started badly, O'Neill stayed with it and in 1885 purchased it for $2,000. With the undisputed ownership of the play, he continued to play the role of Dantes throughout the rest of his life.

O'Neill mounted dozens of road tours of the play and it irrevocably became identified with him in the eyes of countless thousands of playgoers across America. A play that exalted and rewarded the common man, Dale Shaw has recently noted in his study of O'Neill's association with *Monte Cristo*: it was the story of a poor man, wrongly accused, who suffers interminably, avenges himself and finally gains untold wealth and high social status. It was, moreover, O'Neill's own life story, wrote Shaw, and everywhere it toured, "People turned out who had been strangers to the theater."[1]

Because O'Neill stood at the center of the play, he continually made changes in the script. Over the years, incidental characters were abandoned, scenes found to be extraneous were eliminated, and spectacular effects unsuited to the small theaters on the road were either scaled down or dropped completely. By the time O'Neill was ready to appear in the film version for Famous Players, the basic text for *The Count of Monte Cristo* was a simplified version of the Dumas and Webster originals. Simply called the "James O'Neill Working Copy," it has been published and probably reflects the version seen by audiences across the country at the turn of the century.[2] There are five acts and ten scenes. The settings include a Marseilles tavern, the cabinet of Villefort, the house of the Count de Morcerf, the cell of the Chauteau d'If, the Inn Pont du Gard and a forest area at Vincennes.

Although there is almost no physical action, the plot is rather complex. Dialogue, asides and reported action bear a heavy burden since many events either have occurred before the curtain or are transpiring offstage and must be relayed to the viewer through conversations. For example, Act One's first scene takes place near a tavern in Marseilles. It opens after Edmund Dantes has docked the ship *Pharon* at Elba at the behest of its dying captain to pick up a mysterious letter from the exiled Napoleon. This action, which is extremely important since it sets in motion the plot of Danglars, Fernand and Villefort to imprison Dantes on charges of treason against Louis XVIII, is related by means of long stretches of dialogue among the conspirators. Similarly, Act Two relies upon a great deal of expository dialogue. It opens eighteen years after Dantes' arrest and subsequent incarceration in the Chateau d'If. Fernand has adopted Dantes' and Mercedes' son Albert, and Dantes has befriended the mysterious Abbe Faria. Again, all of this is conveyed through speeches made by the characters in, respectively, the apartments of Fernand (now a count) and in the Chateau d'If. Throughout Act Four the nefarious activities of Fernand and Danglars are conveyed through their conversations (and subsequent asides) with the vengeful Count of Monte Cristo. Many other crucial moments in the action occur offstage— Villefort stabs himself offstage, Dantes discovers and plunders the island of Monte Cristo between Acts Two and Three, and Dantes rescues Albert (his son) from marauding Arabs between Acts Three and Four. The only moments of action that *do* occur onstage are the marriage of Edmund and Mercedes in the first act, Dantes' escape from the Chateau d'If at the end of the second act and his final duel with Danglars.

This dependence upon expository dialogue and reported action was a challenge for the filmmakers at Famous Players. Edwin S. Porter and Joseph Golden decided that if written intertitles were used they would be too numerous and too long. Instead, they decided to present chronologically the sequence of events. Thus, all the events leading up to Dantes' false arrest are visualized on film. Dantes is first seen as he takes leave of his invalided father and, after bidding farewell to his betrothed Mercedes, when he boards the ship *Pharaon*. The ship's captain, dying of brainfever, entrusts Dantes with a mysterious letter to Napoleon. This episode is overheard by Danglars. Then Dantes arrives at Elba and delivers the document to Napoleon. Other events only alluded to in the play's dialogue are also here presented on film— Dantes' arrest and initial incarceration in the Chateau d'If, his escape by water, his rescue by a passing ship, his arrival at the island of Monte Cristo, and his discovery and exhumation of the buried treasure. (In the play Dantes first utters the famous line, "The world is mine!" after he escapes from the prison; in the film he utters it upon finding the treasure.)

At the same time the film simplifies the plot by eliminating some of the incidental characters and incidents. The scenes with Noitier, the revolutionary and brother of Villefort, are drastically cut or, in the instance of his publication of defamatory articles about Fernand (in Act Four), deleted altogether. The character of Caderousse, originally implicated in the plot against Dantes (but later to repent and serve as Dantes' servant) is only seen near the opening of the film. All reference to the African exploits of the Count are deleted. Also missing in the film is the catharsis of Dantes when he realizes the tragedy of his vengeful ways. By swearing to kill Albert he had unwittingly sworn to kill his own son. This near-tragedy on his conscience, Dantes decides to let God alone punish the conspirators: "Led by a mean and selfish jealousy, I sought to strike Fernand cruelly to the heart by slaying his son, and it is my heart Thou strikest, and before my weapon Thou placest mine own child. 'Tis justice ..." (66-67).

Many other elements of the play are retained in the film version. The long conversation between Mercedes and Dantes near the beginning of Act One is conveyed on film by a long pantomimed scene. Another long pantomime enacts Danglar and Fernand's drafting of the document to the King's Procurer that implicates Dantes in a plot with Napoleon. The tableau at the end of Act One, Scene Three at the Reserve Inn is transferred to film: the wedding ceremony of Dantes and Mercedes is interrupted by Dantes' arrest and Mercedes' fainting fit which brings down the curtain. Also transferred to film is the long conversation between Dantes and the Abbe Faria in the prison cell wherein we learn of the treasure of Monte Cristo. The three famous scenes where Dantes kills his enemies and mutters, successively, "One!," "Two!," and "Three!" are retained. And, finally, the climactic tableau of Dantes, Mercedes and the kneeling Albert occupies its rightful position at the end of the film.

Despite the differences between the play and the film version, *The Count of Monte Cristo* remains a literal translation of a play onto film. The use of artificial scenery drop curtains and painted backdrops predominates, excepting a few scenes displaying natural locales—such as the scene where Dantes swims away from the Chateau d'If toward the island of Monte Cristo. The setting at the beginning of the film of Dantes' father's room is simply a shallow playing space with only a rude table and chair in front of a painted flat. For the harbor settings at Marseilles there are three artificial settings—a tavern set with a harbor scene painted behind it, a stone wall with a painting of ships' masts behind it, and a tavern exterior backed by a seacoast scene painted on a flat. The interior of the Chateau d'If is nothing more than a shallow playing space backed by a painted flat of a stone wall along a plane parallel to the camera. Soldiers enter and exit by simply passing laterally beyond the edges of the frame, which approximate the proscenium boundaries of a stage.

The artificiality of these settings forces a stiffness upon the acting. O'Neill, of course, is in almost every scene. He stands in the center forestage area and employs the broad gestures and stiff attitudes characteristic of many popular stage actors of the day. This style is all the more strenuous because there are few intertitles to explain the action. It is an example of what Montrose J. Moses called "strenuous acting," (a reliance upon pantomime instead of dialogue; see Chapter One). For example, when Dantes returns from Elba and gives Mercedes a keepsake brooch (seen briefly in one of the two closeup inserts in the film), the furtive Fernand vigorously registers jealousy upstage while the two lovers broadly pantomime their love scene downstage. Their gestures seem choreographed, their hands describing great arcs in the air, their expressions and body movements stiff and jointed. When Dantes conceives his plan of escaping the Chateau d'If by substituting for the dead Abbe Faria, he broadly points first to himself, then to the Abbe, and then knowingly looks toward the camera, lest the viewer be in doubt about his strategy. But probably O'Neill's most awkward moment comes when Dantes learns that Albert is his real son. The subsequent upthrust of O'Neill's arms, the agonized backward tilt of the head, the stiff posture of the body, seem inappropriate for the intimacy of the medium distance camera vantage point.

The tableaux groupings of the original play are duplicated in the film. Tableaux, of course, were common both to the melodrama and the "legitimate" drama of the 19th century.[3] Examples in the film of *Monte Cristo* can be found in the scenes of the marriage ceremony and the final duel. In the first, the ranks of flower girls and attendants serve as a frame for Dantes and Mercedes downstage. When Dantes is suddenly arrested and removed from the room, Mercedes faints and the assembled group freezes stiffly in place. In the second example, the duel between Dantes and Fernand is followed by a reconciliation wherein Dantes embraces Mercedes while young Albert kneels to the right—all of which is held in a prolonged shot from a middle distance vantage point. These studied moments in the film of acting and pose are made more awkward by the fact that the players seem to be performing to the gallery when, in fact, the camera lens is only a medium distance from them, approximating the view from a front row aisle seat. In a word, the artificiality of the pose is heightened by the relatively close scrutiny of the camera lens.

Also enforcing this apparent artificiality of setting and acting is the occasional juxtaposition of the few natural locales with the painted sets. This is apparent when Dantes finds the grotto where Cardinal Spada's island treasure is hidden. Dantes is seen swimming in a real setting of shoals and rocks. But in the next shot he reappears in a blatantly artificial paper-mache cave setting. Worse, when Dantes swings his pick at the painted floor of the cave, he takes care not to make contact with the floor. Instead, he broadly pantomimes the digging movement and, leaning over, pretends to uncover a trap door. This illusion might have been adequate for a theatre house where many viewers were removed at a distance from the action, but for the closer scrutiny of the camera lens, the contrivance of the action is immediately exposed.

It is apparent that the film version of *The Count of Monte Cristo* was planned for audiences familiar with the action of the play. It is not unusual here for a succession of long, sixty-second takes to have no explanatory intertitles. This is especially troublesome in the long dialogue exchanges between Dantes and the Abbe Faria in the Chateau d'If, the conversations between Dantes and Mercedes prior to his arrest, the episode when Dantes confronts the banker Morel, and the argument between Albert and Danglars that precipitates their intended duel. There is no apparent reason why they all should stand around mouthing silent dialogue, unless the audience is expected to know the events. The effect, to today's viewer, is only baffling. (The confusion is further intensified because some of the titles are out of sequence with the events they describe. Several factors could explain these discrepancies—the filmmakers' ineptitude, the rearrangement of some of the titles when the paper print was registered with the Library of Congress in 1913, or the possibility of a subsequent rearrangement of scenes and titles when the film was restored by Kemp Niver's Renovare Company in the mid-1950s.)

Men and Women (The Protective Amusement Company, 1913)

Four of the plays filmed by the Protective Amusement Company, 1913-14, were written by the team of Henry C. De Mille and David Belasco. They were, in order of release, *Lord Chumley* (Lyceum Theatre premiere, August 20, 1888) *The Charity Ball* (Lyceum Theatre premiere, October 20, 1890), *The Wife* (Lyceum Theatre premiere, November 1, 1887), and *Men & Women* (Proctor Theatre Premiere, October 20, 1890)." The collaboration began in 1887 when Daniel Frohman was organizing a permanent company for the regular stock season at the Lyceum Theatre. He was looking for a society play in the mold of the European well made plays of Robertson and Pinero. He turned to his two friends Henry De Mille and David Belasco. Their first play, *The Wife,* in which infidelity was treated with compassion and understanding was a huge success, running 239 consecutive performances. It was revived frequently thereafter for New York audiences—even as late as 1915. *Lord Chumley,* which followed, was a vehicle tailored for E.H. Sothern, who played the title role. *Men and Women* was the last play in the series and presented Maude Adams in her New York debut in the role of Dora Prescott, for whom Frohman had commissioned the part. It ran for over two hundred performances.[4]

These plays appeared at the same time as William Dean Howells' one-act playlets, Bronson Howard's *The Banker's Daughter* and *Shenandoah,* Steele MacKaye's *Hazel Kirke* and *Paul Kauvar,* and Herne's *Margaret Fleming,* and they are usually neglected in favor of them in most examinations of American naturalistic theater.[5] It is true that the De Mille/Belasco series do belong to the drawing room style of the well made play. They employ numerous asides and present a variety of incidental characters and situations. But this series also reveals a tendency in the American drama to deal with contemporary issues and strong situations. Robert Hamilton Ball, in his preface to the published texts of the De Mille/Belasco plays, acknowledges this:

The interest in social and economic themes is evidenced by ... [the] treatment of politics in *The Wife*, of speculation and poverty in *The Charity Ball*, of banking and prison in *Men and Women*. Nevertheless, though [Henry De Mille] plainly had strong opinions on these subjects, they were always in the background of the plays in which he collaborated with David Belasco. (xxii)

Thus, like the well made plays of Scribe, the De Mille/Belasco plays dealt with social issues; these issues, however, were subordinated to the overriding priorities of entertainment.

Men and Women was about the imminent collapse of the Jefferson National Bank during a Wall Street panic. Two of the bank's young cashiers, William Prescott and Edward Seabury, have been speculating with large quantities of the Bank's bonds. The subsequent loss of funds has left the Bank vulnerable for a probable "run" on it. The burden of guilt falls upon Seabury's shoulders and the Bank's Counsel, Calvin Stedman, pushes for a conviction of the youth. But Ned and the Bank are both saved when William Prescott confesses his own guilt. Funds subsequently become available to cover the Bank's losses.

The play presents an appeal for tolerance toward wrongdoers who are trying to redeem themselves. Unbeknownst to anyone, Governor Rodman of Arizona, whose daughter is in love with William Prescott, was himself guilty of bank defalcation in his youth. He sympathizes with Seabury and Prescott's predicament. He, too, it seems, had been pursued years ago by this same Prosecutor, Calvin Stedman. Rodman thus is able to comment on the plight of the ex-convict who can never be forgiven by society:

I was sent to prison for six years. When my trial ended, and, submitting to the decree, I paid the price of my misdeeds, I thought prosecution would cease. But it seems that six years were not enough, for there stands the prosecutor still, and I am as much the convict as when I stood in Auburn prison .... Let a man once wear the stripes of a convict, and the world will permit no new life for him, except through the portals of the grave. (326)

And later in the play when William Prescott finds himself in a smaller situation, he, too, cries out: "I am free to walk the streets, but it must be those that are unfrequented, to escape the humiliation of being passed by former friends who pretend not to see me. I have health, ability, and would be thankful for the meanest position they can offer, but no one will trust me." (334)

The main action in *Men and Women* is concerned with men struggling to keep a bank afloat in a moment of financial crisis. The play's most suspenseful scene occurs during a meeting of the Bank's officers early in Act Three to unmask the defaulter and save the Bank. Yet the defaulter is not the real villain in the standard sense of the melodrama—rather it is the Panic itself. The play's closest candidate to the stock villain of melodrama is the vengeful Calvin Stedman, whose pursuit of two generations of bank defaulters is borne as much out of disappointed love as it is out of a sense of frustrated justice. However, even Stedman in the end reconciles his vengeful ways with the need for compassion. He shakes hands with his intended victim, Ned, and resolves to work toward saving, instead of prosecuting, his other target, William Prescott.

The text of *Men and Women* displays characteristics of staging and exposition that tie it to the traditions of 19th century stagecraft. For example, each of the four acts consists of lengthy dialogues where the characters are split into two separate groups, each group occupying a different part of the stage. While a conversation is occurring on one part of the stage, asides that comment on the dialogue are heard from other parts of the stage. We must accept the convention that, although these characters are very close to one another, they do not hear the words that the audience hears. An aside from one character may reveal, for instance, that Governor Rodman in reality is an ex-convict, but that revelation is not allowed the other characters standing on stage at that moment. The device of the soliloquy is also extensively used. In the play's only "pictorial" moment, William Prescott in a long soliloquy agonizes over the question of whether or not he should reveal his own culpability in the Bank's crisis. At first he speaks of suicide; but gradually he realizes that he must live to face squarely his problems. All the time he is speaking, the moonlight, according to stage directions in Act Three, brightens perceptibly until it has "illuminated the stained-glass window, gradually revealing the picture of the Savior and the Magdalen ... the light from it falling on the bowed head of William" (330). This scene is cited by Lise-Lone Marker in her study of Belasco's stagecraft as an early example of his predilection for dramatic lighting effects.[6] Finally, as we have seen in *The Count of Monte Cristo*, many of the principle actions in the play have already occurred before the curtain's rise for each act. They are related to us by means of lengthy, expository dialogues and asides. Thus, events in Governor Rodman's past—his embezzlement, his arrest, trial and imprisonment—are revealed through dialogue between Rodman and William Prescott at the end of Act One.

As had happened in the film version of *The Count of Monte Cristo, Men and Women* films in chronological order the events referred to in the play's dialogue. The first eight minutes of the film are devoted to a series of *tableaux*, or living pictures, much in the manner that they might be employed in a stage production. For example, a written intertitle will flash on the screen and then be followed by a brief shot of an appropriate figure grouping, the figures relatively motionless throughout the shot. "After a great bank failure," announces the first title, "the bank cashier is charged with embezzlement and placed on trial." This is followed by a courtroom scene where a policeman points to the prisoner and then gestures in dismissal as the man is escorted "offstage"—or beyond the edge of the frame. Then appears another title: "Death then claims the faithful wife," followed by a tableau of a deathbed, a child kneeling before it, and a praying nun hovering over the group. And so on, until Rodman's entire history from trial to imprisonment to repentance to political rise have been explained to us. By this method, we are spared the long exchanges of expository dialogue provided in the play, even if we are left with a series of melodramatic tableaux that remove any sense of subtlety or complexity from the action. By the time the main principles have gathered together in Mrs. Prescott's—the point at which the play begins—the viewer is already well acquainted with their respective histories. However, this use of tableaux robs the film of one of the dramatic highpoints of the original play—the delayed revelation of Rodman's guilty past that originally came *after* we were introduced to him as the respectable Governor of Arizona.

For the most part, the filming techniques merely record the action in such a way as to promote the sense that we are watching a stage play from a center aisle seat. The camera distance is consistently held to medium long shot, which is to say that the figures are seen from head to toe—occasionally from head to knee. The settings they occupy, the offices of Ned and William at the Bank and the home of Bank President Cohen, are shallow-depth box sets. The players enter and exit from the edges of the frame, which is to say that their movements are lateral and never toward or away from the camera. The dual set of President Cohen's meeting room and the adjoining room—which in the play allowed two threads of action to be played out concurrently—is re-created in the film by the device of parallel editing. When Prescott, tortured by his own guilt, leaves the meeting room to sit alone in the next chamber, shots alternate showing Prescott alone and then the assembled officers next door. Thus, cutting takes us back and forth to both locations, whereas in the play we could view both areas simultaneously. Although the action in both play and film is identical throughout this scene (even to the shot of Prescott mutely slipping handcuffs on himself as he accepts his guilt), it is curious to note that the play's pictorial effect of the painting of the Magdalen is abandoned in the film. Instead, Prescott broadly pantomimes his guilt, sans audible dialogue and sans appropriate atmosphere. He simply sits, wrings his hands, and then puts on the cuffs. In contrast to the play, the effect is flat and unconvincing. Throughout this and all other scenes, it should be emphasized, the camera remains fixed in medium distance from the stage occupying a plane parallel to the lens. There are no closeups, except for a few inserted shots of letters and telegrams.

Because *Men and Women* had been a parlor drama, its action confined to libraries, corridors and meeting rooms, there was no need for the film version to employ painted scenery as a substitute for exterior locales. When the few examples of exterior shooting do occur—added scenes showing two shots of a run on a bank, a shot of Rodman's daughter at school leaning against a tree, and one shot of New York's Grand Central Station—they reveal natural locales. For the most part, however, the film's action is confined to the Bank's interior and President Cohen's meeting room.

The chief sin of omission in the film version is the absence of anything resembling the play's plea for social tolerance of ex-convicts. Stedman's obsessive pursuit of Ned Seabury is stripped of its complex motivations and emerges as merely a melodramatic chase. Similarly, Governor Rodman's impassioned pleas for social justice toward repentant criminals are omitted altogether. The bonds between him and the guilty William Prescott are never explored, as they were in the play. The sparing use of intertitles did not permit, apparently, the transfer of these issues to the film. Action, not dialogue, prevailed in the film.

The Squaw Man (Jesse L. Lasky Feature Play Company, 1913)

Edwin Milton Royle's most popular play was a shrewd blend of contradictory elements. It demonstrated some attributes of naturalism yet it utilized plot devices and situations that derived from the style of the regional melodrama. It flung its wild western locales into the teeth of the stiff-upper-lip school of English well made drama. Its juxtaposition of these elements are harsh: English lords go west in America to punch cattle, an Indian maiden sacrifices herself for the sake of a British code of morality (which she never understands) and there is an interracial marriage. The play was first presented by Royle and William Faversham at Wallack's Theatre in New York on October 23, 1905, and ran for 222 performances. William Faversham appeared in the title role and William S. Hart portrayed his nemesis, Cash Hawkins. Dustin Farnum appeared in the revival at the Broadway Theatre on January 9, 1911, which ran for eight performances.[7]

The first act is set on the estate of the Earl of Kerhill in England. Charity money contributed by the men of the 16th Lances has mysteriously disappeared. Captain James Wynnegate, in order to protect the culprit, his cousin, assumes the blame for the loss and is subsequently forced to leave England in disgrace. In the second act the fugitive Wynnegate has reached the American West and manages a ranch in Utah, where he faces the vicious opposition of the villainous rustler, Cash Hawkins. Wynnegate (now "Jim Carston") is saved from being ambushed by Hawkins when an Indian girl, Nat-U-Rich, shoots Hawkins from cover. The third act begins years later after Jim has married the Indian girl out of a sense of duty. Now a "squaw man" outcast, he raises their son Hal with dignity while he fights to keep his ranch operating. When members of the English branch of the Wynnegate family visit the ranch to inform him that his name has been cleared and that the way is open for him to return to England and his title, he sadly realizes that out of duty he must stay with Nat-U-Rich. He decides to send his only son back to England. In the fourth and final act, Nat-U-Rich devises a plan that will enable both Jim and the boy to return to England together: she commits suicide.

The play tried to combine naturalistic concerns (the regional settings of Utah) with the more traditional form of the well made play. Arthur Hobson Quinn praised the play for "its fidelity to actual conditions" which elevated the last three acts beyond mere melodrama.[8] Royle was determined to put the "real Indian" on the stage, based on his own experiences in the American West. In casting for the Indian characters, for example, he secured the services of at least one authentic Ute Indian to insure the proper dialect and speech inflection.

Royle's play attacked racist attitudes toward Indians. "I don't think we ever do these primitive races justice," Wynnegate tells a visitor from England to his ranch. "Here I am a 'Squaw Man'—that is, socially ostracised. You see, we have our social distinctions, even out here" (233). And when he prevents the local sheriff from arresting Nat-U-Rich on charges of the shooting of Cash Hawkins, he declares, "There are cases, Sheriff, where justice is superior to the law. And a white man's court is a bad place for justice to the Indian" (237).

Englishmen and their titles, by contrast, become objects of satiric jabs in the play. In the first act titled aristocrats who marry wealthy Americans in an exchange of money for pedigree, are ridiculed. "Please examine these first-class specimens of the British aristocracy," jokes one character, regarding Wynnegate in the first act. "He has blue ribbons, medals, and a pedigree longer than your purses. He's for sale" (214). And when Jim reaches Utah and is promptly swindled by a canny cattleman, one of the locals comments, "The prosperity of our beloved country would go plumb to Gehenna if an all wise Providence did not enable us to sell an Englishman a mine or a ranch now and then" (220).

Although the play was, for the most part, set in wide open western locales, the playwright made little attempt to exploit them. Most of the action—Jim's discovery that Cash Hawkins is a rustler, his rescue by Nat-U-Rich from a fall down a mountain ravine, Nat-U-Rich's suicide—takes place off stage and is conveyed to us by expository dialogue. The one moment of real physical action is the barroom confrontation in Act Two between Wynnegate and Hawkins. The rest of the time the dialogue conveys the action.

Yet the *implications* of regional color and open air romance were there and the Jesse L. Lasky Company decided to film it as its first release in 1913. Royle enthusiastically joined with the Lasky filmmakers in preparing the script. He noted in 1914 that the movies held certain advantages over the stage for the production of stories like *The Squaw Man*. Whereas a monologue in the play was utilized to describe the incident of Nat-U-Rich's rescue of Wynnegate from the ravine accident, a succession of shots could visually present the same thing in a film. "The weakest part of the melodrama is its dialogue," he said, "and that's why we let them say as little as possible in the melodrama. The situations are told better by actions than by words."[9] Similarly, the use of double-exposure to juxtapose two scenes in the same frame could achieve on film effects not possible on the stage. How much cannot be expressed by these "vision" effects, Royle asked. "A vision on the conventional stage is next to impossible and hardly ever really effective. On the screen a vision seems more natural and can easily be utilized for the highest purposes of the dramatist."[10] The film of *The Squaw Man* presents two scenes where such juxtapositions of elements occur.

This use of double-exposure emphasizes the commitment of the original play—to contrast the lifestyles of the English aristocracy and the American West. In one scene Wynnegate quietly scans the illustrated papers looking for news of his native England while relaxing in his ranchhouse. As he holds before him a society page depicting a drawing of a lady of fashion, the page dissolves into a portrait of the woman he left behind at Maudsley Towers. In the other scene, Jim has been told that he can return to England with honor. As he stands at the right half of the frame pantomiming his nostalgia for home, the left half of the frame dissolves into views of his former life in England—a dinner scene in his old estate followed by a view of his Lancers standing in formation. In the play this sense of nostalgia had been conveyed by a long speech ("I love old England as only an exile can . . . . "), but in the film the uniquely cinematic device of the double-exposure conveys that nostalgia far more effectively and economically.

Another way in which the film realized Royle's ambition to put words into actions was in use of exterior shooting. *The Squaw Man* was one of the first filmed plays to make more than minimal use of natural locales. Many events only alluded to in the dialogue of the play were visualized on the screen without the insistence upon shallow-depth playing areas and painted scenery characteristic of other filmed plays like *The Count of Monte Cristo*. One example is Jim Wynnegate's capture of the rustler Cash Hawkins; another is Nat-U-Rich's rescue of Wynnegate during a roundup from the mountain snows. In the first, a quick succession of shots, each photographed in long distance, depicts Wynnegate and other horsemen chasing down the rustlers. In the second, Wynnegate, after being injured in a fall from his horse during the roundup, wanders aimlessly through the thickening snows. He is rescued by Nat-U-Rich, who has followed him across the slopes and who pulls him from the ravine into which he has fallen. By means of cross-cutting, the shots shift from one character to the other as they both wander through the snows. This is not the continuity cutting characteristic of the theatrical films already discussed; rather, the editing strategy serves to bind together the two principal characters, symbolizing the bonds that will hold them together until her death at the end of the play. The third example presents an event that was not in the original play at all—Wynnegate's passage from England to America.

There is no reference in the play to the story of Wynnegate's voyage; but in the film, there is an extended scene wherein Wynnegate books passage to America. When the vessel catches fire, the passengers abandon ship. This event, while it is merely tacked on to the main narrative and does nothing to add to the essential action of the play, is quite exciting. At least a dozen shots of brief duration reveal, in succession, the heaving ocean, the burning decks of the ship, and the hysteria of the jostling passengers boarding the boats. Needless to say, the effect of the swift pace and the use of natural locales would be quite impossible on the stage.

Yet this is a filmed stage play, and the above sequence is intercut with scenes that remind us of its proscenium origins. During the fire, there is a scuffle below decks between Wynnegate and a pursuing Scotland Yard agent. Although this incident has been added to the story, it is nonetheless photographed in such a way that it seems to occur on a shallow-depth proscenium stage. The edges of the frame approximate the surrounding walls of the cabin room, the depth of the playing area is extremely shallow, and the broad gestures and pantomime are addressed directly to the camera. When this is intercut with the shots of the heaving ocean and the burning ship, we get the jarring juxtaposition of the real with the artificial that was so apparent in *The Count of Monte Cristo.*

Similar problems arise when the artificial interior of the western saloon is contrasted with the natural locations of the open range. On the stage, both the range vistas and the saloon interiors were painted flats. But the use of natural locales in the firm only throw into harsh relief the artificial nature of the interiors. Incidentally, the western saloon is pictured exactly as it was described in the second act of the play, even down to the double doors at the rear of the set through which the arrival of the Overland Limited can be seen. Except for an occasional shift in camera position from a medium to a medium-long shot, the shallow-depth playing area remains in plane parallel to the camera plane. In the sequence wherein Wynnegate and his men chase down the rustlers, shots of the artificial interior of the saloon clash with the natural locales.

For the most part, the acting styles of Dustin Farnum and others in the cast are in the declamatory style prevalent in stage melodramas. This is most apparent in the scenes of the film that correspond to Acts Three and Four, where the action transpires in the dooryard of the Carston Ranch. The dialogues between the English lawyer and Wynnegate (where Jim declares his nostalgia for England) and between Jim and Nat-U-Rich (where Jim announces his intentions to send the boy back to England) consist of prolonged, static shots with numerous broad gestures and posed attitudes. Although they talk at length, only a few explanatory titles are provided. In both scenes the speakers take their positions at opposite ends of frame and remain there in relatively immobile attitudes. The longest take of the film

Mary Pickford's first talking picture was *Coquette* (1929), adapted from the 1927 play by George Abbott and Ann Preston Bridgers.

occurs when the cowboys bid farewell to the little boy. This scene, faithfully taken from the play, presents a line of cowboys "upstage" in the frame; they advance downstage in single file, each presenting the boy with a gift. This action lasts a full two minutes, without any cutting or camera movement whatever. Similar kinds of staging and camera disposition are seen in two other sequences derived from the play—when the brooding Wynnegate fails to see Nat-U-Rich behind him as she steals off with her gun to commit suicide; and when her body is carried back onstage to a grieving crowd standing in a stiff tableau. The character disposition is static, the gestures stiff, the camera unmoving in medium shot.

For the most part, the camera maintains a medium shot position that keeps the characters visible from head to toe in the frame. The cutting, with the exception of the scenes already cited, is simple continuity cutting. There are only three occasions when closeups are utilized. The first occurs during a scene not in the original play. Wynnegate has arrived in New York. While visiting a restaurant, he foils an attempt by a stranger to pick another man's pocket. There appears a close up of a hand slipping into a pocket, crudely approximating Wynnegate's point of view. The second occurs after Jim has been accused by the sheriff of shooting down Cash Hawkins in the saloon. When Jim proffers his pistol, there is a closeup of the gun, revealing that all its chambers are full. And the third closeup depicts a bit of cloth that the sheriff has found, implicating Nat-U-Rich in the shooting.

The final scene in the film contains a blatant theatrical moment. This moment is a faithful translation of the play's final tableau. Nat-U-Rich's body has been found and is brought on stage by the cowboys while Wynnegate sits and broods downstage. Dustin Farnum's exaggerated pantomime is at its most strenuous here as, echoing the original words from the play, he says, "Poor little mother!" to end the film.

The play's sense of social injustice, its satiric attacks on the English aristocracy, and its use of regional dialects (from England to Utah) have been largely omitted. However, at its most effective, the film's use of double-exposure affirms the dominating theme of East meeting West. As for the jarring blends of exteriors and artificial interiors, perhaps that is not far after all from the idea Royle had wanted to capture of the Englishman with his rules and artificial codes adrift in a country that knew no such rules or boundaries. The naturalness of the location settings only reaffirms the artifice of the rest of the setting.

Coquette (United Artists, released 12 April 1929)

George Abbott, the author of *Coquette*, was an important figure in American drama throughout the 1920s and 1930s. He knew almost every aspect of theater production. He had been a student of George Pierce Baker at Harvard at the same time O'Neill was there. He acted in the role of "Dynamite

Jim" in John Howard Lawson's important production of *Processional* in 1924. That same year he wrote (with James Gleason) his first success on Broadway, *The Fall Guy* (which was filmed by RKO in 1930). *Broadway* (cowritten with Philip Dunning and filmed by Universal in 1929) followed in 1926; the rest of the decade saw his staging of John V.A. Weaver's tough *Love 'Em and Leave 'Em*, his participation in the fast, hard-boiled melodrama *Chicago*, the satire of war and revolution in *Spread Eagle*, and the indictment of feminine stereotypes in *Coquette*. He also worked as a musical and dramatic producer/director and was responsible in 1935 for *Three Men on a Horse*. In sum, in the words of Howard Taubman, Abbott was extremely versatile, "for he could put his hand successfully not only to farce, at which he was a master, but to satire, melodrama and social comment."[11]

Coquette was the major hit of the early 1927 Broadway season. Helen Hayes appeared in the title role. The play, at once jazzy and contemporary was, ultimately, tragic in its consequences. More important from the standpoint of the filmmakers, the play had been extremely successful, running 253 performances since its New York premiere on November 8, 1927.[12] When Mary Pickford cast about for a subject for her first talkie, she opted, like so many other filmmakers, to film a stage play. She followed a practice current at the time of taking a "screen test" of the play—i.e., she had parts of the play filmed with the original cast.[13] According to Alexander Walker, she had the test run and promptly pronounced the cast unsatisfactory, except for Miss Hayes, whose part she was determined to play.[14] The resulting film, begun in 1928 and released in April 1929, won the Academy Award for Pickford for Best Actress of the year.

The play's central character was Norma Besant, flirtatious, beautiful and conniving daughter of a gallant of the old South, Dr. Besant. One of her admirers was young Michael Jeffery, who, because of his relative poverty and lack of social connections, was disapproved of by Dr. Besant. But Michael, independent of nature, is easily swayed by Norma's coquettish ways, and she promptly falls in love with him. The disapproving Dr. Besant orders him out of the house. He reluctantly leaves but not before he secretly reveals to Norma that in six months he will return with his position established and win her father over. But when he does return, the outraged Dr. Besant attacks him with a gun and shoots him dead. On trial, Besant can be saved only by Norma, who is told that she must swear that her honor had been "soiled" by Michael and that her father had been justified in avenging her honor. Unbeknownst to anyone, Norma is pregnant. Should that fact come out in court, it would weaken her father's case and ruin her social position. In an ambiguous ending, Norma chooses to save the family honor and her father's reputation by shooting herself.

The play's deceptively light and frivolous tone in the first two acts suddenly turns darker in the third. The portrait of the beleaguered Norma, confronted by the awkward choices occasioned by an unwanted pregnancy, is incisively drawn. In this respect, the play resembles other "women's" plays that had marked the maturation of the American theater after the turn of the century, following the precedent of *A Doll's House* (1879). Early examples of these American plays included a series of one-act plays by George Middleton in 1911-14 (some of which, like "Back of the Ballot" were frankly pro-suffrage), Clyde Fitch's *The Climbers* (1901) and *The Truth* (1907), Eugene Walter's *The Easiest Way* (1908), William Vaughn Moody's *The Great Divide* (1906), Charles Klein's *Maggie Pepper* (1911) and *The Daughters of Men* (1902), and several plays by Rachel Carothers—*A Man's World* (1909), *He and She* (1911).[15] Carothers declared that these plays had great dramatic potential for the modern stage:

> Most of the great modern plays are studies of women. I suppose it is because women are in themselves more dramatic than men, more changing and a more significant note of the hour in which they live. If you want to see the signs of the times, watch women. Their evolution is the most important thing in modern life.[16]

Coquette's concerns with the entrapment of Norma Besant within fixed role expectancies relate it to the above plays. Recalling the tragic Laura Murdoch and Ruth Ghent in, respectively, *The Easiest Way* and *The Great Divide*, Norma Besant is caught midway between two contradictory conditions—that of the chaste yet coquettish Southern belle and that of a sexually fulfilled woman with Michael Jeffery. Early in the play she is counselled by her brother Jimmy not to cause scandals by remaining out late at night. She replies, "But Jimmy, I don't think every man wants a woman upon a pedestal like you and Daddy." "I tell you," he responds, "a man wants a girl down where he can grab her, but he doesn't want every other man in sight grabbing her." To this neat double standard, Norma can only sigh, "That must be how it is" (953). She feels stifled and she admits to a friend later, "sometimes when I seem to be having a good time I'm really bored to death. Didn't you ever think of that? You have to keep up the bluff, or else you won't be popular. But you get awfully sick of men" (27). These words echo those of Laura Murdoch's friend in *The Easiest Way*, who counsels her: "Don't you realize that you and me, and all the girls that are shoved into this life, are practically the common prey of any man who happens to come along? [But] we've got brains. That is a game, Laura, not a sentiment."[17]

Her problems are later compounded by the death sentence hanging over her father. Her father's defense, a lawyer friend assures her, will rest upon the argument that her father was protecting her chastity by dispatching Jeffery. But what of the truth, asks Norma, now aware of her pregnancy—what happens if she can't lie to the jury and they learn instead she is pregnant by Michael? Wentworth replies: "My dear, it makes all the difference between justice and murder. The fact that you are a virgin gives your father the right to defend your name." He explains further that a committee might be appointed by the court "to establish beyond any question that you are a chaste girl." Shocked at this travesty of "justice," Norma cries out brokenly, "I guess if I were dead, the dear old chivalry wouldn't let them . . ." (79). She stops short when the solution occurs to her. When the lawyer offers to marry her, she refuses. At the same time she knows she can't stand the humiliation of physical examination by any kind of "committee." The only other prospect is to stand by and see her father convicted of murder. Act Three ends with a shot ringing out offstage signalling her suicide.

Of all the plays discussed so far this is the first to present any real challenge to the movies' censorship code. No investigation into the problems and challenges of the filmic adaptation of dramatic literature can long ignore this problem. Although there are some changes in the film's narrative continuity, the most *substantial* changes are those adopted to circumvent the censor and tailor the play into a suitable vehicle for Mary Pickford. But the original thrust of the play is ruined.

With few exceptions, the film version of the play is confined to the Besant house, as was the play. Character groupings and dialogue are transferred intact to the film—such as in the long exchange between Norma and Michael when they first declare their mutual love; the argument between Michael and Dr. Besant; the opening dialogue between Norma, her brother Jimmy and Dr. Bisant wherein most of the exposition of past events occurs; and the scene where Jimmy attempts to shield Norma from her father's wrath over her late hours with Michael. In all these scenes the dialogue is retained, word for word. The camera keeps the action in medium shot (only occasionally intercutting for reaction shots or closer views). The action is confined to the shallow-depth interior, all entrances and exits using the right and left sides of the frame. Thus, even though there is the crude editing possible under the multiple-camera arrangement the general effect is that of watching a performance on a proscenium stage.

The film occasionally breaks away from the proscenium illusion. An added scene is the climatic courtroom trial of Dr. Besant. The events are divided into long shots of the courtroom, closeups of Norma and her father and medium shots of the witness stand. Once the camera moves, panning from the pleading face of Dr. Besant to the revolver with which he will end his life in a few moments. Other added scenes contain both cinematic and theatrical effects. For example, when Michael is shot by Dr. Besant, he is not killed at once, as happens in the play; rather, mortally wounded, he languishes until Norma can rush to his side (three brief shots of her running down a city street, across a stream and up a hill). This brief flurry of editing is immediately followed by the deathbed scene. Secondary characters "frame" the scene by hovering about in the background while Norma and Michael reaffirm their love.

For the most part the union of image and sound is synchronous—whenever a sound is heard, its causing agent is seen at the same time. The term "synchronous sound" does not mean "synchronized sound," which designates any kind of recording system where sound is mechanically combined with the film image. A synchronous combination of image and sound emphasizes the *causal* bond between the two. *Coquette*'s use of synchronous sound is typical of synchronized-sound films of the time. Moreover it is characteristic of *Coquette* and most films of the day that when *music* is heard, its source should be seen at the same time. Thus, the music heard during the college dance sequence is the product of an orchestra prominently displayed. However, there are two brief moments that demonstrate the possibilities of the asynchronous blend of image and sound—an increasingly important part of filmmaking by 1929. When the discharge of the pistol, for example, is heard, the camera remains on Norma's face. This combination of image and sound has more dramatic impact than it would displayed in a synchronous way. What the film achieves is an effect impossible to the silent screen. The second example is the title epilogue when the disconsolate Norma returns home alone after her father's death. As her small figure walks away from the camera, the street lights blink on in succession ahead of her. It is at this moment that the only moment of incidental sound occurs as strains of music well up just before and during the appearance of the end title credits. No orchestra seen, the music is an aural element that enhances the dramatic moment.

The acting in *Coquette* is a throwback to the declamatory style seen in the film versions of *The Count of Monte Cristo* and *The Squaw Man*. John Mack Brown, who replaced Elliott Cabot as Michael Jefferys, is the worst offender. His physical stiffness, the unrelieved monotony in his vocal dynamics and inflection, his awkward postures are inappropriate to the part of a young, strong romantic lead. Mary Pickford, surprisingly, fares no better. Despite the fact that she had been known for her subtle acting styles in films for years, this return to theatrical material enforces a studied and forced quality to her movement and voice.

Unfortunately, the filmmakers refrained from confronting the basic thematic commitments of the play. Censorship restrictions imposed by the Hays Office since 1921 were being reinforced by the writing of the new Motion Picture Production Code in 1929 and 1930. Illicit sex and suicide were expressly forbidden.[18] This explains why the film version of *Coquette* avoided the question of Norma's pregnancy and subsequent suicide. In the film it is made clear that Norma is *not* pregnant. Dialogue was added to the film where she informs her maid that she and Michael did not become sexually intimate. This completely changes the dramatic emphasis. Norma's pregnancy had resulted from her rebellious love for Michael and her inability to adhere to the chaste standards imposed upon her by her father and brother;

moreover, her pregnancy represented a threat to her father's defense against the murder charge. Norma's chastity is emphasized and it is her father who must die—his suicide can be construed not so much as self destruction as just retribution for his murder of Michael. The concept of "moral compensation" is served—a method of punishment prevalent in Hollywood films at this time.[19] Much of the individual will, passion and conflict that surrounded Norma in the play is diminished. It is Norma's survival that occasions the film's weakest moment. In a brief dialogue added to the conclusion, she is confronted by her old friend Wentworth. Refusing Wentworth's sympathetic offer to marry her, she states her desire to remain alone. In one of the most ludicrous lines in the history of the movies, she says: "I've got to go home now and help Jimmy with his algebra."

The Green Goddess (Warner Brothers, released 13 February 1930)

William Archer's *The Green Goddess* would have delighted Dion Boucicault. *The Green Goddess* is an improbable blend of canny stagecraft and hoary melodrama—devices that guaranteed the play an extended success. It was first produced at the Walnut Theater in Philadelphia on December 27, 1920 and was brought to the Booth Theater in New York three weeks later where George Arliss continued his triumphant portrayal of the wily Rajah of Rukh. Its popularity continued when Arliss and the producer, Winthrop Ames, took the play to London on September 6, 1923, where it ran for a full year.[20]

When George Arliss brought the play to the screen for Warner Brothers in 1929,[20] he was no stranger to the movies. Although he implies in his book, *My Ten Years in the Studios,* that *The Green Goddess* was his first film role, he had appeared in previous films, including a silent film version of another of his starring vehicles, *Disraeli,* for United Artists in 1921 (co-starring his wife Florence). However, *The Green Goddess* was, at least, his first effort in talking pictures, although its release was held up while his second talkie, another version of *Disraeli,* was released on October 2, 1929. *The Green Goddess* was eventually released in February of 1930.

On the film set, his chief difficulties, Arlis recalled, were the necessity of restraining his acting style; moreover, the filmmakers insisted that the scenes be shot out of order. The importance of the first showed that what he called "the grand manner of the large theater" was inappropriate to the intimate proximity of the camera lens.[21] The second did not allow him to "build up" a role in the way he was accustomed to on the stage. It represented a loss of control on his part. Because he found this so disconcerting, he prevailed upon his director for *The Green Goddess,* Alfred E. Green, to relax this method and allow him to have the scenes shot in their proper relative position to the story.[22]

The film version of *The Green Goddess* is, in my opinion, as close an

Louis Parker's 1921 *Disraeli* was brought to the screen twice by George Arliss. Here he is in the Warner Bros. 1929 version.

imitation by filmmakers of popular proscenium staging and dialogue as we are ever likely to have. It conveys the full text of the dialogue; consequently, like the play, it does not pretend to be more than a vehicle for Arliss' dry asides and satiric barbs at English civilization. Thus, the film exists entirely on the strength of its dialogue and does little to alter the play or "open it out." It would be unthinkable as a silent film, even one with extensive titles. Arliss' *voice* is irreplaceable just as much as the words themselves. Its brittle sharpness, and snaky softness, by turns, function as dramatic elements on their own. As for Arliss' performance, one can only suppose that its polished and urban menace is an accurate reflection of his stage manner. Despite the film's reliance upon techniques of proscenium staging, Arliss' wit constantly propels the film forward, keeping it interesting and briskly paced.

The film preserves intact the play's characters, dialogue, settings, and narrative continuity. Act one of the play is set in a stretch of rocky terrain outside the Rajah's Palace in the country of Rukh. Three travellers crashland their airplane in this remote region and promptly find themselves surrounded by fierce-looking natives. Soon, a splendidly-attired man in a turban arrives to greet them and, in cultivated English, tells them they are his guests. He is the Rajah of Rukh and he explains that his three brothers back in England have been jailed on a murder charge and have been sentenced to be hanged. Understandably, the travellers are puzzled at his subsequent offer of hospitality. Act Two is set in the Rajah's Palace. The hospitality is interrupted by the news that the Rajah is, in reality, holding them as hostages against the execution of his brothers. One condition only does the Rajah offer—that the English lady be permitted to live if she will agree to stay with him and bear him an heir to the throne. Otherwise, the local religion that worships the "Green Goddess" must be appeased and they all must die. The action ends as the prisoners discover a possible means of escape—the Rajah's private wireless by which they hope to send for help. Act Three opens in the Rajah's snuggery, to the rear of which is concealed a smaller room with the wireless machine. The travellers overpower the Rajah's servant and gain entrance to the wireless where they send a call for help. The Rajah and his men break in and shoot the telegrapher. When asked if he had time to get a message transmitted the telegrapher heroically lies with his dying breath that he had not. The unsuspecting Rajah meanwhile prepares for the prisoners' execution on the morrow. Act Four finds the two remaining prisoners in the chamber of the natives' god, the Green Goddess. Confronted with imminent death, the two confess their mutual love. The Rajah enters with his retinue ready for the sacrifice. Once again, he tries to renew his bargain with the woman, this time threatening to torture her lover if she will not relent and marry him. Just as she considers capitulating, rescuing airplanes arrive. The Rajah, sensing defeat, releases the prisoners; and alone at the end, he faces his captors as haughty and witty as ever.

The play's dialogue beautifully matches Arliss' flair for pungent vocal inflection. His Rajah is a blend of the barbaric and civilized man. He sniffs at the primitve style of his people, telling the Major:

> We know very well that we are barbarians. We are quite reconciled to the fact. We have had some five thousands years to accustom ourselves to it. This sword is a barbarous weapon compared with your revolver; but it was worn by my ancestors when yours were daubing themselves blue and picking up a precarious livelihood in the woods (129).

He cheerfully avows his superiority to the superstitious beliefs of his people (admitting that he manipulates the oracle of the Green Goddess), yet he acknowledges that the impending death of the prisoners does not trouble his sensibilities: "But there is a romantic as well as practical side to my nature, and, from the romantic point of view, I rather admire it" (137). Their death would even assuage his sense of his race's long subjugation to English imperialism: "Asia has a long score against you swaggering, blustering, whey-faced lords of creation, and, by all the gods! I mean to see some of it paid tomorrow" (144)! But this *is* a melodrama, after all, and his ambitions to marry the English lady contain all the miscegenistic implications of so many plays in that tradition. For example, when he explains his desire to marry the lady, he tells her, in words recalling Sax Rohmer, "Though I hate the arrogance of Europe, I believe that from a blending of the flower of the East with the Flower of the West the man of the future—the Superman—may be born" (146). All these dialogue exchanges even the asides, are retained in the film. The best example of this is when the Rajah coolly lights a cigarette after his hostages have been rescued and his hopes for a bride have been destroyed and in both play and film he pauses and looks directly at the viewer. "Well, well," he says, "she'd probably have been a damned nuisance."

The film closely imitates the staging of the play. Its only use of exterior shooting comes at the very beginning of the film (as was so often the case with filmed plays of this period) when the crash-landing of the plane is depicted. But once the Rajah has arrived with his retinue, the action settles into an exact duplication of the play's presentation. Except for some intercutting of reaction shots and an occasional change of camera angle, the long stretches of dialogue, the devices of entrances and exits dividing the action into episodes—all remain identical to the proscenium presentation. This is especially apparent in the scene where the Rajah proposes his plan to spare Lucilla Crespin's life. The entire exchange is contained within a medium two-shot filmed entirely without a break. The camera never moves except in one scene where Lucilla is shown to her room and the camera dollies back before her as she traverses the corridor. Another example of identical staging occurs in the scene where Major Crespin manages to send out their call for help by wireless. The main chamber of the snuggery with the smaller wireless room at the rear of the set exactly corresponds to the layout as described in the play. The blocking of the action also is an exact duplication.

Near the end of the film through some dynamic editing, camera angle and duration of the shot become variable. This occurs during the climactic action in the temple of the Green Goddess. Although there is a highly contrived artificial effect of the shadows of the approaching rescue plane showing through the palace window (much as it might have looked on a stage), there is also extensive cutting among various camera placements so that the huge set's space is fully penetrated and exploited for the sake of spectacular effect. And when the airplanes are sighted, a swift succession of reaction shots intensifies the drama. There is even an example of a reverse angle when a shot of the chamber from the vantage point of the entrance is followed by a shot from the reverse angle from a higher vantage point.

Finally, the film's use of sound is also highly imitative of the play. In an early scene the Rajah plays a phonograph recording of Gounod's "Funeral March of a Marionette." Its ironic, brittle sounds provide a fine, dry counterpoint to the dialogue in which the Rajah tells his prisoners that all men are only puppets of fate. This is the only moment of music in the film—and it is directly adopted from the play. The only other time when sound becomes an important, independent element in the action occurs when the lights darken onstage and the prisoners hear the clicking of the telegraph. That sound, disembodied and strange, signifies their dawning hopes and a possible method for escape. It becomes an effective device in the film as well.

The Musical Films—The Cocoanuts *and* Glorifying the American Girl (Paramount, 1929)

The Cocoanuts and *Glorifying the American Girl* brought to the synchronized-sound film, respectively, the musical show and the musical revue. They both were, generally, closely imitative of their theatrical source materials, although they both displayed a few significant moments of cinematic achievement—which will be considered in the second half of this chapter.

The Cocoanuts was written by George S. Kaufman and Irving Berlin. It premiered at the Lyric Theater in New York on December 8, 1925, starring the four Marx Brothers, and thereafter ran for 276 performances. Admittedly, it is difficult to inquire into the exact nature of the original playscript, since the improvisatory nature of the Marx Brothers' style effectively demolished beyond recognition the original outline. By the time the show opened in New York after its Boston tryout, reported Paul D. Zimmerman and Burt Goldblatt in their study of the Brothers, many of the original contributions by Kaufman and Berlin were gone and replaced by elements derived from the Brothers' comic improvisations. During many performances, "the brothers...completely abandoned the script and were improvising scene after scene."[23] David Ewen, in his book on the American musical theater supports this fact, noting that "any resemblance of dialogue and plot to the original concept of the authors is purely coincidental."[245] By the time the brothers were ready to film *The Cocoanuts* at Paramount's Astoria studios in the spring of 1929, the production had been reduced to a flimsy storyline which existed merely to be flattened by the brothers' unpredictable antics, performance after performance.

The story, such as it is, is set in Florida during a real estate boom. Herny W. Schlemmer (Groucho) is in charge of the Hotel de Cocoanut whose only paying guest is the wealthy and haughty Mrs. Potter (Margaret Dumont). Naturally, she is the target of many schemers, including Groucho's attempts to sell her phony real estate, the machinations of one Harvey Yates to steal her fabulously valuable necklace, and the efforts of Chico and Harpo to disrupt her armor-plated respectability. Surrounding the proceedings were several Irving Berlin songs, "A Little Bungalow," "We Should Care," "Lucky Boy," "Florida By the Sea," and "Monkey Doodle Doo."

The film version not only preserved the illusion that the action was taking place on a proscenium stage, but it was also faithful to the improvisational style of the Brothers' show. It remains, according to Zimmerman and Goldblatt, "The best record we have of their vaudeville style," a record of the brothers "at the height of their stage art rather than [as a record] of their film beginnings."[25] Moreover, they conclude, it can be regarded as an accurate record of theatrical styles in the musical theater of the 1920s with "its highly mannered acting, drill-team dance numbers and sentimental stories."[26] Joining the brothers from the original cast was Margaret Dumont, Groucho's perennial foil, who would remain with them throughout their years at Paramount. Only two songs from the original score—"Florida by the Sea," and "Monkey Doodle Doo" were retained in the film; and Berlin wrote a new song, "When My Dreams Come True" as a theme song which is heard at various times throughout the film.

The film opens with a sequence of brief tableaux—beach scenes around the resort hotel; this is followed by the first dance number, a routine with the chorus line performing calisthenics with drill-team precision. Groucho then comes on the scene for his first monologue, an extended speech captured in a sustained, uncut shot. This basic pattern is followed throughout the rest of the film—brief tableaux groupings, dance numbers, and verbal exchanges. Occasionally, one of the brothers interrupts the proceedings and performs a solo on a musical instrument, such as the harp (Harpo) or piano (Chico).

We feel, for the most part, that we are watching a performance on a proscenium stage. The painted drop curtains and flimsy sets predominate. Aside from the opening shots of beach areas, the entire production is limited to shallow-depth playing areas. The blocking in most of the scenes is highly characteristic of plays already discussed in that the incidental characters, and extras frequently occupy a shallow plane upstage while the main characters come downstage to transact their business. This style of staging can be seen in many other filmed musical shows of the period, most notably *The Desert Song* (Warner Brothers, 1929) and *Whoopee* (United Artists, 1930). The players in *The Cocoanuts,* moreover, seem to be playing to an audience. Quite often Groucho will address the viewer just as he did when on stage. This was a standard technique in the Marx' stage productions, simply a variation on the device of the aside in 19th century drama. In this instance, the device served to remind the audience constantly that nothing was to be taken seriously. This implied awareness of an audience had been intrusive and disturbing when it surfaced in many of the silent and sound theatrical films, as we have seen; but here in *The Cocoanuts* it enhanced the satiric purpose. Multiple camera setups, for the most part, recorded the action and the musical routines. Editing served to preserve the continuity. The succession of shots varied only slightly our viewing angle, while the distance of the camera from the action remained uniformly at a medium distance, maintaining the three-quarter length view of the figures. Sometimes, these lengthy scenes were not interrupted by *any* kind of cutting. For example, when Groucho explains economics to his female bell hops early in the film, a three-minute, uncut take preserves the entire speech. It seems as if his amazing eloquence shackled the camera, holding it mesmerized while the words flowed on and on. . . .

One of the funniest scenes in *The Cocoanuts* is based entirely upon a sequence derived from the original stage production. The pronounced artifice of this scene on film and the unabashed sense of its proscenium origins are striking. The boys have been lured to a room which adjoins that of Margaret Dumont. The two rooms are divided by a wall, but the "fourth walls" are left open to the audience—as if we could look into a doll's house. As the action shifts from one room to the other, or occurs simultaneously in each, the film cuts correspondingly from one room to the other. At other moments, the distant vantage point of the camera allows us to see both rooms at once. Thus, the editing scheme merely duplicates the shifting action of the dual set. In a sense, the dual set in the original stage production anticipated—and, indeed, necessitated—the cross-cutting technique in this film.

The film concludes with a tableau that resembles the finale to dozens of musical shows of the period. The entire cast is present at the concluding wedding ceremony. Everyone faces directly toward the camera and reprises the theme song while the brothers wave at us across the imaginary footlights.

Glorifying the American Girl was filmed in the autumn of 1929 at Paramount's Astoria studios. Consistent with Paramount's policy during the early talking period of pairing stage and film personnel, *Glorifying the American Girl* was jointly produced by filmmaker Monta Bell with theatrical impresario Florenz Ziegfeld. Ziegfeld would co-produce another film before his death in 1932—a film version for Samuel Goldwyn of *Whoopee* in 1930.

Both *Glorifying the American Girl* and *Whoopee* preserved on film the styles and concepts of the Ziegfeld show—a style that made his Follies some of the most successful productions in the history of the American musical theater.

According to Robert C. Toll in his portrait of Ziegfeld in *On With the Show* (1976), the Ziegfeld style was born with his production for Anna Held in 1906 of *The Parisian Model*. The show emphasized the female body adorned in a succession of elaborate costumes; and there was a lavish production number with the show girls arranged on stage in the shape of a silver slipper. Such characteristics would reappear again and again in a succession of Follies during the next twenty-two years. Exotic mood and sinuous curve—all components of an art deco style grafted onto the *jugendstil* of the late 19th century—were consistent elements in every Ziegfeld production.[27] This was just as true of Joseph Urban's architectural and set designs as it was of Irving Berlin and Gene Buck's melodies and Lady Duff-Gordon's dress designs. Exoticism combined with elegance and respectability helped Ziegfeld's productions appeal to large audiences in the 1920s.

The contributions of Lady Duff-Gordon to the Ziegfeld style should be examined so that we can better understand what is seen in the films *Glorifying the American Girl* and *Whoopee*. She made the concept of the "show girl" more respectable than that of the "chorus girl." In what is, in my opinion, the finest study of Ziegfeld extant, Rudolph Carter's *The World of Flo Ziegfeld*, the point is made that the show girl was a woman clothed in gorgeous (and often extravagant) clothes who did little more than stand about in "sculptural" poses. By contrast, the chorus girl usually worked hard but had no special identity in the show. She was, typically, merely an anonymous component in the machine-like precision of the chorus line.[28] Lady Duff-Gordon's "living mannequins" had provided the precedent. They had to conform to her standards—learn proper posture and deportment, wear an elusive and masklike expression, and comport themselves in spectacular and sometimes cumbersome gowns. Duff-Gordon's fashion shows in London had had all the flavor of the Ziegfeld productions to come:

> She rounded up beautiful girls from all over, instructed them in proper deportment, and, gorgeously gowned in her latest creations, let them slowly descend the steps of the beautiful Adam's room on Hanover Square.[29]

Many of Duff-Gordon's mannequins went on to become Ziegfeld show girls, while she herself worked with Ziegfeld on most of his Follies productions. The concept of the "living picture," the serpentine patterns comprised of immobile show girls, became the trademark of the Follies. Usually, these women would stand motionless in a variety of poses, each figure framed in a decorative niche. The women would be stacked vertically against the rear of the stage, forming a kind of "human curtain"—sometimes forty feet high.

Glorifying the American Girl and, to a lesser extent, *Whoopee* are documents on film of elements of the Ziegfeld revue. Both, in addition to presenting Ziegfeld stars like Eddie Cantor and Mary Eaton, duplicated famous fashion shows and living pictures. The last half of *American Girl* was devoted entirely to a mini-Ziegfeld revue. After an inserted shot of an open Follies program, the curtains parted to reveal the first of a series of living pictures. The show girls were arranged in upright positions against a backdrop of decorative nautical motifs. Each girl was immobilized within a frame of fishnets, star fish, or sea shells and was herself either draped or undraped (wearing flesh-colored tights). As the accompanying music from the visible pit orchestra surged up on the soundtrack, the camera panned slowly across the tableau, keeping the show girls at a medium distance so that the entire figure of each was visible in the frame. The curtains then closed and after a few seconds opened again onto another tableau—similar to the first, but with the girls this time in slightly different positions against the same backdrop. Following that there were a number of routines with the Ziegfeld headliners—Eddie Cantor appearing in his famous comedy skit about two tailors who victimize a helpless customer, Helen Morgan dressed in black and performing while seated atop a dazzling white piano, and Rudy Vallee singing "Vagabond Lover." The closing number was another living picture designed according to a "butterfly" motif. The show girls wore giant butterfly wings upon their shoulders while above, atop a column, stood Ziegfeld star Mary Eaton. The column slowly lowered to floor level and Eaton stepped out to dance. Her specialty as a Ziegfield star had been balletic dance routines and she duplicates them here. As she danced, a number of show girls stood about the stage in various attitudes—some holding aloft large silver hoops, others merely maintaining sculptural poses against black curtains.

The entire revue appears to have been shot in a real theater. There were occasional inserted shots of two audience members examining each number on the program. Closeups of the program entries preceeded each shot of the stage. The stage was seen only from the audience's perspective—which is to say that the 180-degree line area parallel to the forestage was never broken. Several overhead perspectives and shifts in camera angle merely served to approximate a variety of perspectives from different seats in the house—from the balcony front row, to the rear of the house, to the front row on the center aisle.

Whoopee featured two elaborately staged fashion shows, each filmed in the same manner described above. The first was the "Stetson" dance. The show girls, dressed in western garb, slowly walked toward the camera from a medium distance and continued on past the lens. Their smiles were fixed and their gait measured and deliberate. And another scene, the wedding ceremony near the end of the film, began with the show girls advancing in single file toward the camera, each girl wearing a gown that was an elaborate variation on the prevailing bridal fashion motif. This was followed by a climactic living picture a tableau of show girls arranged in an intricate design and frozen in a sustained, uncut long shot that approximated the view from the first row of a theater balcony.

Artificial scenery in some portions of the film of *Whoopee* clashed with the use of natural locations in other portions. As we have already seen in films like *The Count of Monte Cristo*, the juxtaposition through editing of natural and artificial locales tended to create a jarring disparity. The same problem arose here. For example, an introductory sequence of horsemen galloping across natural desert exteriors was immediately followed by a sudden shift to the artificial scenery of the ranch patio. The horsemen dismounted in one shot within natural settings and entered the patio in the next shot with painted backdrops. Moreover, these exteriors were all filmed by a camera cranking at a speed of approximately eighteen frames per second—the standard rate of filming before the advent of synchronized sound. By contrast, the sound sequences shot on the proscenium stage were filmed at the rate of twenty-four frames per second—the standard rate of filming utilized for sound recording after 1927. Thus, when both silent and sound sequences are projected on sound projectors at twenty-four frames per second, the exterior scenes seem to contain jerky and accelerated movements, while the sound scenes are smooth and natural.[30] Another disparity perceived between the use of artificial and natural locales was that the editing in the silent sequences was swift and fluid—typical of the editing techniques in films before the advent of sound; however, the editing in the sound sequences was limited to a few prolonged and static shots—characteristic of the editing in the early synchronized-sound films. Thus, the techniques of silent and sound filmmaking, along with the use of artificial and real locales, violently collided, throwing into sharp relief that which I shall define in the next chapter as "cinematic" and that which by contrast was merely imitative of the proscenium stage.

Selectively Imitative Theatrical Films

The second group of theatrical films to be discussed here did not imitate theatrical source materials as closely, or indiscriminately, as did the first group. This group might be more properly designed as achieving essentially "cinematic" rather than essentially theatric effects:

1. They contained fewer sequences, or scenes, that relied wholly upon either written intertitles (in the case of silent films) or spoken dialogue (in the case of synchronized-sound films).
2. They employed more editing within the scene with shifts in viewing angle and camera distance. This involved the adopting of complex editing schemes—parallel editing, subjective camera, and flashbacks.
3. They utilized more natural locales and depended less, therefore, upon the use of artificial scenery.
4. They exploited more depth in the frame (deep focus).

5. The acting techniques revealed more restraint in gesture and movement.

6. In the case of the synchronized-sound films, they promoted a more asynchronous combination of image and sound.

The Virginian (Jesse L. Lasky Company, 1914)

The Virginian was Lasky's fourth release, following, in order, *The Squaw Man* (February, 1914), *Brewster's Millions* (April, 1914), and *The Master Mind* (May, 1914). Once again, it afforded Dustin Farnum the opportunity to duplicate a role he had made famous on the stage.[31] Many other film versions followed it—the version of 1923 with Kenneth Harlan, the version of 1929 with Gary Cooper, the version of 1945 with Joel McCrea, and the television series in the 1960s with Doug McClure.

Owen Wister's novel and his subsequent dramatization involved the confrontation between East and West as embodied by the cowpuncher known only as "The Virginian" and Molly Wood, the new school mistress who has recently come to Wyoming from Vermont. The Virginian's blooming romance with the eastern girl is threatened by his allegiance to Western codes—tracking down and hanging rustlers (necessitating his final gunfight with the villain Trampas). In each case, he clashes with Molly's own eastern ethics; and in both cases, it is Molly who must learn and accept the ways of the new land. Both novel and play relied heavily upon verbal exchanges among Molly, the Virginian, and Judge Henry (the Virginian's boss) in delineating these issues.

The play was like other regional melodramas of the time in its attempts to evoke regional color and romance through costume, implied physical action, and dialects. Its supposed accuracy in its attention to detail gave it a naturalistic stature which some critics of the time praised:

The accuracy of detail, and the consequent wealth of true atmosphere, is, there, the chief value of the play. And this qualtiy in "The Virginian" is especially worth while because hertofore the West of the dramatic stage has been—except in such rare plays as "Arizona"—a pictuesque and bloody No-Man's Land. Mr. Wister possesses the knowledge to write of the West with the same photographic accuracy that characterized the late James A. Herne's plays of the East Coast. (iv)

There was really very little physical action in Wister's dramatization, written in 1904. The drama was largely confined to indoor and domestic settings. Wister felt restricted space of the proscenium stage did not properly permit the convincing portrayals of the novel's incidents of cattle roundups, runaway stagecoaches, and mounted pursuits across mountainous areas. He limited the play to four acts and a total of five scene settings, only one of which is an actual range locale—the campfire scene where the rustlers are apprehended by the Virginian and his men. The other settings were, in order, a ranch house interior, a patch of ground between Judge Henry's ranch and the cowboy's quarters, the interior of Molly Wood's home, and a street corner in Medicine Bow. The dialogue carried most of the action—such as the cowboy's futile attempts to dance with Molly in Act One, the "baby-switching" incident in the same act, the Virginian's discovery of Steve's rustling (before the rise of the curtain in Act One), the cattle roundup that precipitates the deadly clash between the Virginain and Trampas in Act Two, the Virginian's rescue of Molly in the runaway stagecoach (before the curtain of Act One), and the trackdown of the rustlers by the Virginian's posse in Act Three, Scene One.

What real sense we have of the exterior locales arose from the dialogue—both in the measured, Eastern accents and diction of Molly Wood, and in the rougher vernacular of the Virginian. Molly's observations captured a certain genteel perspective on the West:

> Oh, how I love it. The glorious dawn, the rivers—clear, fresh and cold. The unlimited prairie and mountains like giant sentinels and the great hearts of its people. Just hearts of children—knowing nothing—caring nothing—living in to-day with no thought of to-morrow (33).

The Virginian's words, like those of Jack Rance in Belasco's *The Girl of the Golden West,* captured a sense of the harsher realities of Western life, as when he tells Trampas: "We've all hit town too frequent to play Sunday on the balance of the gang; we ain't a Christian outfit a little bit and maybe we've mostly forgotten what decency feels like. But I reckon we haven't plumb forgot what it means" (21).

The 1914 film version lacks the verbal richness of the play, its use of natural locations fully exploits its scenic implications. While the play had of necessity remained "stage-bound," the filmmakers (Cecil B. De Mille and Oscar Apfel) freely roamed around mountainous terrains, spotlighting the action against gorgeous backdrops of lake country and rocky slopes. Unlike *The Squaw Man,* moreover, there is seldom felt that sense of excessive, natural frontality in the acting and in the character grouping; nor that sense of a shallow-depth playing area in the scenes. Apfel and De Mille open out the frame, in effect, carving out great expanses of depth through intelligent use of the extreme long shot and deep focus. By contrast to those earlier films that were adapted from the stage, *The Virginian* reveals little of its proscenium origins; rather, it stands closer to the best work of D. W. Griffith and is just now beginning to be recognized not only as an intelligent adaptation of a stage play to the screen, but a remarkably advanced and "cinematic" film for its time.[32]

To be sure, there are moments that are obviously theatrical. There are a few scenes that display artificial sets and shallow playing areas. The first is the brief shot introducing Molly, accompanied by the title, "Back in Vermont, Molly Wood struggles for a living teaching music;" this is followed by a tableau depicting her sighing before a window through which is seen a painted view of a city. The second is the setting of the Saloon of Medicine Bow with its sparse and blatantly artificial props and painted drops. This particular interior is never described in the play, and it seems that the filmmakers, without any guide for their set, merely patched together a passable replica. The camera's distant and static position, particularly during the famous "When you call me that, Trampas, you smile" scene, flattens the action and drains it of any compelling sense of drama. Moreover, there is little character movement forward or backward in space and no use of editing to explore that space from other vantage points and angles in this scene. Finally, the staging of the scene where Molly tries to prevail upon the Virginian not to face Trampas in the gunfight is also obviously theatrical. Molly's room consists of a bare stage area with a single mirror and window through which is visible a painted flat depicting a setting sun beyond the house tops. Because of the paucity of titles, the two characters stand stiffly, broadly gesturing at length their respective emotions—her anguish and his compelling sense of duty.

But in most other ways, *The Virginian* reveals an assured and relatively sophisticated story-telling technique. This is done both through the editing of action, time, and space, and through intelligent handling of the sustained take.

The parallel editing techniques are far in advance of anything seen in the theatrical films already discussed. In one sense this technique emphasizes the clash between East and West that is so crucial to the play. The play opened with Molly having arrived from Vermont and having been rescued from the runaway stage by the Virginian. But the first fifteen minutes of the film are spent in extensive cross-cutting between the actions of Molly in Vermont and the doings of the main characters in Medicine Bow. One narrative thread follows the Virginian's carousings with his friends Steve and Lin McLean, the confrontation with Trampas in the saloon, an episode in a flophouse after a night's drinking, and the first discovery that Steve has been following Trampas in cattle rustling (title: "Pal, stick to rum, cards, and cussin'; keep your icon off another man's cattle."). The other narrative thread follows Molly from her school house in Vermont to her receipt of a letter from the Wyoming school board offering her a job as the school mistress, to her preparations to leave Vermont, to her arrival in Wyoming by train (and later stagecoach), and finally to her rescue from the runaway stage by the Virginian.

These two narratives are intercut through editing at strategic points. The first shot of Molly follows the first shot of the Virginian; Molly's preparations to leave Vermont follow the famous Trampas/Virginian confrontation; her arrival by train follows the sleeping-room incident; her ride by stagecoach interrupts Steve's denunciation as a rustler; and her rescue by the Virginian immediately follows his warning to Trampas to leave Steve alone. The initial moments of transfer between the two narrative threads are "signalled" by explanatory titles setting the scenes. But these titles disappear as the story progresses, so that the shifts back and forth occur more freely. Thus, the four characters—the Virginian, Steve, Molly, and Trampas—are linked and contrasted through cross-cutting.

Just as this first cycle of cross-cutting culminated in the Virginian's rescue of Molly, so too did the technique later function to bring Molly to the rescue of the Virginian after he had been ambushed by Trampas. Act Three of the play opened with the Virginian's men surprising the rustlers at their campfire. They were taken off-stage and hanged, only the Virginian remaining onstage to describe the event. Then a shot was heard and the Virginian, wounded in the back, fell forward. After a time as the night faded into dawn (the only example of pictorial lighting effect in the play), Molly arrived, found him, and carried him away to safety. The film handles this sequence of events in a more dramatically satisfying (and cinematic) way through cross-cutting. The film cuts from the wounded Virginian to Molly writing her letter of resignation as she prepares to return East "where she belongs" (as a title informs us). The shots alternate from the Virginian to Molly and back again until the characters are both united in the same frame when she finds him.

Cross-cutting is also employed in the sequence where the Virginian and his men pursue the rustlers Steve and Trampas. This event had transpired between the second and third acts of the play, but it is fully pictured in the film. Cutting moves us back and forth between the locale of the Virginian's encampment in a cabin and the nearby campfire in the mountains around which Trampas' men are gathered. As the chase progresses, pursuer and pursued are thus united by means of editing.

Cross-cutting functions to build up the tension surrounding the climactic gunfight between the Virginian and Trampas. A comparison of this sequence with the original stage sequence is interesting. The entire fourth act occurred outside the saloon along a narrow street extending across the stage. The gunfight was simply a matter of the Virginian entering from the wings, calling out Trampas' name, and shooting him after Trampas' first shot misses. In the film the editing alternately shifts from the Virginian boldly walking down the middle of the street to shots of Trampas in the distance sneaking along the sides of the building in an attempt to ambush him. Cross-cutting not only builds up suspense (in effect, prolonging the sense of the passage of time) it also functions to contrast the Virginian and Trampas. The Virginian's bravery and Trampas' cowardice had been suggested by a long dialogue and some asides in Act Four of the play; here, they are amply conveyed in the shots showing the different ways each man approaches the other. This kind of staging, by the way, was the model for the filming of the gunfight in the 1929 version directed by Victor Fleming.

Elsewhere in the film, editing is used in ways beyond merely preserving the continuity. Some scenes, for example, reveal a tendency toward intra-scene cutting. The film opens with several shots from a variety of angles of the Virginian riding among the cattle. When Molly alights from the stagecoach, there is a brief closeup of Molly's foot reaching for the stirrup. During the incident of the baby switching (which occurs offstage in the play) editing binds together several people in different locations as they each discover they have come away from the party with the wrong child. This editing scheme is further complicated by some cross-cutting to the culprits, the Virginian and Lin McLean. This comic scene is contrasted later with the tragedy of Steve's hanging and the climactic scene of the gunfight. Both scenes employ editing to convey reactions of the participants to the action. For example, Steve's hanging is conveyed by a shot of his shadow across the ground and a cutaway to Trampas observing the action from some overhanging rocks. The gunfight consists of a shot of the Virginian firing his pistol, a cutaway to Trampas firing in response, and finally to another angle to Trampas as he falls to the ground. In all of these examples, editing functions to analyze an action, breaking it up into a number of discreet units which are then reassembled for dramatic effect.

Editing also introduces a subjective, or point-of-view, dimension to the story. One example occurs while Molly is riding to the western town on the stagecoach. The camera position records the passing scenery from a vantage point just above Molly's position on the box so that we see the countryside as she sees it. Another example occurs during the baby-switching scene when the Virginian and Lin McLean surreptitiously enter the babies' room. This action occurred offstage in the play, but here the camera records it from behind the men's shoulders so that we see the room from their vantage point. At the same time, our gaze shifts from the door that is being opened to the interior of the room, moving from foreground to background, in effect. This shift in our attention is brought about through movement in the frame and not through editing. This is a tiny example of the function of the deep-focus frame.

There are more significant instances of the deep-focus frame in *The Virginian*. Early in the film, just before Molly and the Virginian meet, the Virginian occupies the foreground astride his horse. In the extreme distance can be seen the approaching coach with Molly aboard. Apart from the considerable pictorial beauty of the shot, the depth of the frame brings the two characters together, foreshadowing their eventual meeting; the shot also conveys their contrasting ways of life—Molly on a train balanced on the tracks, the Virginian lolling on his horse, knee-deep in the prairie grass. Elsewhere in the film, there are deep focus shots of the Virginian's pursuit of the errant Trampas. One shot approximates Trampas' point of view. He stands in the extreme foreground and watches the Virginian in the lower distance riding upward toward him. The next shot reverses the spatial configuration, bringing the Virginian into the extreme foreground while above him in extreme long-shot crouches an Indian. In the sustained shot, we see the Indian aim his rifle and fire and the Virginian recoil at the impact of the bullet. The Virginian in turn draws his rifle and fires toward the Indian, who is hit and falls from the saddle. The two figures are diagonally separated by the distance between the lower left and upper right of the frame. As the gun shots are fired, the eye tracks the action from one part of the frame to the other and back again. This kind of intra-shot montage concept would be extensively employed by later filmmakers, William Wyler, Orson Welles, Jean Renoir, and Kenji Mizoguchi.[33] This kind of effect would have been impossible on the shallow-depth stage. In earlier theatrical films, the sustained take was not utilized for *intra*-shot montage so much as to simply record the scene in real time. But these examples in *The Virginian* do not simply record the scene, they enable the viewer to participate in the editing process.

Finally, the film transforms a talky, philosophical play into a visually exciting chain of events, bound together by editing and the use of deep-focus framing. What is lost in the process, unfortunately, is the intellectual and emotional center of the play. The contrasts between Molly's and the Virginian's cultures, although implied visually in the afore-mentioned cross-cutting, do not go beyond the pictorial contrasts. In the play, the Virginian had insisted that because he belongs to the West, he must do its work (53). Those duties include the fundamental assertions of self-governing men—survival of the fittest and protection of one's chief source of livelihood—the land. Against Molly's assertions that America is a land of democracy and equality, he declares that there can be no real equality in the West: "Some holds four aces, and some holds nothing, and some poor fellows get the aces, and no show to play them, but a man has got to prove himself my equal before I'll believe him"(48). Against her out-cry about his lynching his best friend, Steve, without due process of court trial, Judge Henry defends the action, saying, "far from being a defiance of the law, it is an assertion of it. The fundamental assertion of self-governing men" (71). And in opposition to her urging that he refrain from the gunfight with Trampas, the Virginian extends the ideal of self-assertion to his own injured sense of honor:

> Don't I owe my own honesty something? If a man says I'm a thief, and I hear of it, am I to go on letting him spread such a thing of me? Would I sit down in a corner rubbing my honesty and whispering to it: 'There, there, I know you ain't a thief?' No, sir. Not a little bit. What men say about my nature is not just an outside thing. For the fact that I let them keep on saying is a proof I don't value my nature enough to shield it from their slander and give them their punishment. And that's being a poor sort of a cuss. (97)

Because the 1929 version was a talking picture, there were more

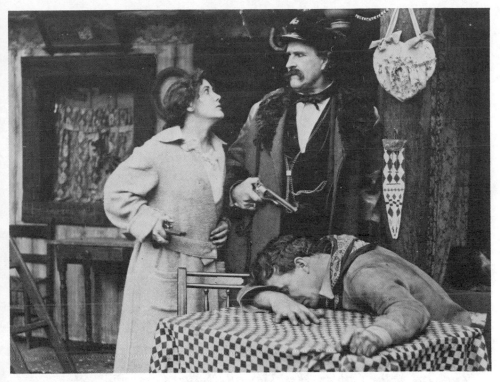

C. B. De Mille and the Lasky Company brought David Belasco's specatcular success, *Girl of the Golden West* (1905) to the screen in 1914. With Mabel Van Buren is House Peters as the wounded "Ramarrez" and Theodore Roberts as Jack Rance.

opportunities for dialogue and some of these ideological conflicts were restored. But the version made in 1914 limits and ignores them. Molly's moral objections to the lynching of Steve are missing altogether. The Virginian's own torn sense of duty at hanging his best friend is conveyed only through the use of a "dream image." When Steve is captured, he is kept in a cabin until sunup. A shot reveals him and the Virginian at opposite ends of the frame in medium shot facing each other, talking. The space in between them dissolves into an image of the two in earlier, happier days. Finally, for the argument between Molly and the Virginian concerning the gunfight, only broad pantomiming and two titles convey the issues. The first title has her saying, "I can't marry a man with blood on his hands; come away with me right now;" and the second has the Virginian responding, "Trampas put Steve's head in the noose. Now he's after me and I must be ready for him."

If the film avoided the artifice of the play's original staging devices, it incurred, as a result, a debility—the simplistic reduction of its moral issues. It was, ultimately, unable to deal with that essentially non-visual dimension of the play, the fundamental issue of the West—the "assertion of self-governing men." As a drama of action and scene conveyed in cinematic terms it was more advanced than the earlier filmed plays. But as a drama of ideas and moral imperatives, it was inadequate.

The Girl of the Golden West (Jesse L. Lasky Company, 1914)

David Belasco realized several ambitions in the writing of *The Girl of the Golden West* in 1905. One had been the desire to create a new part for his protege, Blanche Bates; another had been to write about the land of his boyhood, California; and, finally, he wanted to produce a play full of scenic splendor and detail. *The Girl of the Golden West* brought considerable success and fame to Blanche Bates; because of its realistic staging and celebrated lighting effects, it also brought renewed acclaim to Belasco.[34] Thus, the play was a blend of star vehicle, naturalistic drama, and spectacular stagecraft.

Blanche Bates had already created the part of *Madame Butterfly* for Belasco in 1900 in the play of that name. Her Cho-Cho-San was followed in 1902 by her Princess Yo-San in *The Darling of the Gods*. Now, her role as "The Girl" brought a tougher fiber to the traditionally sentimentalized female roles common to many American plays of the time. It was the first of several western romances to be produced by Belasco—others to follow included the production in 1906 of Richard Walton Tully's *Rose of the Rancho*. *The Girl of the Golden West* was first performed at the Belasco Theatre in Pittsburgh on October 3, 1905; it came to New York on November 13 where it ran for 224 performances. In the original cast with Blanche Bates were Robert Hilliard as Dick Johnson and Frank Keenan as Jack Rance.[35]

The play exemplified those characteristics standard to the spectacle melodrama late in the 19th century: pictorial emphasis (the spectacular scene with exotic and detailed sets), wordless dramatic episodes, and the use of devices we might now call "cinematic"—moving scenery, swift and episodic narrative construction, etc.[36] In a word, it was the kind of play that seemed to anticipate effects appropriate to the motion picture medium. It was only to be expected, therefore, that any cinematic adaptation would be aided by the cinematic implications already imbedded in the concept and the staging. For example, the famous opening scene of *The Girl of the Golden West* consisted of two wordless "pictures" that introduced the viewer to the setting of the Polka Saloon. The first was a view of Cloudy Mountain in the Sierras that was painted on a scrim. As the house lights darkened, the curtain was flown silently and lights were brought to bear upon the second picture, a panoramic view painted on a cloth flat that unrolled downward from the top to the bottom of the proscenium opening. As this vertical diorama unrolled, the viewer saw successively closer views of the Polka Saloon until the Saloon set itself stood revealed behind the diorama. This elaborate opening sequence functioned in much the same way that a "pan" and "tracking" shot would in a motion picture. There were also elaborate stage directions in the playscript involving many moments of wordless pantomime throughout the play. The opening scenes in the first and third acts contained specific directions for the patrons of the Saloon to mill about, shake the snow off their boots, play cards, tell jokes, etc. Their fragmentary speech was intended to provide a barely audible hum or background noise, behind the main action. And, finally, the play contained one crucial moment that might be regarded as the equivalent of a close up in a motion picture. In Act Two Jack Rance visits the Girl in her snow-bound cabin in the mountains while pursuing the bandit, Dick Johnson. At a crucial moment in the conversation, Rance is spattered by blood dripping from the wounded Johnson, who is crouching above him in the loft. In order to emphasize this disquieting revelation to the audience, Belasco instructed that a spotlight be trained on the patch of blood, lest anyone miss it.[37]

The film version of *The Girl of the Golden West* displays moments that are closely imitative of the proscenium staging typical of the period; but, at the same time, the film achieves an overall effect that is more purely cinematic than most theatrical films that preceeded it. The Belasco play had fairly cried out for naturalistic effects of scene and lighting. All work and attention to detail that attempted to transform the stage into a wild and rugged California region failed. Scenic mimesis, said Max Beerbohm in his essay, "The Ragged Regiment," is always doomed to failure. "An art that challenges life at close quarters," Beerbohm wrote, "is defeated through the simple fact that it is not life."[38] But the filmmakers of the Lasky Company had a variety of actual California locations at their disposal—flat plains, broken ground, lake country, and steeply mountainous terrain. Thus, the opening scene in the play was replaced on film by a montage of shots depicting horsemen and wagons traversing the mountain passes. Even the Polka Saloon was not an interior set erected in a studio. It was a three-dimensional set built on location. No longer the flattened, shallow-depth set arranged in a plan parallel to the camera, this set was fully explored by changing camera angles—at one point in the film the angle changes more than 180-degrees. Belasco had tried to view the Saloon set in the play from two different angles on stage in Act One and Act Three. Within seconds on film, the set is more fully explored through changing camera angles than throughout all of the play. Belasco had also worked very hard to achieve complex and naturalistic effects with light in this Saloon interior. Photographs of the original stage production attest to his remarkable achievement in providing the illusion on stage of "outdoor" light.[39] The outdoor set of the Saloon in the film was lit by natural light with an effect impossible to the stage. Instead of the flat lighting of interior sets characteristic of films like *The Count of Monte Cristo, Men and Women,* and *The Squaw Man,* the Saloon of *The Girl of the Golden West* presents a striking blend of light and shadow. The darkened interior is illuminated by shafts of light that pour through the windows and doors. This web and woof of light and dark lends great interest and pictorial beauty to the scene.

This is not to say that low-key lighting as seen in this film is a unique cinematic effect. But it is true that for too long, theatrical films were limited in their lighting effects by the reliance upon painted scenery. Not only did these flats reflect light but they were painted in such a way as to imply their *own* lighting effects. But the Belasco style of lighting came to the film version of *The Girl of the Golden West* in a natural and logical way. The director of the film, Cecil B. De Mille, had been trained in Belasco's style of stagecraft. Both he and his brother, William, had been personally acquainted with Belasco ever since Belasco had collaborated with their father on *The Charity Ball, Lord Chumley, The Wife,* and *Men and Women* in 1887-89. Later, De Mille recalled his experiences with Belasco and how he came to transfer what he had learned to his work in motion pictures. "Trained in that school," he said in his autobiography, "Wilfred Buckland and I decided to experiment...with special lighting effects. What I was after was naturalism: if an actor was sitting beside a lamp, it was crudely unrealistic to show both sides of his face in equal light, so....we began to make shadows where shadows would appear in nature."[40] Thus, some sequences in the film version of *The Girl of the Golden West* benefit from a kind of chiaroscuro lighting. This includes the action in the Saloon and during the middle third of the picture when the action takes place in the Girl's cabin.

Many incidents alluded to in the play's dialogue are visualized and placed in chronological order in the film. For example, the episode concerning Ramerrez' gang holding up the Wells Fargo stage is depicted near the beginning of the film, *before* Johnson (Ramerrez) enters the Saloon (when the action of the play begins). The holdup consists of a series of shots showing Ramerrez' gang laying their trap for the stage—looping a noosed rope over an overhanging tree branch and overruning the guard when the stage is halted. Another extended action sequence—alluded to in the dialogue of Act Three—is visualized in a sequence that marks the film's most exciting moments. This is when Ramerrez is finally traced to the Girl's cabin, chased through a mountain pass, and subsequently captured. This is done through an imaginative interplay of long shots, and medium shots. The chase transpires across a succession of natural backdrops—mountain slopes and a lake area—that provide a nice sense of shifting locale as a complement to the action.

At times the film utilizes an extremely deep-focus frame, a device already noted in *The Virginian*. In the action of Act Two in the play Dick Johnson has gone to visit the Girl in her mountain cabin. As the evening lengthens and the snows intensify, his pursuers surround the cabin. After Johnson leaves the stage, a shot is heard. Johnson returns onstage, wounded. But in the film version, Johnson leaves the cabin and there is a cut to a long shot outside the cabin. A sniper occupies the foreground of the frame and Johnson is seen in the distance, higher in the frame, his figure silhouetted against the ridge. The gun's discharge in the foreground and the fall of the tiny figure in the background consistitutes a beautiful example of the deep-focus shot where the viewer's eye is guided to different areas of the frame—in effect, an intra-shot cut.

Aside from its use of natural locales, one of the most important examples of *The Girl of the Golden West* is its editing. There are several examples of cross-cutting and changes of camera angle within a given scene. When we first see the Girl in her Saloon, the scene is intercut with the bank holdup sequence. The preparations for the hold-up also are intercut with a shot of the Wells Fargo coach leaving town. While Rance plays poker in the Saloon there is a cutaway to Ramerrez riding toward the Saloon to hold it up. And when the wounded Ramerrez lurches back into the Girl's cabin after being shot, there is a cutaway to a shot of the posse closing in on him.

The action in Act Two of the play gave the filmmakers the opportunity for a sophisticated use of intrascene editing. I refer to the famous poker game played between Jack Rance and the Girl in her mountain cabin. The stakes are crucial—the fate of Dick Johnson, who lies slumped over the table throughout the game. In the play, terse dialogue accompanies each deal of the cards. But in the film, each deal is accompanied with closeups of the respective hands of cards, seen over the shoulder of each player. During the third and deciding deal, the Girl surreptitiously draws out cards from her stocking. On the stage, this business would have to be broadly pantomimed so that such a tiny gesture would not go unnoticed. In the film, a medium close shot pans downward with the motion of her hand as she pulls out the cards. This is a good example of a cue from the play being realized in cinematic terms. These closeups are essentially subjective views of the action. In effect, they take the viewer from his seat in a theater house and involve him with the action. Another example of the subjective view occurs earlier in this scene when Johnson is discovered hiding in the loft above Rance's head. At the moment of discovery, the camera angle changes from a head-on view to a vantage point that looks down at Rance from past Johnson's shoulder.

Curiously, if parenthetically, I should note that not all of the cinematic implications of the play are realized. During the key moment of the play— when Johnson's blood spatters down from the loft onto the handkerchief of Rance—the filmmakers have opted for a routine imitation of the original staging. The scene is done in uninterrupted medium shot, although the use of a closeup of Rance's soiled handkerchief might have been expected at this point.

The film of *The Girl of the Golden West* also suffers from an occasional moment when cinematic and theatrical effects seem to clash. The worst example of this comes during and after the arrest of Johnson. While the pursuit and arrest sequence are highly cinematic in execution and effect, the sequence is immediately followed by a static scene where the Girl pleads to Rance to spare the life of her lover. In the play this scene occurred in the Saloon. In the film, it takes place outdoors in a natural locale, but recorded in an uncut take from a static camera. First, we see Johnson tied to a tree with a rope; then the Girl enters from the right edge of the frame (like the right side of the proscenium frame) and runs toward Johnson. Coming right after the chase scene, this moment seems quite flat and uninteresting. The action, while only indirectly derived from the play, is curiously bound to the worst kind of staging with its arbitrary and abrupt entrances and exits.

Much of the action in the play which involves incidental characters and which is primarily verbal is omitted in the film. For example, Act Three of the play opened in the Polka Saloon in wintertime. During the winter months, it seems, the Girl was schoolmistress in a makeshift "Academy" to the rough men in the community. The humor here grows out of the confrontation between primitive men and people of "book learning," although that humor is forced and trite. But in the film, this scene is omitted altogether. Events move from Johnson's convalescence to his subsequent arrest to his near lynching without the intervening nonsense. In the play this had been important as it established a sense of the color and variety of the occupants of the Polka Saloon. Attention was paid to fragments of dialogue and song by characters like Sonora, Billy Jackrabbit, Handsome Charlie, Trinidad, and Sid the Card Sharp. In the film some of these men are there to be recognized by their dress by those who have seen or read the play, but they don't contribute to the action and they are not singled out for our attention. In short, the deletion of the schoolroom scene means the film loses a sense of regional types, but it maintains an uninterrupted narrative.

Unfortunately, the characterization of the Girl in the film is less interesting than in the play. Although Belasco's play eventually sentimentalized the character in Act Three into a traditional feminine stereotype of 19th century melodrama—all sweetness and light—the Girl was at least initially a wordly and tough person. In his stage directions Belasco had described her in these terms:

> Her utter frankness takes away all suggestion of vice—showing her to be unsmirched, happy, careless, untouched by the life about her. Yet she has a thorough knowledge of what the men of her world generally want. She is used to flattery—knows exactly how to deal with men—is very shrewd—but quite capable of being a good friend to the camp boys (62).

Indeed, she was of a tougher fiber than the usual genteel heroines of the contemporary stage. There was for example, this striking speech where she exclaims to Jack Rance during a poker game, "I live on chance money—drink money—card money—saloon money. We're gamblers—we're all gamblers" (85). In the film, however, Mabel Van Buren's portrayal of the Girl is bland from beginning to end. Without the colorful vernacular of the dialogue (most of which is not conveyed by the film's titles), her character seems routine and undefined. Moreoever, Van Buren's robust pantomiming (along with that of Theodore Roberts as Rance) cannot bring life to the characters. Their overplaying is especially obvious when, at the climax of the film, they confront each other during the attempted lynching of Johnson.

Other apsects of the play are lost in this film version's predilection for action as opposed to characterization. Generally speaking, *The Girl of the Golden West* had a tough-minded view of the life of desperate characters in a small mining community. For example, late in Act Three, the Girl said to her lover, Johnson, "Suppose you was only a road agent—an' I was a saloon-keeper: we both came out of nothing' an' we met, but through loving, we're goin' to reach things now—that's us! We had to be lifted up like this, to be saved" (96). The predilection of naturalism for the accidental aspects of life was present in dialogue like this and gave the play a special charm. Occasionally, Belasco's dialogue recalled the novels of Frank Norris and Jack London in its depictions of the cowboys' unvarnished view of life—such as when Jack Rance stated his philosophy of life: "Hold on! Hold on! After all, gents, what's death? A kick and you're off"! (60) But the film version, for all of its attention to a naturalistic view of the wilds of California, fails in conveying anything of the fatalistic world-view of the play.

Both the play and film conclude with an epilogue set in what the play described as the "boundless prairies of the West." As the lovers, the Girl and Dick Johnson prepare to make a new life together for themselves, they face back eastward for a moment toward the rising sun. As might be expected at this point, the filmmakers decided to set the scene in a real locale as opposed to the artificial environment that would have been seen on stage. Nonetheless, the scene is played out as if it were on a stage. A slow "iris-in" reveals the little tableau of the two lovers standing looking at the sky. This corresponds to Belasco's original staging and lighting where gauze curtains rose in combination with the use of blue footlights and borders—in effect, "opening out" the scene for the viewer.[41] The two people pantomime their love for each other in stiffly exaggerated gestures, and they remain relatively motionless in the center of the screen in a sustained take recorded by a static camera. It was as if in this final moment, the filmmakers wanted to reaffirm that this largely cinematic film was, after all, derived from a stage play.

The Taming of the Shrew (United Artists, 1929)

The Taming of the Shrew was not only the first synchronized-sound motion picture version of a Shakespeare play, but one of the few full-length Shakespearean films to come from the American film studios in the 1920s. It starred Douglas Fairbanks and Mary Pickford as Petruchio and Kate, and it was directed by Sam Taylor. As an early all-talking motion picture, it might be expected that, like the sound films *Coquette* and *The Green Goddess*, it would be closely imitative of a proscenium stage production—especially in so far as a reliance upon dialogue was concerned. Such was not the case, however. Sam Taylor's adaptation altered the essentially verbal quality of the play and transformed it into an essentially visual work.[42]

Much of the original play was either altered, deleted, excised, or exploited for its comic potential—a fact which might make purists wince. The Bianca subplot was compressed and diminished in importance, as was the character of Bianca itself. The rival suitors Lucentio and Hortensio were compressed into a single character, Hortensio (played by Geoffrey Wardell), who posed as a combination tutor and music teacher and who eventually won Bianca's heart. This secondary wooing took on a decidedly ancillary importance. The character of Lucentio is absent, but he was, after all, one of Shakespeare's glib and rather dull young lovers in the original. Because the original Hortensio and his lusty widow were removed, the last act of the play had to be compressed and redesigned for the film. Gremio (Joseph Cawthorn) was present, but his role was no longer that of a comic rival suitor for Bianca's hand. And since we also saw very little of Dorothy Jordan's Bianca, the relationship between Kate and her sister as a further means of explaining Kate's shrewishness in the Shakespearean original was all but gone in the adaptation. Anything that might be construed as a soliloquy was also cut. In one instance, the film retained Petruchio's lines at the end of Act Four, Scene One—when he told the audience what he planned to do in order to curb Kate's "mad and headstrong humor"—but Fairbanks speaks to them after he has returned to the dining table on the honeymoon night and has his dog Troilus there to listen. Another change that occurred here, incidentally, was that Taylor has Kate leave her chamber and appear on the balcony above Petruchio so that she hears Petruchio and, thus, learns what he is up to. This eventual understanding was subtly hinted at in the play, but the film makes it so obvious that no one in the audience could miss it.

Many events alluded to in the play's dialogue are visualized in the film. One of the central scenes in the film is Petruchio's arrival at the wedding—an event that is only reported action in the original text. Another key scene, also reported action in the original, is the wedding itself. This scene takes up fully ten minutes in the film and is virtually without dialogue. Another example is the arrival of Petruchio and Kate at his country estate, and even related by Gremio to Curtis in Act Four Scene One ("how her horse fill, and under her horse...in how miry a place; and how she was bemoiled...and how she waded through the dirt....").

In all these instances, the words of the play are transformed to a series of sight gags. This should not be surprising, since the adaptation was made by Sam Taylor, a man trained in silent comedy as a gag writer and director for Harold Lloyd (*The Freshman, The Kid Brother*, 1925-26). Taylor's method of adaptation has been described by Lawrence Irving (son of Sir Henry), who was on the set at the time:

> Day and night [Taylor] was attended by two gagmen—rude, nonsensicals after the Bard's own heart—with faces like battered bantam-weights and an inexhaustible fund of practical comicalities in the Mack Sennett tradition. Whenever dialogue that could not be cut tended to lag, or was reckoned incomprehensible to the ninepennies, they were called upon for a diversion.[43]

Thus, Petruchio's arrival is visualized with Fairbanks riding in to the town *backwards* on an aging nag. He wears a jackboot atop his head and insolently munches on an apple. At the wedding, a series of gags predominate over the few spoken words as Fairbanks continues to munch on the apple, stomps on the foot of the reluctant Kate, and disposes of the apple core by surreptitiously passing it from hand to hand of the bewildered guests present. The camera is very mobile here as it follows in medium closeup the progress of the discarded apple core as it is relayed across the room. The arrival of Petruchio and Kate at the estate is a series of slapstick pratfalls as both tumble on and off the horse into the mud. The wedding feast between the two is an elaborate running gag as Kate continually reaches for food only to have Petruchio snatch it away for his own ingestion at the critical moment. Finally, Kate's arrival and first appearance on screen is heralded by a powerful tracking shot—one of the examples of camera movement being exploited as an expressive device. We have not yet seen her as the camera begins to mount the stairs toward her room, but we sense her fiendish presence through the sounds of horrendous bumping and crashing and the flurry of servants fleeing the closed door. Then the camera moves into the room and, after a slow pan enabling us to survey the disordered room, pans to the left where we finally encounter the proud and angry Kate. Her subsequent confrontation with the equally proud Petruchio relies more upon key closeups than upon lengthy dialogue exchanges. Both characters carry whips and closeups of both are inserted as a visual counterpoint to the words.

The nature of this adaptation, while eminently cinematic when compared to *Coquette* and *The Green Goddess,* nonetheless might trouble those who like their Shakespeare undefiled. Such horsing around and pratfalling may at first seem too physical, vulgar, and farcical, but few would argue that the knockabout additions which the films provide to compensate for this loss are not entertaining.[44]

The Virginian (Paramount, 1929)

This is the first all-talking adaptation of the play by Owen Wister and Kirke La Shelle. By the late twenties filmmakers and audiences alike were beginning to realize the pitfalls of the synchronous union of sound and image. When you hear and see the same thing an audio-visual pleonasm occurs. There was something ridiculous in insuring that every sound had its visual component on the screen, as we have noted in *Coquette* and *The Green Goddess.* On the other hand, if sound could be utilized as a relatively independent element, a different effect was produced. For example, if a pistol shot was heard and an image of a startled facial expression was seen at the same time, a different kind of link between the two was established—one that was not merely causal but which was also symbolic, even poetic. An imaginative combination of image and sound could function like the counterpointing of musical lines in a fugue, as opposed to mere imitation (and I mean the term here in its strictly musical sense). In this way the door was opened to the *expressive* use of the soundtrack, including natural sound, voices and music. These sounds could be used to *inform* the image with additional information as well as with imaginative and symbolic connotations.

From beginning to end, *The Virginian* utilizes sound as a relatively independent expressive element. During the opening credits, for example, we do not hear the expected burst of music that would lapse into silence only to reappear again at the end title. Rather, we hear natural sounds of a cattle roundup—the slap of reins, the whistle of the cowboys, the mooing of the cattle, the muffled hoofbeats of the horses, etc. These sounds constitute a kind of aural mood for the titles. This use of natural sounds extends into the dialogue of the cowboys throughout the picture, and here we have at least the equivalent on screen of the colorful vernacular that had been excised from *The Virginian* and *The Girl of the Golden West* during the silent period. At many times, Trampas launches into bawdy cowboy songs. They give a

Director Victor Fleming starred Gary Cooper and Mary Brian in the 1929 Paramount adaptation of Wister's dramatization of his own novel, *The Virginian*. This theatrical film was shot largely out of the studio on exterior locations.

pungent irony to scenes, as when he sings in the bar prior to the first confrontation with the Virginian (Gary Cooper); then later, after shooting and wounding him from ambush; and again before the fatal gunfight at the end.

Significantly, the extensive location shooting of this all-talking *Virginian*, encouraged the use of natural sound. Just as the location shooting of the silent version enhanced its naturalistic scenic quality, now the location shooting of the sound version provided the natural *sounds* as well as the sights. Director Victor Fleming took not only his cameras but his sound recording equipment to the San Diego County locales. The entire film has almost no studio shooting, or sound-stage recording. The filmmakers devised ways of recording sound with mobile equipment just as the images were captured. Most impressively, they found ways of making natural sounds poetically profound.

The best example of this occurs during the hanging of the Virginian's friend, Steve (Richard Arlen). Natural sounds are heard asynchronously with the images that create a powerfully dramatic scene that points the way toward the subsequent development of the technique in talking pictures. We know already that the two friends had often called to each other by simulating the cry of a wild quail. The sound had come to symbolize the lifelong bond between them. As Steve is hanged the film cuts to his shadow thrown across the grass (as had happened in the silent film version). At the same time we hear the sadly expressive sound of a creaking rope. As the Virginian and a friend ride slowly away, suddenly the cry of a wild quail is heard. "Must be a quail," is all that the friend says, laconically. They ride off. It is a beautiful moment. A natural sound had achieved such significance that when it unexpectedly breaks the silence it works in conjunction with the image of sorrowful, silent men, to create a fine dramatic moment.

Finally, the climactic gunfight, which is staged very much like the one in the silent version, is here informed with an aural counterpoint. As the approaching antagonists near the dramatic moment, the clink of spurs, the scrape of boots on the wooden sidewalk, the soft sighing of the wind around them—all are heard without having to see their visual causes. The sounds— there is no music at this point—coexist with the mounting tension of the cross-cutting so that we *hear* as well as see the developing conflict.

The Musical Films—The Cocoanuts (Paramount, 1929), Glorifying the American Girl (Paramount, 1929), Whoopee (United Artists, 1930), and Paramount on Parade (Paramount, 1930)

Some of the best examples of the use of asynchronous sound in early talking pictures occur in the musical films. Perhaps filmmakers felt that if audiences were prepared to accept the musical show at all—with its conventions that people burst into song at the slightest provocation and that dozens of chorus girls could cavort about in machinelike precision—then audiences could also accept unusual combinations of sight and sound. In the above musical films, as we already know, there are moments when the films closely imitate the sense of a proscenium stage production. On the other hand, there are also moments that strikingly illustrate the early achievements in the asynchronous union of image and sound.

The Cocoanuts, while a closely imitative theatrical film, has two sequences that exploit the possibilities of asynchronous sound. In the first, a romantic dialogue between Mary Eaton and Oscar Shaw is accompanied by background music that quite literally comes from nowhere. Elsewhere, we always saw an orchestra in conjunction with music. Now, there is no visible source. Moreover, the music foreshadows the song that is about to be sung between the two lovers. And when they begin to sing, they pick up the melody that has already been heard. A continuity between words and music has been established that enhances the romantic moment. Far more spectacular in effect is a dance sequence which reveals, according to musical historian Miles Kreuger, the first attempt in a synchronized—sound film to "analyze" the space of a scene in an abstract fashion. The dance choreographers Maria Gambarelli and George Hale were under contract as a team to the Paramount studios, where they had come via the Paramount Publix theater circuit. Gambarelli had been a ballet choreographer for the Capital, Roxy, and Radio City Music Hall. While staging the ballet for the film version of The Cocoanuts, she noted that in one sequence the girls in their fluffy black-and-white costumes looked like flower petals when viewed from a position directly above the action. According to Kreuger, she asked her cameraman, George Folsey, if he could raise the camera and shoot down at the girls from a high angle. He said he could do better than that and he climbed up into the rafters and shot straight down at the action from a perfect perpendicular. The result was a brief shot that lasted on screen for only a few seconds. But it marked a new direction in the presentation and analysis of screen space that would be imitated in dozens of dance sequences during the next few years. The head-on angle of the theater spectator was abruptly changed and a totally abstract image resulted, shattering the customary sense of a framing proscenium. When combined with the music, the result was a poetic expression that temporarily transcended the rest of the film. "It is this brief moment," Kreuger concludes, "that marks the emancipation of the screen musical from its theatrical roots. For the first time the camera offered the moviegoer a new perspective on a theatrical event."[45]

The most imaginative sequence in Glorifying the American Girl is its opening scene. A succession of titles superimposed over images of women announce various incarnations of "glorified" American girls in the 20th century. Tableaux shots of girls in various "domestic" poses—ironing, washing, etc.—are followed by rapid dissolves in which these same women are metamorphosed into dazzling show girls with long trains and headdresses. While all this is happening, other images appear and disappear in superimpositions—a globe of the world with hundreds of chorus girls marching across the surface, crowds of people marching through what looks like a train station. And all the while, underpinning this free mix of images, is an imaginative blend of sounds. There are a number of fragments of Ziegfeld songs, like "A Pretty Girl Is Like a Melody," that rapidly sequence in and out of each other. This union of images and sounds in montage signals an attempt to separate image and sound and recombine them in interesting and imaginative ways. Just as important, sound and image both effect the abridgement of time and space and continuities are no longer natural, but dreamlike. The whole world of the Ziegfeld revue is compressed into two minutes.

Paramount on Parade was a revue that, like *Glorifying the American Girl,* presented its theatrical events on a real stage; nonetheless it employed imaginative combinations of image and sound. The film consisted of many semi-related sketches and musical routines. One sketch, directed by Ernest Lubitsch, utilized music as a satiric commentary on a marital situation. A quarrel is taking place between Maurice Chevalier and Evelyn Brent. The music is heard without any visible source, and we accept it as a counterpoint to the action, underpinning the dialogue with witty commentaries—even mimicking the rhythm and inflection of the speech itself. As Chevalier and Brent alternately sing and speak, each verse is accompanied by a variant in the musical instrumentation corresponding to the tone and diction of the words. For example, the flutter of their lips, the slapping of their hands, the flow of their words, all parallel instrumentation and rhythm in the music. The "My Marine" song with Ruth Chatterton, displays another example of an unusual combination of image and sound. In this mini-musical/dramatic sketch Chatterton portrays a lovelorn streetwalker who sings the song, "My Marine," to some soldiers in a bar. The song begins and an unseen orchestral accompaniment springs up in response. She stops singing abruptly and drops her head to the bar. But the orchestral accompaniment continues uninterrupted and is then succeeded by the same song sung by soldiers' voices. At this point a shot of marching soldiers dissolves into the image. Music bridges space and time; it also acts as the aural correlative of memory and emotion.

The key in achieving moments like those described here lay not only in finding ways to record separately the image and the sound—insuring their relative independence of each other—but in devising methods of putting them back together. The idea of editing *sound* was extremely important in this achievement. As long as films were made with the Warner Brothers Vitaphone system, sound editing was extremely difficult. Although this is not the place for a technical discussion of this point, suffice it to say that because sound was recorded onto wax discs, there was no way of cutting it into discreet units.[46] But when the Fox Movietone system of recording sound on film began to gain popularity over the disc system late in the 1920s, the way was open to cut lengths of film that contained sound in synchronization with the film strips that contained the image. The editor, in effect, now had at his disposal pieces of film that contained discreet units of either image or sound, and he could thus combine them in any way he chose.

In closing, it is amusing to note that when *Paramount on Parade* was made, sound editing had advanced to the point that the filmmaker could flaunt the techniques. There is a moment when Jack Oakie and his dancing partner perform a series of gymnastics where in they literally throw each other around a gymnasium, singing all the while to an orchestral accompaniment. Had such a stunt been attempted a year previously the sound would have been recorded at the same time as the image. A number of microphones would have been placed about the set which would have been turned on and off as the dancing figures came within and subsequently passed out of their range. Thus, their voices would have faded in and out. Also, the physical exertion would have affected the vocal intonations and there would have been telltale breathing and signs of fatigue in the voices. In short, the technical limitations would not have permitted the filming at all! But with the sound-on-film recording technique utilized in *Paramount on Parade,* the song was recorded separately and then synchronized later to the lip movements of the dancers. The image was freely edited into a series of long shots, closeups, and moving camera shots without the worry of simultaneous sound recording. We shall see how this technique of recording sound and image separately was perfected when the musical film, *King of Jazz,* was made in 1930.

The Birth of a Nation (Epoch/Triangle, 1915) and King of Jazz (Universal, 1930)

If any two films could be regarded as marking the end of their respective eras of theatrical imitation, D. W. Griffith's *The Birth of a Nation* and John Murray Anderson's *King of Jazz* are the likeliest candidates. At first glance, they seem wildly dissimilar films—the first mixed fiction with historical fact, the second was simply a musical revue on film; one was silent, the other had synchronized sound; one presented actors that were primarily trained for the screen, the other presented actors and musicians from the variety stage. Yet the two films are comparable in terms of how they relate to the stage. Both were derived from theatrical events. Both were directed by men trained in the theater. And, although both revealed aspects of their theatrical origins, both, ultimately, achieved an entirely cinematic expression. *The Birth of a Nation* fully exploited the potentials of the asynchronous union of image and sound. Finally, both films elicited a critical and popular response that reveals to us a growing understanding at the time of the differences between stage and screen.

The Birth of a Nation was released through the Epoch Producing Corporation in February, 1915. Few films in the history of the medium have aroused more comment and controversy, although this is not the place to discuss its racial and political controversies, which have been examined extensively elsewhere.[47] Rather, I view it in its context as a theatrical film that achieved a powerfully cinematic expression. Although, as we have seen, pictures like *The Virginian, The Girl of the Golden West,* and *Glorifying the American Girl* all showed signs of this kind of achievement, it was *The Birth of a Nation* that for all time freed the motion picture medium from the boundaries of the proscenium frame. Prominent film historian William K. Everson noted this in a recent interview. After the appearance of *The Birth of a Nation,* he said, "stage-bound" movies were a thing of the past: "They were swept aside—the few good along with the many bad."[48]

An indication of the film's complete mastery of cinematic techniques is the fact that its theatrical origins have been totally ignored by most of the standard film history texts.[49] Thomas Dixon had dramatized his novel, *The Clansman,* in 1906. It premiered in New York at the Liberty Theatre under the guidance of the impresario George H. Brennan. In the cast were Holbrook Blinn, Sydney Ayres, and DeWitt Jennings. The play became a popular vehicle for travelling stock companies in succeeding years. In 1912 the Kinemacolor motion picture company announced plans to produce a film version of the play using the original stage cast and the original playscript. The project was abandoned after several reels of film had been made. Purportedly, the footage was closely imitative of the proscenium stage production; subsequently, the footage has disappeared.[50]

D. W. Griffith knew about the stage version of *The Clansman.* In the fall of 1906 he was engaged to appear in a road tryout of another play of Dixon's, *The One Woman,* which followed on the heels of Dixon's success with *The Clansman.* At this time Griffith was struggling for recognition as a playwright and actor. While appearing with a number of touring companies—the Meffert Stock Company, the Ada Gray Company, the Neil Alhambra Stock Company, and the Melbourne MacDowell Company—he had written *The Fool and the Girl,* a naturalistic drama in the style of *Margaret Fleming* and *The Pit.* Although unsuccessful, the play nonetheless gave evidence of Griffith's developing sensibility for cinematic expression.[51] Griffith remembered his association with Dixon when one of the writers for Biograph, Frank Woods, suggested Griffith complete the abandoned Kinemacolor project.

But despite his theatrical background, Griffith was not content to film *The Clansman* as if it were an imitation of the stage production. Since 1908, when he first arrived at Biograph, he had been experimenting with methods of releasing the motion picture from the limitations imposed by the proscenium frame of a stage. For example, the notion that a shot of film should correspond to a given scene in a play was abhorrent to him. As early as his *The Sands of Dee* (1911), Griffith had broken up a story into as many as sixty-eight shots in a reel of film. The shot was, obviously, no longer in itself a complete scene, but a *component* of a scene. The shot could break up the scene into a variety of angles and viewing distances; it could serve as a cutaway to a different action in a different locale; it could be used to move the action forward or backward in time; and the conjunction of shots, each of varying duration, could create temporal and dramatic rhythms. When the Reverend Dr. Stockton, writing in the *Moving Picture World* in August, 1912, attacked Griffith's *Sands of Dee,* he singled out this use of many shots as a reprehensible technique:

A twenty-scene drama is run up to fifty or sixty scene [shots], with an average time length of from fifteen to eighteen seconds each. Acting is not possible. Clarity of story is not possible. Unfolding of plot is not possible. There is a succession of eye-filling scenes, but no stories.[52]

Stockton's editorial declared that a return to "sensible" filmmaking was in order. Other films, such as the closely imitative theatrical films of Porter for Famous Players, were preferable. *They* were the ones that were "really drama" and not "bitten by the lightning bug," as were Griffith's. If Griffith's method were to continue unchecked, the writer concluded, the motion picture medium would be committed to "jumping-jack tendencies" and everything eventually would "drop with a crash."[53]

But, of course, Griffith did continue his experiments and in *The Birth of a Nation* they had their culmination. In all aspects—editing, camera movement, use of natural locales, swift narrative pace through shots of brief duration, the deep-focus frame—*The Birth of a Nation* exploited the resources of the motion picture medium to a degree far surpassing that of previous theatrical films. In William K. Everson's words, it "established movies as an international art and an international industry almost overnight, and influenced the manner of narrative story-telling in American films for at least the next six years."[54] Indeed, it had so transcended its theatrical origins that it was virtually a different work altogether—a symbol, as it were, of the general advancement of the motion picture at the time. "The theater and film were changed thereafter," Everson concluded; "*Birth* didn't do these things first, but it was very, very successful, and that made the difference."[55] Another important film historian, Kevin Brownlow, agrees with this judgment. In a recent letter he told me that in *The Birth of a Nation*..."the classical format of the American motion picture was established—not too far from the best tenets of the stage, but far enough to be a separate art."[56]

Contemporary assessment of the film generally agreed that the motion picture was a unique art form, not dependent upon the stage. Late in February, 1915, advertisements in New York heralding the arrival of the film to local houses boasted that it marked the "Dawn of a New Art which marks an Epoch in the Theatres of the World." Sir Herbert Beerbohm Tree, about to begin work on *Macbeth* for Triangle, declared that the picture signified "the birth of a new art—and a new artist." And Griffith himself, while working on the film, commented to historian Robert Grau that the theater and film must ultimately diverge:

> The conditions of the two being so different it follows that the requirements are equally dissimilar. Stage craft and stage people are out of place in the intense realism of motion-picture expression....[57]

Its success at the boxoffice and with the critics assured its enduring popularity and influence. No longer would filmmakers and public be content with mere photographic imitations of stage plays. Ironically, however, the film's exhibition policy followed that of many previous theatrical films. It "played" in prestige theater houses, including the Clunes Auditorium in Los Angeles, the Liberty Theater in New York, the Colonial in Chicago, the Forrest in Philadelphia, the Atlanta, the Tremont in Boston, the Scala and the Drury Lane in London, and many others. In the assessment of Seymour Stern, who devoted his life to studying the films of Griffith, it challenged the legitimate theater and it won. For example, it broke all the known box-office records in the history of the stage. In the first six months of its national run, it was viewed by more persons than had witnessed all the stage plays in the United States in any given five-year period. Its gross in the New York City area alone, where it ran at five theaters, from March of 1915 to January of 1916, for a total of 6,266 performances, was $3,750,000.[58]

A significant fact beyond these statistics is that this kind of exposure gained for it the attention of "serious" critics everywhere. Before 1915, film criticism on a consistent basis had been sporadic, all too often superficial, and often from anonymous sources in the major newspapers in America. Seymour Stern notes that because of *The Birth of a Nation*, however, motion picture criticism began as a regular feature in the daily press. Articles on Griffith appeared as well, such as a series in the New York *Times* by Henry McMahon, James O. Spearing, and Richard Barry. And other newspapers—notably the New York *Herald-Tribune*, the New York *Globe*, the Boston *Examiner*, the Los Angeles *Times*, and the leading Chicago newspapers—also instituted regular screen departments at this time.

The impact made by *The Birth of a Nation* surpassed anything achieved by theatrical filmmakers in the seven years since the formation of Film d'Art in 1908. Prestige, success, popularity all had been reached. Yet, the achievement came because of a film that had so burst the bounds of the proscenium that its theatrical origins were hardly detectable. Writing in 1929, Gilbert Seldes noted that its subject, its very substance, was no longer a theatrical property; it was the *camera* itself.[59]

There were more than 1,500 shots in the print of *The Birth of a Nation* at its premiere in February, 1915. That contrasts sharply with the mere twenty-eight shots in the most important theatrical film made before it, *Queen Elizabeth*. Moreover, unlike *Queen Elizabeth*, the shots were of all different kinds. They vary from close shots of objects—such as an eye seen through a small hole in a door, a cotton blossom, a pistol, and parched corn in a pan—to distance shots across great expanses of countryside. The camera moves freely in many of these shots—tilting down to take in the dogs at Dr. Cameron's feet, panning across a battlefield, or preceding the riding Clansmen (the camera was mounted on the back of an automobile). Even the shape of the screen varies from shot to shot. No longer was there the "golden mean" of the rectangular screen that approximated the proscenium platform; the screen shape was constantly changing through the use of masks in the camera. Shots of the Camerons at home were in the shape of a circle, while battlefield shots were masked at the top and bottom so that the image becomes a wide, elongated strip resembling today's Panavision frame. Many of the shots were framed in vignette—the image shaded off gradually on all sides into the surrounding ground. Griffith also employed a split-screen technique by which he visualized two events simultaneously instead of cutting from one to the other. This occurred, for example, during the "march to the Sea" sequence, when the screen appeared to be diagonally cut in two. The scene of the burning Atlanta occupied the upper triangle and that of the marchers the lower.

The ways in which these shots are joined are far more complex than anything we have seen in *The Virginian* or *The Girl of the Golden West*. Parallel editing is utilized frequently. The climax of the film is actually a last-minute rescue—or rather two rescues. Action progresses simultaneously in several different places—an office, a room adjoining the office, a street, the exterior and interior of a cabin, and various parts of the countryside. During the sequence depicting the assassination of Lincoln, Griffith cuts from the President's box to the auditorium to the passageway occupied by Booth. There are no less than fifty-five shots in this one sequence alone. Effects are possible in this way not available in the employment of only one or two sustained takes—such as establishing a relationship between the unsuspecting Lincoln and the scheming Booth, not to mention the inclusion of shots of the stage, of Booth's pistol, the audience, etc. The cutting also transports the viewer through time and space by means of flashbacks. For example, when Margaret Cameron refuses Phil Stoneman's proposal of marriage, a shot is inserted that flashes the action back to the death of her brother that had occurred on the battlefield. One flashback sequence, replaces a speech by the "Little Colonel" when he relates "a series of outrages that have occurred."

I do not mean to imply, however, that the entire film is absolutely devoid of references to its theatrical source. There are relatively few dialogue titles and, as a result, some of the action is as broadly pantomimed as anything seen in earlier theatrical films. I refer particularly to the love scenes involving Elsie Stoneman (Lillian Gish) and the moments of terror when Margaret Cameron is driven to commit suicide by the advance of the mulatto villain. Many of the film's historical episodes and allegorical visions are presented in the fashion of theatrical tableaux. The sequence at Ford's Theater is preceded by the title, "And then when the terrible days were over and the healing time of peace was at hand, came the fated night of April 14, 1865." And the final apocalyptic vision (when the god of war is replaced by the figure of Christ) features a title reading, "Liberty and Union, One and inseparable, now and forever." One of the villains, Silas Lynch, is described in a title as leading black people "by an evil way to build himself a throne of vaulting power." In such title sequences, Griffith returns to the style and diction of the theatricalism he knew so well. The title cards convey subject, message, purpose, and editorial comment all at once. Their blend of simplistic morality and allegorical effusions can only remind one of a road company production of *Uncle Tom's Cabin*.

Nonetheless, *The Birth of a Nation* effectively signalled an end to the presumption during the silent period that a motion picture had to closely imitate a theatrical event in order to achieve success and prestige. It also contained within its shifting web of time and space the hint that by abandoning close imitation of the stage the motion picture was on its way toward its own artistic expression.

King of Jazz appeared just fifteen years later in 1930. So much had come between it and *The Birth of a Nation*—the maturity of the silent film by the early 1920s, the coming of sound and the subsequent return to close theatrical imitation by 1928, and the growing sense by 1929 that films could once again abandon that close imitation. *King of Jazz* was one of the first all-talking pictures to create a consistent and dynamic combination of image and sound. Just as *The Birth of a Nation* had woven space and time into a constantly shifting continuum, *King of Jazz* had weakened the natural, or causal bonds between image and sound and created a new kind of combinative possibility between the two.

Its director, John Murray Anderson, must be credited with his achievement. Described by historian Miles Kreuger as "one of the most remarkable people in the theater and an amazingly innovative man with great taste and imagination,"[60] Anderson had previously displayed his talents in the Greenwich Village Follies and Music Box Revues throughout the 1920s. These musical revues were noted for their high degree of imaginative and stylized staging.[71] Anderson had created, for example, what he called the "ballet ballad." This concept used a song as the core for an elaborate fantasy involving light changes, dance sequences, songs, scrims, and curtains to achieve bizarre effects. In a word, long before Anderson came to Hollywood's Universal studios in 1929, he had strained at the physical restrictions of the proscenium. Although he acknowledged that he knew nothing about movies upon his arrival, he was already prepared to seek the flexibility in time, space, and sound that he would achieve in the film medium. *King of Jazz,* while relatively unknown today, was a highly influential achievement in its time and influenced methods of sound and image recording for decades to come. For a long time, *King of Jazz* was regarded as a "lost film"—that is, its materials were withdrawn from circulation and consequently have remained unseen by generations of filmgoers. It was not until 1970 that the American Film Institute, in cooperation with the Library of Congress, presented a restored print for screening. Yet, the film is still generally unavailable, and one searches in vain through the many recent film texts and, in particular, to histories of the early sound period for a mention of it.

John Murray Anderson was a practical man. He realized that achieving on film the scale, color, and sound of a musical revue would be extremely difficult. How was he to film hundreds of dancers on vast sets and, at the same time, adequately record the variety of sounds needed—from solo voices and instruments, to massed choruses and instrumental combinations? We have already seen how the dance sequence in *Coquette* was a chaotic jumble of sounds because of the lack of control in modulating the voices, the musical instruments, and crowd noises. Anderson's solution was to further develop the concept of recording the image and the sound separately. Steps had been taken in this direction, as we have seen, in portions of *Glorifying the American Girl* and *Paramount on Parade* (which was being filmed at the same time as *King of Jazz*). There were two reasons for utilizing this technique, Anderson explained. The first was, simply, to insure the best possible sound recording environment: "You can't get perfect sound conditions yet on a stage while shooting a big scene. There are poor acoustics, extraneous noises...."[62] The second reason lay in the need to restore complete mobility to the camera and flexibility to the editing process. By varying the camera setups, by moving the camera, by restoring the freedom to cut quickly and easily from angle to angle and forward and backward in time, one could avoid the limitations seen all too frequently in *Coquette* and sections of *Glorifying the American Girl.* Like Griffith, Anderson saw no necessity in retaining the correlation of shot to scene, in retaining strict continuities in real time and space, in utilizing shallow-depth playing areas. In addition, he saw no need to record image and and sound directly and simultaneously. By recording them separately, he could *recombine* them in striking and unusual ways. Further, no longer would the editing be mere continuity cutting—the use of sound bind together a sequence of shots.

Musical rhythm, for Anderson, became such a linking device. The duration of the given shot and its juxtaposition with other shots could be determined by the metrical dimension of the music. Given a certain rhythm in the music, the shots could be combined so that each one would last a given number of beats of time in synchronization with the musical rhythm. Anderson did not just want to *record* a revue on film; he wanted to *create* an entirely new event.

The formulas of the revue—and their subsequent incarnation on film—have already been discussed. *King of Jazz,* unlike most of the musical films of its time, strays so far from the revue form as to become cinematic event. In some scenes it exploits the resources of superimpositions and double-printing—most notably when Paul Whiteman first presents his band. He opens a suitcase, takes out a miniature platform, sets it on a table, and then spills from the bag a group of tiny musicians who rush to the platform. Another sequence in the film is entirely animated—reminding us that Walt Disney's "Steamboat Willie," the first synchronized-sound animated film, had appeared a year earlier. This cartoon relates the fantastic story of how Whiteman first earned the title of "King of Jazz." As the film progresses, more and more novel effects are introduced, climaxed with the imaginative rendering of Gershwin's *Rhapsody of Blue.* For this sequence a "miniature" band is concealed in a gigantic blue piano (the film is in Technicolor). The music is visually counterpointed with a succession of images, each dissolving into the other and each illustrating through color and composition the shifting moods and harmonies of the music. The rhythm of the dissolves is determined by the rhythm of the music.

These scenes are indicative of the uniquely cinematic character of the film—even though the basic structure relates to the traditional theatrical revue. But the effects would be impossible to achieve on the stage. This fact was not lost upon contemporary critics who greeted the film in May, 1930. For example, Richard Dana Skinner of *The Commonweal* noted that "nothing could better illustrate the growing flexibility and range of the talking color screen than the general excellence, variety, charm and occasional imaginative interludes of *King of Jazz.*" In singling out Anderson's direction, Skinner noted that his tendencies for pictorial spectacle have always been limited on the stage; that now they can work "in a medium made to his order and temperament." *King of Jazz* achieved "a unit of mood between music and vision utterly impossible on the stage."[63]

The preceding discussion should make it clear that theatrical films made early in both periods were more closely imitative of theatrical source materials than those made late in the periods. This is also generally true of the hundreds of other theatrical films that appeared in both time periods. This is only a general observation, however, because there were exceptions to the rule. But the point is that roughly midway through 1912-15 and 1927-30 a change in attitude regarding the validity of close imitation in theatrical films can be discerned. This change represents nothing less than a new, or at least enriched, perception of the nature and potentials of the motion picture medium—not just as an extension of the stage but, more importantly, as an independent medium of artistic expression. Theatrical films by their very existence stimulated this discussion and were themselves barometers whereby the results of that discussion were visible on the screen. Such points are examined in detail in the next chapter.

Notes

[1]Dale Shaw, *Titans of the American Stage* (Philadelphia: The Westminster Press, 1971), p. 113.

[2]*Monte Cristo by Charles Fechter as Played by James O'Neill*, in J. B. Russak, ed., *America's Lost Plays*, Vol. XVI (Princeton: Princeton University Press, 1941). All quoted passages are taken from this section.

[3]In referring to the pictorial aspects of plays like *The Count of Monte Cristo* and *Arrah-na-pogue*, A. Nicholas Vardac in *Stage and Screen* (Cambridge: Harvard University Press, 1949) frequently uses the term "tableau" to refer to a wordless, pictorial scene of brief duration and limited movement on the part of the players. See pp. 59-63.

[4]Henry C. De Mille and David Belasco, *Lord Chumley*, in Robert Hamilton Ball, ed., *The Plays of Henry C. De Mille, America's Lost Plays*, Vol. XVII (Princeton University Press, 1941). All quoted passages are taken from this edition.

[5]For a good introduction to this subject, see "The Rising Tide of Realism in the American Drama," *Current Opinion*, October 1913, pp. 250-51.

[6]Lise-Lone Marker, *David Belasco: Naturalism in the American Theater* (Princeton: Princeton University Press, 1975), p. 80.

[7]Edwin Milton Royle, *The Squaw Man*, in Burns Mantle and Garrison P. Sherwood, eds., *The Best Plays of 1899-1909* (New York: Dodd, Mead and Co., 1944). All quoted passages are taken from this edition.

[8]Arthur Hobson Quinn, *History of the American Drama from the Civil War to the Present Day* (New York: F. S. Crofts & Co., 1943), p. 124.

[9]"Edwin Milton Royle," *The Moving Picture World*, February 21, 1914, p. 930.

[10]*Ibid.*, p. 930.

[11]Howard Taubman, *The Making of the American Theatre* (New York: Coward-McCann, Inc., 1965), p. 185.

[12]George Abbott and Ann Bridgers, *Coquette* (New York: Samuel French, 1929). All quoted passages are taken from this edition.

[13]Historian of the musical film, Miles Kreuger, has noted that the practice of filming stage shows directly from the stage was a common practice by the early 1930s. These films were used as "guides" for projected film adaptations. MGM, for instance, by 1931 had shot complete, sound records of such stage productions as *Private Lives*, *The Cat and the Fiddle*, *Grand Hotel*, and scenes from *Strange Interlude*. The respective casts of these productions were paid by the studio for these performances. These versions were utilized only as guides and the footage was not actually incorporated into the subsequent film versions. (Miles Kreuger interviews with the author, May 26, 1979 and March 3, 1980, in Hollywood California.)

[14]Alexander Walker, *The Shattered Silents* (New York: William Morrow, 1979), p. 92.

[15]For a good introduction to this "feminist" oriented drama, see Emma Goldman, *The Social Significance of the Modern Drama* (Boston: Richard Badger, 1914). See also my "The New Woman on Stage: Women's Issues in American Drama, 1890-1915," *Helicon Nine: The Journal of Women's Arts and Letters*, No. 7 (Winter 1982), pp. 6-19.

[16]Quoted in Lois C. Gottlieb, "Obstacles to Feminism in the early Plays of Rachel Crothers," *Papers in Women's Studies*, Vol. II, No. 2, University of Michigan, Ann Arbor, p. 71.

[17]Eugene Walter, *The Easiest Way*, in John Gassner, ed., *Best Plays of the Early American Theatre* (New York: Crown Publishers, Inc., 1967), p. 660.

[18]The text of the Motion Picture Code can be found in Murray Schumach, *The Face on the Cutting Room Floor* (New York: William Morrow and Company, 1964), pp. 279-92.

[19]See Alexander Walker, *Sex in the Movies* (Baltimore: Pelican Books, 1968), p. 192-93. Walker explains that the principle of the Code was "the belief that the sinful can be redeemed through the technique of penance. In the censorship manual this goes under the name of 'moral compensation'. It means that whoever commits a sin or a crime in a film must be made to suffer remorse, or repentance, or retribution—the degree of each to be apportioned to the gravity of the offence."

[20]William Archer, *The Green Goddess*, in Burns Mantle, ed., *Best Plays of 1920-21* (Boston: Small, Meynard and Co., 1921). All quotations taken from this edition.

[21]George Arliss, *My Ten Years in the Studios* (Boston: Little, Brown and Co., 1940), p. 55.

[22]*Ibid.*, p. 53.

[23]Paul D. Zimmerman and Burt Goldblatt, *The Marx Brothers at the Movies* (New York: G. P. Putnam's Sons, 1968), pp. 19-20.

[24]David Ewen, *The Complete Book of the American Musical Theater* (New York: Holt, Rinehart and Winston, 1970), p. 93.

[25]Paul D. Zimmerman and Burt Goldblatt, pp. 19-20.

[26]*Ibid.*, p. 20.

[27]Robert C. Toll, *On With the Show* (New York: Oxford University Press, 1976), p. 301.

[28]Randolph Carter, *The World of Flo Ziegfeld* (New York: Praeger, 1974), p. 60.

[29]*Ibid.*, p. 57.

[30]For a discussion of film speeds in the silent era, see William K. Everson, *American Silent Film* (New York: Oxford University Press, 1978), pp. 56-57.

[31]Until the present time, the play script of *The Virginian* has not been anthologized nor has it appeared in any series of publications, such as the Samuel French series. Apparently the only version extant is the script for the London production as revised by Wister and given to his cousin, Lady Alice Butler. This version was then given to N. Orwin Rush who published it in 1958 in Tallahassee, Florida. Mr. Rush comments in his preface: "I have never seen a printed copy of the play, and the United States Copyright Office in the Library of Congress has informed me that the dramatized version of the story was never copyrighted. This leads me to beleive that this edition of the classic, considered the father of today's movie and television westerns, may be the only play version easily available." (v) Rush's publication bears no publisher's imprint, only the legend: "Tallahassee, Florida, 1958." All quotations are taken from this edition.

[32]See William K. Everson, p. 59. Although he only briefly refers to the film, saying it brought "a spectacular dimension denied to the stage version," the passage is, nonetheless, one of the few references to the film in history texts.

[33]A classic discussion of the deep-focus frame aesthetic can be found in Andre Bazin's essay, "The Evolution of the Language of Cinema," reprinted in Andre Bazin, *What Is Cinema?* (Berkeley and Los Angeles: University of California Press, 1967), pp. 23-40.

[34]David Belasco, *The Girl of The Goldest West*, in Montrose J. Moses, ed., *Representative American Dramas: National and Local* (Boston: Little, Brown, and Co., 1929). All quotations are from this edition.

[35]For an examination and reconstruction of the play's original production, see Lise-Lone Marker, *David Belasco: Naturalism in American Theatre*, pp. 139-60.

[36]See the extended discussion of melodrama in Vardac's *Stage to Screen*, pp. 20-67.

[37]See Lise-Lone Marker, p. 155.

[38]Max Beerbohm, "The Ragged Regiment," reprinted in *Yet Again* (New York: Knopf, 1923), p. 230.

[39]See Lise-Lone Marker for photographs of the stage production.

[40]Cecil B. De Mille, *Autobiography* (Englewood Cliffs, New Jersey: Prentice-Hall, 1959), p. 115.

[41]Lise-Lone Marker, p. 154.

[42]For an extensive analysis of the Fairbanks/Pickford film version of *The Taming of the Shrew*, see John C. Tibbetts and James Welsh, *His Majesty the American: The Cinema of*

Douglas Fairbanks, Sr., (Cranbury, New Jersey: A. S. Barnes, 1977), pp., 175-84.

[43]Quoted in Roger Manvell, *Shakespeare and the Film* (New York: Praeger, 1971), pp. 24-25.

[44]John C. Tibbetts and James Welsh, p. 180.

[45]Author's interview with Miles Kreuger in Hollywood, California, May 3, 1980.

[46]For a description of attempts to edit sound on wax discs, see John C. Tibbetts, "Now Hear This: Bernard Brown Talks About the Hollywood Sound Man," *American Classic Screen*, September/October 1978, pp. 36-38, 40, 42.

[47]An especially fine account of the controversial aspects of *The Birth of a Nation* can be found in Arthur Lennig, *The Silent Voice* (New York: Walter Snyder, 1969), pp. 32-49.

[48]William K. Everson, p. 55.

[49]Even in a film history text that is heavily oriented toward the history of the theatrical film, A. R. Fulton's *Motion Pictures* (Norman, Oklahoma: University of Oklahoma Press, 1960), it is stated that the film was based on Dixon's novel. There is no mention of the play at all (p. 82).

[50]The most complete account of this project I have found is in Jack Spears, *The Civil War on the Screen* (Cranbury, New Jersey: A. S. Barnes and Co., 1977), pp. 32-34.

[51]See Robert M. Henderson, *D. W. Griffith: The Years at Biograph* (New York: Farrar, Straus and Giroux, 1970), pp. 19-20. The theater would continue to play an ambiguous role in Griffith's sensibility. For example, he often cited as influences on his work a variety of novels, poems, classical painting; but rarely did he make any references to plays or stagecraft at all. Yet most of his best-known films were based on stage plays. One-act versions of famous plays and literary works were his principal source for his Biograph literary adaptations. Russell Merritt claims in his fine study on Griffith and the theater that many memorable moments in Griffith films were directly borrowed from stage plays—such as the baptism in *Way Down East* (derived from Minnie Maddern Fiske in the staged *Tess of the d'Urbervilles*), the vendetta of Jacques-Forget-Not in *Orphans of the Storm* (derived from the "One! Two! Three!" of James O'Neill in *The Count of Monte Cristo*), and the last-minute rescue in *Intolerance* (derived from none other than Thomas Dixon's *The One Woman*, in which Griffith himself performed). See Russel Merritt "Rescued from a Perilous Nest: D. W. Griffith's Escape from Theatre into Film," *Cinema Journal*, Vol. 21 no. 1 (Fall 1981), pp. 2-29.

[52]Quoted in Epes Winthrop Sargen, "The Photoplaywright: Scenes and Leaders," *The Moving Picture World*, Vol. 13, No. 6 (August 10, 1912), p. 542.

[53]*Ibid.*, p. 542.

[54]For a concise overview of *The Birth of a Nation*, see William K. Everson, pp. 72-89.

[55]Author's interview with William K. Everson in New York City, November 10, 1979.

[56]Letter to author from Kevin Brownlow, November 16, 1979.

[57]Quoted in Robert Grau, *The Theater of Science* (New York: Benjamin Blom, 1969), p. 86.

[58]This assessment and many of the statistics quoted in these passages are from the unpublished papers of Seymour Stern, from which several articles on *The Birth of a Nation* have been extracted. I use this material with the cooperation of Ira Gallen, literary executor of the Stern papers.

[59]Gilbert Seldes, *An Hour with the Movies and the Talkies* (Philadelphia: J. B. Lippincott Co., 1929), pp. 75-76.

[60]Author's interview with Miles Kreuger in Los Angeles, May 3, 1980.

[61]The Music Box Reviews were mounted for the Music Box Theatre of Irving Berlin in New York. There were editions for 1921, 1922, 1923 and 1924. Howard Taubman describes them: "Not pinchpenny affairs, they were handsomely and imaginatively designed and staged; they were so resourceful technically that it became a matter of wonder when a performer just walked out instead of materializing from some mysterious spot in the set." (See Howard Taubman, *The Making of the American Theatre* (New York: Coward McCann, Inc., 1965), p. 197.

[62]Quoted in Harry Lang, "He Didn't Know How," *Photoplay Magazine*, 1930, reprinted in Miles Kreuger, *The Movie Musical: From Vitaphone to 42nd Street* (New York: Dover, 1975), pp. 186-87.

[63]Richard Dana Skinner, "King of Jazz," *The Commonweal*, Vol. XII, No. 3 (May 21, 1930), pp. 80-81.

Chapter Six

Stages in Development:
New Definitions For Stage and Screen

The two surges of theatrical films in the 1912-1915 and 1926-1930 periods brought in their wake a clamor of voices from critics, artists, laymen, and technical people. Some deplored the practice of movies borrowing from the theater and from stage plays. Others applauded. Still others adopted a wait and see attitude. And if the motives were questioned, the results were even more hotly debated. Was there such a thing as "cinematic" as opposed to "theatrical"? Could (or should) the two be blended? And what claims to "art" did the film medium potentially have, considered apart from the theater?

Even in one of the most blatantly theatric of theatrical films—Famous Players' *The Prisoner of Zenda* (1912)—at least one critic singled out certain aspects that seemed unique and deserving of comment. Writing about the climactic chase and duel scenes, the critic observed: "...numerous rapidly changing scenes dovetail[ed] into each other in a manner that excites the interest of the spectator."[1] In another publication, *The Moving Picture World,* the reviewer praised the occasional use of natural locales in the photography of those same scenes. "The audience," the writer declared, "mostly composed of theatrical people and perhaps somewhat inexpert in moving picture work, was quick to appreciate these advantages of the new invention and broke into applause whenever the action of the drama was carried on in the theatre of Nature."[2]

Such films displayed some of the effects hitherto common primarily to non-theatrical films, like chases and newsreels. The sole purpose of these latter kinds of films had been to inform or entertain the blue collar audiences of the nickelodeons. But after 1912, theatrical features like *The Prisoner of Zenda* brought these effects to a different kind of audience—"theatrical people...somewhat inexpert in moving picture work...." Moreover, these effects became more pronounced and visible when perceived within the context of an otherwise blatantly theatrical film. Now, for the first time, serious questions arose as a result. Was it really useful—and artistically legitimate—to simulate theatrical effects on the movie screen? Did this imitation serve only to block original and creative work in movie making? Should filmmakers strive instead only to achieve effects on the screen that were different from those of the proscenium stage? What, specifically, were these effects, and how could they be utilized to promote on film a distinctively different kind of artistic expression, one only tangentially related to that of the stage?

The appearance of the theatrical features—both silent and sound—played a significant role in the first important formulations of cinematic theory. Strangely enough, this fact has been either undervalued or totally ignored in at least three important histories of film theory—Guido Aristarco's *Storia delle teoriche del film*, Henri Agel's *Esthetique du cinema*, and J. Dudley Andrew's *The Major Film Theories*. Although Professor Andrew, for example, notes that most theories of film begin "with questions generated by individual films or techniques,"[3] he fails to cite the many specific *theatrical films*—silent and sound—that helped generate these theoretical formulations. When *The Birth of a Nation* and *King of Jazz* appeared in, respectively, 1915 and 1930, major theoretical works were also being written. Hugo Muensterberg's *The Photoplay: A Psychological Study* (published a year later), Vachel Lindsay's *The Art of the Moving Picture*, and Luigi Pirandello's *Si Gara! (Shoot)* all were written in 1915. Rudolf Arnheim's *The Art of the Film* and writings by Vsevolod Pudovkin (later collected in 1933 under the title of *Film Technique and Film Acting*) were written in 1929-30. All of these works established the basis for later formulations of formal, realistic, phenomenological, and semiotic film theory—André Bazin's writings (collected under the series of volumes entitled, *What is Cinema?*, 1967-71), Siegfried Kracauer's *Theory of Film* (1960), Jean Mitry's *Esthetique et psychologie du cinema* (1963-65), and Christian Metz's *Film Language: The Semiotics of the Cinema* (translated into English in 1974).[4] All of these formulations grappled in common with the issues and questions that first arose from the appearance of theatrical films.

Nontheatrical news films and chase films first presented on the movie screen a number of effects that would eventually be adopted in the theatrical films as well. The men who made the newsreels and chase films in the years prior to the emergence of feature-length films in 1912 were not concerned with imitating theatrical events. Like the so-called "primitive" photographers in France and England in the middle of the nineteenth century, these filmmakers simply sought to preserve on film what Raymond Fielding in his definitive *The American Newsreel* has called "actualities"—documents of unstaged reality like parades, fires, battlefields, and sporting events.[5] Sometimes these films merely recorded events; at other times they were incorporated into simple stories and chases. In his study of early American filmmaking, *American Film History Prior to 1920*, Anthony Slide has observed that these non-theatrical filmmakers "had no pretensions as to their products being works of art." Moviemaking was a practical experience and they were interested only in "manufacturing a commodity."[6]

News films and chases have always been popular with audiences. The applause that greeted their use of natural locales anticipated reaction to the natural locales seen in *The Prisoner of Zenda*. It was an actuality, a short film depicting waves breaking upon Dover Beach in England, that brought the most applause to Edison's first program of projected films on April 23, 1896, at Koster and Bial's Music Hall in New York. Thomas Armat, an associate of Edison's at the time, recalled that "when it was thrown upon the screen the house went wild; there were calls from all over the house for 'Edison,' 'Edison,' 'speech,' 'speech.' "[7] The production of thousands of actualities from all over the world stemmed from that time. Some of the producers included Oskar Messter in Germany; Charles Pathé in France ("The Czar's Arrival in Paris" and "March Past of the Light Cavalry"); Cecil Hepworth and S. Mitchell in England ("The Clyde Regatta" and "The Henley Regatta"); and Edison, Vitagraph, and Biograph in America (including Edison's series of locomotive films—"The Black Diamond Express," "The Philadelphia Express," "The Fast Mail, Northern Pacific R.R.," etc.). By 1911 the practice had begun of combining these short actualities into a reel, establishing the newsreel format, in the "Pathé's Weekly" series. The newsreel thus became a standard item in the bill of films at nickelodeons. These films, according to Fielding, "provided a predominantly photographic kind of news coverage long before most newspapers and magazines of the period began to do so."[8]

Not only were actualities included on the first bills of silent films, but they also comprised an important part of the first programs of synchronized-sound films. The news films, along with the theatrical shorts, introduced to American audiences in 1927 the Fox Movietone sound-on-film system. The first program of sound news films utilizing the Movietown process was shown at the Sam Harris Theater in New York on January 21, 1927, fully eight months before the release of *The Jazz Singer* from Warner Brothers. The Fox studios then began producing a synchronized-sound version of the newsreel with a series called "Fox Movietone News," which premiered at the Roxy Theater in New York on October 28, 1927. Apart from their emphasis upon sound, these films generally recalled actualities of the silent period in their choice of subject matter—"Niagara Falls," "Army-Yale Football Game at the Yale Bowl," "The Vatican Choir Singing at the Tomb of the Unknown Soldier," the dynamiting by engineers of the Cono-wingo Bridge in Maryland, and a series of interviews with celebrities like Mussolini, Conan Doyle, and George Bernard Shaw.

The emphasis upon location photography in these silent and sound films had a significant impact upon the filmmaking process. While the theatrical filmmakers had built proscenium-style stages and arranged the action around the fixed camera, the news filmmakers took their camera *to* the action. This sometimes meant that it was impractical to mount the camera to a fixed tripod. Whereas the action in theatrical films transpired in a plane parallel to the lens and restricted the players to a shallow-depth playing area, news films liberated the camera and allowed it to *move* with the action. Just one of many examples was a news film made in 1901 in San Francisco. The camera was mounted on the front of a moving trolley car as it took a journey down Market Street. In effect, the viewer's eye was swept along in an uninterrupted movement. The exigencies of location shooting and sound recording forced the development of more portable cameras and recording techniques not needed in the theatrical films. Devices like the French Lumière camera and the De Proszynski Aeroscope camera—a handheld, motor-driven camera with a stabilizing gyroscope—were developed for use by the combat photographers.[9] For the synchronized-sound news films, techniques were developed that enabled filmmakers to edit the soundtrack as well as the image. For example, as Fielding notes, when the individual news items were assembled into a newsreel, editors, in order to provide smooth transitions among the individual films, began to add narration and music to the already-recorded sound track. This marked an early example of *mixing* different sound tracks together into a composite sound track. This control over the elements of sound eventually enabled filmmakers to achieve asynchronous combinations of image and sound. In this sense, the synchronized-sound news films were far in advance of the theatrical films of the time, which, as we know, relied for the most part upon direct sound recording.[10] And, finally, just as the cameras had to be made portable to follow events in natural locales, so too were sound recording techniques developed that were more mobile and flexible than those used on the sound stages. Instead of the fixed microphones common to the early theatrical films, the news films utilized boom microphones and "fish-pole" microphones which could follow the action. Thus, just as the news films were able to take portable cameras to the action, so could they also take portable microphone systems to it as well.

Sometimes camera coverage of a developing story forced filmmakers to alter the continuities of space and time. Thus, the correlation of one-shot-to-one-scene was completely shattered. In "The Demolition of the Star Theater in New York" (1901), to cite just one example at random, the sense of real time was altered through a manipulation of shots. A camera crew was assigned to film the demolition, which was to take a full day. Obviously, it was impractical to film the work of the entire day. Instead, time-lapse photography was utilized. Twenty-four camera exposures of the wrecking operation were taken every four minutes for a total of eight hours. When the completed motion picture was projected upon movie house screens, the dismantling of the building seemed to take but a few minutes and at a spectacularly swift speed. Eight hours of "real" time were compressed to mere minutes of "screen" time.

Like the news films, chase films did not imitate theatrical events. They recorded movement and incident against the backdrops of natural locales, using mobile cameras, strategies of parallel editing and intra-scene cutting. In sum, they generally abolished what had been sensed in theatrical films— the surrounding proscenium frame. "Given the stress on movement," William K. Everson had recently noted, "as many films as possible were shot outdoors. This not only gave rise to the chase...as a movie staple but also led to the utilization of intensely cinematic devices in shooting those chases."[11] Needless to say, there was no equivalent to this on the stage. Stage chases— say, in the French farces of Feydeau and Labiche—were necessarily confined to the proscenium frame, with figures appearing and disappearing through doors and windows. In America, Dion Boucicault had strained the mechanics of the stage to the utmost in depicting chases in his *Arrah-na-Pogue*, yet the lightning speed of scene change and the naturalism of the locales remained beyond his resources.[12]

It is necessary to examine some chase films made before 1905 in order to gain a sense of how they radically differed from contemporaneous theatrical films. In *The First Twenty Years*, historian and archivist Kemp R. Niver discussed some pertinent examples of film chases. A chase film, he explained, "begins with one person fleeting from another, with the number of pursuers increasing as the film progresses."[13] In the "Pick-pocket" (Gaumont, 1903), a thief is pursued through, successively, city streets, open fields, and finally a lumber yard. At each stage of the chase, more police and more bystanders join in. Although the film is only 129 feet long, it employs more than ten different camera positions, each in a natural locale—almost half of the total camera positions employed in the feature-length *Queen Elizabeth*, made eleven years later! In 1904, Biograph released "Personal," an important chase film that in popularity and sophistication of technique excelled most of the theatrical films of the day. When a French count rashly advertises for a wife, he is subsequently overwhelmed with applicants. And so begins the chase. Its popularity was extraordinary. A year after its release it was described in a trade journal as "the most popular [of the chase films] and continues in active demand at the present time."[14] The "take-off point" was Grant's Tomb in New York City, and the pursuit progressed through a series of natural locales, including hillsides, back roads, and a brook. In each successive shot the number of running figures increased. Sometimes they ran directly toward (and past) the camera lens; sometimes they ran laterally across the frame as the camera panned to follow them. One of the most famous chases of the time was, of course, Edwin S. Porter's *The Great Train Robbery* (Edison, 1903). Yet it was probably influenced by a film from Great Britain, *A Daring Daylight Burglary*, which Porter saw before beginning his own film. *Burglary* was directed by Frank Mottershaw for the Sheffield Photo Company. This rare film, long thought to have disappeared, has recently been found in the archives of Eastman House in Rochester, New York. Its use of editing, moving camera, compression of time, and location shooting was far in advance of any theatrical film of the time. As two policemen chase a burglar, the natural locales shift from, successively, the initial setting of a walled in garden, to a policeman on the street witnessing the event, to a cliff, to the stepping stones over a stream and finally to a country railway station where the criminal is finally apprehended. In some of the locales, as in the garden, the shot is interrupted by a cut. In this instance, the camera position changes from a head-on angle (characteristically used in theatrical films) to an overhead view of the policemen scrambling over the rooftops. Intrascene editing is also employed in Biograph's "The Lost Child" (1904). A passing stranger is pursued as the suspected kidnapper of a child. As the succession of briefly held shots depicts the chase, more and more pursuers join in. When the man is finally caught, the pursuers snatch away his market basket to retrieve the baby. At that moment, the scene is interrupted by a closeup, which reveals the basket's contents to be a guinea pig! The correlation of one shot for each scene—typical of theatrical films—is broken for the sake of heightening the dramatic revelation. The nickelodeon audiences of the day enjoyed this kind of entertainment, wrote Hugo Muensterberg in 1915, with its "flashlike quickness" of action and cutting. By the time theatrical features like *The Prisoner of Zenda* appeared in 1913, "the rapid change of scenes has meanwhile been put into the service of much higher aims."[15]

In these examples it is apparent that the devices and effects of news and chase films were the result of practical considerations rather than consciously artistic ambitions. It is useful to think of the men who made these films as the civilized equivalents of the primitive artisans that Claude Levi-Strauss has called "bricoleurs." Writing in *The Savage Mind*, Levi-Strauss defined the bricoleur as someone who carried out a task without benefit of special training or tools. Rather, he used tools "collected or retained on the principle that they may always come in handy"; and he used them in special ways to cope with the problem at hand: "In the continual reconstruction from the same materials, it is always earlier ends which are called upon to play the part of means."[16] This concept can be applied to the techniques of the early filmmakers. For example, a cameraman who worked on many chase films at this time, Glen MacWilliams, has discussed his methods of working. He carried about with him many different materials in the event they would "come in handy." Sawed-off broomhandles could serve as levers to pan the camera and gelatine could be used to coat the edges of the lens in order to "soften" the focus of the image. There was nothing self-conscious about these activities; rather, as Waldemar Kaempffert has writen, the "artist" simply followed the lines of least resistance in overcoming difficulties with available means.[18]

Thus, the early filmmakers would not film a chase against artificial backdrops when they could work more conveniently in real locales. (Besides, it was easier to shoot outdoors before 1906 since indoor lighting was not yet practicable.[19]) Moreover, because the early filmmakers worked with a silent medium, they saw no practical reason for letting their players stand motionless while declaiming extended dialogue that would never be heard; better to keep the people in motion in situations that demanded little, if any, dialogue. If a particular moment of the story needed dramatic emphasis, it made no sense to keep the camera fixed at a medium distance from the action—a closer view was preferable.

These statements were developed "on the spot," as it were. Filmmakers were working with a medium whose resources were as yet undetermined and which had no history or system of training. The painter, the musician, the architect, the stage player all had either academies or at least traditions of achievement as inspiration and example. Those filmmakers who worked either in ignorance or in defiance of the tenets and practices of other artistic media were preparing the way for the more conscious achievement to come in the motion picture.

Dissatisfaction with Closely Imitative Theatrical Films

Although, as has been seen in Chapter Three, there was a body of critical writing that praised and promoted the production of closely imitative theatrical films, by 1913 there was an increasing body of commentary that objected to these films. One year after the release of *Queen Elizabeth*, Robert Grau, an influential vaudeville promoter and commentator, flatly stated that *Queen Elizabeth* no longer satisfied him; that its theatrical nature now seemed irritating. "A majority of those who had seen these pictures on the screen," Grau noted, "would emphatically state that they did not wish to renew the experience...."[20] A year later Louis Reeves Harrison, one of the most prominent motion picture commentators in America, expressed his own growing weariness with closely imitative theatrical films. Imitation may have been "amusing" at first, he declared, "but it is doubtful whether people now care to be amused in that way." He concluded that filmmakers should cease such ambitions, "for screen visualization is an entirely different art, at its best when freed from the artificial limitations imposed by dramatic construction for stage performance...."[21] At this same time, even Daniel Frohman, who had actively worked with Zukor to produce theatrical films for Famous Players, expressed some reservations about close imitation. "The creative director must elaborate many of the episodes of a play before he can use the camera on it," Frohman said. "Incidents which are only casually referred to in the dialogue [of a stage play] must be visualized on more complete lines."[22] And, perhaps not surprisingly, D. W. Griffith was quoted in 1914 as being dissatisfied with theatrical films in general. "The conditions of the [stage and screen] being so different," he said, "it follows that the requirements are equally dissimilar. Stage craft and stage people are out of place in the intense realism of motion picture expression...."[23]

These remarks indicate a growing disillusionment with theatrical films. That they represented a wide-spread discussion through the industry is demonstrated by the fact that at precisely this time a series of articles questioning the validity of theatrical films appeared in *The New York Dramatic Mirror*. We will recall that in 1911 and 1912 the *Mirror* vocally supported the ambitions of theatrical features. Yet in March of 1913 a different attitude became apparent in its series of articles collectively entitled, "The Evolution of the Motion Picture." Representatives from several quarters of picture making—including editors, directors, and cameramen—wrote about the ways in which the motion picture differed from theatrical events. As far as my own research has been able to determine, this marked the first time in motion picture history that a consistent body of commentary came to bear upon this subject. Part Three in the series, for example, was written by Horace G. Plimpton, a studio director for the Edison Company. He noted that the artificiality of stage scenery was inappropriate for the film medium. Painted flats and shallow-depth stages should not be employed in films, Plimpton said. What he called "realism in scenery" was a "keynote" in the advance of the motion picture. He praised what he observed in more and more films as "the tendency...towards greater naturalness and towards the elimination of artificiality." He also objected to a tendency common to theatrical films—employing too many titles to approximate the dialogue of play: "There have been too many subtitles. It is surprising to see the extent they use sub-titles abroad. One often follows another, some of them run over to a second sub-caption, and most of them are very long. You can't hold a spectator with a long subtitle."[24] Part Seven in the series of articles was written by the screenwriter Captain Leslie T. Peacocke, a scenarist for the Universal studio. Peacocke admitted to substantial differences between the craft of playwrighting and screenwriting. His remarks reveal a recognition of the film medium as a unique form of expression. Even the finest playwright, he noted, is a poor scenario craftsman unless he understands the pictures. "Where a play has a cast of ten and utilizes three of four acts in the telling, the same story on the screen would require fifty to sixty people...and forty to fifty scenes would be needed...." He acknowledged that the playwright's reliance upon dialogue was inappropriate to movies. The screenwriter should be adept, by contrast, to what he called "situation building." Scenes should be short in a movie, he said, referring to the number of shots in a film. "The eye tires of a scene after thirty or forty seconds. A good scenario averages thirty-five to fifty scenes in a single reel and sixty to one hundred scenes in a two-part drama."[25] Finally, other articles in the series discussed the new challenges movies brought to traditional theatrical styles of acting. Those remarks will be dealt with in their place later in this chapter.

This dissatisfaction with closely imitative theatrical films—felt both within and without the filmmaking community—culminated in the writing and publication of three important works on film aesthetics in 1915. Vachel Lindsay's *The Art of the Moving Picture*, Hugo Muensterberg's *The Photo-Play: A Psychological Study*, and Luigi Pirandello's *Si Gara (Shoot!)* all sprang from objections to this kind of imitation. The writers all agreed that imitation was blocking original work in motion pictures; moreover, they argued that artistic recognition be given to those characteristics of news films and chases that revealed the film medium's unique potentials. For example, Chapter Twelve in the Lindsay book was entitled "Thirty Differences Between the Photoplays and the Stage." In defining what Lindsay regarded as the essential differences between the effects of both media, he selected two filmed plays that represented the worst and best in theatrical films. Sarah Bernhardt's *Camille* was a failure because it was too closely imitative of a proscenium stage production:

> ...every group [is filmed] entire, and taken at full length. Much space is occupied by the floor and the overhead portions of the stage setting. It lasts as long as would the spoken performance, and wherever there is a dialogue we must imagine said conversation if we can. It might be compared to watching *Camille* from the top gallery through smoked glass, with one's ears stopped with cotton.[26]

By contrast, Griffith's *Judith of Bethulia* (1913) was applauded by Lindsay as a filmed play which exploited the inherent potentials of the film medium. He generalized:

> ...in order to be real photoplays the stage dramas must be overhauled indeed, turned inside out and upside down. The successful motion picture expresses itself through mechanical devices that are being evolved every hour. Upon these many new bits of machinery are founded novel methods of combination in another field of logic, not dramatic logic....(186)

Lindsay especially admired the abandonment in *Judith of Bethulia* of the lateral exits and entrances common to most filmed plays. *Bethulia* broke that illusion of a stage playing space by utilizing a device that was already prevalent in chase films. In *Judith*, wrote Lindsay, "the hero or villain in exit strides past the nose of the camera, growing much bigger than a human being, marching toward us as though he would step on our heads, disappearing when largest." There was what Lindsay called "an explosive power" about this device. After citing several examples of the ways cinema could depart from theatrical models, Lindsay concluded with a prophecy that filmmakers would soon totally abandon theatrical imitation. "The photoplays of the future will be written from the foundations for the films. The soundest actors, photographers, and producers will be those who emphasize the points wherein the photoplay is unique" (197). These remarks were especially timely, I should emphasize, because at that moment production companies like Ince and Griffith's Fine Arts studio were building their own writing departments for the production of original scripts, written in a manner suited to the possibilities of camera movement and cutting.

In *Film: A Psychological Study*, Hugo Muensterberg also proposed that the motion picture could only achieve artistic identity by abandoning theatrical imitation. "[Movies] can never give the esthetic values of the theater," Muensterberg said; "but no more can the theater give the esthetic values of the photoplay." Artistic potentials inherent in the film medium and its manipulation could never be exploited by imitation of the stage: "Each art should have its particular method for fundamentally changing reality" (60, 69). Muensterberg's proposals for an aesthetic of cinema will be examined in later pages of this chapter.

Less well known than these two books is Luigi Pirandello's *Si Gara* ("*Shoot!*"). It, too, expressed a dissatisfaction with closely imitative theatrical films. Pirandello's involvement with playwrighting began at the same time that he began to write movie scenarios. This is not to imply, however, that he thought the two media at all comparable in their techniques and effects. *Si Gara* made it clear that he regarded them as independent means of expression. In this, Pirandello's first extended work on the cinema, there was a slim narrative thread concerning the activities of an Italian cameraman (dubbed by his colleagues, "Shoot") which gave Pirandello the excuse to speculate on the nature of the film medium. What emerged clearly from this strange tale was Pirandello's conviction that the concept of the "artificially arranged scenes" of Méliès' theatrical films should be totally discarded. Cinema was a unique medium capable of unique effects and should be regarded separately from the other arts.[27] Before we can examine Pirandello's theories about the unique nature of film, however (as well as the theories of Muensterberg), we need to first jump ahead fifteen years to note that by 1930 a renewed chorus of dissatisfied voices was attacking the second cycle of closely imitative theatrical films.

A brief survey of this dissent makes it clear that, again, the negative reactions came from a wide spectrum of commentators. As early as the release of *Tenderloin* from Warner Brothers in March, 1928, there were signs that the public was weary of the strictly synchronous combination of sound and image, the endless stretches of dialogue, and the return to the artificial props and static camera characteristic of the filmed plays of 1912. In his recent study of the early talkies, *The Shattered Silents*, Alexander Walker wrote that this film evoked for the first time a derisory audience response. Audiences would no longer accept the mere novelty of synchronized sound:

...the vocal characterization seemed either inadequate or in some way excessive to audiences who had come along expecting novelty, but did not yet know how to account for the film's technical or dramatic shortcomings except by laughing at them...for people were now beginning to discriminate between the novelty of audible talk and the *quality* of what was said— as well as the competence of *how* it was recorded.[28]

And a review for *Variety* suggested that "unless the novelty of the screen talking is strong enough to overcome the picture itself, the talking picture appears to be a matter of the voice and calibre of the dialogue to be employed...stripped of its mechanicals, *Tenderloin* is a very ordinary crook meller."[29] This and other theatrical films were discussed at some length in a book that appeared in 1929 by Gilbert Seldes called *An Hour With the Movies and the Talkies*. Seldes wrote that the renewed reliance upon stage plays was ruining the movie industry. He saw this as a return to the disastrous policies followed by Zukor and Famous Players in 1912: "[Zukor's] idea was all wrong and was proved wrong within a year or two after its inception; and now with the talking pictures, his idea returns, verified by the unquestioned authority of experience." Further, the talking picture would never progress toward original expression as long as it imitated stage plays: "It has not found the way yet and will not so long as it merely records stage-plays." Incessant, tedious stretches of dialogue is not the answer; the movies must again realize the value of silence and music: "Until the talkies discover masters of dialogue *who can create a new system of speech* [italics mine] for themselves, they should lean on music; it is a confession not of defeat, but of purpose to succeed." Several theatrical films were cited by Seldes as examples of the failure of imitation—*Broadway* (based on the play by Jed Harris, Philip Dunning, and George Abbott in 1926), *Bulldog Drummond* (based on the play in 1925 by "Sapper"), and *The Cocoanuts* (based on the musical comedy in 1925 by George S. Kaufman and Irving Berlin). *Broadway* retained "as much of the stage dialogue as possible, perhaps because the producers had counted the words and calculated exactly how much each word cost them...." The same complaint was aimed at *Bulldog Drummond*. As for *The Cocoanuts*, "so little change was made that at times one felt as if the talkie had actually been taken from the wings in the theatre of the original production." Seldes concluded his attacks with the somewhat tepid prophecy that some artistic merit might after all arise from these ashes: "[They] may create something pleasing, perhaps significant and beautiful, of their own."[30]

Also writing in 1929, Luigi Pirandello launched his own attack upon the new cycle of theatrical films. We recall that in *Si Gara* in 1915 he had already declared that film and theater were separate and independent media. Now, fifteen years later, he saw the presence of synchronized sound as a threat that might bring the two together. In an article printed in the *New York Times Magazine* he spoke out against the practice of theatrical imitation:

> ...it is not the theatre that is asking to become cinema, but the cinema that is begging to be turned into theatre; and the greatest victory which the cinema can ever hope to achieve in invading more and more the theatrical domain, will be that of becoming a more or less bad photographic and mechanical copy of the theatre...

This was a dangerous course for filmmakers to pursue, Pirandello concluded, for the cinema "is destroying itself in order to become a photographic and mechanical copy of the theatre...."[31]

In proposing alternative directions to theatrical imitation, theorists like Lindsay, Muensterberg, Pirandello, Eisenstein, Pudovkin and others formulated the first approaches toward a synchronized-sound film aesthetic. For the first time, the effects already common to news films and chase films were regarded in a serious and consistent way as contributing to this aesthetic.

Breaking the New Proscenium

Although Vachel Lindsay questioned the artistic validity of theatrical films, he saw artistic potentials in the kinds of chase films I have already described, grouping them into a category he called "action films." Action films have not been taken seriously, he wrote, because they have played primarily in the nickelodeons of the slums. Yet effects of the action film were appearing more frequently in prestige pictures—such as Griffith's *Judith of Bethulia*. The advantages of this type of film included the ability of filmmakers to shoot out of doors and by editing to link together series of brief shots. Speed was of the essence: "The story goes at the highest possible speed to be still credible." It was not possible for a stage presentation to rival such a swift pace. The action film, he declared, "can reproduce a race far more joyously than the stage." At the same time, Lindsay admitted that action films by their very nature do not provide "adequate means for the development of any full grown personal passion." Character studies are more the province of the stage. In action films characters "are but types, swiftly moved chessmen." Instead, the real characters in these films are machines and places that come alive for the viewer through the manipulation of pieces of film (36-40).

This last point needs elaboration since it brought Lindsay to some brief speculations involving the creation of a special continuum of space and time in the motion picture. Devices of editing could interweave different locations in alternating series of shots so that they become, in effect, active agents in the action. The shift from one to the other created a kind of "silent" dialogue that bridges space and time:

> By alternating scenes rapidly, flash after flash: cottage, field, mountain-top, field, mountain-top, cottage, we have a conversation between three places rather than three persons. By alternating the picture of a man and the check he is forging, we have his soliloquy.

Upon such editing strategies, concluded Lindsay, "are founded novel methods of combination in another field of logic...." (189). This was not the logic of scene construction as found on the stage, but something else. Lindsay did not elaborate further about this other "field of logic" but his remarks served as a proper introduction to the theories of Hugo Muensterberg, whose speculations on the nature of the continuum of space and time stand at the beginnings of all formalist film theory.

After cataloguing his objections to theatrical films, Muensterberg noted that the logic of shot construction in movies differed from the dramatic logic of the construction of stage scenes. The theater was a medium bound by the continuities of space, time, and causality. He explained that theatrical events constituted "a complete continuity of the physical events: no cause without following effect, no effect without preceding cause" (79). By contrast, the motion picture, because of editing, could overcome the forms of the outer world—namely space, time, and causality. He summed up this view:

> The massive outer world has lost its weight, it has been freed from space, time, and causality, and it has been clothed in the forms of our own consciousness. The mind has triumphed over matter and the pictures roll on with the ease of musical tones. It is a superb enjoyment which no other art can furnish us (95).

Therefore, the cinema was an art form since it could overcome reality (62). All of the effects and devices present in the news films and chase films here found artistic justification in Muensterberg's theory—the swift successions of shots, the mobile camera, the intercutting of closeups, the compression of time, the interweaving of various locales through schemes of editing (74). The logic of shot construction, Muensterberg concluded, was akin to the "inner movements of the mind.... [The shots take the viewer] here and there...[turning] to the present and then to the past: the photoplay can equal it in its freedom from the bondage of the material world" (79).

Muensterberg's theory, however, represented only one aspect of film theory; for the non-formal (or "realist") theory of film, we must turn again to Pirandello's *Si Gara*. Muensterberg had insisted that the total aesthetic capacity of film was not limited merely to the transmission of the forms of the natural world. It might whet our appetite for the aesthetic experience of nature, but it could never be a substitute for such experience. Manipulation of the film elements by cutting and camera movement created a continuum of space and time that transcended the real world's laws and approached the workings of the mind. However, in *Si Gara*, Pirandello questioned this formalistic practice and called its results "idiotic fictions" (87). The motion picture medium was essentially realistic in nature; there should be no alteration of time and space. In words that might be regarded as extending the pronouncements made in 1857 by Lady Elizabeth Eastlake concerning the unique nature of the photographic plate (and which anticipated realist film theory), Pirandello insisted that the true province of film was the same as that of the photographic plate—the capacity to represent reality with the least deception of any existing artistic medium (87). Again, we recall the chase and news films. The use of natural locales and the capacity of the camera to go to and follow news events that were unstaged were basic cinematic achievements for Pirandello. The manipulation applauded by Muensterberg could, for Pirandello, only lead to the "imaginary construction of scenes and action" (150), whereas an untampered document of the real world could present life as it comes, without selection and without plan: "...the actions of life as they are performed without a thought, when people are alive and do not know that a machine is lurking in concealment to surprise them" (150). Only in this way, concluded Pirandello, could cinema be used so that people could see themselves clearly and learn a great deal about each other. "Ah," exclaims the cameraman Serafino in *Si Gara*, "if my profession were destined to this end only" (151)!

Although Pirandello does not address the issue specifically, it seems clear that such a view would not countenance the alteration of the continuities of time and space. The time and the space within which an event occurs should remain relatively intact—which is to say that the integrity of each should be preserved. Taken to its extreme it would seem that Pirandello wanted to establish on film the very continuum of physical existence. And since 1915 there have been many attempts to make films which follow these precepts quite uncompromisingly. For example, in the 1920s the artist Fernand Leger dreamed of a film that would last twenty-four hours and record the same amount of time in the life of a man and woman.[32] More recently, some of the films of Andy Warhol, such as "Empire State Building," have realized similar ambitions.

These formal and realist theoretical formulations—coming on the heels of intensive activity in theatrical film making in 1912-15—departed radically from the hitherto accepted idea that the artistic identity of motion pictures depended upon how closely a film could simulate the illusion of a theatrical event. Artistically valid precedents, therefore, were found not in theatrical films but in actualities and chases. However, with the introduction to film of synchronized sound in 1927, the climate surrounding the artistic ambitions of filmmakers changed. Suddenly, as we know, the theatrical imitation was again intensively pursued. But by 1930, at the end of this second cycle of theatrical filmmaking, another reaction set in against the practice. This time, however, a new element had to be considered in the theories that followed— synchronized sound.

We have already noted that there was some dissatisfaction with the synchronous combination of image and sound—the linking of sound with the image of its causing agent—in the early theatrical feature films. In addition to being committed, for the most part, to simulating the illusion of a theatrical event, Warner Brothers' *The Green Goddess*, Paramount's *Interference*, and United Artists' *Coquette* also employed sound in such a way that we heard sound and speech and saw their causing agents at the same time. This practice could become a threat to cinema, predicted Hugo Muensterberg in 1915. He wrote that when synchronized sound eventually came to film, its misuse could severely impair the advance toward cinematic accomplishment. "If we could see and hear at the same time," he said, "we do indeed come nearer to the real theater, but this is desirable only if it is our goal to imitate the stage" (87-88). Thirteen years later, in 1929, Ernest Betts echoed those words when he wrote that "the moment a film actor speaks he is placing a limitation on his own medium."[33]

What kind of combination of image and sound could avoid these pitfalls? As early as 1923, Dr. Lee De Forest, who worked throughout the decade to develop a system of recording sound on film, argued that recorded sound could be combined with the image to promote an entirely new kind of artistic expression:

> [A]n entirely new form of screen drama can be worked out taking advantage of the possibilities of introducing music and voice and appropriate acoustic effects not necessarily throughout the entire action, but here and there where the effects can be much more startling or theatrical, if you will, or significant, than is possible by pantomime alone.[34]

Within the next seven years, this view would find more detailed and extended theoretical and practical application in the work of Sergei Eisenstein and Vsevolod Pudovkin in Russia, Edmund Goulding and George Abbott in America, and René Clair in France.

The earliest important formulation of the uses and techniques of asynchronous sound came from Eisenstein and Pudovkin in 1928 and 1929 (although a few years would pass before either could bring these theories to their films). In a joint statement written in August, 1928, Eisenstein and Pudvokin questioned the kinds of sound/image combination that had been so prevalent in the American theatrical films. A "misconception of the potentialities within this new technological discovery may not only hinder the development and perfection of the cinema as an art, but also threatens to destroy all its present formal achievements...." When all sounds were strictly linked with the images of their causing agents, sound then functioned purely "on a naturalistic level, exactly corresponding with the movement on the screen..." They feared that this use of synchronized-sound would lead to "an epoch of its automatic utilization for 'highly cultured dramas' and other photographed performances of a theatrical sort." As a counter theory, they proposed that filmmakers should work toward what they termed the "distinct non-synchronization" [of sound] with the visual images...."[35] ("Non-synchronization" of course means here non-synchronization of sound with the image of its causing agent. It does not preclude the most careful synchronization—after choice of what to synchronize—with some other image, arbitrarily chosen for expressiveness of the resulting linkage.) A year later Pudovkin spoke further on this idea to the American photographer

Margaret Bourke-White, who reprinted his remarks in her book, *Eyes of Russia* (1931). His clear understanding that sound can function as a counterpoint to the image is clear:

...the sound film is a new medium which can be used in entirely new ways. Sounds and human speech should be used by the director not as a literal accompaniment, but to amplify and enrich the visual image on the screen. Under such conditions could the sound film become a new form of art whose future development has no predictable limits.[36]

That same year, in his book, *Pudovkin on Film Technique*, Pudovkin wrote, in words recalling Muensterberg, that this use of sound would not destroy the freely shifting continuum of space and time that had been achieved in the latter years of the silent cinema. Unfortunately, he added, "it is not generally recognized that the principal elements in sound film are the *asynchronous* [italics mine] and not the synchronous." The image strip and the sound strip (his reference to sound recorded on a separate film strip) must "not be tied to one another by naturalistic imitation but connected as the result of the interplay of action." Thus, in conclusion, not only can the filmmaker "edit different points in space, but can cut into association with the image selected sounds that reveal and heighten the character of each.... This is a simple and obvious form for counterpoint of sound and image" (184 86).

Elsewhere, other filmmakers propounded similar theories—although, unlike Pudovkin, they were to put them into practical usage *before* the end of 1930. In America, Edmund Goulding, a director for Paramount at this time (his theatrical films included *Reaching for the Moon* and *Paramount on Parade*) and a scenarist for Metro-Goldwyn-Mayer *(Broadway Melody)*, questioned the strict causal combination of image and sound that was so prevalent in films of that day. Like Pudovkin, Goulding felt that an image could be seen without having always to hear its causing agent; or, putting it another way, an image could be matched with a sound that related to it in a poetic sense rather than merely a causal one—"the roaring mob in the street will be heard and not cut to."[37] Goulding was able to inculcate these concepts into *Paramount on Parade* (see Chapter Five) and in his scenario for *Broadway Melody* (to which I will return later in this chapter). Another American filmmaker, George Abbott, who had come to Paramount in 1928 after years of experience on Broadway, also experimented with the theories and practices of asynchronous sound. He published his views in *Vanity Fair* in April, 1929. In his two short films—*The Bishop's Candlesticks* and *Carnival Man*—he had tried to utilize the devices of asynchronous sound, but since the two films are unavailable for study today, we have to rely upon his words for an idea of his achievement. Abbott denounced current practices in combining sound and image. The "present ineffective makeshift of reproducing a lengthy scene in talk" should be abandoned. Instead—in words that again echo Pudovkin, sound should supplement the image, not merely accompany it in a causal way: "The use of sound as a collaborator with pantomime can be of tremendous dramatic value." He cited as a precedent on the stage Eugene O'Neill's device of what Abbott called the "inner soliloquy" in *Strange Interlude* (1927). O'Neill's characters would sometimes stand motionless on stage, their mouths closed, while voices speaking interior monologues were heard offstage. Because the actor's mouths did not move, the sound that was heard related to the actors in a poetic, rather than a directly causal way. Abbott predicted that this kind of sound/image combination would be utilized far more effectively on film— that speech did not always have to have a causal link with the lip movements of the actors—"[The actor] thinks the thoughts and the words are heard, which is really far more reasonable."[38] Implicit in Abbott's theory is the independent recording and editing of sound and image. Since 1929, many films have appeared that utilized these techniques in interior monologue— including a film of *Strange Interlude* in 1932 and Luis Bunuel's *Los Olvidados* in 1951.

Of all the theorist/filmmakers discussed here, René Clair in France most successfully brought his theories to the filmmaking process. Like other filmmakers, Clair's theories resulted from his questions regarding current practices in theatrical films—many of which were American films he had seen in France in 1929 and 1930. To him, these films constituted a regrettable return to the closely imitative theatrical films from 1912-15; yet, he saw in a few of them the promise of a more imaginative combination of sound and image. Always a filmmaker devoted to the achievement on film of the fluid continuum of space and time that Lindsay and Muensterberg had promoted, Clair wrote in 1929 that the use of synchronized sound posed a threat to that accomplishment. Too many sound films—(he cited the American theatrical films *Give and Take* and *Strange Cargo*)—reduced the role of sound "to the role of a mere gramophone record, the whole spectacle aiming only at the closest possible...reproduction of the stage play...[containing] interminable spoken scenes."[39] On the other hand in Clair's opinion, two other American theatrical films, *Broadway Melody* and *Show Boat*, held out a better promise for the future. They revealed an occasional use of asynchronous sound that broke the strictly causal link between sound and image. In this sense, Clair was extending the theories of Lindsay and Muensterberg. Just as they had proclaimed that cinema could transcend the causal connections of space and time, now Clair employed the same concept regarding image and sound. By working with a double system of sound and image recording, the filmmaker could be liberated from having to reproduce *all* the sounds accompanying a given image. Sounds could be *selected* as carefully as the photographed objects. This meant that sounds could then be *recombined* with images in ways that, by turns, utilized sound as both literal accompaniment and as poetic augmentation. The work of Edmund

Goulding in *Broadway Melody* was especially admired by Clair. In one scene of the film an actress's anguished face is shown on the screen while, on the soundtrack, we hear the noise of a door being slammed and a car driving off. Two events are thus tied together—the sorrow of the actress and the departure of her lover. We did not need to see the door slam and the car drive away. The visual emphasis was the woman's face and the selected sounds functioned as a dramatic augmentation of that image. Goulding's technique was applauded by Clair: "It may well be that this first lesson taught us by the birth pangs of a new technique will to-morrow [sic] become this same technique's law."[40] Clair was also enthusiastic about another device utilized by Goulding—using sound to *replace* the shot. In one scene the screen faded to black while the sobbing of the actress continued to be heard on the soundtrack. In this instance, the aural component of the film carried the entire burden of information and dramatic emphasis.[41]

Clair began to employ these kinds of sound/image combinations in his first synchronized-sound films in 1929 and 1930—*Prix de beaute, Sous les toits de Paris,* and *Le Million.* In *Prix de beaute,* for which Clair wrote the script, a climactic scene was obviously modeled after Goulding's work. An actress is watching a film in a movie house. While the camera records a tight closeup of her face, sounds are heard of an event occurring offscreen. A shot is heard. Her face stiffens in pain and then freezes into a deathmask. At the same time, other sounds—the sounds of the projected movie she is watching—are also being heard. All the sounds heard relate to the actress' face only in a dramatic sense. The sounds of the movie-within-a-movie provide an ironic counterpoint to the image of the actress; the gunshot sound is the basic action of the scene. What we *see,* however, is only a woman's face; which, taken by itself, would have had little dramatic significance. In his first directed talkie, *Sous les toits de Paris* (known in the United States during its release in 1929 as *Under the Roofs of Paris*), he uses sound to replace the shot, just as Goulding had done. During a climactic fight in a trainyard, Claire obscures the action of a fist fight by keeping the screen dark. The action is conveyed instead by a number of selected sounds—the screeching and whistling of passing locomotives and the grunts and blows of the combatants. Probably the most impressive moment in the film is an extended take, a vertical descent across the face of an apartment building. As the camera descends, we get glimpses through the rows of windows of inhabitants inside. Each person's voice is heard, in succession, maintaining the continuity of a song. By the time the camera reaches the street level, we have heard the entire song sung by several participants in turn. This effect, which could never have been achieved through the limitations of single-system sound recording, uses sound to express the poetic unity of the apartment building's inhabitants. And in both this film and *Le Million* (released one year later), Clair counterpoints images with a variety of non-naturalistic sounds. For example, throughout *Le Million,* actions are accompanied by unexpected sounds—such as the crash of a cymbal or the thump of a drum when a man falls. (There are many more examples of Clair's use of asynchronous sound in these films, and the reader is urged not only to see the films but to read the complete analyses of each contained in Celia McGerr's *René Clair* (1980) and Lucy Fischer's article, "René Clair, *Le Million,* and the Coming of Sound."[42])

Clair's achievement, in summary, is the direct outgrowth of the theories of Eisenstein and Pudovkin and the practical achievement of American theatrical filmmakers like Edmund Goulding. We can trace his accomplishments, moreover, further back to the first crude technological advances in asynchronous sound first seen in the early synchronized-sound newsreels. In Clair's hands these crude innovations became the means of artistic expression. In Lucy Fischer's words, Clair "took an almost accidental technological side effect and elevated it to a purposeful aesthetic strategy."[43] The formalist theories of Muensterberg had at last found their counterpart in asynchronous sound in the talkies. Recorded sound was now a vital part of the fluid continuum of space and time in the cinema, not just an ancillary element.

Acting in the Cinema

At the same time that discussions about theatrical films contributed to the first theoretical formulations about space, time, and sound in film, the nature of acting in film was also investigated. We already know when stage actors came in great numbers to the movies in the 1912-15 and 1927-30 time periods, they encountered many problems. The underlying assumption concerning acting had been, as I have shown, that the actor might perform to the camera in the same way he would perform to an audience across the footlights in a theater house. However, the results on film in movies like *The Count of Monte Cristo* and *Coquette* (see Chapter Five) demonstrated that some techniques of stage acting were inappropriate to the medium of film. Especially in the closely theatrical films, like *Queen Elizabeth* and *The Count of Monte Cristo,* the relative closeness of the camera lens to the actors threw into sharp relief their exaggerated declamatory style; the occasional moments of location photography and the sequences of relatively swift editing seemed to minimize the importance of the actor and emphasize scene pacing in the story. In the case of the early synchronized-sound film, the actor had to adjust to the microphonic environment of the early sound stages. In the more cinematically advanced theatrical films late in the 1912-15 and 1927-30 periods, moreover, the problems of the stage-trained actor grew more acute. *The Girl of the Golden West* and *King of Jazz* created on film entirely cinematic illusions—respectively, the shifting continuum of space and time and asynchronous sound. Strategies of editing were more sophisticated, there was more location photography, the shots were of briefer duration, scenes were intercut more with closeups and flashbacks, etc. In other words, the increasing use by filmmakers—theatrical or otherwise—of the devices of the chase and the news film—seemed to place the stage actor at more and more of a disadvantage.

This can be seen in a brief survey of commentary from both time periods. In the 1912-15 years Zukor's Famous Players, Lasky's Feature Play Company, Brady's World Film Company, and the Triangle Film Corporation all began with the assumption that stage actors could transfer their skills to the movies with no problems of adjustment. Yet, within two years after the brave fanfare surrounding the appearance on film of Sarah Bernhardt, James O'Neill, Minnie Maddern, Fiske, and James K. Hackett, Adolf Zukor expressed doubts about the idea. Will Irwin, Zukor's biographer, notes that Zukor began to realize as early as 1914 that "the great stars of the 'legitimate stage' were educated and set in another kind of technique, gesture, posture, and expression which seemed natural behind the footlights [but which] appeared strained and forced on the screen."[44] This was because of the relative closeness of the camera lens to the actor—especially in medium and close shots—which made the declamatory style of acting unnecessary. The stage actor, wrote Henry Albert Phillips that same year, "has to mould himself to new requirements, demanding of him oftentimes a more exquisite art than the spoken drama comprehends."[45]

William De Mille of the Lasky Company also spoke out about the challenges to stage acting techniques presented by the intimate lens. He had come to Lasky in 1914 to script films for his brother Cecil and had had, himself, extensive experience on the stage. He quickly perceived some of the problems stage actors faced in the filmmaking process:

> Previous success on the stage was no handicap, mind you, but it counted for very little; every stage actor who appeared on the screen had to start again from scratch, and make his own way in competition with the field.... Robbed of their voices, and seen for the first time in that almost indecent intimacy which is the method of screencraft, players from the stage found their personalities changed. In many cases their vocal art had been the basis of their success; without it they were lost.[46]

William Brady of the World Film Company saw other challenges to the stage actor in the effects of the chase film and news film which were now being more regularly employed in theatrical films. He explained that movies were, increasingly, both "a struggle for good photography" and an attempt to take the action from the stage "to the open air." In words foreshadowing Vachel Lindsay's description of the "action film," Brady complained that actors were unable to "build up" a role on film as they had been able to do on the stage—the decreasing length of shots and the documentation of real locales were superseding the actor in importance. What he called the "emotional speed" of the camera left the players with little time or opportunity to develop their characterizations. In short, the years of training behind every stage actor were of little value to their film careers.[47]

Nowhere was this conclusion more apparent than at the Triangle Film Corporation. I have already shown that of all the studios founded on the premise of bringing stage actors in their most famous roles to the screen, Triangle actually produced the fewest theatrical films that could be regarded as closely imitative. *The Lamb* and *Macbeth,* to name only two theatrical films, were typical in that they employed extensive location photography and a highly cinematic sense of space and time through sophisticated editing. The inability of actors like Sir Herbert Beerbohm Tree and De Wolf Hopper to utilize their stage training in such sophisticated films confirmed a general feeling that a different kind of training was needed for the film actor. Conversely, actors who had been trained entirely in the film medium were proving to be stronger boxoffice attractions for Triangle. As Kalton Lahue says in his recent history of Triangle, *Dreams for Sale:*

> Audiences deserted the theaters which ran Triangle plays and as a result, exhibitors began to rebel against the high rentals necessitated by the increased production costs, which reflected the high salaries of the stage stars and their unfamiliarity with camera techniques.[48]

And in 1915 *Variety* reported that Triangle producers were discovering for themselves that stage actors were not adjusting to the film medium; that, as a result, "the picture people have been sorely disappointed on more than one occasion."[49] The conclusion for Triangle and the other theatrical production studios at the end of the 1912-15 period was, perhaps, inevitable—the policy of contracting stage players for the movies was modified, if not discontinued. Early in 1916 the *New York Dramatic Mirror* indicated that this decision was becoming an industry-wide policy:

> Today the producers, equipped with accumulated wisdom, shy like scared rabbits at the bare notion of engaging certain "legitimate" stars. These latter may be recognized leaders in their own profession, but they are not "screen types," a phrase rather hard to define exactly, so far as the limitations of the outsiders are concerned, but pregnant with meaning regarding the suitability of camera candidates.[50]

If the techniques of stage acting were unsuited to the film medium, what special conditions then applied to the film actor? Some of the earliest attempts to define the special nature of film acting appeared in theoretical formulations already quoted from in this chapter—Lindsay's *The Art of the Moving Picture* and Muensterberg's *The Photoplay: A Psychological Study.* It will be recalled that Lindsay regarded the actors in the "action film" as "types" and "swiftly moved chessmen." Elsewhere in his book, he noted, "It is a quality, not a defect, of all photoplays that human beings tend to become dolls and mechanisms, and dolls and mechanisms tend to become human"

(53). Implicit in his remarks is the idea that the actor is always subordinated to the devices and effects of film—the scene transitions through editing and the flat, two-dimensional nature of the movie screen. It was not through a catalogue of acquired training in techniques and gestures that the film actor could function; it was, rather as a plastic physiognomy and form that the actor was subject to the manipulations of the director and editor. In differentiating this phenomenon from a stage performance, Lindsay noted, "The stage-production depends most largely upon the power of the actors, the movie show upon the genius of the producer." Further, actors and things were equals in a motion picture: "The performers and the dumb objects are on equal terms in his paint-buckets" (194). This is to say that the screen actor does not control his performance in the same way that a stage actor does. For example, stage actors have an approximate notion of how they look to the eyes of their audiences, and they can hear and gauge their own voices accordingly. Screen actors, however, "have not the least notion of their appearance" (196). Only the film's director or producer "holds to his eyes the seven-leagued demon spy-glass called the kinetoscope" and determines how an audience will eventually perceive the total motion picture (196).

Muensterberg's discussion of film acting touches upon and extends Lindsay's ideas. Muensterberg acknowledges that actors on the screen have not the substance—or, therefore, the control—of stage actors. On the stage the players appear in scenes that proceed "just as they would happen anywhere in the outer world" (59). They are men "of flesh and blood with really plastic bodies" who stand before the audience. But on the silent screen the situation is totally different: "The color of the world has disappeared, the persons are dumb, no sound reaches our ears" (59). Further, the actors themselves are flattened onto a two-dimensional screen: "The essential point is rather that we are conscious of the flatness of the picture." It will be recalled that earlier in this chapter I referred to Muensterberg's statement that in the motion picture the weight and causality of the real world are overcome. Similarly, the presence of the screen actor becomes, on the screen, a part of this "weightless continuum" of space and time; for the actor as well as the physical world, "the idea of heaviness, solidity and substantially must be replaced by the light flitting immateriality" (77). How, then, can the screen actor, whose substantialness is no more or less than the weightlessness of the world around him, function to convey to a viewer feelings of emotion and dramatic effect? No doubt, admits Muensterberg, an emotion which, in the case of the screen actor, is deprived of sound and substantial physical presence, has lost its power. Yet that loss is counterbalanced by the consequent importance of the actor's every facial and physical movement: "...gestures, actions, and facial play are so interwoven with the psychical process of an intense emotion that every shade can find its characteristic delivery" (48). The use of the closeup—a device impossible to a theatrical presentation—"can strongly heighten the impression.... The enlargement by the close-up on the screen brings this emotional action of the face to sharpest relief" (48). Moreover, the closeup can make expressive "actors" out of a performer's hands and feet and out of inanimate objects. It can "show us enlarged a play of the hands in which anger and rage or tender love or jealousy speak in unmistakable language" (48).

If it is true that the screen actor's technique is largely controlled by the filmmaker's manipulation of pieces of film through editing (which includes, of course, employment of the closeup), then is it possible that the screen actor does not necessarily need to have any dramatic training at all? Muensterberg seems to say so, and his words recall for us the use of non-actors and unstaged events in the news films of which I have spoken earlier in this chapter. The player in a film, he said, must possess only the required attributes of a desired "type" in order to be effective as a screen actor. Film actors "need no art of speaking and no training in delivery;" consequently, they do not need the "artificial make-up of the stage actor," either, because they can be naturally fitted for the given role. If a director needs to cast a brutal boxer, for example, he would not, like the stage manager, have to try to transform a clean, neat actor into a vulgar brute by means of make up; rather he could seek out "the real thing" (to borrow a phrase from Henry James) (50). We may regard this notion as comparable to the idea that location shooting, instead of artificial scenery, was proper to cinematic expression—so, too, could non-actors, instead of trained players, be proper to film acting. This idea was soon to be implemented into the work of filmmakers as diverse as Robert Flaherty and Dziga Vertov in the 1920s and Luchino Visconti and Roberto Rossellini in the 1940s.

By the time synchronized-sound was introduced to the film medium in 1927, the majority of the most successful film actors were largely trained in the film medium (see Chapter Two). Yet the subsequent return to intensive theatrical film making brought about a renewed influx of stage-trained actors into the film industry. While the actors trained in the film medium temporarily withdrew to the sidelines, again the stage-trained players came to the fore. Not surprisingly, however, they faced the same kinds of problems working in the film medium as I have described in the 1912-15 period. But there was a significant difference to be found in this second cycle of theatrical film making—synchronized-sound. Now an assumption arose that stage-trained *voices* would benefit these actors. But again, stage training proved to be of little value in performing on the screen. As Elaine Ogden writes in *Photoplay* in 1930, the stage players "have more to overcome than the screen folk. They must forget entirely [their] old technique."[51]

What were the special problems faced by actors in synchronized sound films of the 1927-30 period? Why did the stage-trained actors generally fail in these films? And what did these failures reveal about the special nature of acting in the synchronized-sound film? In order to answer these questions, I have divided the remainder of this section into two parts. The first part will describe some of the physical restraints imposed upon the actor by the environment of the early sound stages. The second part will describe specifically some of the peculiar problems the actor faced before the first crude microphone systems.

The early sound stages presented the stage actors with unexpected challenges. We already know that many of the first sound stages were either erected upon the stages of theater houses or were built to resemble these theater stages. Yet, in significant ways, the sound stages were different. For example, stage actress Peggy Wood wrote that before coming to movies she had been accustomed to the illuminating barrier of the stage footlights; yet, on the movie sound stage, actors "know they will have to perform before a cylinder hanging within a few inches of their heads and that at the other end of the wire running from that microphone sits a deity called the mixer, up in his little room, listening with appalling coldness to their histrionic efforts."[52] In the days before 1930, that cylindrical microphone so restricted the actor's movements that he was reduced to almost complete immobility. Sometimes during the theatrical films of 1912-15 the actor had amplified his gestures and movements; now the opposite extreme proved to be the case—he was able to move very little. Until the microphone could be freed from its fixed moorings by the invention of the boom, the actor had to learn to live (and act) under this system.[53]

There were other differences. The soundproofed studios kept out not only outside sounds, but the outside air as well. Heavy carpeting, double doors, and the smothering woven asbestos coverings were necessary soundproofing, but they added to the already abnormal heat. The blazing artificial lights also intensified the heat. The temperature, likely to be ninety-eight degrees during the Hollywood summers, was now apt to be a hundred and fifteen in the studios. These great concrete stages with four hundred tons of structural steel and more than twelve hundred cubic yards of concrete and two-ton doors contained recording apparatus so delicate that it could register the slightest sound. When the whistle shrilled for the cameras to begin turning, an inadvertent sneeze or cough could cost thousands of unnecessary dollars. Moreover, the actors had to wear special rubber shoes lest their footsteps be too audible; and under their clothing might be a rubber suit to prevent the unwanted sounds of rustling fabrics. All this time, during the filming process, the cameras would creep up, encased within thousands of pounds of soundproofing (lest the camera's whirring register with the microphones), looking like wartime tanks on rubber rollers. In sum, it was a nightmarish world surrounding the hapless actor—the heat and discomfort, the total silence, the absence of an audience, the limited mobility.[54] But while such physical restrictions threatened the years of training of the stage actors, there were other, perhaps worse, terrors in store for them. To describe these, I will have to turn now to the problems presented to the stage actor's voice by the microphone.

As early as the Edison experiments with synchronized sound before 1915, there were predictions of some of the problems microphones would present to actors. While Edison was making his decision as to whether or not to discontinue his Kinetophone system of sound recording (sound-on disc process), C. H. Wilson, Vice-President and General Manager of the Edison Phonograph Company, wrote his recommendations. He advised that films with synchronized-sound would pose too great a threat to the actor. The motion picture "gets over," he wrote, because of the actor's appearance and not because of his voice. In addition, too many popular actors' voices would not record properly—it would be impossible to obtain satisfactory results in the endeavor.[55] The Edison experiments ended after a studio fire.

It has always been true that the human voice is altered by the recording process; but in 1914, when Wilson offered this advice to Edison, this alteration amounted to distortion. The Kinetophone system imparted a metallic quality to the voice and its amplification system was insufficient— either from the recording standpoint (voices had to be within twenty feet of the sound horn to record at all) or the reproduction standpoint (the sound could not be amplified without further distortion). It is hardly surprising, therefore, that commentators of the time would complain of the "dehumanization" of the actor's voice.[56] The effect worsened when the image and sound got out of "synch" with each other.

Fifteen years later, although sound engineering techniques had improved somewhat, the same problems accompanied the early talkies. It was still quite unpredictable whether an actor's voice would register "properly" or not. Tests were demanded of everyone, including the stage-trained personnel. What was ultimately reproduced might bear little similarity to the original voice. Pickup on high frequencies was quite limited on the electromagnetic recording apparatus. Thus, the overtones were cut off on many voices, giving them a hollow-bottom-of-the-barrel sound. Sibilants were also cut off. The effect was that of a lisp.

In order to achieve the best voice recording, the microphones on the sound stages had to be fixed at pre-determined distances and angles from the actor. Director Paul Sloane has left an account of the effect this had on the acting techniques of the players. Unfortunately, he wrote in *Theater Magazine* late in 1928, placement of the microphone—and not the dramatic purpose of the play—dictated the figure placement on the stage. "The actors must to a great extent completely disregard the logical and dramatic positions and groupings which the scene demands," he wrote. Instead, they had to stand "at just so many inches from the microphone; their heads at just such an angle; their voices at just such a level, varying the position of their heads as the quality of their voice changes...."[57]

Soon, the sound engineers were able to predict how a voice would record; from there, it was but a step to find ways to "improve" a voice through the recording process. As a result, the voice was even further altered. Writing in 1929, actress Louise Closser Hale described some of these techniques. For example, by manipulating knobs on the sound mixing board, a "small" voice could be changed to one with a fuller tone; conversely, a strident one could be subdued and lowered. Regardless of any stage training, the voice was subject now to a new kind of challenge in the movies and, as Hale concluded, "we must among other terrifying lessons, learn to appear natural in a new way."[58] Neither the stage voice nor the non-trained "natural" voice was superior to the other before the common challenge of the microphone—both could be adjusted by the sound engineers.

If we accept that control of the actor's gesture and voice resided in the hands of the filmmaker and that virtually anyone could perform and speak on the screen as a result, what responsibilities, then, did the actor have? Commentators late in 1929 sharply disagreed on this question. On the one hand, Luigi Pirandello seemed to lament this loss by the actor of his physical and vocal control. "The film actor," he said, "feels as if in exile—exiled not only from the stage but also from himself." He is "deprived of reality, life, voice, and the noises caused by his moving about." He is like a ghost, the helpless creation of a machine.[59] On the other hand, Vsevolod Pudovkin was not dismayed by the situation. The motion picture represented to the actor a world of discontinuities in sound and image. Even though the film actor, unlike the stage actor, "is deprived of a consciousness of the uninterrupted development of the action,"[60] this did not necessitate the "killing and mechanicalisation of the actor" (146). Rather, it became the challenge the screen actor would have to confront: ". . . the discontinuity of the actor's work must never be ignored, but always treated as a difficulty to be overcome" (244). He had to approach each camera setup, each recording session, each fragment of speech as just a part of the total mosaic of the finished film. This means that the actor's responsibility is to know and understand the relative position each of these fragments will eventually occupy. At the same time, Pudovkin says, the screen actor must learn to abandon what the stage actor had worked so long to learn—how to impart a beginning and an end, a shape, to each scene. Instead, the screen actor "must be able to act his short piece without beginning or end and in the absence of that which eventually will influence the content of his acting by interaction with it on the screen" (256). In this way, each fragment can flow into the others so that a *larger* unity is achieved. Moreover—and we recall an earlier statement of Muensterberg—the screen actor has to learn that subtle shades of vocal intonation must accompany the correspondingly subtle gestures and expressions of the physical acting. The proximity of the microphone was no less close than that of the camera.

Inflated intonation would be just as inappropriate to this situation as exaggerated gesture. "In practice disappears from the actor's work the element of special study of voice production and strength of tone, which in the film actor, need only be strong enough to cover the distance separating him from his colleague; in other words, as strong as would be requisite in the conditions of actuality" (321). In conclusion, Pudovkin says that such awarenesses on the part of the actor are consistent with the manipulation of film by the director and "permit these possibilities to be maintained and exploited to maximum advantage...." (269).

The Symposium on the Synchronized-Sound Film Conducted by the Academy of Motion Picture Arts and Sciences, 1929

During the fall of 1929, the Academy of Motion Picture Arts and Sciences, which had been formed in 1927, sponsored a symposium about the synchronized-sound film and its relation to the theatre. Traditionally, it had always been part of the function of an Academy to become involved with matters of definition concerning the arts. For example, to cite just one instance, the French Academy had responded to the *Le Cid* controversy in 1637 with Jean Chapelain's position paper reaffirming the proper allegiance of the theater to the Aristotelian unities.[61] Now, in 1929, the motion picture industry was undergoing a technological revolution. Was the silent film medium now to be consigned to oblivion? What was the future of the synchronized-sound film? What was the current state of technological development in synchronized-sound? And what part did theatrical imitation play now in the sound revolution? All of these questions were discussed by representatives of the film industry. The symposium marked the first time that members of the industry were able to get together and address themselves to the above issues.

Formation of the Academy marked an important step in the development of the motion picture industry. According to David O. Selznick, its establishment in 1927 was initially intended to promote the aims of past Academies—technical research and the exchange of artistic and scientific views.[62] It had five branches representing the production personnel involved in filmmaking—production, writing, directing, acting, and technical research. Its practical functions included the public recognition of its annual Awards presentations, the institution of a research facility for the preservation and study of historical papers (now called the Margaret Herrick Library), and an arbitration system by which various matters—from labor disputes to technical standards, could be evaluated.[63] And, like all academies traditionally, cultural discussion and debate, as well as public promotion of the arts in education, were also priorities.

The symposium grew out of this last priority. In the fall of 1929, representatives from the motion picture industry met on a weekly basis at the

University of Southern California campus. Actors, directors, writers, set designers, producers all discussed the nature and aims of the movie industry—specifically, the imitation of the theater and how this would be affected by synchronized sound. The four-month symposium was transcribed at the time; until recently, however, the transcriptions have not been published. Recently, in conjunction with the Academy and the National Film Society, I gathered together the surviving typescripts, edited, annotated, and published them.[64] In my opinion, they constitute an invaluable resource for the study of the theatrical film in 1927-30. They represent a contemporary overview of how filmmakers regarded their own medium at a time of crisis in redefinition and assessment.

It takes but a moment to place the symposium—entitled "Introduction to the Photoplay"—in an immediate context. In the months immediately prior to the symposium, some important early talkies had already appeared— some of them theatrical films: *The Lights of New York, The Singing Fool, The Terror, Interference, The Doctor's Secret,* and *Broadway Melody* (July, 1928 to February, 1929). Throughout the remainder of 1929—during and just subsequent to the Academy's symposium—the following major talkies, most of them theatrical films, were released: *Alibi* and *The Desert Song* (April, 1929), *Thunderbolt* (June, 1929), *The Cocoanuts* and *Hallelujah* (August, 1929), *Rio Rita, Applause,* and *The Taming of the Shrew* (October, 1929), *The Virginian* (November, 1929), and *Sunny Side Up* and *Dynamite* (December, 1929). Theatrical films in this second group were generally more cinematically advanced—which is to say they were selectively rather than closely imitative of stage plays—than those of the first group. Thus, the span of the symposium coincided with a remarkably fertile period in the development of the synchronized-sound film. Moreover, the speakers were themselves involved in making many of these films and, therefore, could bring to their presentations an immediate grasp of the problems and possibilities of synchronized-sound. Art designer William Cameron Menzies, writer/producer Paul Bern, writer Clara Beranger, producer Irving Thalberg, actor Conrad Nagel, and director William De Mille all referred to their work. Menzies, for example, spoke of the demands upon set designing caused by the new acoustic sound stages (at that time, he was designing two theatrical films, *Alibi* and *The Taming of the Shrew*). While William De Mille spoke about trying to free the fixed microphone to allow the actors and camera more freedom on the set, he was completing his first talkie, *The Doctor's Secret.* And while Conrad Nagel described the new challenges to acting technique brought by the microphone, he was acting in Cecil B. De Mille's *Dynamite*.

The symposium may be broken down into the categories already under discussion in this chapter—the nature of the continuum of space and time on film, the potentials of asynchronous sound, and acting on film. Generally, what is most impressive about the symposium is that, although there are the expected pronouncements that silent pictures will survive the sound revolution—such as Paul Bern's declaration, "I hope the silent picture will remain because it is important" (81), and that the presence of synchronized-sound would eliminate the swift cutting characteristic of silent pictures, such as William De Mille's assertion that quick cutting "is simply terrible in its jostling effect—it jangles the nerves" (325)—the predictions are remarkably farsighted. They reveal a consciousness on the part of filmmakers that they must break away from the stranglehold of theatrical imitation.

Conrad Nagel and William De Mille discussed the spatial nature of the talking picture. In describing this new film for United Artists, *The Swan*, Nagel noted that it "was shot almost as we would shoot a silent picture," with "individual closeups taken separately from the long shots or medium shots." The technique of recording sound and image separately was returning this flexibility to the filmmakers. Just a year and a half ago this had not been so, remembered Nagel:

> In the beginning, of course, this was a great difficulty as long shots had to be shot sometimes running eight and ten minutes at one time and all the different angles and different sizes had to be taken. This was due to the fact that it was absolutely necessary to use only one sound track without interrupting it. Now, however, this sound can be broken up. (208)

Director William De Mille noted that the breaking of spatial continuities with shifts in camera position and with closeups was important, but difficult. In dialogue scenes, for example, one character's speech and the listener's reaction can be included in the same shot, as opposed to the days of the silent cinema when an intervening subtitle would be followed by a reaction shot of the listener. "But in the talking picture the reaction has to come while the other character is speaking...which means we have a double close-up so that it brings in both the listener and speaker" (325). This is, of course, a variant on what René Clair applauded in the work of Edmund Goulding—the "closeup" of a listener while the voice of another actor is heard. Moreover, De Mille predicted that freeing the microphone from its fixed position on the sound stage could promote this flexibility of sound and image juxtaposition. "Now that we are freeing the microphone," he said, "we can take it out—we can make noise scenes in the street.... We are freeing ourselves from these artificial restrictions...." Thus, the director could move from long shot to closeup, balancing the sweep of the one with the intimacy of the other without being restricted by the microphone" (334).

Benjamin Glazer and Paul Bern spoke of the necessity of returning the synchronized-sound film to the compression of time characteristic of the maturity of the silent film. Glazer calls this technique the condensing of action to its strictest essentials: "For instance, if the action we want to show begins at this end of the table and finishes at that end, we can give you its beginning and its conclusion, leaving out the inessential part between. That cannot be done on the stage" (94). Paul Bern referred to the device of the "fade-out" as a way of altering the passage of time: "The fade-out device is most valuable; it suggests quickly the passage of time; it enables us to leave an episode at its high point of interest, without wearying the audience by getting the actors off the stage to bring new ones on, as must be done in the theatre....."(75).

The use of asynchronous sound was advocated by Benjamin Glazer, Irving Thalberg, and William De Mille. "I can give you a closeup of a sound," said Glazer, "just as I can give you a closeup of a person." Accordingly, Glazer advocated that a filmmaker select sounds just as carefully as he would select images: "It is within my power to exclude any sound, without offending your sense of reality. For as I show you only what action I want you to see, likewise, I let you listen only to what sounds I want you to hear" (95). He gave as an example a scene from one of his first writing assignments, the adaptation of the play *Burlesque* into a film for Paramount. An actor has achieved success while leaving his wife behind. The night of his opening, he decides during a party to telegram his wife with news of his good fortune. While people crowd around the actor to congratulate him, the telegram is brushed off the table onto the floor. "That discarded telegram," Glazer continued, "becomes in the story a symbol of the husband's neglect of the wife who made his success possible. In the scene I show that telegram in closeup, nothing else but the telegram, with feet passing over it, kicking it around. But through it all you hear the voices of all who are in the room. What they say, unseen, tells you of the man's success, but the mute telegram, which is all you see, tells you that the wife has been...discarded, forgotten" (94).

Irving Thalberg described the asynchronous use of background music in a film. In *Broadway Melody*—the film so often cited by René Clair as indicative of the advances of asynchronous sound—there were scenes in which music is heard but whose source is not seen. Thalberg's analysis of the concept is worth quoting at length:

First of all, in connection with this particular scene, we were aware of the possibility that the playing of an orchestra in connection with a scene where no orchestra was present might shock the audience. We observed the reactions of the first audiences with interest and were prepared, if necessary, to recall the picture and devise some other method because we knew from experience how strong the play instinct, referred to by Mr. Bern in his lecture, really is—how far the audience will really go, in adjusting itself. They had accepted the illusion of depth, spoken titles, and many other things because they came to the theatre to play—to make believe. Entertain them and they will not be critical of details of technique, such as the one referred to. Besides, it is customary for a man to sing with musical accompaniment. It makes the song sound better. When we are in a theatre we do not look to the pit every time a song is sung to see if the orchestra is there—we take the musical accompaniment for granted. (129-130)

Benjamin Glazer, on the other hand, deplored such "borrowing" from the precedents of the theater. It was an artistic mistake, a case of "putting sounds where they have no reason to be" (101). William De Mille agreed, saying that the only excuse for such devices was to cover the "waits" between exchanges of dialogue. He rejected musical accompaniment to dialogue sequences; instead, it was preferable to develop what he called "overlapping dialogue." He explained, "I think I was one of the first directors to try an ensemble vocal effect—I let them interrupt each other just as people do when they are talking in a group.... Half the words are lost because they are meant to be lost. We are very sure that you don't lose the words we want you to hear" (336-37).

It was generally recognized by all that the talkies brought new challenges to acting techniques. The consensus of opinion resembles remarks I have already quoted from Muensterberg and Pudovkin. For example, William De Mille asserted that the drama was a story "which finds its best expression through physical acting." But the motion picture brings the camera so close to the actor that "just raising of an eyelid can be made more powerful than the big broad gestures in the theatre used to be." This intimacy of gesture and voice is "a beautiful new intimacy of the spoken work which gives us so much more than pantomime alone can give." De Mille concluded that this sense of restraint and modulation necessary in the actor's voice was the aural equivalent of a closeup (326).

A sharp conflict in attitudes arose, however, regarding the suitability of the stage-trained voice for the talkies. Conrad Nagel adopted the view that had led to stage-trained actors coming to the movies in the first place—that stage training qualified actors for the film medium. "The good actor has to spend years developing good diction and, if he is a good artist, once he has mastered this phase of his art he will be unconscious of that fact. They will merely enjoy his performance because they will distinctly hear every word he says." This is important, concluded Nagel, because ""the microphones and the recording are so perfect that the tiniest shading of the voice can be reproduced and be effective in a large theatre" (206). Benjamin Glazer disagreed. The stage actor had had to learn to project his voice for everyone in the theater house. In the case of voice recording for movies, however, that was no longer necessary. "We try to keep away from stilted, unreal tones and the possessor of a trained voice is apt to be voice-conscious. In the microphone, every nuance of tone can be picked up at its source, so to speak, so a trained voice is not really necessary" (102). The "natural" voice is more effective because it is more realistic (102). Glazer's attitude was soon adopted by others, as we have seen in the writings of Pudovkin. Of course, the dialogue best suited to this natural vocal inflection should stress conversation, as opposed to oratorical speech. Clara Beranger, who had just finished scripting *The Doctor's Secret* at the time of her presentation, noted that the dialogue should be suited to the drawing room rather than for the gallery of the theater house. That is why, in her opinion, the playwright was generally unsuited to the movies: "We have to get dialogue that is conversational; that is poignant, compact, and will carry the action forward." That is why, Beranger concluded, "to get the right form of 'talkie' dialogue, stage and screen writers will have to study the new medium for a new method of expression" (150).

There is a special excitement contained in the foregoing survey of comment from the Academy's symposium. The speakers knew that as filmmakers they were at this time poised between the ambitions of theatrical imitation and the possibilities of a more cinematic kind of achievement. It was a moment of decision for them, and Clara Beranger described their predicament:

The talkies are a combination of the stage and the screen; and at present we are wondering how much they are going to borrow from either or both of these mediums. From the stage they get language and psychology. But if they follow the stage too closely they do not get a motion picture but a photographed stage play. The tempo is too slow and the audience resents it. If they follow the motion picture they can get that fluidity of action which the picture audiences have learned to like. The stage picks out the big dramatic moments and leaves out what goes on between the acts. In pictures we have tried to fill this in. But since you can have much less plot in a talking picture than a picture without sound, we are going to have difficulty in knowing just what to keep and what to throw away (149).

What conclusion, if any, came from the symposium regarding the future of the talking picture—theatrical or otherwise. Perhaps Frank Woods expressed the prevailing mood best when he said, "With the addition of sound to help create the illusion of reality, the motion picture may possibly become the art expressive of all arts in the same sense that the printing arts have been described as the art preservative of all arts" (60).

Finally, it is significant that these attempts to discuss and formulate the nature and goals of the sound film should have occurred within an academic context. The motion picture industry had, for the most part, pursued a policy of imitating the theater since the turn of the century; now, in 1929, that policy was being vigorously questioned in an atmosphere of consistent and orderly debate. Imitation had ultimately resulted, for the filmmakers, in a process of redefinition. Form now on, the term "theatrical film" would no longer imply a motion picture that was closely imitative of theatrical sources; rather, it would denote a kind of film that while it revealed its theatrical origins, was, nonetheless, a fully realized expression. The words of Sir Joshua Reynolds in his "Sixth Discourse" (1784), while referring specifically to the education and development of painters, apply to this moment in the history of film: "It is a common observation that no art was ever invented and carried to perfection at the same time.... By imitation only, variety, and even originality of invention, is produced" (65).

Postscript: The Influences Motion Picture Production Have Had Upon the Production of Stage Plays, 1896-1930

The "photographic realism" of the motion picture—especially in spectacles and the news and chase films—was imitated in stage plays in basically two ways. First, there were attempts to recreate on stage the amplitude of scale and realistic detail common to the spectacle film; second, there were attempts to recreate on stage the intimacy, the intensely observed and realized detail of a more "intimate" cinema—that kind of cinema described by Vachel Lindsay of places and objects. Some examples will suffice to make the point. In the first instance, according to A. Nicholas Vardac in his definitive *Stage to Screen*, a number of theatrical spectacles clearly derived from motion pictures. When *Quo Vadis* and *Ben Hur* were produced on American stages in 1899, a number of motion picture "Passion Plays" (of which one, the Biograph version in 1896 has already been discussed in Chapter Four) had already been successful on movie house screens. According to Vardac, the stage productions of *Quo Vadis* and *Ben Hur*—to name only two examples—subsequently contained effects common to these films— numerous scenes and elaborately detailed "stage pictures." These approached photographic mimesis to such an extent that they could be considered the equivalents of photographs. The stage entrepreneurs utilized the proscenium frame boundaries to enclose, in effect, spectacular pictures that rivalled the mass and scale of long shots of film.[65] This imitation of photographic realism, however, was not restricted to spectacle. David Belasco's series of chamber dramas from 1900 to 1912—*The Auctioneer* (1901), *The Music Master* (1904), *The Easiest Way* (1909), and *The Governor's Lady* (1912)—all exhibited a realism that exploited interiors of other kinds or specific areas. Vardac notes that Belasco's drive for verisimilitude imitated that capacity of the motion picture and "strove, through the drama of intimate realism, to outrival the screen...."[67] So detailed was the playwright Eugene Walter's description of Laura Murdock's shabby Bowery tenement in the preface to the Second Act of *The Easiest Way*, for example, that Belasco went to a Bowery hotel and bought the entire interior of one of its dilapidated rooms—down to the patched furniture, threadbare carpet, tarnished and broken gas fixtures, and even the faded wall paper. There are many other examples of such concern in Belasco's productions.[68] In another example, the playscript of Edward Sheldon's *Salvation Nell* (1908) was replete with detailed descriptions of the setting of the Empire Bar in the First Act. Photographs of the Minnie Maddern Fiske production at the Hackett Theatre in November, 1908, attest to the fidelity in the stage production to Sheldon's photographic concept.[68]

Many of these dramas were topical social dramas that derived much of their power from their realistic effects on the stage. Indeed, *Salvation Nell*, without its superbly realized sense of scene, was little more than a routine melodrama. In a recent study of these plays, Maxwell Bloomfield claims the photographic realism often overwhelmed the dramatic action. Playwrights like Sheldon, Walter, and Veiller "grew increasingly absorbed in technical details, seeking to reproduce with absolute fidelity the external conditions described by fact-finding reporters." As a result, these plays, in Bloomfield's opinion, "degenerated into a series of carefully contrived photographs, authentic 'still lifes' depicting the interiors of police stations, brothels, and tenement houses."[69] And for the influential theater critic, William Winter, these "pictures" threatened the charm and artifice of traditional scenic theatrical conceptions: "The stage has been disgraced by the putrescent.... Eugene Walter's photographic abomination of 'The Easiest Way'...."[70]

We know already that when filmmakers imitated theatrical illusion, it was realized that the two media were really incompatible in being conjoined. Similarly, playwrights and entrepreneurs of the stage began to discover that such imitation on their part of photographic realism was futile. No matter how they tried, they could not realize on the stage more than a momentary illusion of a photograph or of a real place; moreover, maintaining that sense of illusion was impossible.

At this point it is pertinent to note a parallel to this situation involving one aspect of the interaction between photographers and painters in the nineteenth century. Baudelaire had attacked in 1859 what he felt to be the influence of photography upon painters in attempting to render the surfaces of realism. Dreams were disappearing, he said, and were being replaced by the vulgarity of the commonplace.[71] As the century waned, however, more and more painters agreed that the mechanical reproduction of Nature by the camera could not be challenged by the brush. Recently, Susanne K. Langer has contended that these artists felt a sense of futility as a result. This led many of them, she wrote, to make of painting "once more an art of pure form [which] was again, in certain instances, restricted to two dimensions."[72] The literal transcription to canvas of realistic effects was increasingly supplanted by more nonrepresentational works. Indeed, Picasso asked why the artist should persist in depicting subjects that could be transcribed so much more faithfully by the camera:

> Photography has arrived at a point where it is capable of liberating painting from all literature, from the anecdote, and even from the subject.... So shouldn't painters profit from their newly acquired liberty...to do other things?[73]

It is, of course, absurdly simplistic to imply that the emergence during the last quarter of the century of movements in painting like Impressionism and Post-Impressionism, Symbolism and the Nabis was entirely the result of a counter-reaction to photographic realism; however, it would be short-sighted not to attribute to these movements apprehension of the unique propensities of the camera and the folly of attempts to compete with them.

Just as many painters had retreated from the futility of rivaling photographic realism late in the 19th century, so can we trace a similar retreat on the part of many theatrical people after 1910. In words that seem to echo those of Picasso, Eugene O'Neill described what he felt to be a general distaste felt in many quarters about photographic imitation:

> It represents our Fathers' daring aspirations toward self-recognition by holding the family kodak up to ill-nature. But to us their old audacity is blague [sic]; we have taken too many snapshots of each other in every graceless position; we have endured too much the banality of surfaces.[74]

Too long had the stage disguised itself as a parlor, wrote Francis Fergusson in his discussion of naturalistic drama in *The Idea of a Theatre*. Many playwrights felt it was time to abandon such ambitions and return the stage to its prominence as a *stage*.[75] Fergusson cited Pirandello's *Six Characters in Search of an Author* (1921) as an example. Pirandello, said Fergusson, did not believe in the stage as a "photograph of a parlor" but as an arena of symbolic enactment which accommodates "the primitive and subtle medium of the dramatic art."[76] The very dependence of the stage upon artifice, which so many had tried to disguise, was now free to declare itself openly *as* artifice—or disappear altogether.

Perhaps Pirandello's attitudes might have themselves been influenced by the motion picture. Pirandello was involved with filmmaking all his life, as I have already noted earlier in this chapter. Once again we turn to his *Si Gara* for insights into how Pirandello's theatrical attitudes were shaped by his involvement with movies. The book is full of filmmakers who have become mere observers of the life around them—perceiving life with the detachment of a motion picture camera. In plays like *Six Characters*, however, we can see the playwright delving beyond naturalistic surfaces, rejecting photographic mimesis, refusing to find enduring truths in mere exterior surfaces. This play extended a movement already under way in many countries through groups like Jacques Copeau's Theatre du Vieux Colombier in 1913 and the experiments of Evreinov and Meyerhold in Russia. Brockett and Findlay in *A Century of Innovation* refer to the theater of Copeau as "perhaps the most important event in the French theatre of the time. . . ."[77] Like Pirandello, Copeau declared his own dissatisfaction with photographic mimesis in his "Essay on the Renovation of the Drama: the Theatre du Vieux Colombier (1913)." He called for a complete rejection of this realism and for a return to the bare stage where the proper attention could be fully focused upon the actor.[78] This trend toward what we might call the "theatricalization" of the theater found a powerful voice in Evreinov and Meyerhold at the Moscow Art Theater during the 1909-1920 period. Herbert Marshall in his study of Russian Theater has said that both men opposed the idea of getting an audience to forget they were in a theater; rather, they "must be made acutely conscious of that fact. . . ."[79] In Evreinov's treatises, *The Theatre As Such* (1912), *Pro Scene Sua* (1913), and *The Theatre in Life* (1915-1917), he explained that all men had a "will for the theatre," a drive to "play-act." Like Pirandello, Evreinov's convictions led him to remind his audiences continually that they were watching a *stage*. Evreinov even wrote several plays that dealt with stage directors and erstwhile actors (see especially his *The School of Stars*, 1911). As for Meyerhold, his production of *Mystery Bouffe* (1918), as described by H. W. L. Dana, began with a small army of workers quite literally tearing down the curtain from the proscenium. "They were going to do away with the curtain which separated the actors from the audience," said Dana. The action "was to pass freely from the stage to the auditorium and from the auditorium to the stage." Moreover, it was Meyerhold's avowed ambition at this time "to present a theater house without benefit of curtain, footlights, or proscenium arch."[80] In Meyerhold's work, as stage designer Mordecai Gorelik has written, the Theatricalists "established once and for all that the stage is an acting platform onto which 'life' is brought only through translation into stage values."[81] For the Theatricalists, naturalism, or realism, remained the province of the motion picutre rather than of the theater.

It is misleading, however, to infer that the movement toward theatricalism was simply a counter-reaction against the naturalistic capacities of the motion picture. Many of the popular and experimental plays that might be classified as "expressionist" or "constructivist" in Germany, Russia and America presented effects that in themselves are comparable to those of motion pictures. I refer to their episodic construction—a mosaic of acts, scenes, and episodes that pass quickly, one to the other, before the eyes. As early as 1912, theatrical commentator Claude Hagen, writing in *The Stage in the Twentieth Century*, noted that the successions of brief shots in films was influencing the work of playwrights. "Producers of photo plays," he said, "have set the pace to be followed." He enumerated some of the effects perceptible in contemporary drama, including what he termed the "rapid change of scenes."[82] And other commentators noted throughout the next fifteen years an increasing tendency in stage plays to split up the action into numerous brief units, much in the same way that editing in motion pictures fragmented the action into a series of brief shots. Pudovkin cited Meyerhold's production of Ostrovski's *The Forest* as an example. Meyerhold broke up the action into many scenes and episodes by means of which two actors are guided throughout a whole province in Russia without ever leaving the stage. In this and other plays, noted Pudovkin, Meyerhold and others were attempting to borrow or adapt to the stage cinematic effects (236). It was an ambition, however, fraught with difficulties. In Pudovkin's view, the technique of rapid scene changing, while easily effected in the motion picture, was inordinately difficult to do on the stage. A stage performance what was "cut up into one-and-two-minute bits," he explained, "would presuppose entirely new engineering inventions enabling scenic changes at the speed of lightning, enabling the spectator to transfer his attention from one point of stage space to the other with the speed of the successive bits" (236). Thus, he declared the ambition was misguided. Nonetheless, since the inception of motion pictures in the 1890s, there had been many attempts to design stages that would permit rapid scene changes. In 1892 Steel MacKaye, envisioned and designed what he called a "Proscenium-Adjuster." It was calculated, said Vardac, "to provide a greater flexibility in the pictorial arrangement of the stage." The change from a panoramic view to a "closeup" "could be handled instantaneously by enlarging and contracting the proscenium opening at will."[83] In MacKaye's words, scenes could be changed "without a moment's delay and almost imperceptibly to the audience...."[84] The project was never completed and MacKaye died shortly afterwards. A few years later, in 1909, the "New Theatre" was founded in New York City. Its construction included elaborate provisions for complex revolving stages, elevator stages, light curtains, and other devices to effect rapid scene changes. The project failed, noted Claude Hagen in 1912, but in his view it forecast the nature of future stagecraft. Hagen described his own "ideal" theater in terms that could be describing the perceptual experience of watching a film. It would have a revolving stage upon which a number of stage sets could be arranged at one time, "thus permitting scenes to be moved into position rapidly, silently."[85]

As plays like Meyerhold's *The Forest* were broken up into more and more episodes of brief duration, it was, perhaps, inevitable, that the nature of stage time and space could be made to approach that of cinema. If we recall the formulations of Muensterberg in 1915, we know that there was a growing perception that the created illusion of a film "is not bound by the rigid mechanism of space and time." By contrast, it had been widely understood that the created illusion within the proscenium frame of the theater was "bound not only by space and time," but "controlled by the same laws of causality which govern nature." Muensterberg insisted upon this point. On the stage there was "a complete continuity of the physical events: no cause without following effect, no effect without preceding cause" (79). Even though the playwright might interrupt the continuous flow of time—such as gaps in time between the divisions of acts and scenes—he is, nonetheless, "bound by the fundamental principle of real time, that it can move only forward and not backward. Whatever the theater shows us in any previous moment" (77-78). In the motion picture, on the other hand, the sense of continuity in time and space is bound up only in the viewer's own attention, memory, imagination, and emotion: "The freedom of the mind has triumphed over the unalterable law of the outer world" (78).

Yet, after 1910—and this is a date that I am rather arbitrarily assigning— a large number of plays, especially those classified as "expressionist," attempted to present on stage a succession of events relatively free of the chronological, cause-and-effect principle of construction Muensterberg described. Two plays appeared in 1914 that, acording to Muensterberg, attempted to imitate the cinematic arrangement of scenes. In describing the effects in Roi Cooper Mergrue's *Under Cover* (1914) and Elmer Rice's *On Trial* (1914) Muensterberg rather drily commented, "It is interesting to watch how playwrights nowadays try to steal the thunder of the photoplay and experiment with time reversals on the legitimate stage." For example, the third act of *Under Cover* is played on the second floor of a house; it ends with a mysterious explosion. The fourth act, which plays downstairs, begins a quarter of an hour *before* the explosion. In other words, the fourth act functions as a flashback. In *On Trial*, which Muensterberg describes as coming the "nearest to a dramatic usurpation of the rights of the photoplay". (78), the entire structure of the action consists of a number of flashbacks. In the main setting, a courtroom, one witness after another begins his testimony—at which point the action flashes back to the events being described. Incidentally, the "cinematic" nature of both plays was not lost upon filmmakers—both were made into films, respectively, by Famous Players in 1916 and by Warner Brothers in 1928.

At this same time plays began appearing elsewhere that revealed a far more complex arrangement of scenes. In his recent study of German expressionism as performed on American stages, *The Hooded Eagle*, Peter Bauland describes the style in terms that sound definitely cinematic. Since Hasenclever's *Der Sohn* had appeared in Germany in 1914, Hasenclever writes, theatrical construction of scenes abandoned the kinds of logic described by Muensterberg. The rapid succession of scenes (or *stationen*) constituted "the rejection of conventional causal developments, transitions, and details of plot" formerly characteristic of the theater. The results on stage yielded "an unrelieved, episode, and fragmentary structure which the expressionist believes is a more accurate depiction of humane experience than a logically constructed pattern."[86] Thus, returning to Muensterberg's remarks, the world of the stage has approached that of the cinema. It "has been freed from space, time, and causality, and it has been clothed in the forms of our own consciousness." One of the most celebrated expressionist plays was Ernest Toller's *Man and the Masses*, and it contains examples of these cinematic tendencies. Its construction is episodic; each episode is brief, consisting of one highly emotionally charged "picture" that, in turn, is quickly succeeded by the next picture. The sequence of the seven pictures moves from a workingman's tavern, to a dream vision of the stock exchange, to a worker's hall, to a "dream vision" of a trial, back to the workmen's hall, to a "dream vision" of a jail cell, and to the "real" depiction of a jail cell. There is no strict sense of chronology, no strict progression in time and space. The only "order" apparent in this structure is the alternation of dream visions with reality; otherwise, the links that bind the scenes together are emotional links—that is, for example, a scene of the stock exchange is followed by the scene of the workers' hall. The ironic juxtaposition of both elicits our emotional outcry at the injustice and manipulation of the masses at the hands of unscrupulous capitalists. This arrangement of scenes reflects the cinematic effects that had long been present in the work of D. W. Griffith—to name just one filmmaker. In his early one-reeler, "A Corner in Wheat" (1909), for example, scenes of the Wheat Exchange in Chicago alternated with scenes of starving workers. Later in Pudovkin's *The End of St. Petersburg* (1927), we again saw this device of ironic juxtaposition through the manipulation of shots—scenes of soldiers in combat alternating with shots of the stock exchange profiting from munitions sales.

Other expressionist plays also exhibiting these cinematic effects reached American audiences during the 1920s through the auspices of the Theater Guild—Eugene O'Neill's *The Emperor Jones* and *The Hairy Ape*, Elmer Rice's *The Adding Machine*, Susan Glaspell's *The Verge*, John Howard Lawson's *Processional*, and an adaptation of the German play, *Johannes Kreisler*. Bauland says that *Kreisler* had "forty-one scenes presented in the rapid succession of a movie scenario. Its sentimental story was told in flashbacks, not as the historical events occur but as they appear to Kreisler in his feverish recollections."[87] In her recent study of expressionism, Mardi Valgemae's *Accelerated Grimace* also suggests that the effects of motion pictures influenced the form of plays like *The Hairy Ape, The Adding Machine, Roger Bloomer*, and *Processional*. Specifically, she says, Robert Wiene's film, *The Cabinet of Dr. Caligari*, influenced much of this work. O'Neill saw the film in the summer of 1921, for example. He noted to a friend soon afterward: "I saw 'Caligari' and it sure opened my eyes to wonderful possibilities I had never dreamed of before."[88] Six months later, O'Neill quickly recast a now lost short story containing the germ idea of *The Hairy Ape* in the form of a play characterized by set distortion characteristic of expressionism. Valgemae succeeds in tracing connections between the arrangements of images in both film and play. The structuring of the episodes, or pictures, in *The Hairy Ape* and other expressionist plays, concludes Valgemae, is dependent upon subjective states of the main characters—Yank, Zero, Roger Bloomer, and Dynamite Jim. Similarly, *The Cabinet of Dr. Caligari* was structured according to the subjective state of the insane "Dr. Caligari."[89]

In addition to the foregoing kinds of influences perceptible in plays and stagecraft, the motion picture began to be incorporated as an *element* in theatrical events. The utilization of films as part of the theatrical event was regarded as avant-garde when Orson Welles inserted film footage into his production of *Too Much Johnson* for the Mercury Theater in 1937;[90] yet such attempts can be traced back to the beginnings of cinema in the 1890s. Writing in *The North American Review* in September, 1896, George Parsons Lathrop speculated that the new "Vitascope" of Edison—the projected motion picture—might have a proper place in stage productions. Is it possible, he asked, that the Vitascope could be so used "as to make painted scenery unnecessary in plays performed by flesh and blood actors; or is it likely, at any rate, to replace that to some extent and to become a valuable adjunct in certain particulars of scenic effect upon the stage?" In short, could the motion picture play a part in "heightening theatrical verisimilitude?" Seizing upon the capacity in cinema for capturing realism, Parsons contended that Vitascope could capture events "absolutely from life" and, through the device of rear-projection, project the images behind the actors. In addition, people could be photographed and, through this projection, the film could be combined with the "real" figures on the stage.[91]

Soon, films did indeed become integral parts of stage productions. Stage and screen personality John Bunny utilized motion pictures during his engagement at Hammerstein's Victoria Theatre in 1913. His comedy routine opened with a film of himself asleep in bed. A frantic stage manager races through the streets to wake him up and drag him back to the theater. The skit ended with the "real" John Bunny bursting through the curtain. This kind of skit was typical of many other vaudeville routines. On more ambitious and complex levels, Meyerhold and Erwin Piscator used projected photographs and moving pictures in their stage work. In *The Earth Rampant* and *Give Us Europe* (1923-24), Meyerhold used them as both "backdrops" for the action and as self-contained episodes. Erwin Piscator found that projected maps of city streets functioned better as scenic devices than painted backdrops. For his work at the Berlin Volksbuehne in the 1920s—such as *The Flags* and *Storm Over Gothland*—Piscator used films as essential elements of the drama. For *Hurrah, We Live!* (1927), he used newsreels at various points in the action to explicuate the past history of the main character. In this case, the device of the flashback was used by means of movies. And for his dramatization of Tolstoy's *Rasputin* (1927), Piscator placed several film screens about the theater in order to present a number of events simultaneously.

It is appropriate to end this book with Erwin Piscator, for he was not intimidated by the motion picture—either as an inspiration for effects or as an element to be used on the stage. He boldly called upon theatrical producers and writers to use the devices of the film, wherever appropriate, to promote "the interchange on stage between light and 'film light,' " and the complete motorization of the stage in order to burst dynamically "the static illusion of the present stage" and overcome its "limitations." These remarks are from some formulations Piscator made in 1929, near the end of the second period of imitation discussed in this paper. The stage, he wrote, could properly incorporate the motion picture—even television (in which experiments had already begun)—in many ways:

Film and television would be used in combination with the stage, for stage close-ups. Imagine the other fields, both psychological and epic, such combinations would open! Contrasts between the conscious, spoken thought could be revealed. Monologues would be visualized; the inner colloquy could be externalized, the actor talking to his own screen image. Asides made visible motives traced to their sources—all this could be done by contrasting new over-dimensional material (by means of projections referring to the outside world) with human material (the actors on the stage, the actual scene). Film could be used as atmosphere for fantasy, or as moving background, or as chorus: interpreting, prophesizing, philosophising.[92]

Thus, imitation of film by theater people was a reciprocal dynamic that could lead to new developments and enriched perceptions concerning both the theater and the motion picture. The motion picture was an art form of the twentieth century; now, as Piscator forecast, by means of the motion picture the stage could be brought into the new century as well.

Notes

[1]"Hackett on the Screen," *The New York Dramatic Mirror*, Frebruary 26, 1913, p. 28.

[2]W. Stephen Bush, "The Prisoner of Zenda," *The Moving Picture World*, March 1, 1913, p. 871.

[3]J. Dudley Andrew, *The Major Film Theories: An Introduction* (New York: Oxford University Press, 1976), p. 5.

[4]See Hugo Muensterberg, *The Photoplay: A Psychological Study* (New York: Dover Print, 1970); Vachel Lindsay, *The Art of the Moving Picture* (New York: Liveright reprint, 1970); Luigi Pirandello, *Si Gara*, trans. C. K. Scott-Moncrieff (New York: E. P. Dutton, 1926); Rudolph Arnheim, *The Art of the Film* (Berkeley: University of California Press, 1957); Sergei Eisenstein, *Film Form and the Film Sense* (Cleveland and New York: World Publishing Company, 1968); Andre Bazin, *What is Cinema?* (Berkeley: University of California Press, 1968); Siegfried Kracauer, *Theory of Film* (New York: Oxford University Press, 1970); Jean Mitry, *Esthetique et psychologie du cinema* (Paris: Editions Universitaires, 1963, 1965); and Christian Metz, *Film Language: The Semiotics of the Cinema*, transl. Michael Taylor (New York: Oxford University Press, 1974).

[5]Raymond Fielding, *The American Newsreel* (Norman, Oklahoma: University of Oklahoma Press, 1972), p. 4. This definitive history of the news film and newsreel presents this concise definition of the term, "actuality": "Actualities are short scenes of everyday people and events—unmanipulated activity of more or less general interest. It is with the humble actuality that one begins not only the history of the newsreel but also the history of all motion pictures."

[6]Anthony Slide, *American Film History Prior to 1920* (Metuchen, New Jersey: Scarecrow Press, 1978), p. 63.

[7]Thomas Armat, "My Part in the Development of the Motion Picture Projection," *Journal of the Society of Motion Picture Engineers*, Vol. XXIV (March 1935), p. 247.

[8]Raymond Fielding, p. 47.

[9]The De Proxynski Aeroscope camera was a portable, compressed-air camera with gyroscopic attachment which weighed only fourteen pounds, including 320 feet of film. For most information on technological developments in filmmaking during the Frist World War, see Kevin Brownlow, *The War, The West, and the Wilderness* (New York: Oxford University Press, 1979), pp. 3-219.

[10]Raymond Fielding, p. 167.

[11]William K. Everson, *American Silent Film* (New York: Oxford University Press, 1979), p. 22.

[12]For a detailed examination of this famous chase scene in *Arrah-na-Pogue*, see A. Nicholas Vardac, *Stage to Screen* (Cambridge: Harvard University Press, 1949), pp. 25-31.

[13]Kemp R. Niver, *The First Twenty Years* (Los Angeles: Locare Research Group, 1968), p. 46.

[14]This quotation from the *Biograph Bulletin* is quoted in Kemp R. Niver, p. 57.

[15]Hugo Muensterberg, *The Photoplay: A Psychological Study* (New York: Dover reprint, 1970), p. 14. All quotations are taken from this edition.

[16]Claude Levi-Strauss, *The Savage Mind* (Chicago: University of Chicago Press, 1966), pp. 17-21.

[17]See John Tibbetts, "Glen MacWilliams: Following the Sun with a Veteran Cameraman," *American Classic Screen*, Vol. 3, No. 3 (January-February, 1979), pp. 32-39.

[18]Waldemar Kaempffert, "Invention as a Social Manifestation," reprinted in Charles Beard, ed., *A Century of Progress* (New York: Harper and Brothers, 1930), p. 21.

[19]Perhaps the best account of the history of motion picture lighting extent is Charles W. Handley's "History of Motion-Picture Studio Lighting," in Raymond Fielding, ed., *A Technological History of Motion Pictures and Television* (Berkeley and Los Angeles: University of California Press, 1967), pp. 120-24.

[20]Robert Grau, "A Word About Celebrated Stars in Photoplays," *The Motion Picture Story Magazine*, February 1913), p. 127.

[21]Louis Reeves Harrison, "Stage Plays," *Moving Picture World*, April 11, 194, p. 185.

[22]"Daniel Frohman Talks Pictures," *Moving Picture World*, April 11, 1914, p. 194.

[23]Quoted in Robert Grau, *The Theater of Science* (New YOrk: Benjamin Blom, 1969), p. 86.

[24]Horace G. Plimpton, "Evolution of the Motion Picture, Part Seven: From the Standpoint of the Photo-Playwright," *New York Dramatic Mirror*, July 23, 1913, p. 25.

[26]Vachel Lindsay, *The Art of the Moving Picture* (New York: Liverright reprint, 1970), p. 185. All quotations are taken from this edition.

[27]Luigi Pirandello, *Si Gara*, trans. C. K. Scott-Moncrieff (New York: E. P. Dutton, 1926). All quotations from this edition.

[28]Alexander Walker, *The Shattered Silents* (New York: William Morrow and Co., 1979), p. 48.

[29]Quoted in Alexander Walker, p. 52.

[30]Gilbert Seldes, *An Hour with the Movies and the Talkies* (Philadelphia: J. B. Lippincott Company, 1929), pp. 50-154.

[31]Luigi Pirandello, "Pirandello Views the 'Talkies,'" *The New York Times Magazine*, July 28, 1929, p. 1.

[32]See Siegfried Kracauer, *Theory of Film* (New York: Oxford University Press, 1970), pp. 63-65.

[33]Ernest Betts, "Why Talkies are Unsound," *Close Up* (April 1929), p. 23.

[34]Quoted in Rosalind Rogoff, *Sound and Film—The Long Engagement*, unpublished Masters Thesis, University of California at Los Angeles, 1973, p. 57.

[35]Quoted in Jay Leyda, *Kino: A History of the Russian and Soviet Film* (New York: Collier Books, 1973), pp. 278-79.

[36]Quoted in Jay Leyda, p. 280.

[37]Edmund Goulding, "The Talkers in Close-Up," *Variety*, June 13, 1928, p. 7.

[38]George Abbott, "The Big Noise," *Vanity Fair*, April 1929, p. 79.

[39]René Clair, "The Art of Sound," reprinted in Richard Dyer MacCann, ed., *Film: A Montage of Theories* (New York: E. P. Dutton & Co., INc., 1966), p. 41.

[40]*Ibid.*, p. 43.

[41]*Ibid.*, p. 42.

[42]See Celia McGerr, *René Clair* (Boston: Twayne Publisher, 1980), and Lucy Fischer, "René Clair, *Le Million*, and the Coming of Sound," *Cinema Journal*, Vol. XVI, No. 2 (Spring 1977), pp. 34-50.

[43]Lucy Fischer, p. 42.

[44]Will Irwin, *The House That Shadows Built* (New York: Doubleday, Doran and Co., 1928), p. 183.

[45]Henry Albert Phillips, "The New Literary Profession," *Motion Picture Magazine*, October 1914, p. 82.

[46]William de Mille, *Hollywood Saga* (New YOrk: E. P. Dutton and Co., 1939), pp. 145-46.

[47]Quoted in J. Sidney McSween, "Players of the Film Drama," *Theatre Magazine*, October 1912, p. x.

[48]Kalton Lahue, *Dreams for Sale* (Cranbury, New Jersey: A. S. Barnes, 1971), pp. 83-84.

[49]"Stage Stars in Hollywood," *Variety*, December 10, 1915, p. 3.

[50]"New Industry Policy," *New York Dramatic Mirror*, September 16, 1915, p. 24.

[51]Elaine Ogden, "Inside the Monitor Room," *Photoplay*, July 1930, p. 77.

[52]Quoted in Rosalind Rogoff, "From Silence to Sound," *American Classic Screen*, March/April 1977, p. 33.

[53]For a fine discussion of these problems, see "Interview With Hal Mohr" in Leonard Maltin, ed., *Behind the Camera* (New York: Signet Books, 1971), pp. 91-138.

[54]See John Tibbetts, "Following the Sun," pp. 32-39.

[55]Quoted in Rosalind Rogoff, *Sound and Film*, p. 40.

[56]*Ibid.*, p. 33.

[57]Paul Sloane, "Hysteria Talkerfilmus: New Movie Malady," *Theatre Magazine*, October 1928, p. 70.

[58]Louise Closser Hale, "The New Stage Fright: Talking Pictures," *Harper's Monthly Magazine*, September 1930, pp. 420-41.

[59]Quoted in Walter Benjamin, "The Work of Art in the Age Mechanical Reproduction" reprinted in Gerald Mast and Marshall Cohen, eds., *Film Theory and Criticism* (New York: Oxford University Press, 1974), pp. 612-32.

[60]Vsevolod Pudovkin, *Film Technique and Film Acting*, transl. and ed. by Ivor Montague (London: Vision Press, 1968), p. 137.

[61]For an overview of the *Le Cid* controversy, see Julian M. Kaufman, *Appreciating the Theater* (New York: David McCay Co., Inc., 1971), pp. 176-77.

[62]Paul Michael, *The Academy Awards: A Pictorial History* (New York: Crown Publishers, Inc., 1968), p. ii. David O. Selznick in the Foreward laments that the glamor of the Academy Awards has overshadowed the "substantial contributions to the inauguration and advancement of cinematic techniques." (ii) For a definitive history of the Academy, see Pierre Norman Sands, *A Historical Study of the Academy of Motion Picture Arts and Sciences: 1927-47* (New York: Arno Press, 1973).

[63]Robert Sklar in his *Movie-Made America* (New York: Random House, 1975) argues that one of the prime motivations in the formation of the Academy in 1927 was the effort of Actors Equity Association to organize the movie players. The producers set up the Academy "to function more or less as a company union" (84). It proved to be more effective, however, in the arbitration of disputes of a technical nature. For example, in September, 1930, the Technicians Branch, in conjunction with the Directors and Producers Branches, met to consider the artistic, technical, and economic advantages of adopting the standard width of film. All arguments in favor of increasing the screen's horizontalism were defeated by Sergei Eisenstein, then working for Paramount. The standard rectangle of 1:1.33 was retained. See Arthur Knight, *The Liveliest Art* (New York: Mentor, 1957), pp. 306.08.

[64]See John Tibbetts, ed., *Introduction to the Photoplay* (Kansas City and Los Angeles: The National Film Society, 1977). All quotations are taken from this edition.

[65]Sir Joshua Reynolds, *The Sixth Discourse*, reprinted in John Gassner, eds., *The Nature of Art* (New York: Crown Publishers, 1964), p. 374.

[66]A. Nicholas Vardac, *Stage to Screen*. Vardac notes that the stage presentation of *Ben Hur*, which premiered on November 29, 1899, at the Broadway Theatre, placed an emphasis, from first to last, "upon the pictures." Its use of many scenes, oftentimes employing little dialogue, proved that the stage was trying to approach the standard of the early motion picture. Nonetheless, Vardac claims that its audience, already accustomed to some of the possibilities of the movies, was not overly impressed. He cites the reaction of one reviewer who said, "The only way to secure the exact sense of action for this incident in a theatre is to represent it by Mr. Edison's invention" (80).

[67]*Ibid.*, p. 134.

[68]See Lise-Lone Marker, *David Belasco: Naturalism in the American Theater* (Princeton University Press, 1975).

[68]At least one critic, Louis V. Defoe of the New York *World*, was disturbed at the play's "too great emphasis" on "photographic externals." See Eric Wollencott Barnes, *The Man Who Lived Twice: The Biography of Edward Sheldon* (New York: Charles Scribner's Sons, 1956), p. 52.

[69]Maxwell Bloomfield, "Muckraking and the American Stage: The Emergence of Realism, 1905-1917," *The South Atlantic Quarterly*, Spring, 1967, p. 177.

[70]"Is the American Theater Deteriorating?" *Current Opinion*, Vol. LV No. 6 (December 1913), p. 413.

[71]Charles Baudelaire, "The Modern Public and Photography," reprinted in Beaumont Newhall, ed., *On Photography* (New York: Watkins Glen, Century House, 1956), pp. 104-07. Baudelaire's review of the 1859 Salon contained this statement: "Each day art further diminishes its self-respect by bowing down before external reality; each day the painter becomes more and more given to painting not what he dreams but what he sees. Nevertheless, it is a happiness to dream, and it used to be a glory to express what one dreamt. But I ask you! Does the painter still know this happiness?" (107)

[72]Susanne K. Langer, *Reflections on Art* (New York: Oxford University Press, 1961), p. 319.

[73]Quoted in Van Deren Coke, p. 299. Georges Bracque is also quoted in this regard: "...painting is getting closer and closer to poetry, now that photography has freed it from the need to tell a story" (299). Coke offers this general observation about photography's impact upon this group of painters: "Photographs have aroused some artists to throw off the baggage of tradition...." (301)

[74]Quoted in Oscar Cargill, ed., *O'Neill and His Plays: Four Decades of Criticism* (New York, 1962), p. 525. Ironically, as O'Neill acknowledged in 1926, it was a play of "photographic" surfaces that helped inspire him in his life in the theater. In a letter to Edward Sheldon, O'Neill said that *Salvation Nell* "first opened my eyes to the existence of a real theatre as opposed to the unreal—and to me, then hateful—theatre of my father, in whose atmosphere I had been brought up." (Quoted in Eric Wollencott Barnes, pp. 42-53).

[75]Francis Fergusson, *The Idea of a Theatre* (Princeton, New Jersey: Princeton University Press, 1949), pp. 186-93. He uses the term "action of the parlor" in referring to the naturalistic drama of Ibsen, Chekhov, and Strindberg.

[76]*Ibid.*, p. 193.

[77]Oscar G. Brockett and Robert R. Findlay, *Century of Innovation* (Englewood Cliffs, New Jersey: Prentice-Hall, 1973), p. 222.

[78]Brockett and Findlay, pp. 222-23.

[79]Herbert Marshall, *The Pictorial History of the Russian Theatre* (New York: Crown Publishers, Inc., 1977), p. 50.

[80]Barrett H. Clark and George Freedley, eds., *A History of Modern Drama* (New York: Appleton-Century Crofts, Inc., 1947), p. 450.

[81]Mordecai Gorelik, *New Theatres for Old* (New York: E. P. Dutton and Co., Inc., 1962), p. 305.

[82]Claude L. Hagen, "The Twentieth Century Stage, Mechanically," in Robert Grau, *The Stage in the Twentieth Century* (New York: Broadway Publishing Company, 1912), pp. xxv-xxvii.

[83]A. Nicholas Vardac, p. 143.

[84]*Ibid.*, p. 143.

[85]Claude L. Hagen, p. xxvii.

[86]Paul Bauland, *The Hooded Eagle* (Syracuse: Syracuse University Press, 1968), p. 67.

[87]*Ibid.*, p. 75.

[88]Quoted in Mardi Valgemae, *Accelerated Grimace* (Carbondale and Edwardsville, Illinois: Southern Illinois University Press, 1972), p. 34.

[89]*Ibid.*, p. 33.

[90]See Joseph McBride, *Orson Welles* (New York: The Viking Press, 1972), p. 23.: "There have been a few furtive mentions, largely unheeded by film historians, of a film he shot in 1938 for use in a Mercury Theatre stage production, William Gillett's farce, *Too Much Johnson*. The film was never shown publicly because Welles decided not to bring the play to Broadway after a summer stock try-out. He reportedly shot a twenty-minute silent prologue to the play, and ten-

minute films to introduce the second and third acts.... Sadly, the only copy of the film was destroyed in an August 1970 fire at Welles' villa in Madrid...."

[91] Erwin Piscator, "The Theatre Can Belong to Our Century," in Eric Bentley, ed., *The Theory of the Modern Stage* (New York: Penguin Books, 1976), pp. 472-73.

[92] *Ibid.*, pp. 472-73.

Bibliography

Allen, John. *Vaudeville and Film*. New York: Arno Press, 1980.

Andrew, J. Dudley. *The Major Film Theories: An Introduction*. New York: Oxford University Press, 1976.

Arliss, George. *My Ten Years in the Studios*. Boston: Little, Brown and Company, 1940.

Arliss, George. *Up the Years from Bloomsbury*. New York: Blue Ribbon Books, 1927.

Arnheim, Rudolf. *Film As Art*. Los Angeles: University of California Press, 1957; paper edition, 1971.

Atkinson, Brooks. *Broadway*. New York: The Macmillan Company, 1970.

Ball, Robert Hamilton, ed. *The Plays of Henry C. De Mille, Written in Collaboration with David Belasco*. America's Lost Plays, no. XVII. Princeton: Princeton University Press, 1941.

_____. *Shakespeare on the Silent Screen*. New York: Theatre Arts, 1973.

Balshover, Fred J. and Miller, Arthur C. *One Reel a Week*. Berkeley and Los Angeles: University of California Press, 1967.

Baral, Robert. Revue: *The Great Broadway Period*. New York: Fleet Press Corporation, 1962.

Barnes, Eric Wollencott. *The Man Who Lived Twice: The Biography of Edward Sheldon*. New York: Charles Scribner's Sons, 1956.

Barsacq, Leon. *Caligari's Cabinet and Other Grand Illusions: A History of Film Design*. Boston: New York Graphic Society, 1976.

Bauland, Paul. *The Hooded Eagle*. Syracuse: Syracuse University Press, 1968.

Bazin, André. *What Is Cinema?* Selected and translated by Hugh Gray with a Foreword by Jean Renoir. Berkeley and Los Angeles: University of California Press, 1967.

Beerbohm, Max, ed. *Herbert Beerbohm Tree*. London: Hutchinson and Company / 1920?/

Bernheim, Alfred L. *The Business of the Theatre*. New York: Benjamin Blom, Inc., 1932.

Blum, Daniel. *Great Stars of the American Stage*. New York: Greenberg, 1952.

Brockett, Oscar and Findlay, Robert R. *Century of Innovation*. Englewood Cliffs: Prentice-Hall, 1973.

Brown, Karl. *Adventures with D. W. Griffith*. New York: Farrar, Straus, and Giroux, 1973.

Brown, Maurice F. *The Life and Works of William Vaughn Moody*. Carbondale and Edwardsville: Southern Illinois University Press, 1973.

Brownlow, Kevin. *Hollywood: The Pioneers*. New York: Alfred A. Knopf, 1980.

_____. *The War, the West, and the Wilderness*. New York: Oxford University Press, 1979.

Calderwood, James L. and Toliver, Harold, eds. *Perspectives on Drama*. New York: Oxford University Press, 1968.

Cambon, Glauco, ed. *Pirandello: A Collection of Critical Essays*. Englewood Cliffs: Prentice-Hall.

Canham, Kingsley. *John Cromwell*. New York: A. S. Barnes and Company, 1976.

Cargill, Oscar, ed. *O'Neill and His Plays: Four Decades of Criticism*. New York, 1962.

Carter, Randolph. *The World of Flo Ziegfeld*. New York: Praeger, 1974.

Chapman, John and Sherwood, Garrison P., eds. *The Best Plays of 1894-1899*. New York: Dodd, Mead and Company, 1955.

Churchill, Allen. *The Great White Way*. New York: E. P. Dutton and Company, 1962.

Clark, Barrett H. and Greedley, George, eds. *A History of Modern Drama*. New York: Appleton-Century-Crofts, Inc., 1947.

_____. *Intimate Portraits*. New York: Dramatists Play Service, 1951.

Cooke, Alistaire. *Douglas Fairbanks: The Making of a Screen Character*. New York: Museum of Modern Art, 1940.

Costello, Donald. *The Serpent's Eyes*. Notre Dame: University of Notre Dame Press, 1965.

Crane, W. H. *Footprints and Echoes*. New York: E. P. Dutton and Company, 1927.

Curtis, Dan. *James Whale*. Metuchen and London: Scarecrow Press, 1982.

Dart, Peter. *Pudovkin's Films and Film Theory*. New York: Arno Press, 1974.

De Mille, Cecil B. *Autobiography*. Englewood Cliffs: Prentice-Hall, 1959

De Mille, William. *Hollywood Saga*. New York: E. P. Dutton and Company, 1939.

Deutelbaum, Marshall, ed. *"Image" on the Art and Evolution of the Film*. New York: Dover Books, 1979.

Dickinson, Thomas H. *The Case of American Drama*. Boston and New York: Houghton Mifflin Co., 1915.

Dickson, Antonia and Dickson, W. K. L. *Edison's Invention of the Kineto-Phonograph*. Los Angeles: Pueblo Press, 1939.

Dimeglio, John E. *Vaudeville U. S. A.* Bowling Green: The Popular Press, 1973.

Edmonds, I. G. and Mimura, Reiko. *Paramount Pictures*. San Diego and New York: A. S. Barnes and Company, 1980.

Eisenstein, Sergei. *Film Form and The Film Sense*. Edited and translated by Jay Leyda. New York: World Publishing Company, 1968.

Everson, William K. *American Silent Film*. New York: Oxford University Press, 1978.

Ewen, David. *The Complete Book of the American Musical Theater*. New York: Holt, Rinehart and Winston, 1970.

Felheim, Marvin. *The Theater of Augustin Daly*. Cambridge: Harvard University Press, 1956.

Fell, John. *Film and the Narrative Tradition*. Norman: University of Oklahoma Press, 1949.

Fielding, Raymond. *The American Newsreel: 1911-1967*. Norman: University of Oklahoma Press, 1972.

_____ *A Technological History of Motion Pictures and Television*. Berkeley and Los Angeles: University of California Press, 1967.

Frazer, John. *Artificially Arranged Scenes*. Boston: G. K. Hall and Company, 1979.

Freeburg, Victor Oscar. *The Art of Photoplay Making*. New York: Arno Press reprint, 1970.

Frohman, Daniel. *Daniel Frohman Presents*. New York: Claude Kendall and Willoughby Sharp, 1935.

Fulton, A. R. *Motion Pictures*. Norman: University of Oklahoma Press, 1960.

Gagey, Edmond M. *Revolution in American Drama*. New York: Columbia University Press, 1947.

Gassner, John and Quinn, Edward. *The Reader's Encyclopedia of World Drama*. New York: Thomas Y. Crowell Company, 1969.

Geduld, Harry M. *The Birth of the Talkies: From Edison to Jolson*. Bloomington: Indiana University Press, 1975.

Goldman, Emma. *The Social Significance of the Modern Drama*. Boston: Richard Badger, 1914.

Gowans, Alan. *The Unchanging Arts*. Philadelphia and New York: J. B. Lippincott Company, 1971.

Grau, Robert. *The Stage in the Twentieth Century*. New York: Broadway Publishing Company, 1912.

_____ *The Theatre of Silence*. New York: Benjamin Blom reprint, 1969.

Green, Abel and Laurie, Joe. *Show Biz*. New York: Henry Holt and Company, 1951.

Green, Fitzhugh. *The Film Finds Its Tongue*. New York: G. P. Putnam's Sons, 1929.

Hall, Ben M. *The Best Remaining Seats*. New York: Bramhall House, 1961.

Hammond, Paul. *Marvellous Melies*. New York: St. Martin's Press, 1975.

Hampton, Benjamin. *A History of the American Film Industry*. New York: Covici, Friede, 1931.

Haver, Ronald. *David O. Selznick's Hollywood*. New York: Alfred A. Knopf, 1980.

Henderson, Robert M. *D. W. Griffith: The Years at Biograph*. New York: Farrar, Straus, and Giroux, 1970.

Herron, Ima Honaker. *The Small Town in American Drama*. Dallas: Southern Methodist University Press, 1969.

Higham, Charles. *Warner Brothers*. New York: Charles Scribner's Sons, 1975.

Hochman, Stanley, ed. *A Library of Film Criticism: American Film Directors*. New York: Frederick Ungar Publishing Company, 1974.

Hopper, De Wolf. *Once a Clown, Always a Clown*. Boston: Little, Brown, and Company, 1927.

Hoyt, Harlowe R. *Town Hall Tonight: Intimate Memoires of the Grassroots Days of the American Theatre*. Englewood: Prentice-Hall, 1955.

Irwin, Will. *The House that Shadows Built*. New York: Doubleday, Doran and Company, 1928.

Jobes, Gertrude. *Motion Picture Empire*. Hamden: Archon Books, 1966.

Kahn, E. J., Jr. *The Merry Partners: The Age and Stage of Harrigan and Hart.* New York: Random House, 1955.

Kauffman, Stanley, ed. *American Film Criticism.* New York: Liveright, 1972.

Kaufman, Julian M. *Appreciating the Theater.* New York: David McKay Company, 1971.

Knepler, Henry. *The Gilded Stage.* New York: William Morrow and Company, 1968.

Kobal, John. *Gotta Sing Gotta Dance.* New York: Hamlyn Publishing Group, 1970.

Koon, Helene and Switzer, Richard. *Eugene Scribe.* Boston: Twayne Publishers, 1980.

Kracauer, Siegfried. *Theory of Film.* New York: Oxford University Press, 1970.

Kreuger, Miles, ed. *The Movie Musical: From Vitaphone to 42nd Street.* New York: Dover Books, 1975.

——— *Show Boat: The Story of a Classic American Musical.* New York: Oxford University Press, 1977.

Krutch, Joseph Wood. *The American Drama Since 1918.* New York: Random House, 1939.

Lahue, Kalton. *Dreams for Sale.* Cranbury, New Jersey: A. S. Barnes, 1971.

Lawson, John Howard. *Film: The Creative Process.* New York: Hill and Wang, 1967.

Lennig, Arthur. *The Silent Voice.* New York: Walter Snyder, 1969.

Lewis, Emory. *Stages.* New Jersey: Prentice-Hall, 1969.

Leverton, Garrett H., ed. *The Great Diamond Robbery and Other Recent Melodramas,* America's Lost Plays, vol. VIII. Princeton: Princeton University Press, 1940; Indiana University Press, 1963.

Leyda, Jay. *Kino: A History of the Russian and Soviet Film.* New York: Collier Books, 1973.

Limbacher, James L. *Four Aspects of the Film.* New York: Brussel, 1968.

Lindan, George W. *Reflections on the Screen.* Belmont: Wadsworth Publishing Company, Inc., 1970.

Lindsay, Vachel. *The Art of the Moving Picture.* New York: Macmillan, 1915.

Lounsbury, Myron. *The Origins of American Film Criticism.* New York: Arno Press, 1973.

MacCann, Richard Dyer, ed. *Film: A Montage of Theories.* New York: E. P. Dutton and Company, Inc. 1966.

Maltin, Leonard, ed. *Behind the Camera.* New York: Signet Books, 1971.

——— *The Movie Factory.* New York: The Popular Library, 1976.

Mantle, Burns and Sherwood, Garrison P., eds. *The Best Plays of 1899-1909.* New York: Dodd, Mead and Company, 1944.

——— *The Best Plays of 1909-1919.* New York: Dodd, Mead, and Company, 1933.

Marker, Lise-Lone. *David Belasco: Naturalism in the American Theatre.* Princeton: Princeton University Press, 1975.

Marshall, Herbert. *The Pictorial History of the Russian Theatre.* New York: Crown Publishers, Inc., 1977.

Matlaw, Myron, ed. *American Popular Entertainment: Papers and Proceedings of the Conference on the History of American Popular Entertainment.* Westport: Greenwood Press, 1979.

Marx, Arthur. *Goldwyn.* New York: W. W. Norton and Company, 1976.

McGerr, Celia. *Rene Clair.* Boston: Twayne Publishers, 1980.

McLaughlin, Robert. *Broadway and Hollywood: A History of Economic Interaction.* New York: Arno Press, 1974.

Meserve, Walter, ed. *The Complete Plays of W. D. Howells.* New York: New York University Press, 1960.

——— *An Outline History of American Drama.* Totowa: Littlefield, Adams and Company, 1970.

Middleton, George. *These Things Are Mine.* New York: The Macmillan Company, 1947.

Milne, Tom. *Mamoulian.* Bloomington: Indiana University Press, 1969.

Moses, Montrose J. *Famous Actor-Families in America.* New York: Benjamin Blom reprint, 1968.

——— *The American Dramatist.* Boston: Little, Brown and Company, 1911.

——— and Gerson, Virginia. *Clyde Fitch and His Letters.* Boston: Little, Brown, and Company, 1924.

Muensterberg, Hugo. *The Photoplay: A Psychological Study.* New York: Dover Books reprint, 1970.

Munden, Kenneth W., executive editor. *The American Film Institute Catalogue of Motion Pictures Produced in the United States, 1921-1930*. New York and London: R. R. Bowker Company, 1971.

Munro, Thomas. *The Arts and Their Interrelations*. New York: The Liberal Arts Press, 1949.

Nannes, Caspar Harold. *Politics in the American Drama as Revealed by Plays Produced on the New York Stage, 1890-1945*. Philadelphia: University of Pennsylvania Press, 1950.

Nathan, George Jean. *Testament of a Critic*. New York: Alfred A. Knopf, 1931.

Niver, Kemp R. D. W. *Griffith: His Biograph Films in Perspective*. Los Angeles: Locare Research Group, 1974.

———. *The First Twenty Years: A Segment of Film History*. Los Angeles: Locare Research Group, 1968.

———. *Klaw and Erlanger Present "Famous Plays in Pictures."* Los Angeles: Locare Research Group, 1976.

——— *Motion Pictures from the Library of Congress Paper Print Collection, 1894-1912*. Berkeley and Los Angeles: University of California Press, 1967.

North, Joseph H. *The Early Development of the Motion Picture*, New York: Arno Press, 1973.

Nye, Russel. *The Unembarrassed Muse*. New York: The Dial Press, 1970.

Ormsbee, Helen. *Backstage with Actors*. New York: Thomas Y. Crowell Company, 1938.

Perry, John. *James A. Herne: The American Ibsen*. Chicago: Nelson Hall, 1978

Phelps, William Lyon. *Essays on Modern Dramatists*. New York: Macmillan, 1921.

Phillips, Rev. Gene, S. J. *George Cukor*. Boston: G. K. Hall, 1982.

Pirandello, Luigi. *Si Gara*. Translated by C. K. Scott-Moncrieff. New York: E. P. Dutton, 1926.

Pratt, George C., ed. *Spellbound in Darkness*. New York: New York Graphic Society, Ltd. 1973.

Praz, Mario. *Mnemosyne: The Parallel Between Literature and the Visual Arts*. Bollingen Series, No. 16. Princeton and London: Princeton University Press, 1974.

Pudovkin, Vsevolod. *Film Technique and Film Acting*. Translated and edited by Ivor Montague. London: Vision Press, 1968

Puggi, Jack. *Theatre in America: Impact of Economic Forces, 1870-1967*. Ithaca: Cornell University Press, 1968.

Quinn, Arthur Hobson. *History of the American Drama: From the Beginning to the Civil War*. New York: F. S. Crofts and Co., 1946.

Rahill, Frank. *The World of Melodrama*. University Park: Pennsylvania State University Press, 1967.

Ramsaye, Terry. *A Million and One Nights*. New York: Simon and Schuster, 1964.

Rogoff, Rosalind. "Sound and Film—The Long Engagement." Unpublished Masters Thesis, University of California at Los Angeles, 1973.

Rosenberg, Bernard and Silverstein, Harry, eds. *The Real Tinsel*. New York: Macmillan Company, 1970.

Sachs, Curt. *The Commonwealth of Art*. New York: W. W. Norton and Company, 1946.

Sands, Pierre Norman. *A Historical Study of the Academy of Motion Picture Arts and Sciences: 1927-47*. New York: Arno Press, 1973.

Sarris, Andrew, ed. *Interviews with Film Directors*. New York: Avon Books, 1969.

Seldes, Gilbert. *An Hour with the Movies and the Talkies*. Philadelphia: J. B. Lippincott Company, 1929.

Shaw, Dale. *Titans of the American Stage*. Philadelphia: The Westminster Press, 1971.

Simonson, Lee. *The Stage Is Set*. New York: Harcourt, Brace and Company, 1932; Theatre Arts Books reprint, 1970.

Sinclair, Upton. *Upton Sinclair Presents William Fox*. Los Angeles, California: By the author, 1933.

Sklar, Robert. *Movie-Made America*. New York: Random House, 1975.

Slide, Anthony. *American Film History Prior to 1920*. Metuchen: The Scarecrow Press, 1976.

———. *The Big V: A History of the Vitagraph Company*. Metuchen: The Scarecrow Press, 1976.

———. *The Kindergarten of the Movies: A History of the Fine Arts Company*. Metuchen, New Jersey: Scarecrow Press, 1981.

———, ed. *Selected Film Criticism, 1896-1911*. Metuchen and London: Scarecrow Press, 1982.

———, ed. *Selected Film Criticism, 1912-1920*. Metuchen and London: Scarecrow Press, 1982.

Sobel, Robert. *A Pictorial History of Vaudeville.* New York: Citadel Press, 1961.

Spears, Jack. *The Civil War on the Screen and Other Essays.* Cranbury: A. S. Barnes, 1977.

Spehr, Paul. *The Movies Begin: Making Movies in New Jersey, 1887-1920.* Newark: The Newark Museum, 1977.

Spiegel, Alan. *Fiction and the Camera Eye.* Charlottesville, University Press, 1976.

Stagg, Jerry. *The Brothers Shubert.* New York: Random House, 1968.

Stanislavski, Constantin. *My Life in Art.* New York: Theatre Arts Books, 1952.

Stanton, Stephen S., ed. *Camille and Other Plays.* New York: Hill and Wang, 1957.

Steiner, Max. *Notes to You.* Unpublished autobiography in the possession of Max Steiner's widow, Leonette Steiner.

Sullivan, Victoria and Hatch, James. *Plays by and About Women.* New York: Random House, 1973.

Talbot, Frederick A. Moving Pictures: How They Are Made and Worked. Charlottesville, University Press, 1976.

Tarkington, Booth. *On Plays, Playwrights, and Playgoers.* Selected and edited by Alan S. Downer. Princeton: Princeton University Library, 1959.

Taylor, John Russel. *The Rise of the Well Made Play.* London: Methuen and Company, Ltd., 1967.

Taubman, Howard. *The Making of the American Theatre.* New York: Coward-McCann, Inc., 1965.

Thomas, Tony. *Music for the Movies.* Cranbury: A. S. Barnes, 1977.

_____ and Terry, Jim. *The Busby Berkeley Book.* New York: New York Graphic Society, Ltd., 1973.

Tibbetts, John C. and Welsh, James M. *His Majesty the American: The Films of Douglas Fairbanks, Sr.* Cranbury. A. S. Barnes, 1976.

_____ *Introduction to the Photoplay.* Los Angeles and Kansas City: The National Film Society, 1977.

_____ The Triangle Film Corporation.'' Unpublished Masters Thesis, University of Kansas, 1975.

_____ "The Stage/Screen Exchange: Patterns of Imitation in Art, 1896-1930." Unpublished Doctoral Dissertation, University of Kansas, 1982.

Toll, Robert C. *On with the Show.* New York: Oxford University Press, 1976.

Valency, Maurice. *The Flower and the Castle: An Introduction to Modern Drama.* New York: Macmillan, 1963.

Valgemae, Mardi. *Accelerated Grimace.* Carbondale and Edwardsville: Southern Illinois University Press, 1972.

Vardac, A. Nicholas. *Stage to Screen.* Cambridge: Harvard University Press, 1949.

Walker, Alexander. *The Shattered Silents.* New York: Oxford Press, 1979.

Walls, Howard Lamarr. *Motion Pictures, 1894-1912: Catalogue of Copyright Entries.* Washington: Library of Congress Copyright Office, 1953.

_____ *Motion Pictures, 1912-1939: Catalogue of Copyright Entries.* Washington: Library of Congress Copyright Office, 1951.

Zierold, Norman. *The Moguls.* New York: Coward-McCann, Inc., 1969.

Zimmerman, Paul D. and Goldblatt, Burt. *The Marx Brothers at the Movies.* New York: G. P. Putnam's Sons, 1968.

Miscellaneous Articles

Abbot, George. "The Big Noise." *Vanity Fair,* April 1929, pp. 79, 110.

"Are Movies a Menace to Drama?" *Current Option,* Vol. 62 (May, 1917), p. 331.

Ashby, Clifford. "William H. Crane: The Old School of Acting and the New." *Drama Survey,* Vol. 3, no. 3 (Winter 1964), pp.

Bakshy, Alexander. "The Movie Scene: Notes on Sound and Silence." *Theatre Arts Monthly,* February, 1929, pp. 97-107.

_____ "The Talkies." *The Nation,* Vol. 128, no. 3320 (20 February 1929), pp. 236-38.

Barnard, Charles. "The Theatre—A Publishing House." *Godey's Magazine,* June 1893, pp. 760-62.

Barnes, Howard. "Talkie Town." *Theatre Magazine*, Vol. LII (July 1930), p. 36.
———— "Twilight of the Producing Titans." *Theatre Magazine,*, Vol. LII (April 1931), pp. 18-19, 60.
Barnouw, Erik. "The Magician and the Movies." *American Film*, Vol. III, no. 6 (April, 1978), pp. 8-13.
Belasco, David. "Stage Realism of the Future." *The Theatre*, Vol. XVIII, no. 151 (September 1913), pp. 86-90.
Bennison, Martin J. and Witham, Barry B. "Sentimental Love and the Nineteenth Century American Drama." *Players*, Vol. 49 and 5 (Summer 1974), pp. 127-29.
Betts, Ernest. "Why Talkies Are Unsound." *Close Up*, April, 1929, pp. 22-24.
Billboard. "Editorial." Vol. 18, no. 37 (15 September 1906), p. 16.
Bloomfield, Maxwell. "Muckraking and the American Stage: The Emergence of Realism, 1905-17." *The South Atlantic Quarterly*, Vol. LXVI, no. 2 (Spring, 1967), pp. 165-78.
Brown, Karl. "The Great D. W." *Sight and Sound*, Vol. 42, no. 3 (Summer, 1973), pp. 160-65.
"Camera Drama Versus Spoken." *Current Opinion*, Vol. 59 (December 1915), p. 405.
Charques, R. D. "The Future of Talking Films." *Fortnightly Review*, Vol. 132 (July 1, 1929), pp. 88-98.
Condon, Frank. "Over the Bridge to the Movies." *The Saturday Evening Post*, Vol. 204 (January 16, 1932), pp. 31-48.
"Costly Sneezes in Talkie' Land." *Literary Digest*, Vol. 99 (October 20, 1928), pp. 58, 60, 62.
Coward, Edward. "Sir Herbert Tree, England's Actor Knight." *Theatre Magazine*, Vol. XXII, no. 183 (May 1916), pp. 289-91.
Dale, Alan. "Dramatic Critics and Photoplays." *The Theatre*, Vol. XXII (June 1916), pp. 344-46, 64.
"Directors on Sound." *Take One*, Vol. 6, no. 2 (January, 1978), pp. 23-26.
"Disraeli Speaks." *Literary Digest*, Vol. 105 (21 April 1930), p. 19.
Eaton, Walter Prichard. "Actor-Snatching and the Movies." *American Magazine*, Vol. 80 (December 1915), pp. 32-37, 58, 62, 64.
———— "The Menace of the Movies." *American Magazine*, Vol. 76 (September 1913), pp. 55-60.
Eppes, William D. "The Empire Theatre." *Marquee*, Vol. 10, no. 3 (Summer 1978), pp. 3-15.
Findlay, Robert R. "The Emperor Jones: O'Neill as Scene Designer." *Players*, October-November 1969, pp. 21-24.
"The Fine Arts: The Kinetoscope." *The Critic*, Vol. 24, no. 638 (12 May 1894), p. 330.
Fletcher, Beaumont. "The Heart of Maryland." *Godey's Magazine*, February 1896, p. 180.
Fortune Magazine. "Color and Sound on Film." Vol. 2 (October 1930), p. 33.
Fox, Julian. "Casualties of Sound." *Films and Filming*, October 1972, pp. 34-40.
———— "Casualties of Sound" (part two). *Films and Filming*, November 1972, pp. 33-40.
Gillespie, Patti. "James A. Herne—A Reassessment." *Players*, Vol. 51, no. 2 (December-January 1976), pp. 66-69.
———— "Plays: Well-Constructed and Well-Made." *Quarterly Journal of Speech*, Vol. 58, no. 3 (October 1972), pp. 313-21.
———— "Plays: Well-Complicated." *Speech Monographs*, Vol. 42 no. 1 (March 1975), pp. 20-28.
Gomery, Douglas. "Tri-Ergon, Tobis-Klangfilm, and the Coming of Sound." *Cinema Journal*, Vol. XVI, no. 1 (Fall 1976), pp. 51-61.
Gottlieb, Lois C. "Obstacles to Feminism in the Early Plays of Rachel Crothers," *Papers in Women's Studies*, Vol. II, no. 2 (University of Michigan, Ann Arbor), pp. 71-89.
Grau, Robert. "A Word About Celebrated Stars in Photoplays." *Motion Picture Story Magazine*, February 1913, p. 127.
Hale, Louise Closser. "The New Stage Fright: Talking Pictures." *Harper's Monthly Magazine*,
Hazlitt, Henry, "Pictures from Plays." *The Nation*, Vol. 133 (September 30, 1931), p. 343.
Henderson, Brian. "Mise en Scene: The Long Take." *Film Comment*, Vol. 7, no. 2 (Summer 1971), pp. 6-11.
Herne, James A. "Art for Truth's Sake in the Drama." *The Arena*, Vol. XVII (February 1897, p. 364.
Herring, Robert. "Twenty-Three Talkies." *Close Up*, February 1930, pp. 113-29.

Hinton, A. Horsley. "Truth to Nature in Photography." *Camera Work*, No. 4 (October 1903), pp. 42-43.

Houghton, Donald E. "Two Heroes in One: Reflection Upon the Popularity of *The Virginia.*" *The Journal of Popular Culture*, Vol. IV, no. 2 (Fall 1970), pp. 507-17.

Ince, Thomas H. "The Stage Star and the Screen." *Motography*, February 5, 1916, pp. 299-300.

Is The American Theatre Deteriorating?" *Current Opinion*, Vol. LV, no. 6 (December 1913), pp. 413-14.

Is the Realism of the Stage Running to Seed?" *Current Literature*, Vol. LII, no. 1 (January 1912), pp. 88-89.

Jannings, Emil. "Why I Left the Films." *Living Age*, Vol. 338, (1 July 1930), pp. 554-57.

Jessel, George. "Why I Alternate on Stage and Screen." *Theatre Magazine*, Vol. XLVII, no. 323 February 1928), p. 22.

Kevles, Barbara. "Slavko Vorkapich on Film as a Visual Language and as a Form of Art." *Film Culture*, No. 38 (Fall 1965), pp. 1-44.

Knight, Leonard. "Beerbohm Tree in America." *Theatre Survey*, May 1967, p. 39.

Kovacs, Katherine Singer. "Georges Melies and the 'Feerie.'" *Cinema Journal*, Vol. XVI, no. 1 (Fall 1976), pp. 1-13.

Kupferberg, Audrey. "The Jazz Singer." *Take One*, Vol 6, no. 2 (January, 1978), pp. 28-32.

Lane, Lupino. "To Talk or Not to Talk—in Pictures," *Theatre Magazine*, Vol. XLVII, no. 329 (August 1928), pp. 28, 58.

Lathrop, George Parsons. "Stage Scenery and the Vitascope." *North American Review*, Vol. 163 (September 1896), pp. 377-81.

Lenauer, Jean. "The Sound Film: Salvation of Cinema." *Close Up*, April 1929, pp. 18-21.

Manski, Al and Navarro, Dan. "Hollywood Goes to Court: The Trial of Mary Dugan." *American Classic Screen Magazine*, Vol. 5, no. 2 (March-April 1981), pp. 29-32.

Marble, Arthur L. "George Arliss and the Merger of Stage and Screen." *Photo-Era*, (Vol. 65 (September 1930), pp. 178-79.

Masefield, Joseph. "Feature Filmmaking Returns to Astoria." *Making Films in New York*, December-January 1976-76, pp. 22-24.

Mawson, Harry P. "The Movies." *The Theatre*, Vol. XVI, no. 137 (July 1912), pp. 18-22.

Maxwell, Perriton. "Why Compare the Stage with the Screen?" *Theatre Magazine*, Vol. XLV (March 1927), p. 16.

Merritt, Russell. "Nickelodeon Theaters: Building an Audience for the Movies," *Wide Angle*, Vol. 1, no. 1, pp. 4-7.

Merrit, Russell. "Rescued from a Perilous Nest: D. W. Griffith's Escape from Theatre into Film." *Cinema Journal*, Vol. 21, no. 1 (Fall 1981), pp. 2-30.

Meserve, W. J. "An Earnest Purpose." *Players*, Vol. 48, no. 2 (December-January 1973), pp. 61-64.

McCreary, Eugene C. "Louis Delluc, Film Theorist, Critic, and Prophet." *Cinema Journal*, Vol. XVI, no. 1 (Fall 1976), pp. 14-35.

McLean, Albert F. "US Vaudeville and the Urban Comics." *Theatre Quarterly*, October-December, 1971, pp. 47-52.

McSween, J. Sidney. "Players of the Film Drama." *The Theatre*, Vol. XVI, no. 140 (October 1912), pp. 112, ix-x.

MgLinchee, Claire. "Belasco Magic." *Players*, Vol. 43, no. 1 (October-November, 1967), pp. 12-15.

Mickunas, Algis. "Philosophical Pragmatism and American Narrative Films." *Wide Angle*, Spring, 1976, pp. 13-21.

Nathan, George Jean. "Falling Star System." *The Theatre*, Vol. XV, no. 131 (January 1912), pp. 12-14.

Onosko, Tim. "RKO Radio: An Overview." *The Velvet Light Trap*,, no. 10 (Fall 1973), pp. 2-5.

Patterson, Frances Taylor. "Will Hollywood Move to Broadway?" *New Republic*, Vol. 61, 5 (February 1930), pp. 297-99.

Patterson, James A. "Bohemian Iconoclast: James Gibbons Huneker." *Players*, Vol. 43, no. 4 (April-May 1968), pp. 112-17.

Patterson, Joseph Medill. "The Nickelodeons: The Poor Man's Elementary Course in the

Drama." *The Saturday Evening Post,* Vol. 180, no. 21 (23 November 1907), pp. 10-11.

Perry, John. "The New Theatre." *Quarterly Journal of Speech,* Vol. 58, no. 3 (October, 1972), pp. 322-26.

Pirandello, Luigi. "Pirandello Views the 'Talkies.' *The New York Times Magazine,* 28 July 1929, pp. 1-2.

Pitts, Michael R. "Popular Singers and the Early Movie Musicals." *Classic Images,* no. 72 (November 1980), pp. 10-11.

"The Promise of the American Theatre." *Current Opinion,* Vol. LIV, no. 6 (June 1913), p. 472.

Reuss, Prince Henry. "Talkies and the Stage." *The Living Age,* Vol. 339 (November 1930), pp. 298-300.

Richardson, Dorothy M. "Continuous Performance." *Close Up,* June 1929, pp. 31-37.

Riddle, Melvin M. "Screen Portrayal." *The Photodramatist,* September 1922, pp. 9-10.

"The Rising Tide of Realism in American Drama." *Current Opinion,* Vol. LV, no. 4 (12 May; 1894), p. 330.

Robinson, Alice M. "James A. Herne and His 'Theatre Libre' in Boston." *Players,* Vol. 48, no. 5-6 (Summer 1973), pp. 202-09.

Rogoff, Rosalind. "Edison's Dream: A Brief History of the Kinetophone." *Cinema Journal,* Vol. XV, no. 2 (Spring 1976), pp. 58-68.

———. "How Hollywood Found a Voice: The Transition from Silent To Sound, 1926-1931." *The Los Angeles Film Calendar,* Vol. 2, no. 4 (August 1976), no pagination.

———. "How Hollywood Found a Voice" (Part Two). *The Los Angeles Film Calendar,* Vol. 2, no. 5 (September 1976), no pagination.

Savage, Richard. "Trying Out for the Movies." *Theatre Magazine,* Vol. XXIII, no. 180 (February 1916), p. 75.

Selwyn, Edgar. "Speaking of Talking Pictures." *Theatre Magazine,* Vol. LI (January 1930), pp. 30, 70.

Sherwood, Robert E. "Beyond the Talkies—Television." *Scribner's Magazine,* Vol. LXXXVI, no. 1 (July 1929), pp. 5-9.

Shinn, Everett. "Reportorial Sketching." *Time Magazine,* October 29, 1945, p. 94.

Skinner, Richard Dana. "King of Jazz." *The Commonweal,* Vol. XII, no. 3 (21 May 1930), pp. 80-81.

Slide, Anthony. "Evolution of the Film Star." *Films in Review,* December 1974, p. 593.

Sloan, Paul. "Hysteria Talkerfilmus: New Movie Maladay." *Theatre Magazine,* Vol. XLVIII, no. 331 (October 1928), pp. 26, 70.

"Solving Some Problems of the Talkies." *Literary Digest,* Vol. 100 (January 19, 1929), pp. 40, 43-44.

Smith, Milo L. "The Klaw-Erlanger Bogeyman Myth." *Players,* Vol. 44, no. 2 (December-January 1969), pp. 70-75.

Staiger, Janet. "Mas Produced Photoplays." *Wide Angle,* Vol. 4 no. 3, pp. 12-27.

Stern, Seymour. "Kaleidoscopia: Literature of the Films." *The Greenwich Village Quill,* Vol. 19, no. 4 (October 1926), pp. 32-39.

Tassin, Algernon. "The Drama as a Moral Force." *Good Housekeeping,* Vol. XLIX, no. 6 (December 1909), pp. 644-49.

Taylor, Francis Henry. "Realism with a Purpose." *Parnassus,* Vol. III, no. 5 (May 1931), p. 3-5.

Tibbetts, John C. "Interview with Sound Engineer Bernard Brown." *American Classic Screen Magazine,* Vol. 3, no. 1 (September-October 1978), pp. 33-38, 40, 42, 46.

———. "Glen MacWilliams: Following the Sun with a Veteran Cameraman." *American Classic Screen Magazine,* Vol. 3, no. 3 (January-February 1979), pp. 32-39.

———. "The Real Thing: Arguments Between Art and Science in the Work of P. H. Emerson and H. P. Robinson." *The Journal of Popular Culture,* Vol. 4, no. 1 (Spring 1981), pp. 149-72.

———. "The Stage Goes West: Owen Wister's 'The Virginian.' " *Illinois Social Studies Quarterly.*

———. "The 'New Woman' on Stage: Women's Issues in American Drama, 1890-1915." *Helicon Nine: The Journal of Womens Arts and Letters,* No. 7 (Winter 1982), pp. 6-19.

Titus, Warren I. "The Progressivism of the Muckrakers." *Midcontinent American Studies Journal,* Vol. 1, no. 1 (Spring 1960), pp. 10-16.

Trimmer, Joseph F. *"The Virginian:* Novel and Films." *The Illinois Social Studies Quarterly,* Vol. 35, no. 2 (December 1972) pp. 5-18.

"What They Really Get—Now!" *Photoplay Magazine.* March 1916, pp. 28-29.

"When the Dumb Actor Speaks." *Literary Digest,* Vol. 97 (June 2, 1928), p. 29.

Wills, J. Robert. "Olive Logan vs. the Nude Woman." *Players,* Vol. 47, no. 1 (October-November 1971), p. 39.

Wilson, Edmund. "Movietone and Musical Show." *The New Republic,* Vol. 55 (July 18, 1928), pp. 226-27.

Wilstach, Claxton. "Light and Sound on the Stage." *Godey's Magazine,* August 1906, pp. 183-89.

Witham, Barry. "Owen Davis: America's Forgotten Playwright." *Players,* Vol. 46, no. 1 (October-November 1970), pp. 39-45.

Worth, Sol. "Film as a Non-Art." *The American Scholar,* Vol. 35, no. 2 (Spring 1966), pp. 322-34.

Additional Periodicals (represented herein are those publications that have an extensive number of articles cited in this study)

The New York Dramatic Mirror (Arranged chronologically)

"Many Notable Films." Feburary 13, 1909, p. 12.

"The Spectator." February 21, 1912, p. 24.

"The Assassination of the Duc de Guise." February 26, 1909, p. 13.

"The Spectator." January 10, 1912, p. 28.

"The Spectator." January 31, 1912, p. 51.

"The Spectator." February 7, 1912, p. 28.

"The Spectator." February 21, 1912, p. 29.

"The Spectator." February 28, 1912, p. 32.

"The Spectator." February 28, 1912, p. 28.

"The Spectator." March 13, 1912, p. 24.

"The Spectator." March 26, 1912, p. 24.

"The Spectator." April 3, 1912, p. 24.

"Reviews of Feature Subjects." April 10, 1912, p. 26.

"The Spectator." April 10, 1912, p. 26.

"The Spectator." June 12, 1912, p. 24.

"Reinhardt's Mystery Play in Pictures." June 26, 1912, p. 22.

"The Spectator." July 3, 1912, p. 31.

"Theatrical Stars in Pictures." July 10, 1912, p. 34.

"Bernhardt as Queen Elizabeth." July 1912, p. 31.

"The Spectator." July 17, 1912, p. 24.

"The Spectator." October 23, 1912, p. 25.

"The Spectator." February 19, 1913, p. 25.

"Klaw and Erlanger New World Project." March 19, 1913, p. 13.

"The Octoroon on Film." May 7, 1913, p. 26.

"A Good Little Devil." May 14, 1913, p. 25.

"Suggestions and Comments." July 2, 1913, p. 24.

"Suggestions and Comments." July 11, 1913, p. 23.

"Advertisement." July 30, 1913, p. 26.

"Suggestions and Comments." September 3, 1913, p. 25.

"Review of *Arizona.*" September 24, 1913, p. 32.

"Making a Picture Director." January 13, 1914, p. 62.

"Review of *The Billionaire.*" April 8, 1914, p. 39.

Muensterberg, Hugo. "Psychology of the Photoplay." June 3, 1916, p. 35.

Howland, Delavan. "The Stage Supreme." June 17, 1916, p. 3.

The New York Times (arranged chronologically)

Hall, Mordaunt. "Review of 'Interference' " November 17, 1928, p. 23.

Tree, Herbert, "The Worthy Cinema." January 30, 1916, p. 8.

"Review of 'Don Quixote.' " December 20, 1915, p. 11.

"Review of 'The Hometowners.' " October 24, 1928, p. 26.
"Review of 'The Letter,' " March 8, 1929, p. 30.
"Review of 'Macbeth.' " June 17, 1916, p. 28.
"Review of 'The Trial of Mary Dugan.' " March 29, 1929, p. 21.

The Moving Picture World (arranged chronologically)
"The Factor of Uniformity." July 24, 1909, pp. 115-16.
"The Essanay Company Out West." December 4, 1909, p. 801.
"Too Near the Camera." March 25, 1911, pp. 633-34.
Sargent, Epes Winthrop. "The Photoplaywright: Scenes and Leaders." August 10, 1912, p. 542.
"Jesse L. Lasky in Pictures." January 3, 1914, p. 35.
Advertisement. February 7, 1914, pp. 696-97.
Harrison, Louis Reeves. "Review of 'The Squaw Man.' " February 29, 1914, pp. 1068-69.
———— "Stage Plays." April 11, 1914, p. 185.
Bush, W. Stephen. "Belasco on Motion Pictures." June 13, 1914, p. 1513.
"Shuberts and World Film in Big Deal." June 20, 1914, p. 1700.
Hackett, James K. "Hackett's Strong Arguments for Pictures." July 1914, p. 1701.

Photoplay Magazine (arranged chronologically)
"What They Really Get—Now!" March 1916, pp. 28-29.
Larkin, Mark. "The Truth About Voice Doubling." July 1929, pp. 32-33, 108-110.
"Trials of the Talkies." July 1929, pp. 52-53, 113-16.
Hall, Prof. Leonard. "How to Make a Talking Picture." August 1929, pp. 52-53.
———— "Revolution in Hollywood." August 1929, pp. 39, 100.
Hoffman, Jerry. "Westward the Course of Tin-Pan Alley." September 1929, pp. 38-39, 94, 98-99.
York, Cal. "The New Broadway." October 1929, pp. 42-43, 138-40.
Fenton, Maurice. "The Birth of the Theme Song." November 1929, pp. 66, 136.
Carr, Harry. "The Microphone—The Terror of the Studios." December 1929, pp. 29-30, 124-26.
Busby, Marquis. "Strange Talkie Tricks." February 1930, pp. 51, 94.
Hall, Prof. Leonard. "Are Stage Actors Stealing the Screen?" April 1930, pp. 44-45, 104.
Ogden, Elaine. "Inside the Monitor Room." July 1930, pp. 76-77, 100.

Variety (arranged chronologically)
"Vitaphones Play Talking Films as Road Show Substitutes." March 28, 1928, p. 5.
Goulding, Edmund. "The Talkers in Close-Up." June 13, 1928, p. 7.
"Review of 'The Pullman Porters.' " June 27, 1928, p. 14.
"Talkers in Closeup." June 13, 1928, p. 7.
"Fox Assembling 1st for Talker." July 4, 1928, p. 5.
"Vaudevillians Most in First 100% Talking Film, 'The Lights of New York.' " July 11, 1928, p. 27.
"Review of 'The Swell Head.' " July 18, 1928, p. 14.
"Tests Start at Paramount's New L. I. Sound Studios—1st Full Length in Nov." July 25, 1928, p. 7.
"Film People Who Can Talk." July 25, 1928, p. 5.
"Broadway Legit Producers Tying Up with Talker Makers on New Plays," July 25, 1928, p. 49.
"Dialogue Menace." August 15, 1928, p. 44.
"Review of 'Across the Border.' " August 29, 1928, p. 15.
"Plays Mostly; No Theatre Deal." September 19, 1928, p. 5.
"Talkies on Ordinary Stages." October 3, 1928, p. 4.
"Transparent Backgrounds." October 10, 1928, p. 4.
De Mille, William C. "No Stage Director or Writer Required for Talkers." October 17, 1928, p. 4.
"Sarnoff's Talker Views." October 24, 1928, p. 3.
"Review of 'The Bath Between.' " November 28, 1928, p. 15.
"Heyday for Legitimate Talent." December 5, 1928, p. 43.
"What Sound Has Done." March 13, 1929, pp. 1, 60.
"Review of 'The Letter.' " March 13, 1929, p. 14.
"About One-Third Silent for 1929-30." March 20, 1929, p. 7.

"Vita's Play Talking Films as Road Show Substitutes?" March 28, 1929, p. 5.
"11 Legits Sites Playing Films." April 10, 1929, p. 49.
"Review of 'Coquette.' " April 10, 1929, p. 25.
"Review of 'Thru Different Eyes.' " April 17, 1929, p. 22.
"Musical Firms' 'Tie-Ups.' " April 17, 1929, p. 71.
"Overhead Trolleys for Sets." April 24, 1929, p. 7.
"Review of 'Madame X.' " May 1, 1929, p. 17.
"205 Stagey People West." May 1, 1929, p. 57.
"Review of 'Bulldog Drummond.' " May 8, 1929, p. 20.
"Review of 'The Knife.' " May 29, 1929, p. 26.

Plays Cited (The following plays have more than a casual relevance to this study)

Abbott, George and Bridgers, Ann. *Coquette*. New York: Samuel French, 1929.

Archer, William. *The Green Goddess*. In Mantle, ed. *The Best Plays of 1920-21*. Boston: Small, Meynard and Company, 1921, pp. 124-61.

Belasco, David. *The Girl of the Golden West*. In Moses, Montrose J., ed., *Representative American Dramas: National and Local*. Boston: Little, Brown and Company, 1929, pp. 47-97.

De Mille, Henry C. and Belasco, David. *Men and Women*. In Ball, Robert Hamilton, ed., *The Plays of Henry C. De Mille*, America's Lost Plays, Vol. XVII. Princeton University Press, 1940; Indiana University Press, 1965, pp. 269-342.

Dumas, Alexandre and Fechter, Charles. *The Count of Monte Cristo*. In Russak, J. B., ed., *Monte Cristo and Other Plays*, America's Lost Plays, Vol. XVI. Princeton: Princeton University Press, 1940; Indiana University Press, 1965, pp. 1-70.

Fitch, Clyde. *The Climbers*. New York: Macmillan and Company, 1906.

Herne, James A. *Margaret Fleming*. In Quinn, Arthur Hobson, ed. *Representative American Plays*. New York: Appleton-Century-Crofts, 1966, pp. 515-44.

Klein, Charles. *The Lion and the Mouse*. New York: Samuel French, 1906.

_____ *Maggie Pepper*. New York: Samuel French, 1916.

Moody, William Vaughn. *The Great Divide*. In Gassner, John ed. *The Best Plays of the Early American Theatre*. New York: Crown Publishers, Inc., 1967, pp. 361-97.

_____ *The Faith Healer*. In Quinn, Arthur Hobson, *Representative American Plays*. New York: Charles Scribner's Sons, 1941, pp. 831-48.

Rice, Elmer. *On Trial*. In Rice, Elmer, *Seven Plays*. New York: The Viking Press, 1950, pp. 3-61.

_____ *The Adding Machine*. In Rice, Elmer, *Seven Plays*. pp. 64-108.

Royle, Edwin Milton. *The Squaw Man*. In Mantle, Burns and Sherwood, Garrison P., eds. *The Best Plays of 1899-1909*. New York: Dodd, Mead and Company, 1944, pp. 207-41.

Sheldon, Edward. *Salvation Nell*. In Gassner, John, ed. *Best Plays of the Early American Theater*. New York: Crown Publishers, Inc., 1967, pp. 557-616.

Toller, Ernst. *Man and the Masses*. In Watson, E. Bradlee and Pressey, Benefield, *Contemporary Drama: European Plays*. New York: Charles Scribner's Sons, 1934.

Walter, Eugene. *The Easiest Way*. In Gassner, John, ed. *The Best Plays of the Early American Theatre*. New York: Crown Publishers, Inc., 1967, pp. 617-76.

Wister, Owen and La Shelle, Kirke. "The Virginian: A Play in Four Acts." Tallahassee, Florida, 1958; typed, mimeographed and printed by N. Orwin Rush.

Letters

Kevin Brownlow to John Tibbetts, November 16, 1979.

Paul Spehr (Archivist for the Library of Congress Film Division) to John Tibbetts, January 24, 1980.

Interviews (arranged chronologically)

Author's interview with Glen MacWilliams (Hollywood cameraman), May 21, 1978.

Author's interviews with Bernard B. Brown (Hollywood sound engineer), June 7-8, 1978.

Author's interview with Kemp R. Niver (of the Locare Research Group), July 28, 1978.
Author's interview with Miles Kreuger (of the Institute of the American Musical), May 24, 1979.
Author's interview with William K. Everson, November 10, 1979.
Author's interview with Paul Spehr (of the Library of Congress), November 11, 1979.
Author's interview with Audrey Kupferberg (of the American Film Institute), November 12, 1979.
Author's interview with Miles Kreuger, May 3, 1980.
Author's interview with Anthony Slide, October 22, 1980.
Author's interview with Kevin Brownlow, October 24, 1980.

Index